INGRES

MANUEL JOVER

Cover :
La Grande Odalisque
1814, oil on canvas, 91x162 cm
Paris, Musée du Louvre.

Editorial Director : Anne Zweibaum
Editorial Coordination : Christine Marchandise
Design : Sandrine Roux/Caroline Keppy
Picture Research : Héléne Orizet
Copy Editor : Jack Liesveld
Photo Engraving : Groupe Horizon-Géménos, France

Publication N° 316,
ISBN : 2-87939-289-6
Printed in Italy.

MANUEL JOVER

INGRES

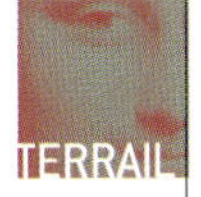

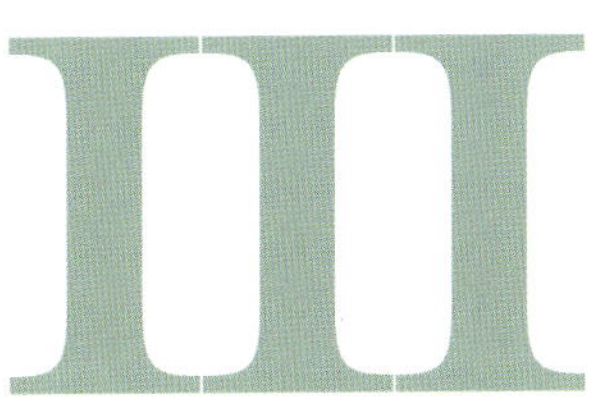

A Paradoxical Modernity

At the threshold of the oeuvre, at the dawn of the career, Ingres' *Self-Portrait* at twenty-four leaves no doubt as to the sheer force of a truly exceptional personality. The princely pose, one hand holding the stick of chalk for the sketch and the other on the heart, the haughtiness of the face with its disdainful mouth, and the intensity of the look directed outwards at the viewer – and at himself – all express an almost violent self-consciousness and determination. Is he already preparing the words he will write a few years later: "There comes a time when an artist of genius feels somehow swept along by his own capacities and every day does things he thought he could not do...I think I am that man." The time may not yet have come fully, but the artist knows what he is capable of.

When he left David's atelier three years before, he already had his Prix de Rome scholarship and had wasted no time. In just a few years he had become his master's technical equal and had totally emancipated himself from David's esthetics; and even more importantly he had laid the groundwork for an original personal style running counter to that of David and his school. The *Self-Portrait* reveals enormous energy and will: clearly this is a man to be reckoned with.

More than half a century later another self-portrait, at the age of seventy-eight, shows the same arrogance and irascibility. The gaze is tormented, but has lost nothing of its interrogative intensity.

"In my opinion," wrote Baudelaire in 1855, "the faculty that has made Monsieur Ingres what he is – the powerful, unchallengeable, uncontrollable dominator – is willpower, or rather an enormous abuse of willpow-

Self-portrait at the Easel
1804, oil on canvas, 77x61 cm
Chantilly, Musée Condé

er. In brief he was what he is now from the very outset. The energy in him means he will remain so until the end: just as he has not changed, he will not age."[1]

Other accounts are in the same vein. Physically and temperamentally Ingres changed scarcely at all over the years.

"A small, portly man, short arms and legs, a Southern face with dark eyes and pronounced features; simply dressed in the bourgeois manner. One would take him for a notary were his hair not parted down the middle like that of Poussin and Raphael." Thus Auguste Barbier described him[2]. More viciously, Théophile Silvestre compared him to a "Spanish priest."

His character was without ambiguity. All his life he would hold fast to the same certainties, defending them with an absolute intolerance. He suffered no contradiction and was hermetically closed to dialogue. Highly emotional, he could be brought to tears by beauty, or problems with his work. Given to fits of enthusiasm and rage, he openly proclaimed his passions and vented wild threats and imprecations. Misunderstood and under-appreciated during the first twenty years of his career, he never deviated by an inch from the course he had set himself, despite times of financial difficulty and even poverty. But when his first successes in Paris brought with them power and influence, Monsieur Ingres became the unlovable sectarian leader his contemporaries delighted in mocking. Théophile Gautier, although an admirer of the work, summed up the public figure thus: "The religion of art, of which he was the most devoted priest, gave Ingres a truly pontifical look. All his life he guarded the Holy Ark and carried the Tables of the Law." [3]

The oeuvre too, from beginning to end, remained true to itself, as if from the very beginning it had found its definitive level, temperature and horizons. There is something puzzlingly enduring about an art whose perfection can seem timeless, innate and unbreachable, but which is founded on insoluble contradictions.

The first of these was the unresolved tension between his artistic "instinct" – the so to speak natural capacities Ingres was endowed with – and his willpower, or rather that "enormous abuse of willpower." His "instinct" was an exceptional sensitivity to nature and living forms, which he could grasp and transcribe plastically as no one else could. Thousands of dazzling drawings, painted studies and large nudes, together with the incomparable gallery of portraits he left, bear witness to his powers.

But his willpower drove him to identify, at whatever cost, with a tradition and a doctrine – Classicism – of which he saw himself as the heir and savior, in the face of the developing modern movements he called "artistic anarchy." It was in the name of this tradition, to which he sometimes hewed too closely, and this doctrine he sometimes applied to the letter, that he would produce

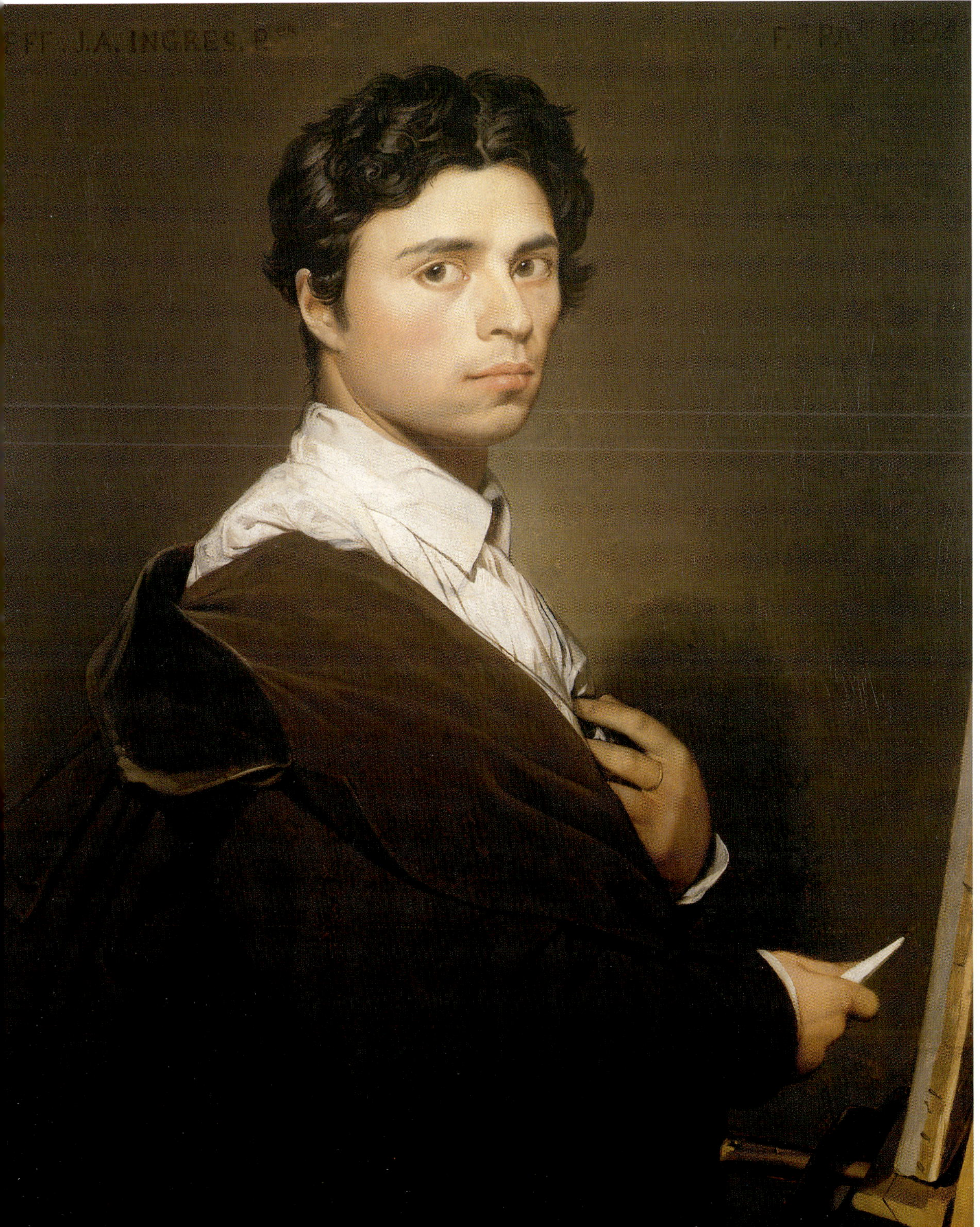
J.A. INGRES.
1804

his most dubious, least personal works – but the ones he considered the most important: those belonging to the "noble genre," his large historical paintings.

"In him," wrote Robert de la Sizeranne, "we see the most perfect example of the self-mistaken genius, who sees himself as someone else and wants that someone to be granted the supreme honors."[4] And Louis Gillet would write, "His case is a memorable example of a clash between one man's genius and his ideas, between nature and nurture, between what is truly himself and what comes to him from others. Whence all the misunderstandings he is subject to..."[5]

Ingres, then, emerges as an artist divided, weakened by his contradictions and clashing instincts. For Baudelaire, capable of recognizing his rarest gifts, Ingres was "bereft of the energetic temperament that forges the destiny of a genius." In his case, Baudelaire said, "Imagination, the queen of all the faculties, has vanished," having been sacrificed "on the altar of tradition and the Raphaelesque idea of the beautiful."[6]

All of which is sound observation. And yet...

And yet things are not quite so simple. For while these clashing instincts often did harm, they could also give rise to new and original ideas. The Classical archetype, drawn from the depths of antiquity and the Renaissance, could be applied to the charms of a grand bourgeois lady of the Second Empire. The quest for abstraction could be combined with the most acute realism, and the stylistic drive brought to bear on living forms. These daring, highly controlled mixes of disparate elements sometimes ended in disaster. But mostly they resulted in astonishing masterpieces, and in the final analysis it is to this way of thinking and this artistic process that Ingres owes the originality and paradoxical modernity of his painting. The process involves a kind of laboratory of forms, drawn from nature and a host of different traditions, then recast and brought together in often odd, sometimes utterly disconcerting combinations. There is no better summary of this experimental eclecticism and the astonishment it generated than Théophile Silvestre's marvelous sentence: "Monsieur Ingres has nothing in common with us: in the middle of the 19th century he is a Chinese painter lost among the ruins of Athens."[7]

Baudelaire too attempted to define the sensation of eccentricity the master's works produced: "This feeling, difficult to describe and made up, in unknown proportions, of unease, *ennui* and fear, makes you think vaguely of the weakness caused by rarefied air, the atmosphere of a chemistry laboratory, the sense of being caught up in a fantasy world – or rather, a world that imitates fantasy, with a population of automata that troubles our senses with its excessively visible and palpable strangeness." He went on to add, "It is almost a negative sensation, if it can be put that way."[8]

What he is reacting to here is the artificiality of a painting which, for all its realism, is much more focused on itself than on nature.

And that was what interested the painters of the early 20th century.

The Ingres oeuvre has never met with unanimous, unqualified approval. Today, as in the past, certain aspects of it remain totally indefensible. At the same time, other aspects are inimitable, and the best works have something truly unique about them. They disconcert, like fruits caught forever in all their vigor. These are works issuing from a willed, obstinately and artificially cultivated youthfulness whose enduring freshness has no source other than desire: a lover's passion for the human form, preferably in its feminine version; an artistic passion experienced as a religion of the beautiful.

I

A Youth

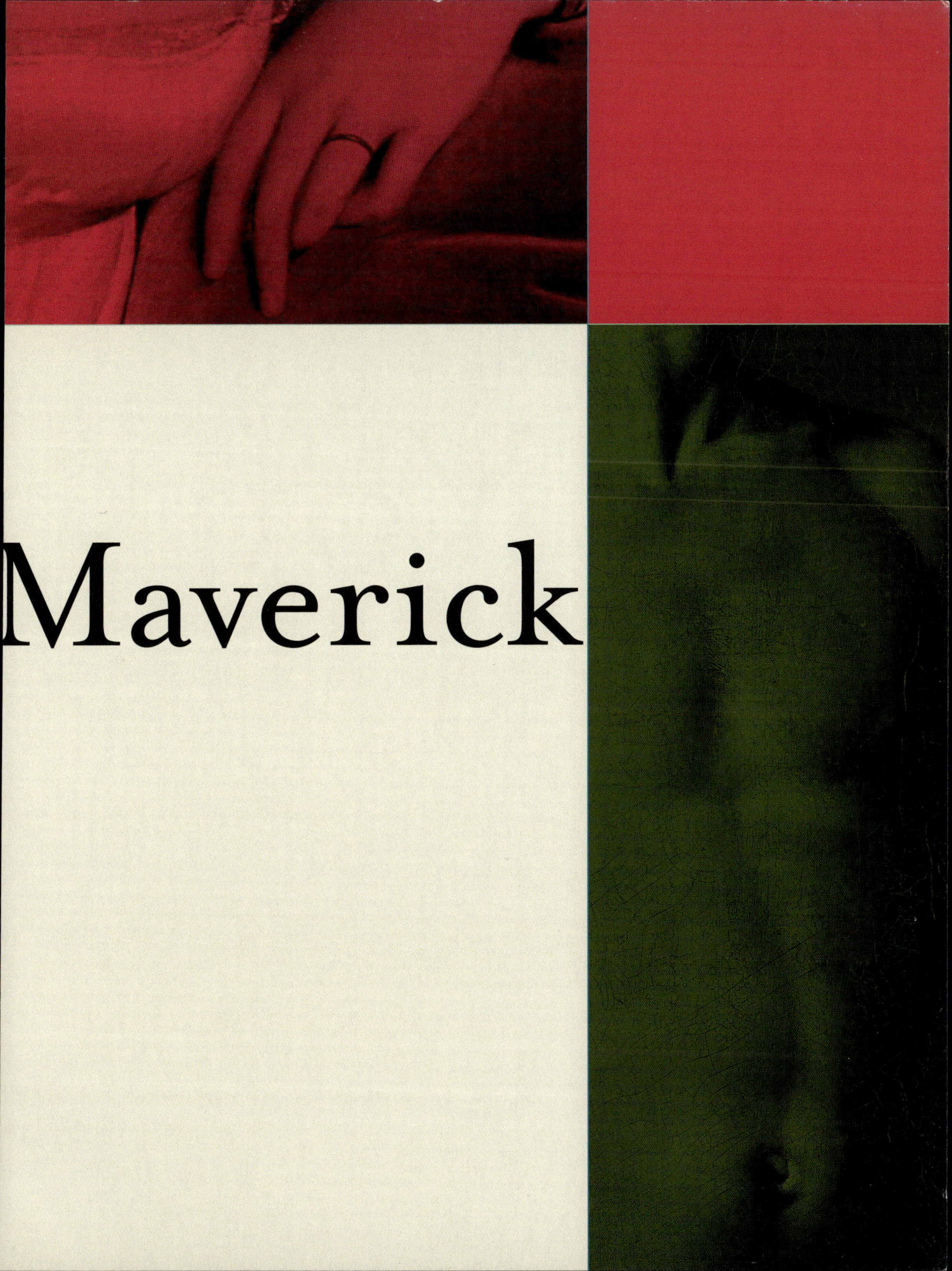
Maverick

Raised Amid Red Chalk

When seventeen-year-old Jean-Auguste Dominique Ingres left Montauban in 1897 to enroll in David's atelier in Paris, his art studies were already well advanced. His initial training had come from his father Jean Marie Joseph Ingres, ornamental sculptor, painter, architect and drawing teacher: in other words the all-purpose artist for polite Montauban society.

The French Revolution had put a premature stop to the boy's other studies, but his father had kept a close eye on his art training. "I was raised amid red chalk," he would say later. "My father, a musician and painter, intended me to be a painter and taught me music as a pastime. This excellent man, after giving me an enormous portfolio of three or four hundred prints of Raphael, Titian, Correggio, Rubens, Teniers, Watteau and Boucher – a bit of everything – found me a teacher in Toulouse, Monsieur Roques, who had been

Portrait of Jean-Charles-Auguste Simon
1793–94, black chalk and white chalk highlights on white paper, 41x36 cm
Orléans, Musée des Beaux-Arts

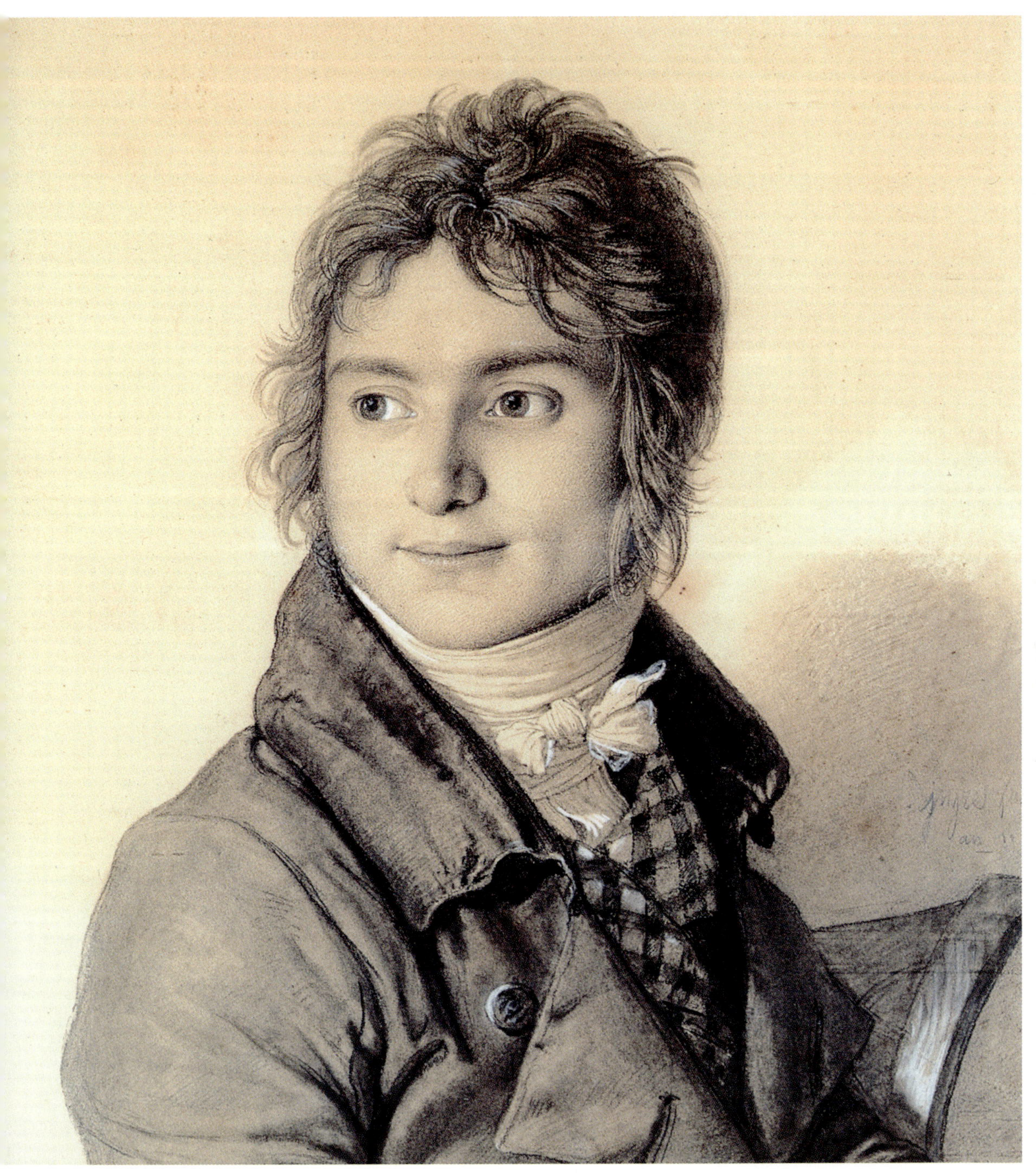

a pupil of Vien." [9] The conscientiousness of this double teaching program, plus the father's ambitions for his son, were major factors in Ingres' imperious urge towards painting. Music remained a second passion, and Ingres played the violin – apparently with real skill – all his life.

In Toulouse as in Paris, academic training was divided into different classes, each one a stage to be mastered before moving on to the next. The first of them involved drawing the parts of the body from prints; the second, "complete figures"; and the third, drawing from "low reliefs or sculpture in the round." It was only at the fourth stage that students worked from the life until able to "compose" – to create for themselves. More than elsewhere, painting in Toulouse had resisted changes in taste, holding to the standards of a Classicism whose models were Raphael and the great achievements of the 17th century. Joseph Roques also familiarized the young Ingres with the Neoclassical esthetic, thus making him highly receptive to David's teaching.

A brilliant student, Ingres was very soon conscious of a vocation not as a painter, but as a history painter. This was no small difference: to be a painter was to turn out all sorts of pictures, portraits, decorative panels and illustrations – the kind of utilitarian objects Ingres Senior made. History painting, by contrast, was a noble, intellectual activity. By showing the most exemplary human actions – borrowing from religious texts, ancient history or mythology, while meeting the obligation of *inventing* a composition with figures that made these actions intelligible – the history painter could compete with the other intellectual disciplines, and philosophy in particular. Such was the requirement of a "hierarchy of the genres" drawn up during the Renaissance, rigorously theorized by the Royal Academy of Painting and Sculpture under Louis XIV, and destined to survive, to a greater or lesser extent, until the late 19th century. According to this hierarchy the portrait, whose primary function was to *copy* the physical likeness of the subject, was a subordinate genre. Nonetheless Ingres took it up early, doubtless under pressure from his father: a painter had to make a living and one of the main sources of income was the portrait. The genre, once restricted to the kings and great ones of this world, had been democratized, and now every bourgeois with a reasonably comfortable lifestyle wanted to have his portrait painted.

Ingres was thirteen or fourteen when he drew his *Jean Charles Auguste Simon* portrait. The work reveals real mastery of drawing, together with the overmeticulousness and clumsy touches of the beginner. But what radiance of features, what fullness of form, what delicacy of contour! Life flows to the tip of the pencil and rises in full flower from the depth of the paper.

It is no small matter that this exceptional ability should appear so soon and so forcefully: it was, perhaps, the most innate single gift of a painter who was to become the greatest portraitist of his century. Even if it was in spite of himself: he would have preferred a career devoted entirely to the "elevated" genre of history painting.

18

The "Pure Greek Manner"

After the fall of Robespierre David had narrowly escaped death. Imprisoned in 1794, then amnestied with the coming of the Directory, he decided to give up politics completely and devote himself exclusively to his art and his atelier. But History, this time in the person of Napoleon Bonaparte, was once more about to tug at his sleeve.

His atelier, the focal point for European Neoclassicism, was probably the most important in Europe, and simply being one of his students meant a certain fame. When Ingres arrived such earlier students as Fabre, Wicar, Girodet, Gérard and Gros were already masters in their own right, and the atelier was welcoming a new generation of young artists.

In his book on David, Etienne-Jean Delécluze, a fellow student who went on to become an art critic, mentions the newly-arrived Ingres as someone who "not only stood out for the candor of his character and disposition, but immediately provided proof of a genuine talent...In the school he was among the most studious, and this inclination, together with his gravity and the absence of what is called *esprit* in France, meant that

Jacques Louis David
The Sabine Women
1799, oil on canvas, 385x522 cm
Paris, Musée du Louvre

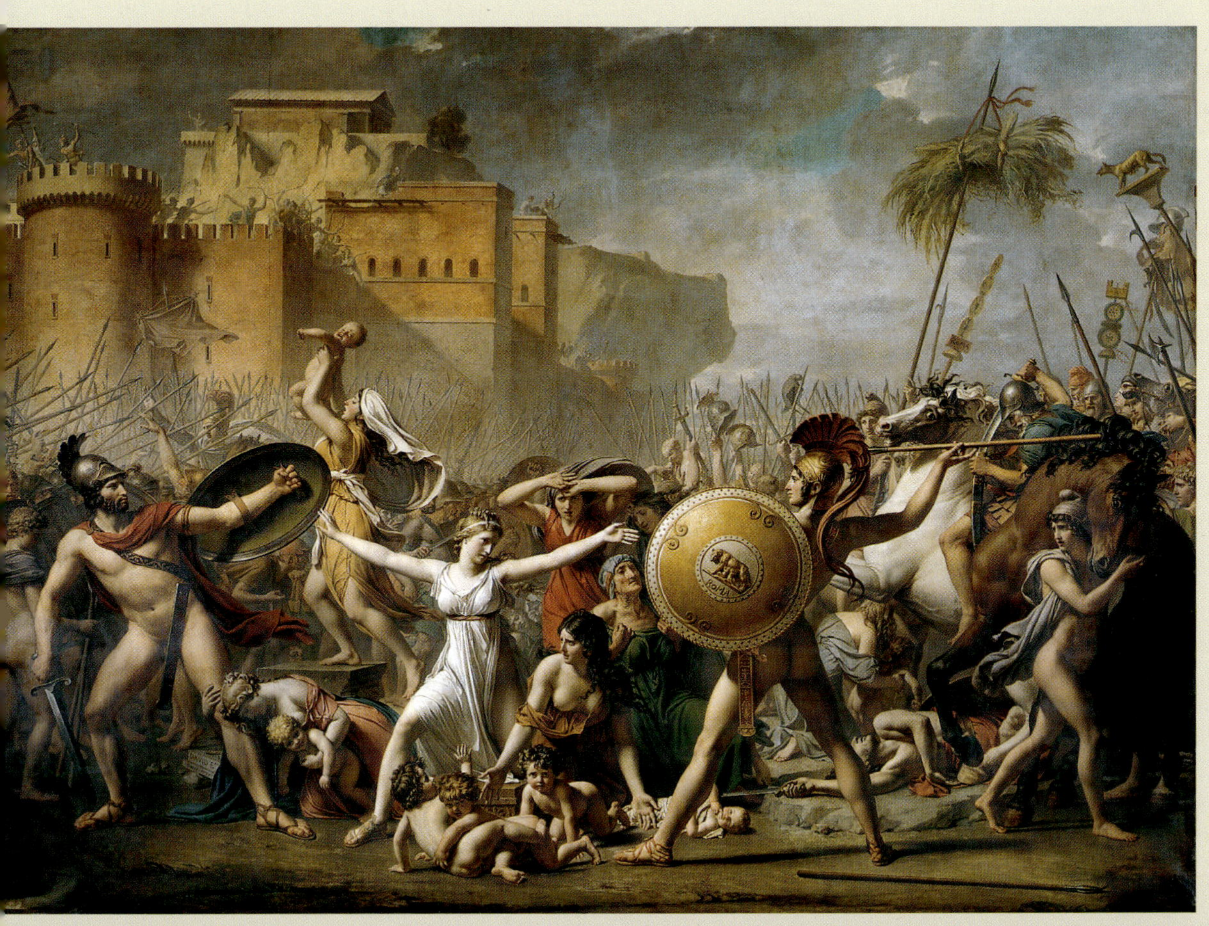

he took very little part in the crazy goings-on around him. He studied more seriously and with more perseverance than most of his fellow students."[10]

Delécluze was "very struck by the first figure Ingres painted in the atelier. Everything that now characterizes the talent of this artist – the subtlety of contour, the true, deep feeling for form, the extraordinary accuracy and assurance of relief – were already there to be seen in his first efforts. No one failed to notice these qualities, and although some of his comrades, and David himself, pointed out a tendency to exaggeration in his studies, everybody was struck by his capacities and acknowledged his talent."

In 1797 David was working on his large painting *The Sabine Women*: "I've undertaken something quite new. I should like to take art back to the principles followed by the Greeks." His intention was to work "in the pure Greek manner." Exactly what he meant by this is not easy to say, since the notion is clearly not an objective one: rather, it reflects the dream of an artist and an era that projected their current aspirations into an imagined or reconstructed past. For David, however, it meant bending his "Roman" style of the 1780s, with its rigorous realism of anatomy and perspective, towards a greater purity of form. His intention was to purify his drawing, clarify his composition using the frieze approach of the classical low reliefs, and portray his heroes naked.

The urge to regenerate art and society by rediscovering and imitating the exemplars of simplicity, virtue and purity provided by ancient Greece and Rome was an obsession throughout the last years of the 18th century. It permeated all the work of the Neoclassical movement, from the architecture of Claude-Nicolas Ledoux to revolutionary discourse, and was the source of the great "reform" of which David had been the leading advocate in the 1780s.

The Neoclassical esthetic tied in with the theories of the German philosopher Winckelmann and his interpretation of Greek art: the Greek esthetic ideal, he said, corresponded to the desire for moral elevation of the producing society; it was the reflection and the symbol of that society. This art set out to express nobility of soul and the idea of the divine through the simple, serene beauty of naked bodies, the restraint of their poses and the purity of their forms and contours. The "untranscendable" art of Greek statuary was the result not of copying nature, but of choosing all that was most beautiful in what nature produced. Thus, to create a single ideal figure, certain artists in antiquity had used several young women as models, taking what was best from each.

Working from these presuppositions, Winckelmann had developed a theory of "ideal beauty" that stipulated the absolute necessity of imitating the masters of antiquity and copying nature solely through their examples.

Based on the study and unqualified admiration of Greek statuary – known, however, only through Roman copies – this notion meant that painting, instead of

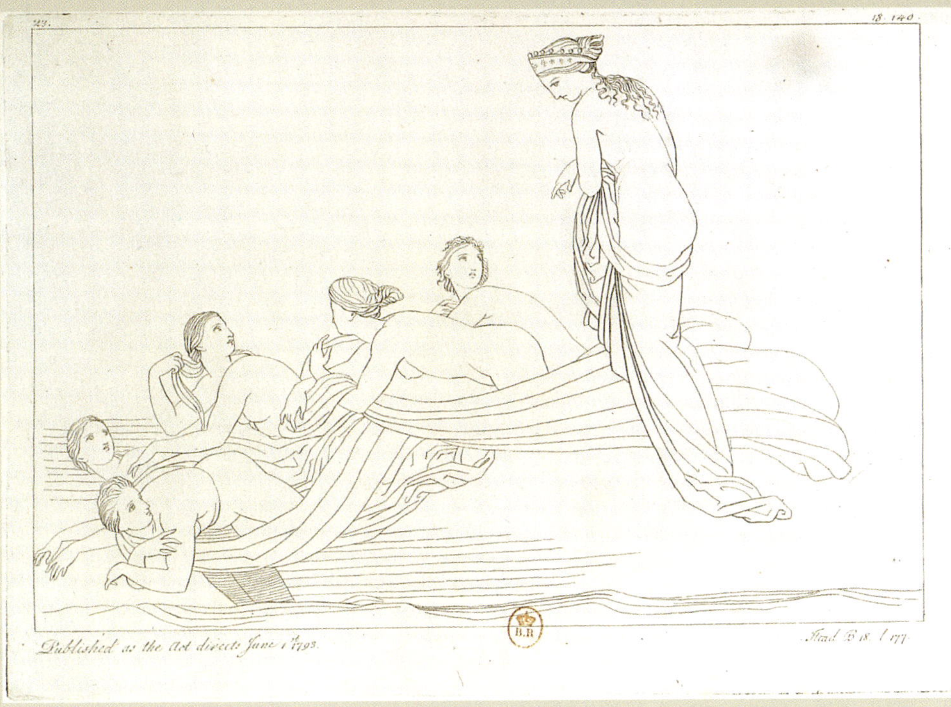

John Flaxman
Illustration for Homer's Iliad *(pl. 23)*
Thetis Ordering the Nereids to Descend into the Sea, 1793,
Paris, Bibliothèque Nationale de France

John Flaxman
Illustration for Homer's Iliad *(pl. 25)*
Thetis and Euronyme Receiving the Infant Vulcan, 1793,
Paris, Bibliothèque Nationale de France

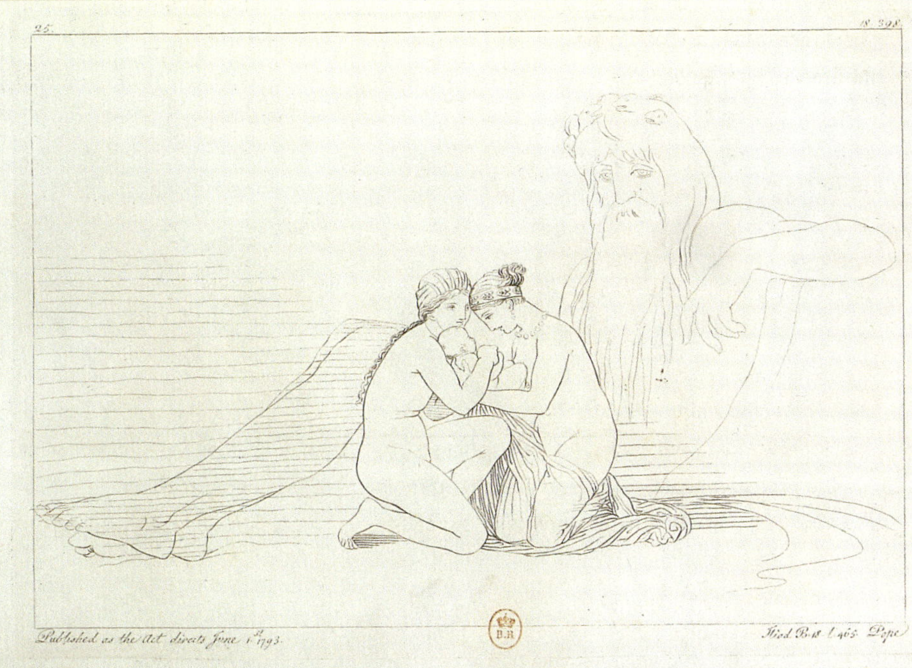

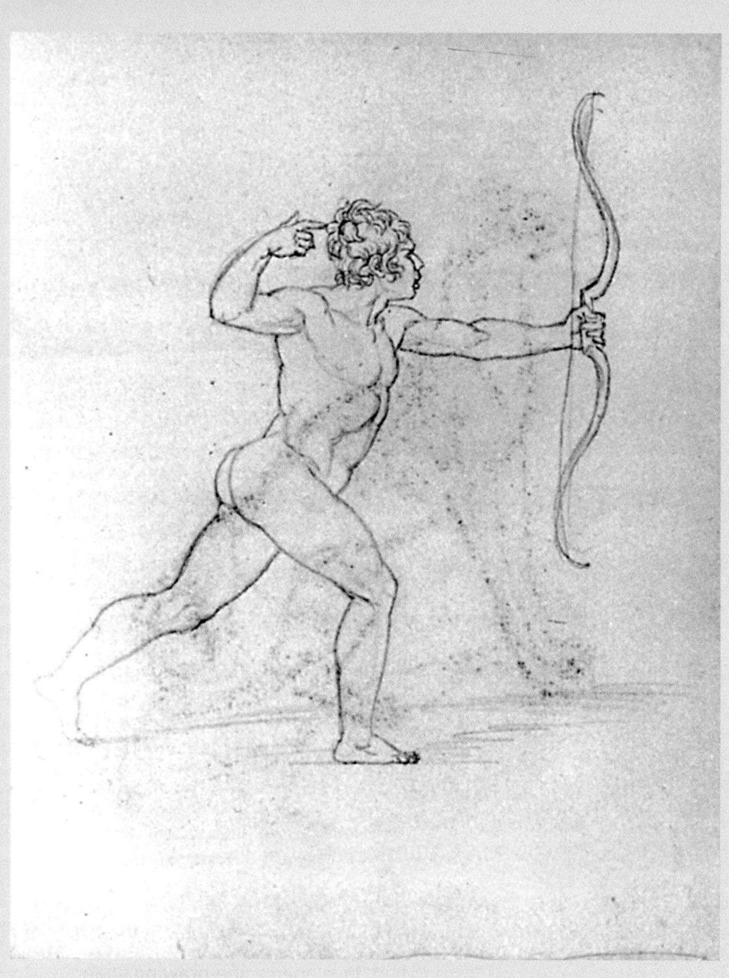

Fleury-Richard
Academic Male Nude
1796-1800, pencil on paper,
20x15.4 cm
Lyon, Musée des Beaux-Arts

seeking a direct relationship with nature, began to imitate sculpture. *The Sabine Women* shows that despite his immense talent, David himself failed to avoid this trap. As Régis Michel has put it, "In adapting painting to statuary, he petrifies it in the sculptural coldness of the chisel. And not without dogmatism: this is the ideal of an antiquarian." [11] Indeed, this antiquity-inflected ideal rapidly fossilized into the stereotypes and studio formulae which, once the Revolutionary period was over, would mark the output of the school of David.

In the closing years of the century the triumphal arrival in Paris of treasures plundered during Bonaparte's Italian campaign gave fresh impetus to the passion for Greek art. In David's atelier some students outstripped the master in their quest for "pure Greek." Calling themselves the "Thinkers" or the "Beards," Maurice Quay and his followers proclaimed their exclusive veneration for ancient art, Homer, the Bible, Ossian and Greek sculpture up until Phidias. Not content with reforming the arts, these Young Turks also saw themselves changing the way people lived, and paraded through Paris dressed as Agamemnon and other Greek figures. In their eyes even David's painting was impure, a point of view that ultimately got them thrown out of the atelier.

However these "Thinkers" were taking the new paths of an artistic primitivism that others would later bring to full flower.

There was a craze at the time for the most ancient Greek objects: the painted vases which, it was believed, revealed Greek art at its highest point of purity and simplicity. The most noble subjects, taken from Homer and mythology, were treated here using the simplest means of all: line. While sculpture, necessarily a rendering of volume, is inevitably destined to a certain realism, line alone suffices to convey the essential – the idea – through figures made all the more eloquent by their simplification. Line, what is more, possesses a decorative, unifying function that can underpin the visual harmony of the composition. As the Englishman John Flaxman had totally understood, these two seemingly opposed functions – the ideal and the decorative – can in fact make a perfect marriage. Flaxman had developed a line-drawing style – figures in profile, no indication of volume – directly inspired by Greek vases, and his plates for the *Iliad* and the *Odyssey* in 1793 met with enormous success. In France Bénigne Gagnereaux was making similar line drawings. Flaxman had a considerable influence, especially on Ingres: the latter would make artistic capital out of this primitivist esthetic, markedly different from the Neoclassical canons in that it drew on two-dimensional Greek vase representations or ancient low reliefs, and not on statuary.

Dissidence

The young artist still had to prove himself. He won the Grand Prix for a painted figure in 1801 and 1802, each time with a superb *Academic Study of a Male Torso* going far beyond the standard nude. The sheer energy of the drawing and composition, and above all a vibrant sensitivity to the beauty of the human form – to its "Venusness," you might say, even when the bodies in question are male – set these works apart from the Neoclassical nude and its rhetoric of virile heroism.

The goal of the studies in an atelier like David's was the supreme distinction, the Prix de Rome scholarship, which entitled the winner to a four-year residence at the Académie de France in Rome. There he would round off his studies via direct contact with ancient art and the work of the Italian masters. If the work of the young artist during his stay in Rome met the standards of the Institut de France, the doors of the Salon were open to him on his return and his career virtually assured.

After an initial failure, Ingres won the Prix de Rome in 1801, when the examination subject was taken from the *Iliad*: *Achilles Receives the Envoys of Agamemnon*. With its figures inspired by classical statues, its naked, muscular warriors, its very "Poussin" landscape and background characters, and its strict archeological observation, the work initially seems to match David's teaching. However a closer look reveals flagrant divergences. Facing the motionlessly sculptural group of the envoys, examples of a "Roman" heroism thoroughly in the style of the master, Achilles and Patrocles reflect a quite different esthetic. These two figures are marvelously alive, mobile, and full of the youthful, sensual grace that gives the picture its beauty. The painter seems entirely focused on these bodies with their tapering limbs, vividly supple contours and infinite subtlety of relief. This relief, however, indicates no volume; on the contrary, it provides flat, chiseled shapes with only the slightest of projections, exactly as on a low relief. What the painter is working on here is principally the linearity of the work. And from here on in, in the interests of enhancing the rhythmic sequence of curves and their interplay between the two sides of the canvas, Ingres does not hesitate to sacrifice anatomy or, better still, "fake" it: Ajax's thigh, on the right of the picture, bulges monstrously, and his entire leg is lit so as to set a firm, tense, luminous arc against the sinuous adolescent limbs to the left. Here we catch that "fondness for exaggeration" that was already worrying his teacher and his fellow students, and which in the future would take on greater emphasis and provoke ever-increasing criticism. Moreover it is clearly neither the dramatic action – fairly weak: the figures are only talking – nor the moral content of the subject that interests the artist most, but the formal issues.

His divergences from the norm became rapidly more marked. As Napoleon's Consulate was unable to cover the expenses of the most recent Prix de Rome winners, they had to wait several years before leaving for Italy. After leaving David's atelier, Ingres was given a studio in the former Capuchin convent, where Gros, Girodet, and his ex-fellow students Granet and Bartolini also had theirs. According to Delécluze's account, "Monsieur Ingres and his friend Bartolini, the sculptor from Florence, shared two cells, and nearby was Monsieur Bergeret, a friend and admirer of Monsieur Ingres. These three artists, whose work at the time was focused on the Italian artists of the Renaissance, made up a kind of academy of their own within the convent. They let no one in and we had only a vague idea of what they were doing in their mysterious studios." This secrecy is hardly surprising if we consider the small *Venus Wounded by Diomedes* painted by Ingres at this time; for despite its grace the work is pure heresy in terms of Neoclassical orthodoxy.

Neoclassicism approached classical subject matter as a vehicle for morality and philosophy, foregrounding exemplary heroes – mostly Roman – as embodiments of civic virtues inherent in the post-revolutionary Republic. And as we have already seen, it did so using a plastic language inspired by ancient statuary.

For *Venus Wounded by Diomedes*, however, Ingres drew on two-dimensional material: painted Greek

Academic Study of a Male Torso
1800, oil on canvas, 99x80 cm
Montauban, Musée Ingres

Academic Study of a Male Bust
1801, oil on canvas, 102x80 cm
Paris, Ecole Nationale Supérieure des Beaux-Arts

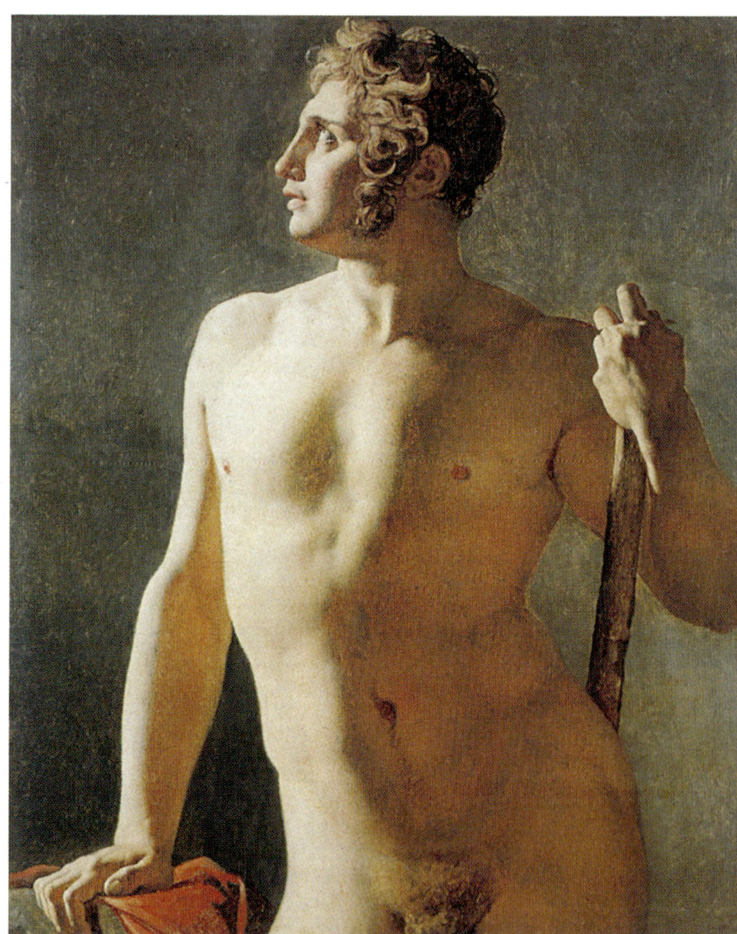

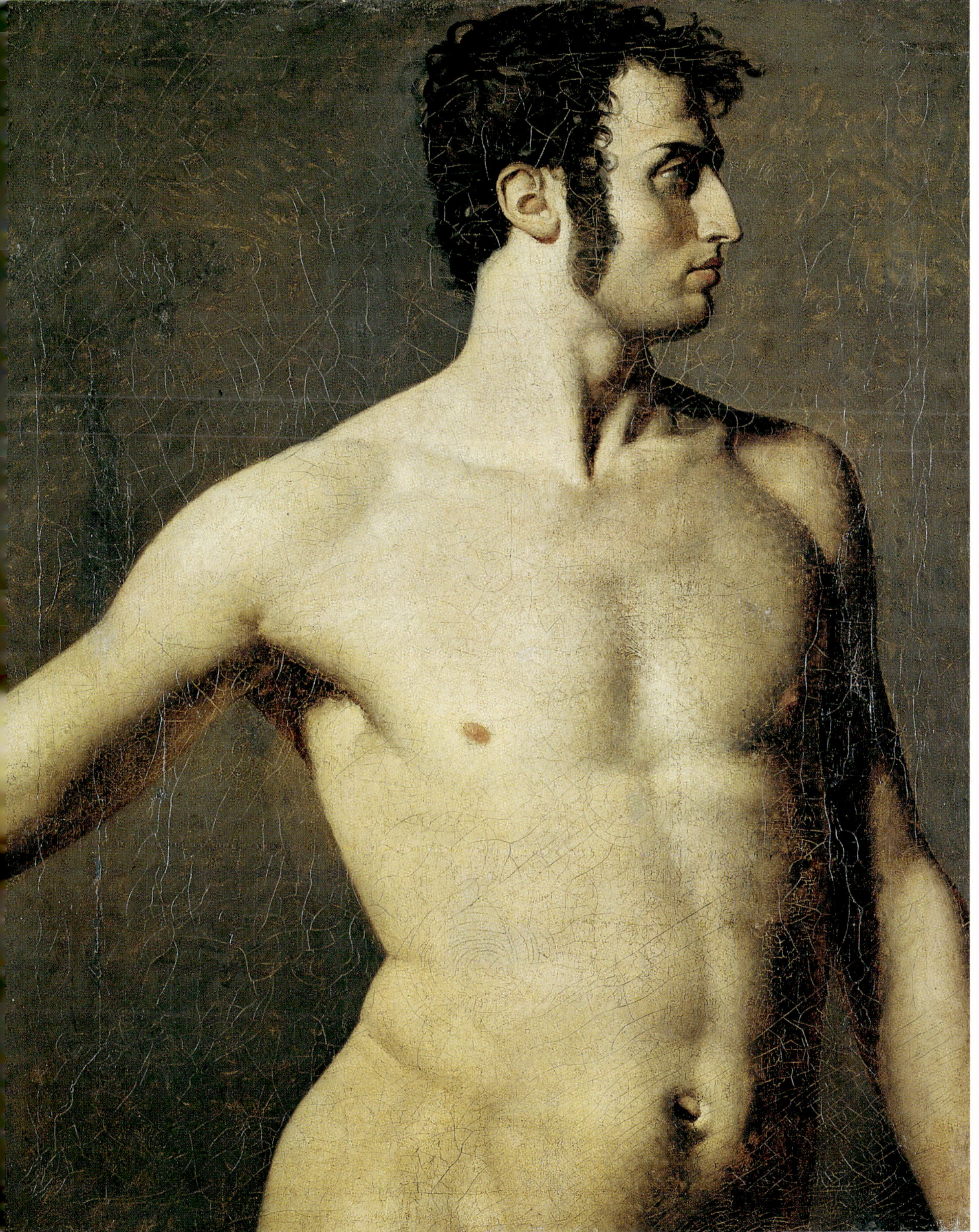

Léon Matthieu Cochereau
Interior of the Studio of David
1814, oil on canvas, 90x105 cm
Paris, Musée du Louvre

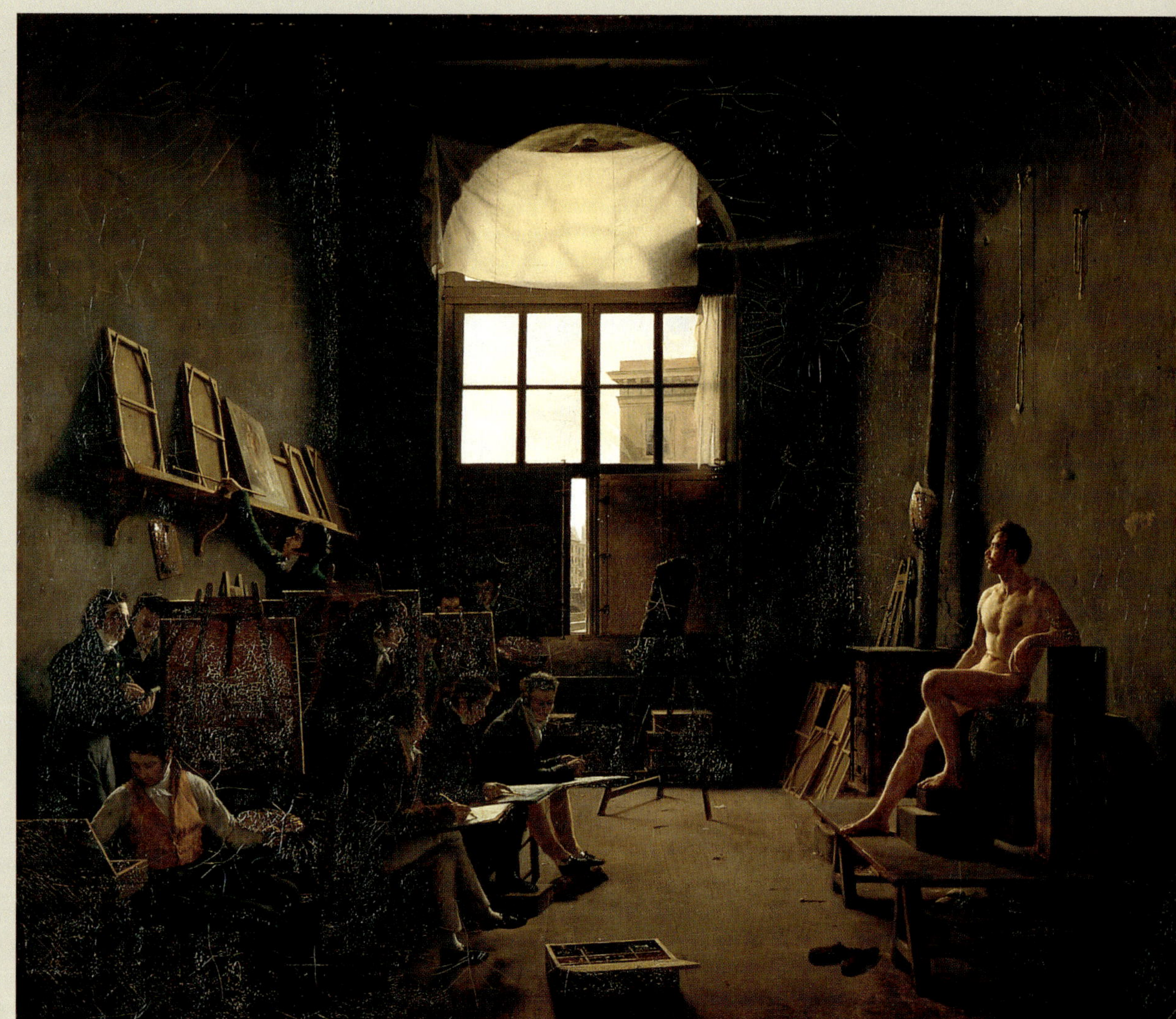

vases, low reliefs and ancient cameos. The horses and chariot are quite literally copied from an engraving taken from a vase. The artist clearly delights in accentuating the flatness and exacerbated linearity of the figures, and to such an extent that they lose all bodily, spatial and moral depth. He is in search of the purity of form discovered by early civilizations, but in the interests of a beauty taking us back to the founding myths, not of any moral values that might be associated with the subject. In doing so he reduces art to a question of style and personal taste: no mean venture, in that this means the very function of painting is at stake.

A further point of interest is that this small painting uses a distinctive feminine silhouette, whose forms are stylized and whose limbs are too sinuous. This type of figure, later used in many different forms, was already to be found in a delicious little drawing, *Hermaphrodite and the Nymph Salmacis*.

In the drawing the nymph is embracing the young man, who rejects her advances. The legend has it that she begged the gods to unite their bodies and her prayer was granted: Hermaphrodite became both man and woman.

The overstated expression of amorous passion is seized here in the extension of simplified forms defined solely by their contours. The two bodies form a single unit, without depth yet opened at its centre by a "niche" or little "window" exactly focused on the sexual organs, facing but not touching each other. This is an odd detail in relation to the anomalous reflection in the water: in the Greek fable it is Narcissus, not Hermaphrodite who studies himself in the water of a spring. Ingres has merged the two mythological heroes, and the water, as mirror, intensifies the image of the nymph's ardor – a point to be remembered when a mirror appears in Ingres' future female portraits.

With their "pear-shaped" torso, extended neck, strictly upright posture and utter physical fluidity, Venus and even more so Salmacis are the first examples of the typically Ingres figure that would reappear in the large Thetis of some years later. At the same time a certain imaginary conception of woman comes to the surface here: a sensual, supple, malleable creature, a sort of amorous octopus of which this drawing provides the initial curving movements; and which, in the closing phase of the oeuvre, will spread its countless arms in the circular space of the *Turkish Bath*.

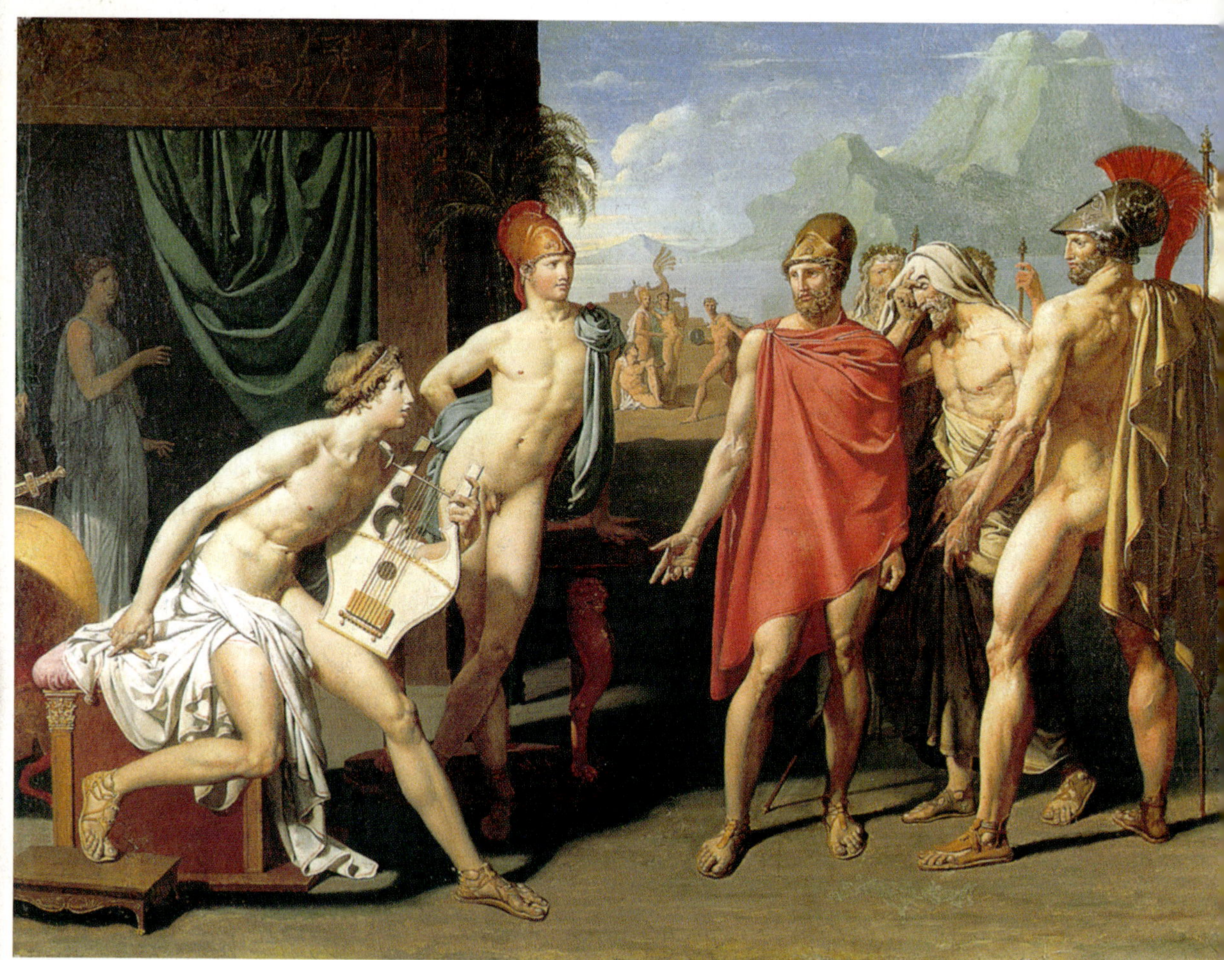

Achilles Receives the Envoys of Agamemnon

1801, oil on canvas, 110x155 cm

Paris, Ecole Nationale Supérieure des Beaux-Arts

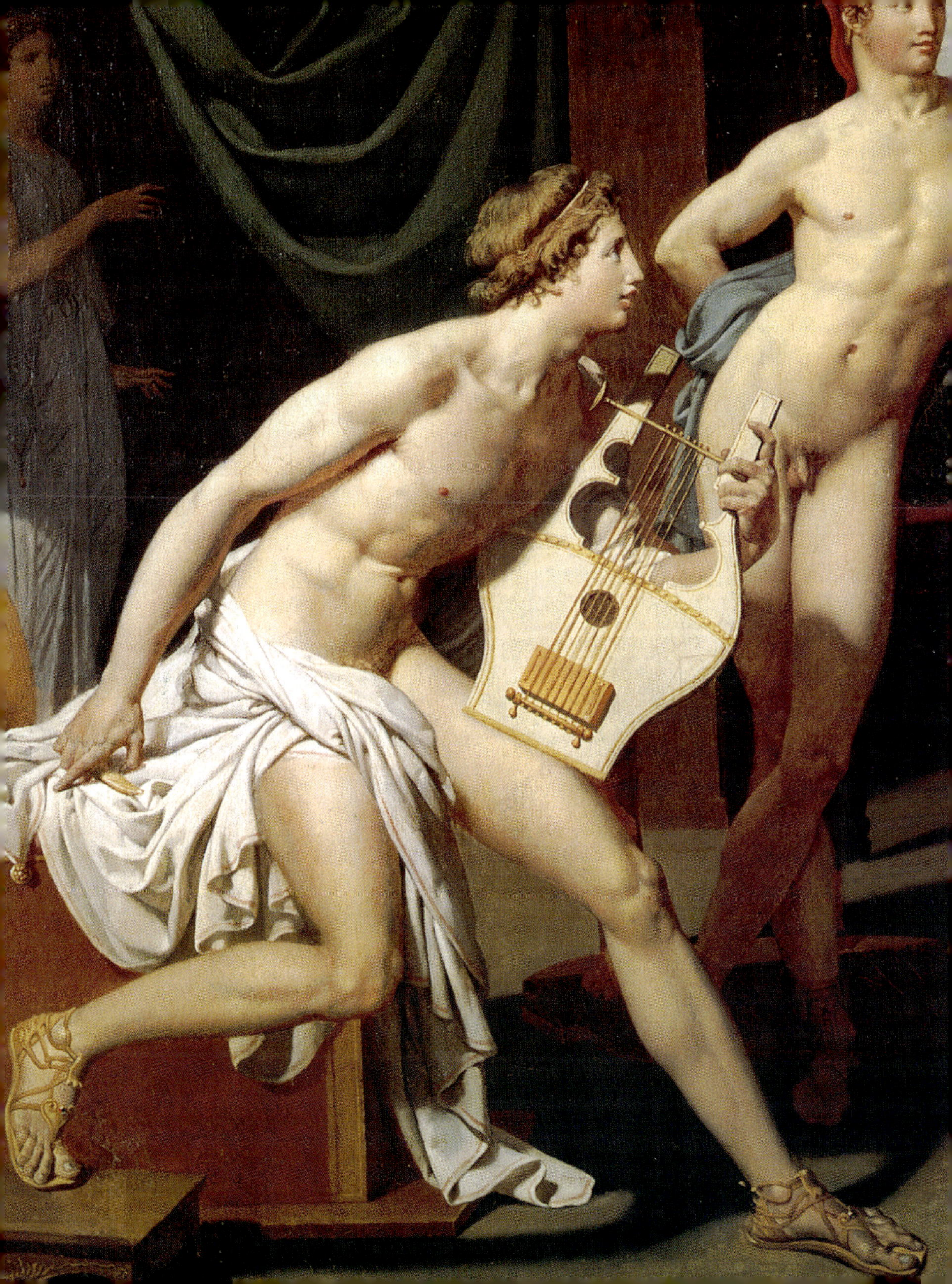

Venus Wounded by Diomedes
1810, oil on canvas, 26.5x33 cm
Basel, Kunstmuseum

W. Tischbein
Collection of Engravings from Ancient Vases
(vol. I, pl. 23)
1803, Diana Received by Apollo at Delphi
Paris, Bibliothèque Nationale de France

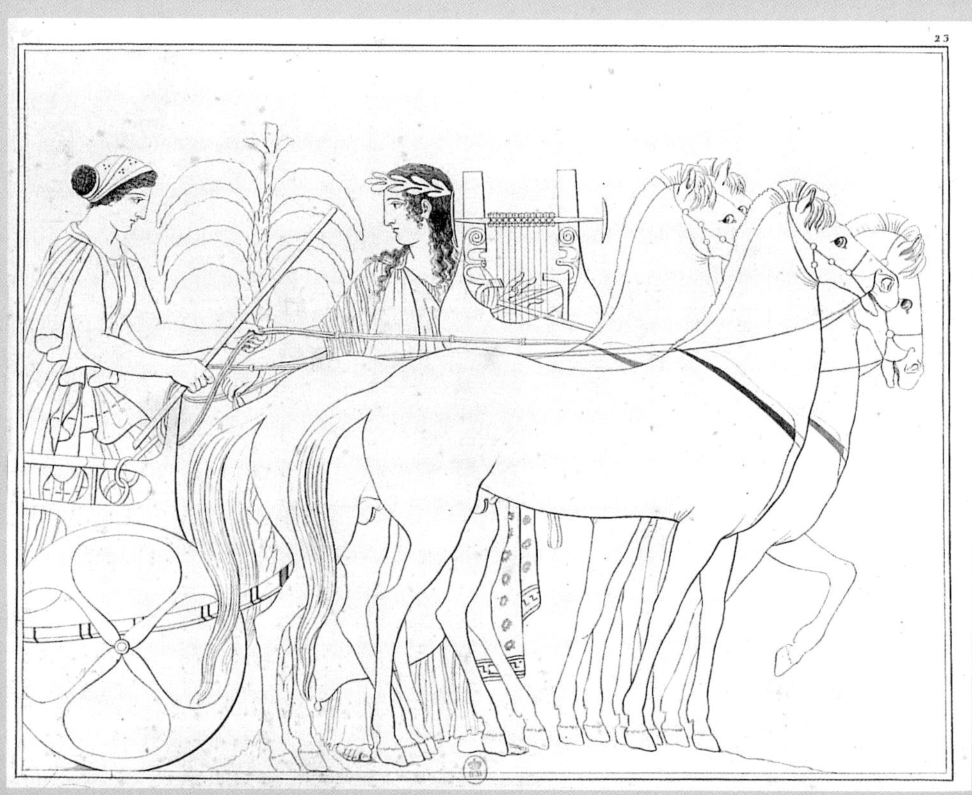

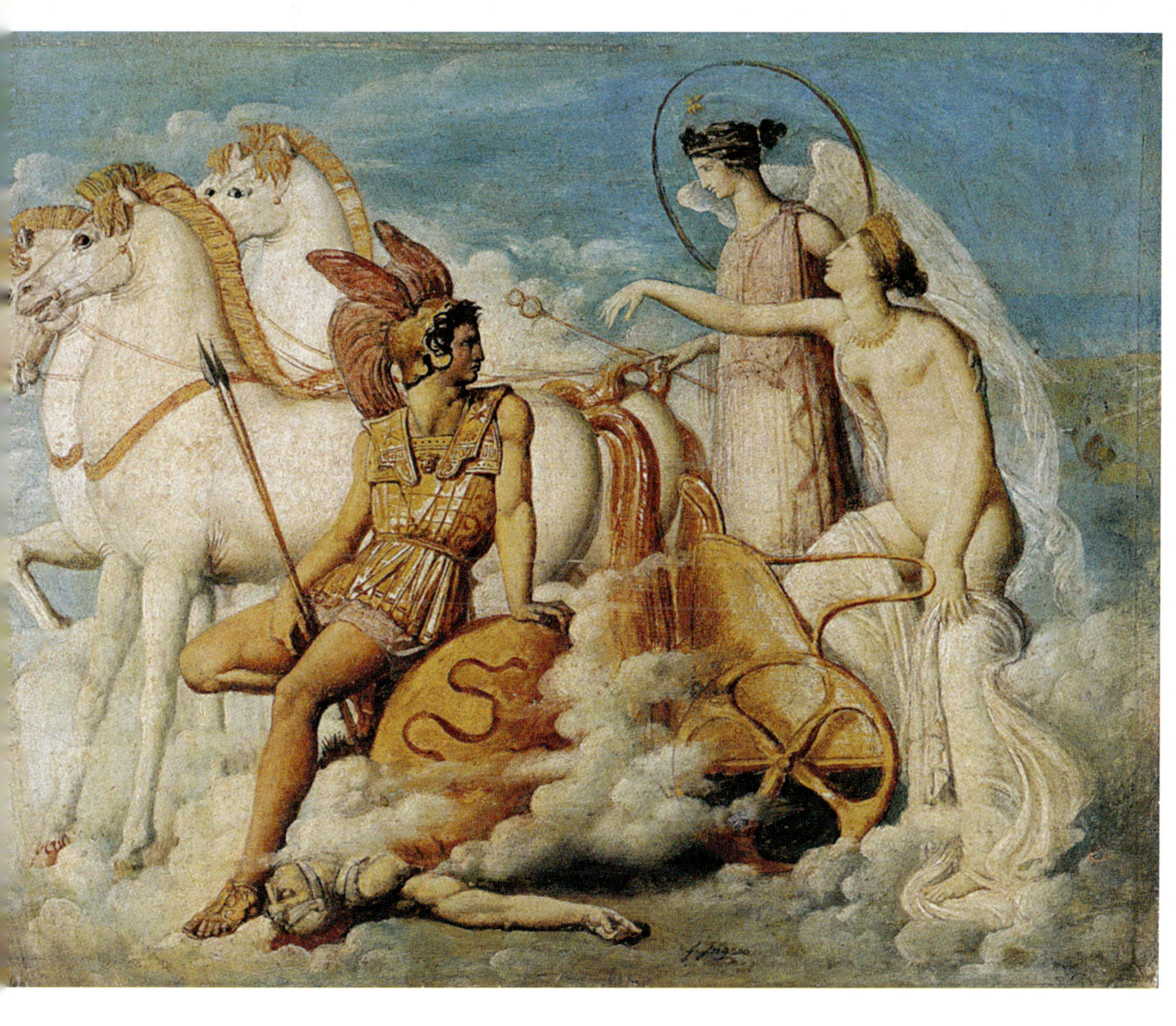

Hermaphrodite and the Nymph Salmacis
undated, pencil and watercolor on paper
17.6x17.2 cm
Montauban, Musée Ingres

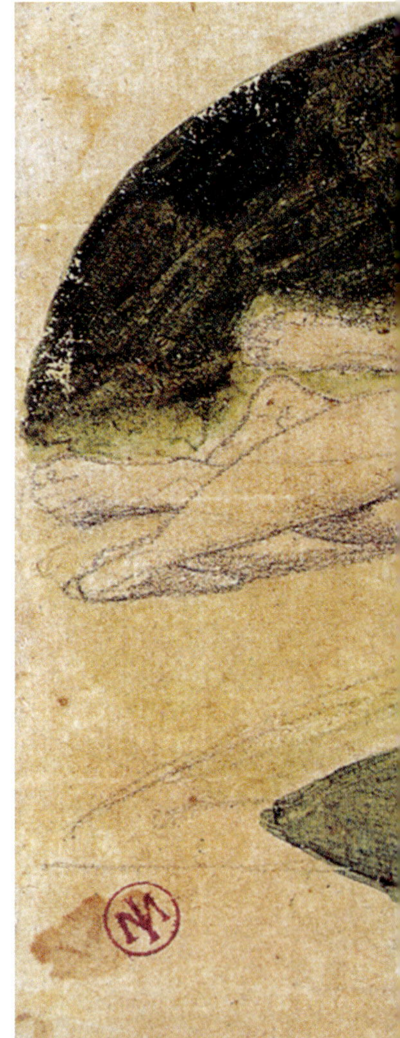

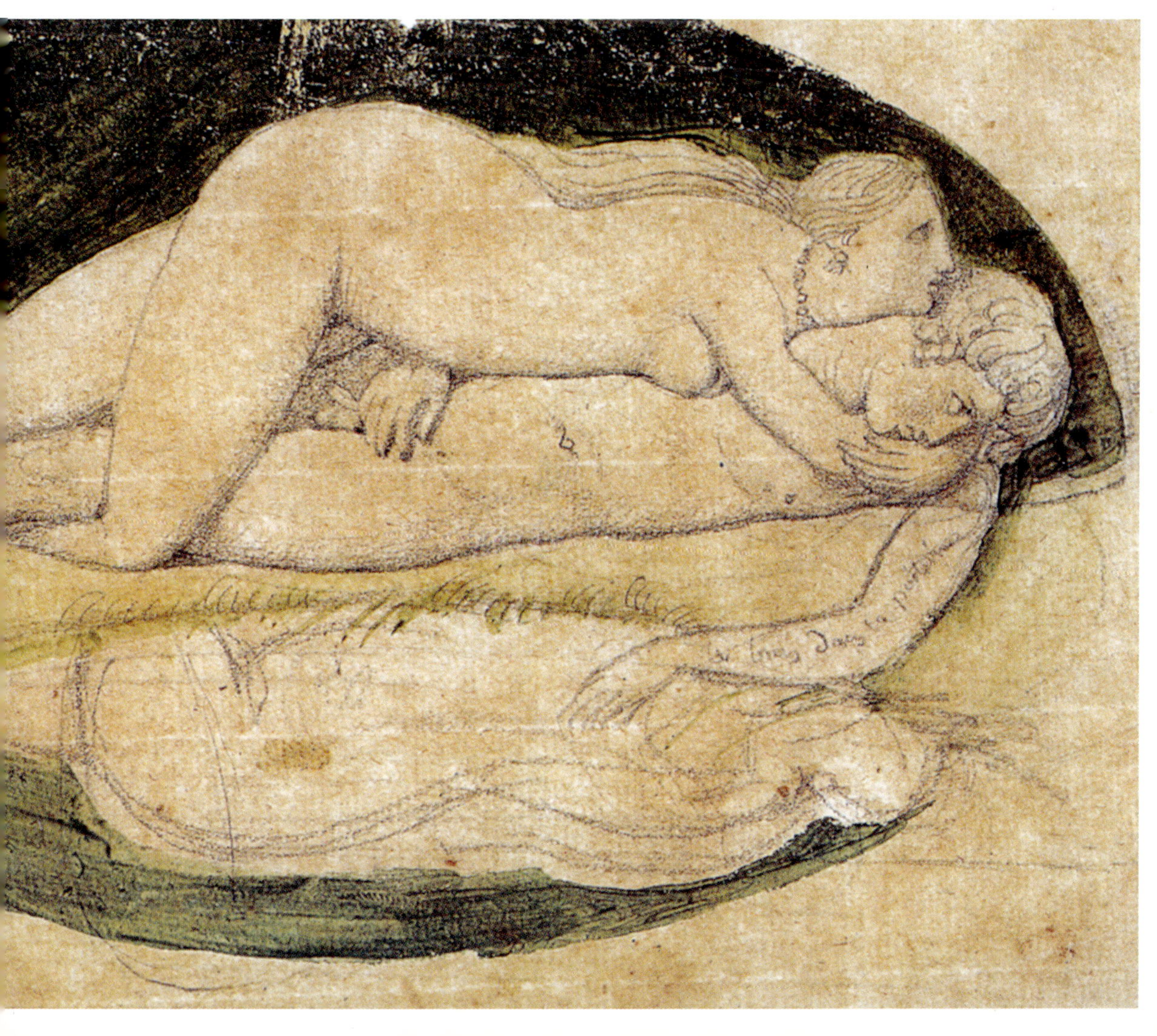

Portraits I

It was thanks to his friend Lorenzo Bartolini that Ingres deepened his knowledge of the Italian painters of the Renaissance, and especially the Florentine masters. This latter tradition, which enjoyed no special status at the time, would become one of his main sources of inspiration, notably in the field of the portrait: his *Portrait of Lorenzo Bartolini*, painted during this period, contains clear references to Bronzino's *Portrait of a Young Man*, also known as *Portrait of a Sculptor*, now in the Louvre. This half-length portrait shows the subject's face in three-quarter view as he holds an object – a fragment of an ancient statue – emblematic of his social function and his moral and intellectual identity. But where the artist's most overtly avails himself of the Florentine Mannerists Bronzino and Pontormo is in the authority and clarity of a monumental style: assurance of composition, generosity of the simplified forms, and purity of drawing. At the same period, in his *Napoleon Bonaparte in the Uniform of the First Consul*, he opts for a scrupulous realism in the rendering of detail, proof of his close interest in the Northern tradition of the Flemish Primitives and Holbein.

In the years 1804-06 Ingres painted a series of portraits that are a kind of initial, sudden flowering of masterpieces. In quick succession came the *Self-portrait at the Easel*, the portraits of Philibert, Marie-Françoise and Caroline Rivière, and the *Portrait*

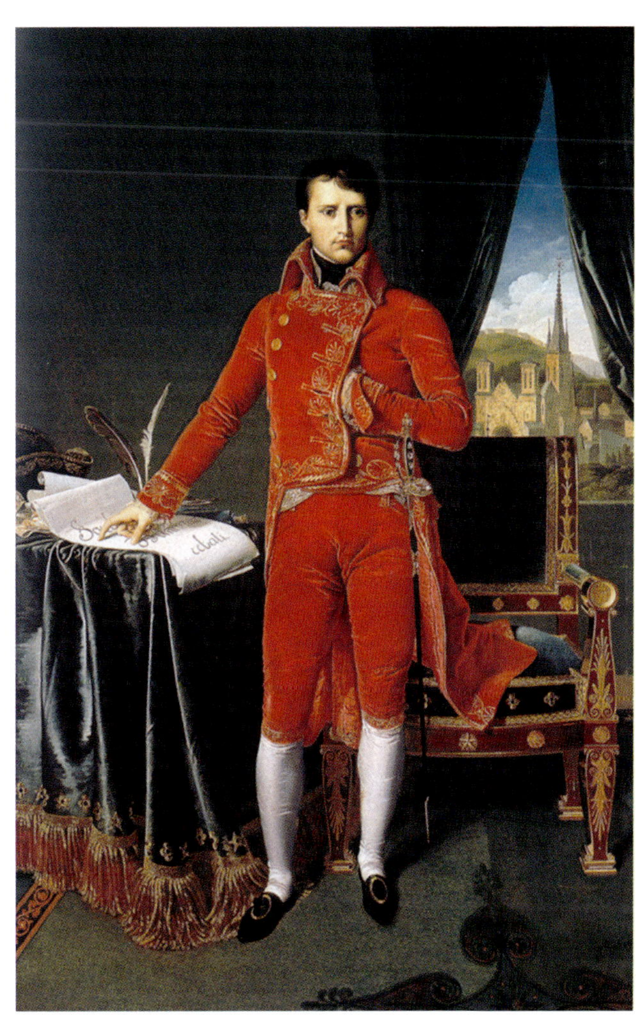

Napoleon Bonaparte in the Uniform of the First Consul
1803, oil on canvas, 227x147 cm
Liège, Musée d'Armes

Portrait of Philibert Rivière
1805, oil on canvas, 116x89 cm
Paris, Musée du Louvre

of Madame Aymon (known as *La Belle Zélie*).

At the age of twenty-five Ingres was in a state of grace, in full possession of his painterly means. With utter confidence these works proclaimed a new esthetic whose force seemed to put the work of all his contemporaries in the shade. By comparison the best of David's portraits appear prosaic, those of Gérard stand exposed in all their fake delicacy, and those of Girodet are frankly leaden.

The keynote of this esthetic is the extreme sharpness of the technique, as if the image were bathed in a diamond-like luminosity. There is little depth of field and little emphasis on volume: the figures are thus set on a very shallow plane strictly parallel to the picture surface, and defined by forms and lines of great fullness, chosen for their expressive and *decorative* capacities. At the same time this linear "abstraction" is balanced by the density of the lovingly modeled living forms and the acute realism of the details and textures.

The resultant picture is a total composition all of whose plastic components are given the same intensity: Mademoiselle Rivière's boa and mustard-colored gloves, Madame Rivière's shawl and Madame Aymon's kiss-curls are no less important than the oval of their faces or the line of their shoulders and neck. Most often neutral, the backdrop is not mere empty space, but a dense plane that sets off the contours.

Ingres' intention was not simply to show a person and point up a personality, but to create a thoroughgoing work of art, a total manifestation of his conception of beauty. And this beauty, while it takes truthful account of the subject, is essentially tied to the style, the "manner," and thus to requirements of a purely artistic nature.

The technique is impeccable, bringing the same unfailing virtuosity to all aspects of the picture, including skin, folds, accessories and furniture.

The paint shows the same evenness: Ingres neither exaggerates nor skimps, using no impasto but leaving no "hollow areas" either. As he would say later, transparent shadows are out: they have to be "filled" with white. All his shades of color have equal covering-power, their combined result being a single, uniform pictorial "layer" marked by density and seamlessness. His mastery of paint – used precisely, sufficiently and almost parsimoniously – would remain visible in the least of his painted studies. In the finished pictures, the same economy of means is brought to bear on the creation of structure and the rendering of relief; there is, however, great sophistication in the use of the final glazes, an additional smoothness that gives his surfaces their incomparable enameled look.

The image is smooth, as if seen through glass or, as critic Gaétan Picon so accurately put it, in a mirror. Ingres' pictures combine all the appearance of reality with a perfection and a vividness that are not of this world.

His realism, sometimes described as photographic, is not at all that of the painters of reality. Curiously,

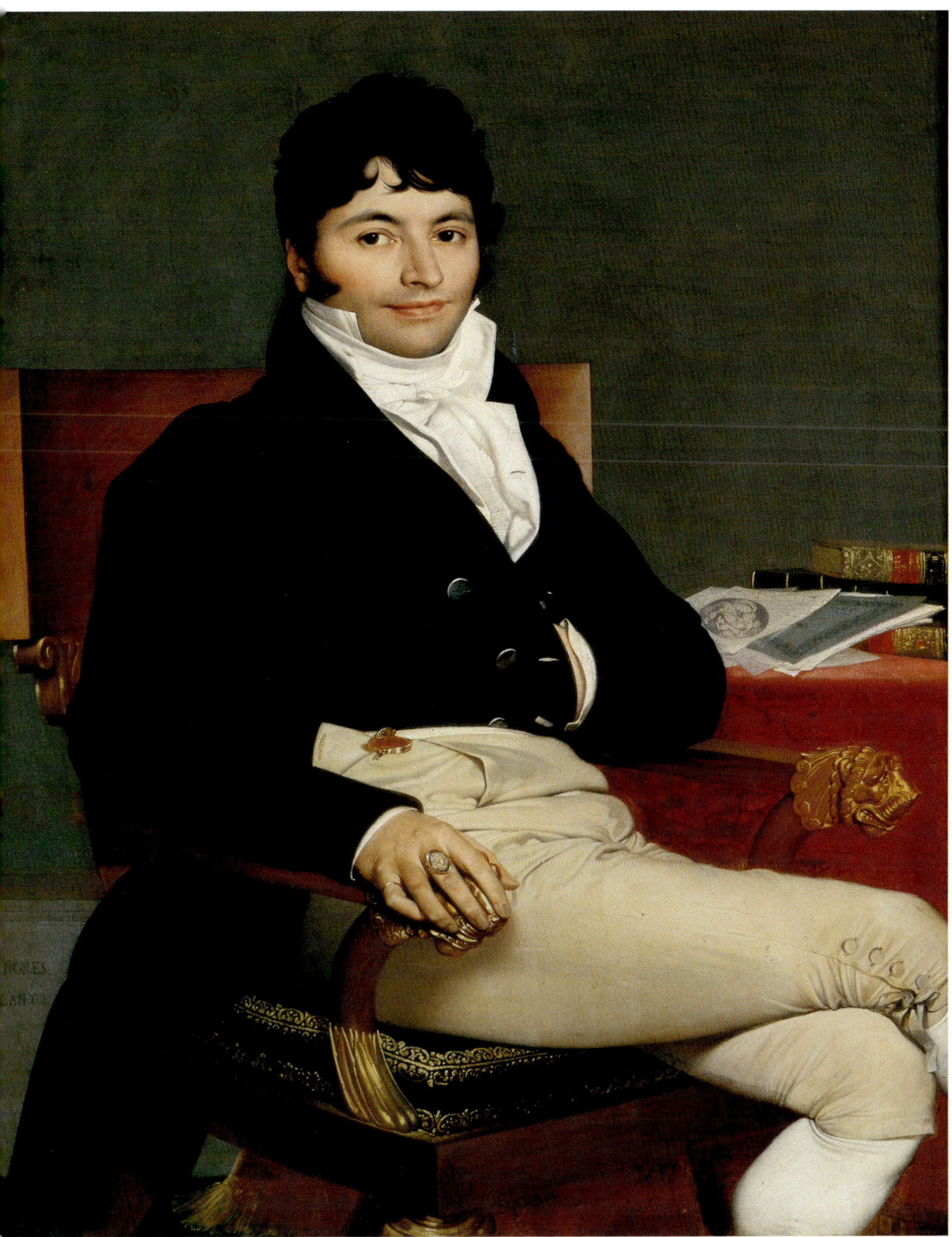

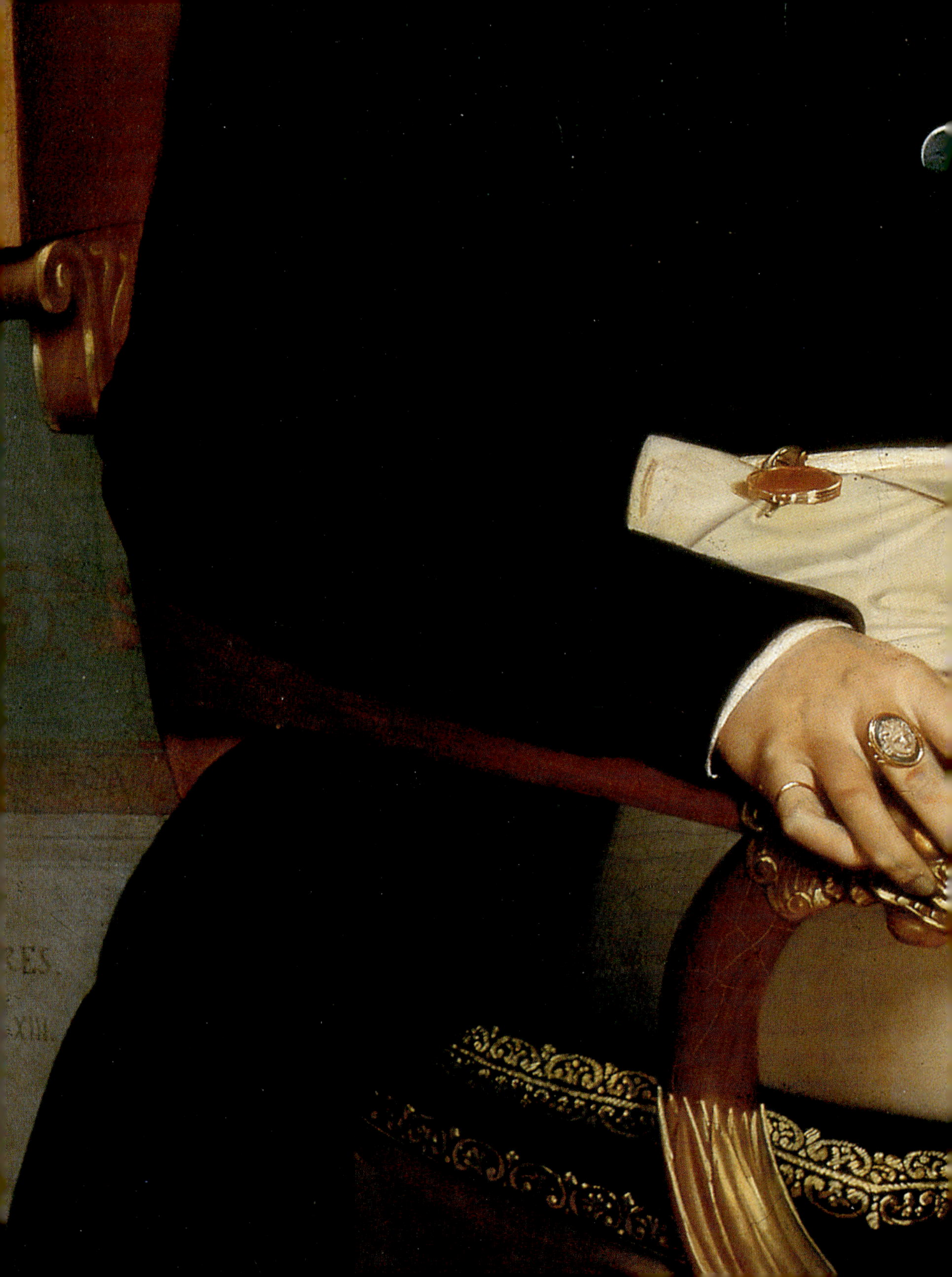

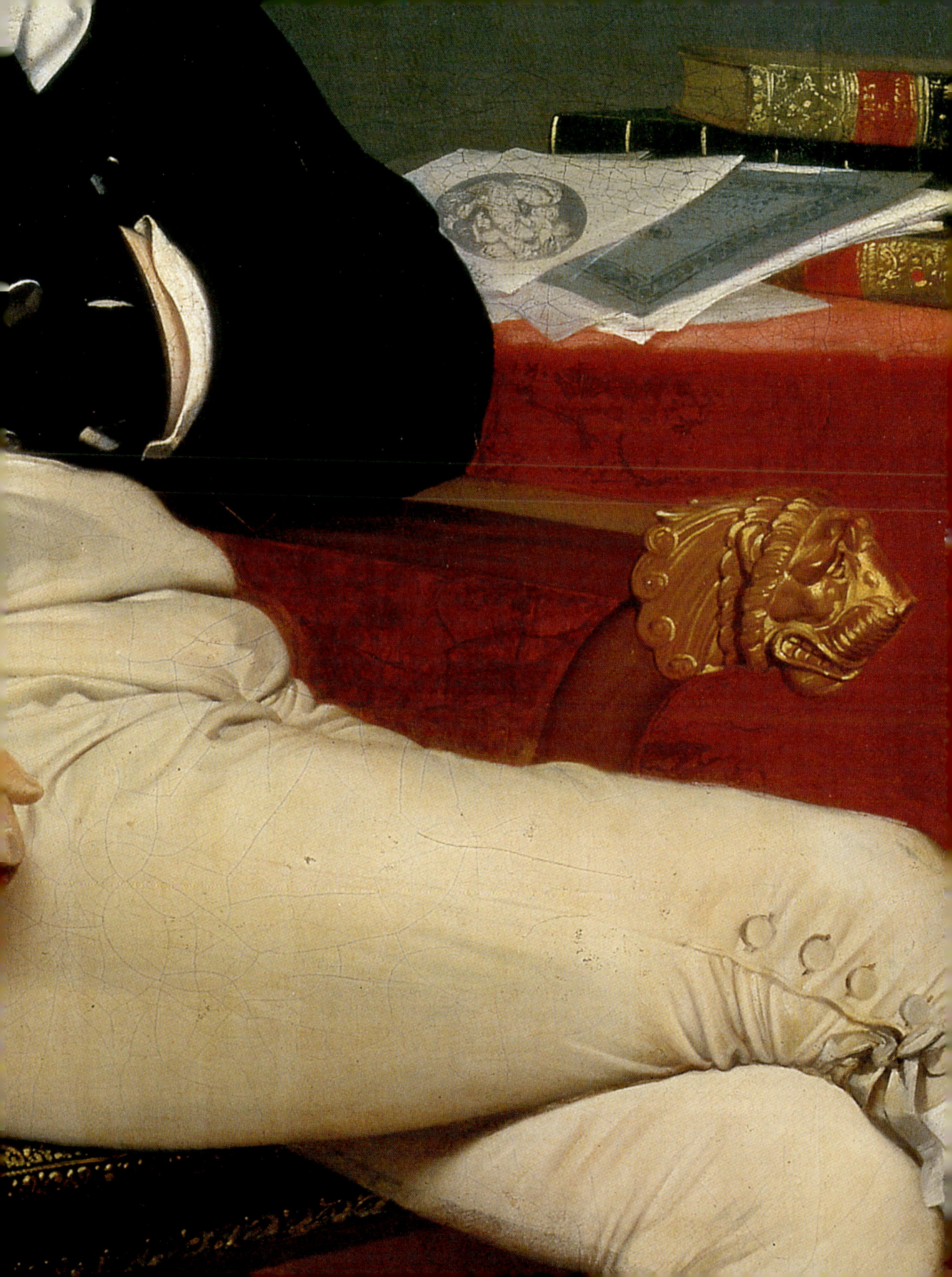

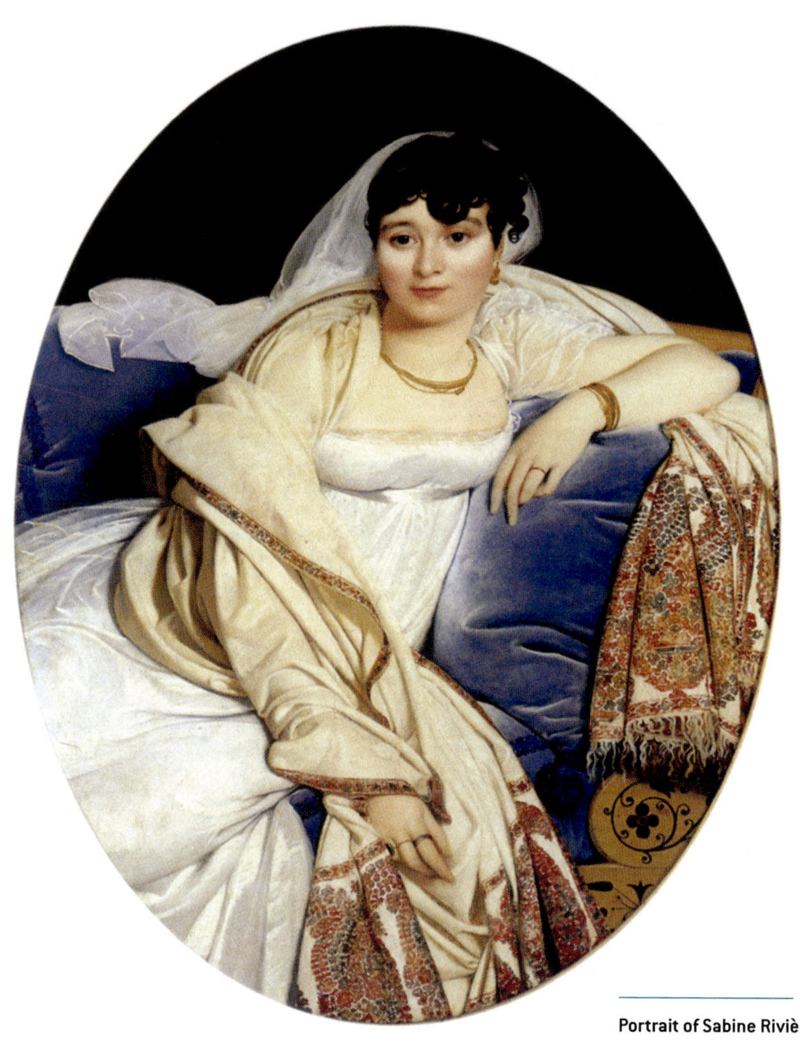

Portrait of Sabine Rivière

1805-6, oil on canvas, 115x90 cm

Paris, Musée du Louvre

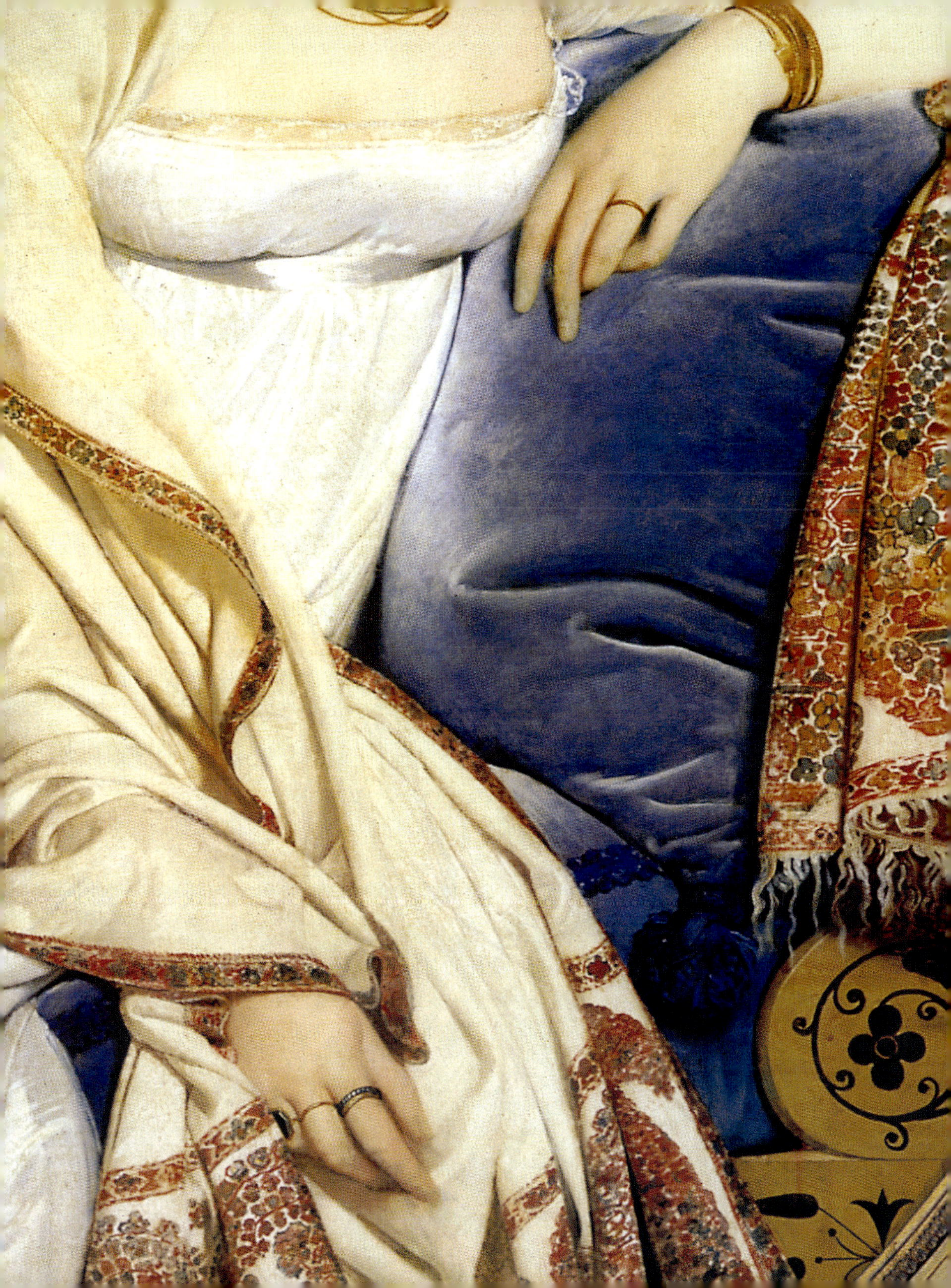

by its excessive precision – and as if the painting increased the sharpness of our eye – it verges on the opposite. This strange state of affairs goes a long way towards explaining the fascination his pictures exert. The eye is inundated with their visual overabundance: the fullness of the bodies, the skin, the velvet, the muslin, the chased jewelry are offered to us as patent and palpable. And yet they have lost the transitory feel of reality: the quiver of life has left them. These forms, figures and textures are frozen in an abstract perfection; seized for all eternity, they are now part of an immutable order – that of beauty according to Ingres.

Of all these works, the *Portrait of Sabine Rivière*, with its abstract play of swirling lines given harmony by the oval frame, the lively restraint of its colors, and its crystalline light, best conveys this impression of the miraculous apparition of a reality that is rich, entire and spirited, yet trapped in the ice of an unworldly perfection. This in no way excludes emotion, however. In Ingres' female portraits a sort of emotional vibrancy, or emotivity, everywhere signals the commitment of their creator.

Ingres has a characteristic approach to his female subjects. From one portrait to another we find the same full, smooth flesh, supple and somehow malleable; the same too-large, too-gentle eyes, always just slightly dreamy and with a touch of mannered melancholy; a psychology just out of reach, as if of a languorous soul; and the same pleasure in finding a harmony between clothing, jewelry and exposed skin. Special attention is given to the placing of the head and neck on the shoulders: a recurring "plastic theme" in itself and the locus of a true erotic crystallization. In this part of his pictures – in the luminous planes of the face, in the roundness and softness of shoulders and throats, in the near-imperceptible yet so moving crease that quickens the curving cylinder of always over-long necks – the paint attains, if not the temperature of desire, at least the luminosity of a dazzled, sated gaze. This hollowing-out of the throat, this filling-out or elongation of the neck are found time and again in his portraits and figures, as one of the clearest marks of Ingres' eroticism.

Portrait of Madame Aymon (known as ***La Belle Zélie***)
1806, oil on canvas, 59x49 cm
Rouen, Musée des Beaux-Arts

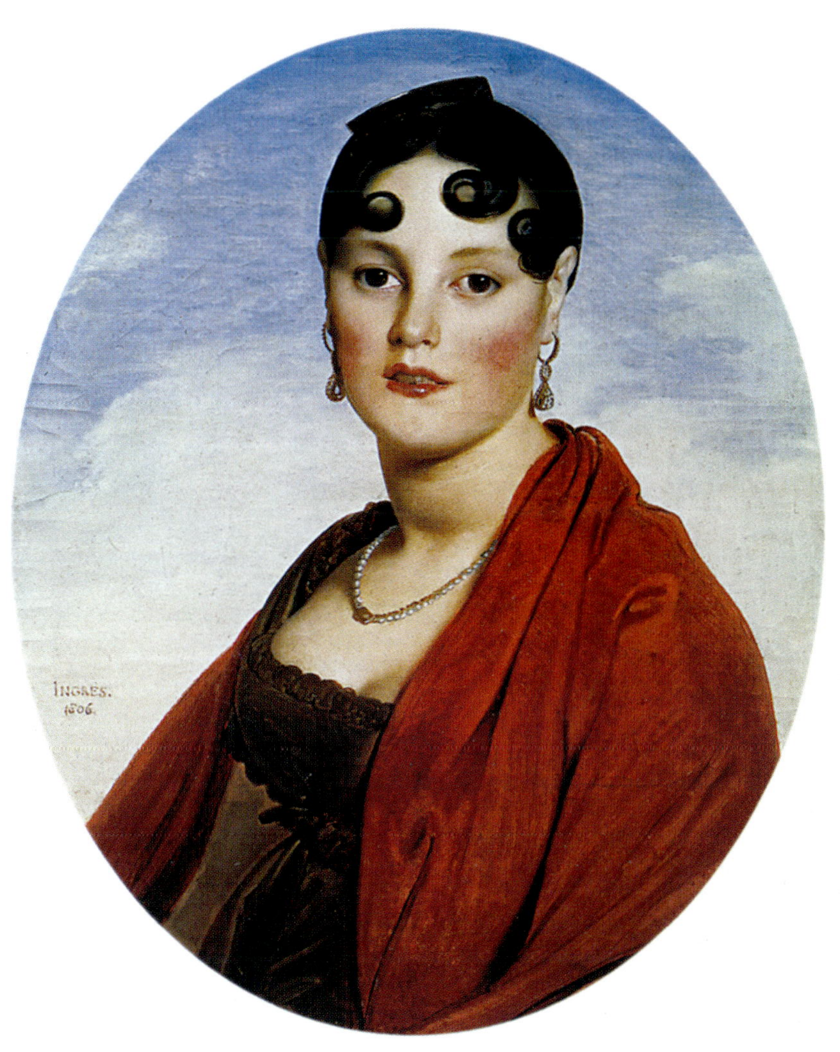
INGRES.
1806.

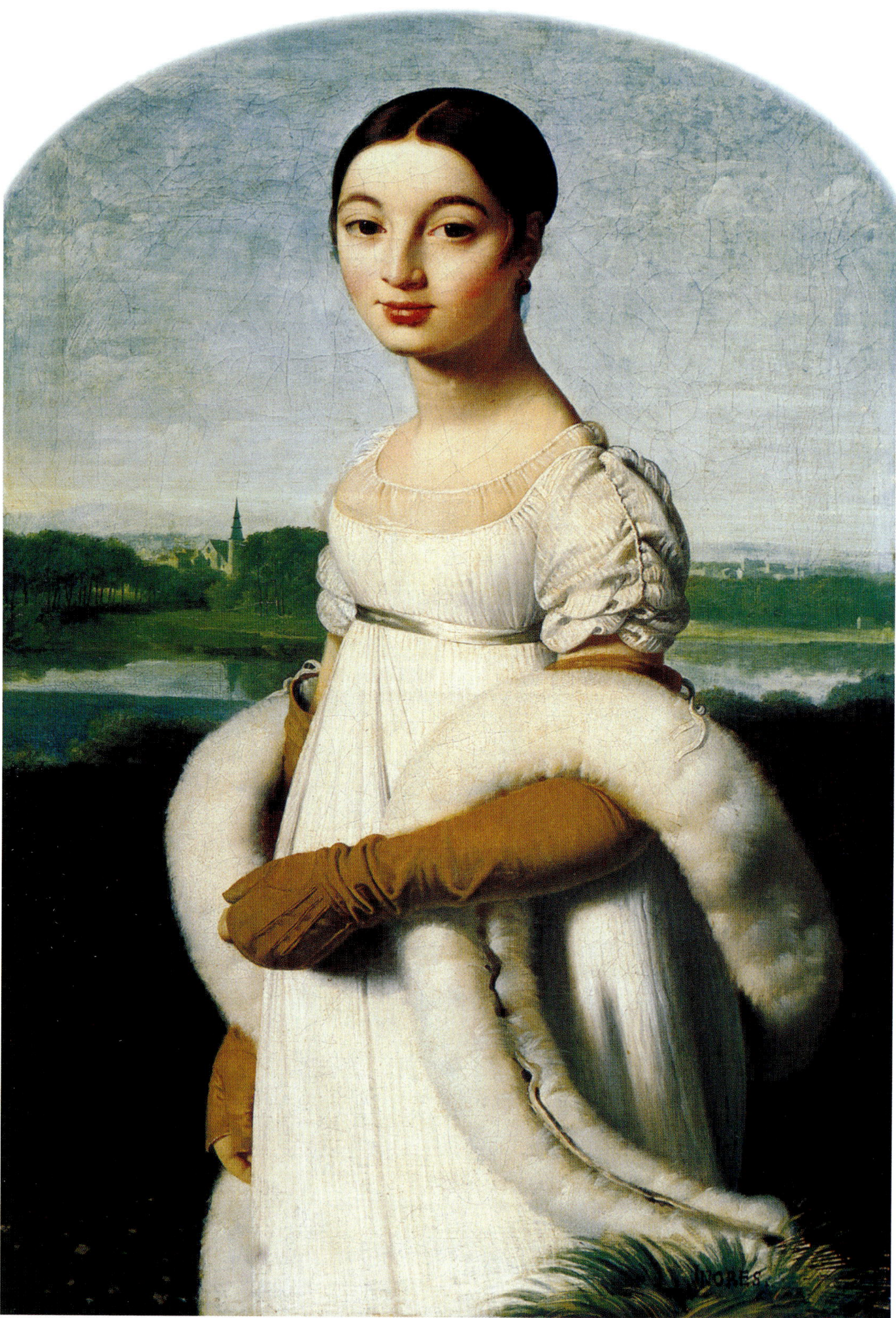

Portrait of Caroline Rivière
1805-6, oil on canvas, 99x64 cm
Paris, Musée du Louvre

Gothic, Primitive, Barbarous

When they were shown at the 1806 Salon, the Rivière family portraits were disparaged as stylistically dry, but this was nothing compared to the criticism heaped on *Napoleon as Jupiter Enthroned*. This second official portrait shows Bonaparte dressed for coronation and anointment, with all the insignia of power – the scepter of Charles V, and the hand of justice and the sword of Charlemagne – and in a pose clearly derived from Roman, Byzantine and Carolingian prototypes identifying the imperial figure with a deity. This presentation fitted perfectly with the notion of imperial power Napoleon himself had wanted to convey via the choice of Carolingian regalia for the coronation ceremony.

The work was received with stupefaction. For one commentator it had been "painted by moonlight," for another it was "Gothic and barbarous." The critic Pierre Chaussard wrote, "Monsieur Ingres' intention is nothing less than to take art back four centuries, to its infancy, to a revival of the manner of Jan van Eyck." [12] Chaussard's list of failings included a "coldly illuminated outline" and "the most bizarre effects;" the head was "dry," the colors were "inaccurate and too pale;" and the shading, "fragmented or forced, wearies the eye and

Napoleon as Jupiter Enthroned
1806, oil on canvas, 260x163 cm
Paris, Musée de l'Armée

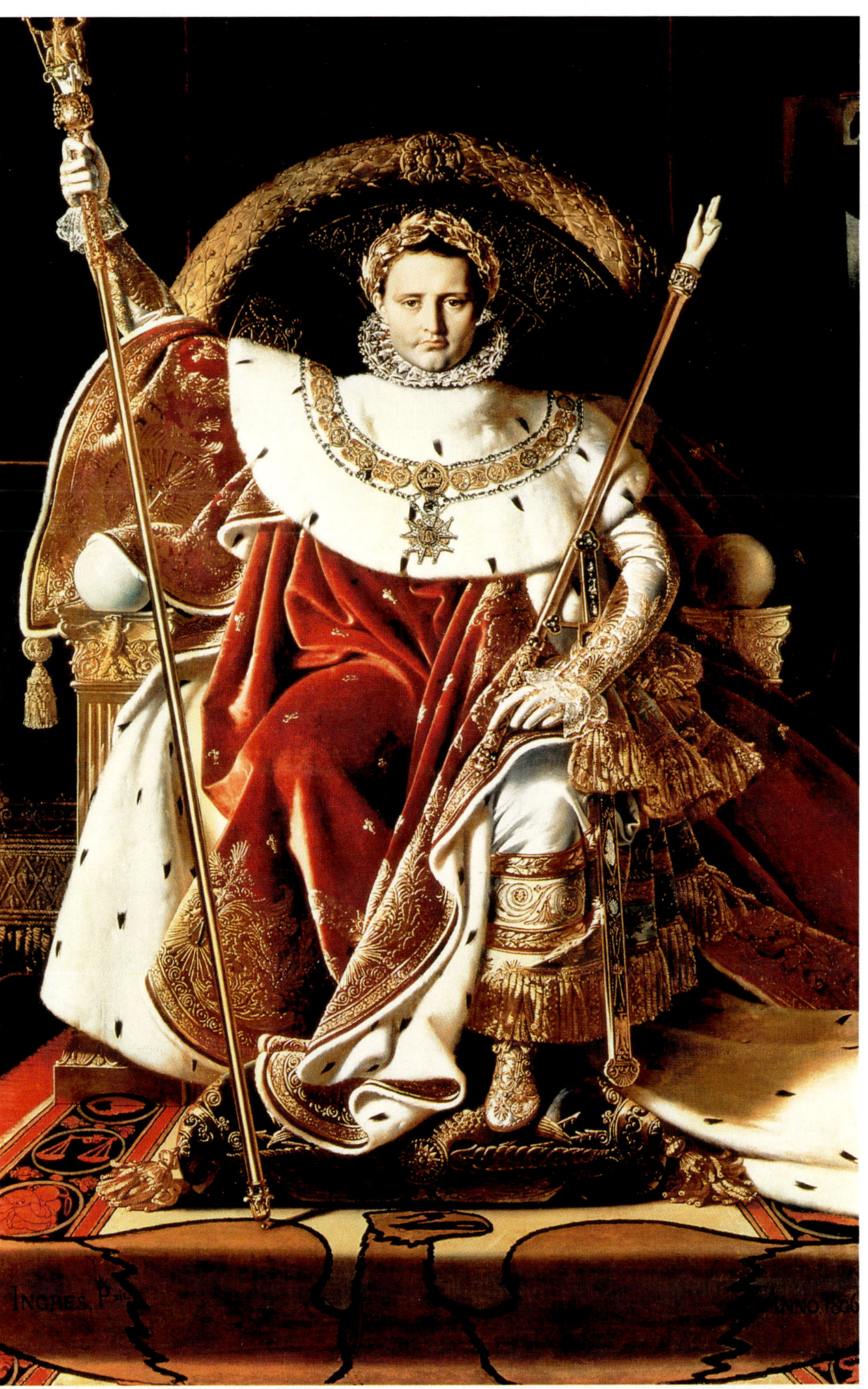
INGRES. P
NNO 1806

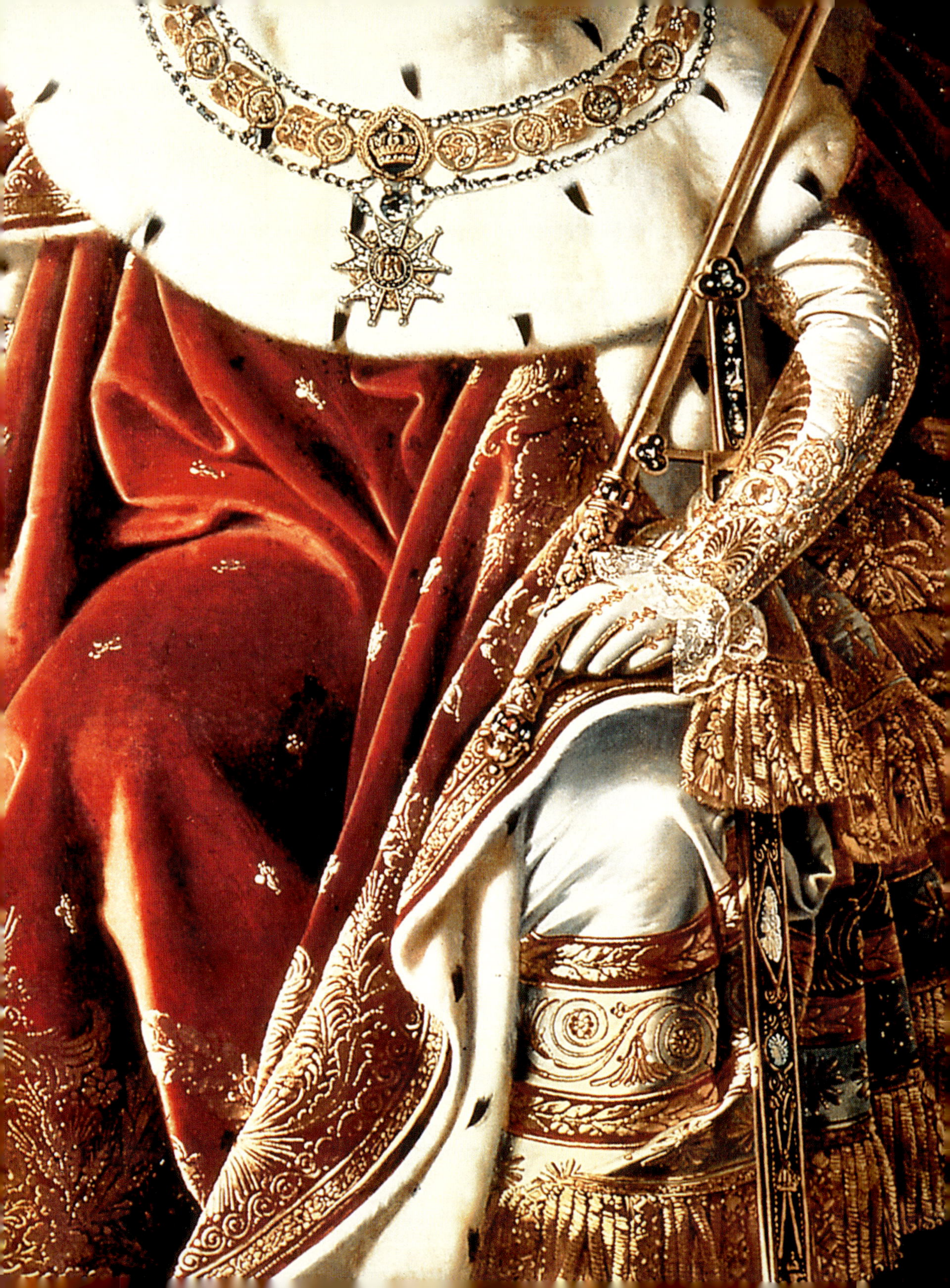

destroys the overall effect." He did, however, acknowledge the "delicacy of the brushwork, and the sophistication of the finish."

The criticisms were justified, and today the work's strangeness still shocks. Yet it suffices to cover the head, with its labored, iconic portentousness, to reveal a truly spellbinding painterliness. The glow of gold in shadow, the texture of red velvet and immaculate ermine, the sparkle of embroidery and lacework, the chasing on the insignia and the throne: these and a host of other details claim the attention with a hypnotic insistence and clarity, and seen in this light the faults picked out by Ingres' contemporaries – the illuminated manuscript look, the weirdness, the tonal fragmentation, the moonlight effect – become virtues. Can we speak of realism here? It is true that Ingres had in mind the Flemish "Primitives" he was being compared to, and the Van Eyck whose work he may well have seen in Paris. And he does imitate, to the point of making it his own, their meticulous realism, the precision in the rendering of texture, and their attention to the least gleam of light. But to what end? This is not a realistic rendering. On the contrary, it is as abstract as a Byzantine Christ, as unreal as some figure from mythology. This is a hybrid, part portrait, part allegory, an elevation of political reality to the status of myth in which the "total" realism of the details is at the service of idealization.

As incompatible as such a work may be with modern taste, it points up a highly distinctive form of artistic exploration and a most characteristic agenda. We know already of Ingres' interest in Greek art, vase painting, Flaxman's engravings and the Florentine masters. Here, in an eclecticism that would always be part of his working method, we see him drawing on Byzantine models and the Flemish Primitives. Nineteenth-century artistic eclecticism often produced superficial stylistic mixes and works with no character of their own, a weakness to which Ingres himself sometimes fell victim, but on most occasions his eclecticism was a form of experimentation. In these early years of the century, when the official esthetic was the ancient rhetoric of Neoclassicism, such experiments represented a form of dissidence for which the artist is still paying the price.

II

Ingres in Italy
The

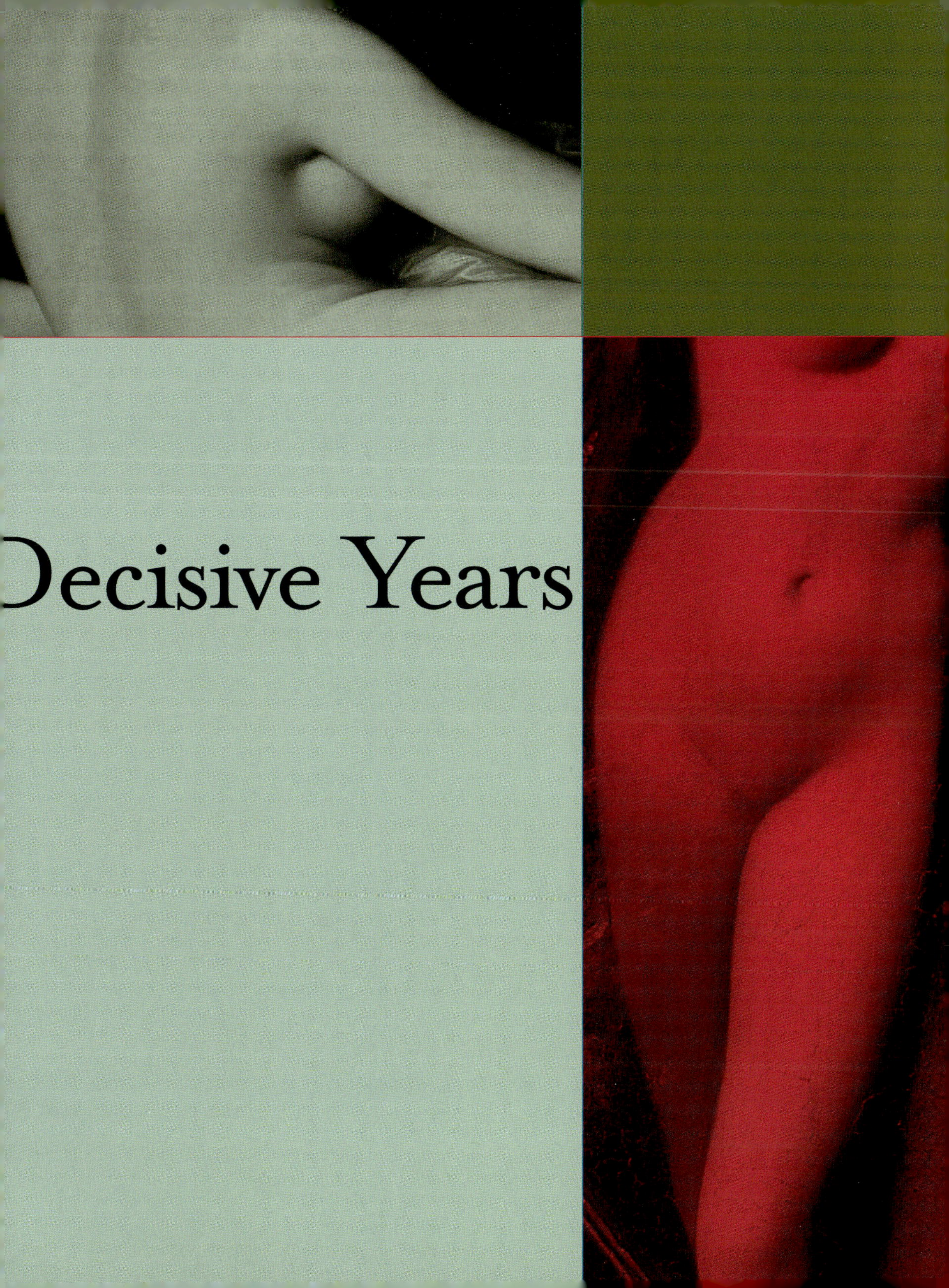

Decisive Years

"I Would Willingly be the Required Revolutionary"

Ingres, however, was not on hand to confront his critics. Even before the Salon opened he had to leave Paris for Rome to take up his new post as director of the Académie de France there.

Of course the criticism came to his ears in Rome, and his correspondence is full of anger and indignation. "I know exactly what is being done to me in Paris. Is the Salon to be the stage for my shaming? I am the victim of ignorance, bad faith, and calumny, and from you, my friends, I receive no comfort. Those scoundrels waited until I was gone to destroy my reputation...And not being there, I cannot defend myself. I might sacrifice my life, or that croaking, jealous horde might one day cease its noise, but I beg you, take pity on me in my despair. Since my arrival in Rome I have had no news of you; I swallow insults night and day, I am dying of worry, I have never been so miserable!...I knew I had plenty of enemies. I have never been complacent about that and never will be. My greatest wish is to rush to the Salon and expose them, there in front of my works; those works bear no resemblance to theirs, and the more I advance the less they will resemble them."[13]

We may smile at the boastful tone, the raised voice, the noisy sentimentality and the inability to put up with criticism – all part of the persona – but at the same time we see an Ingres fully conscious of his own value and originality, refusing all compromise and imbued with a disquieting reformist zeal: "Yes, art is in need of reform and I would willingly be the required revolutionary. But patience, I'll work so hard at it that maybe it will happen one day; my ambition is totally

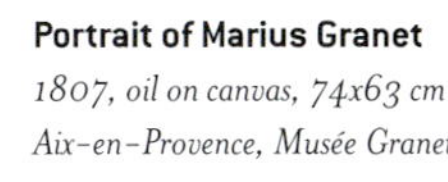

Portrait of Marius Granet
1807, oil on canvas, 74x63 cm
Aix-en-Provence, Musée Granet

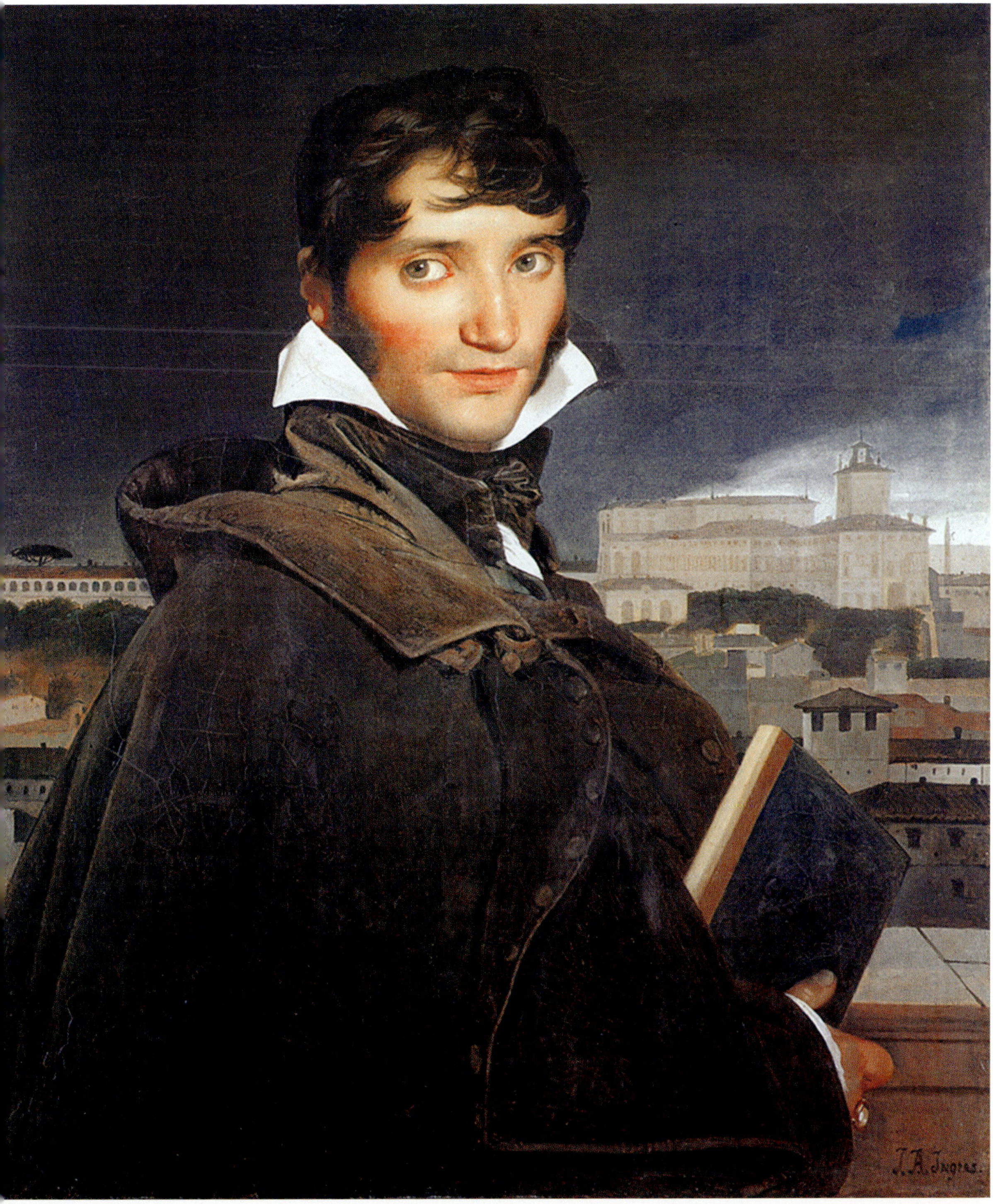

focused on that."[14] How can we not think here of the revolutionary ardor of his master, David, the great "regenerator" of art in the 1780s before becoming the arbiter of the French art scene for several decades?

Much later, of course, Ingres himself would become a major reformer and the powerful leader of a school.

Created at the instigation of Colbert and Le Brun in 1666, almost twenty years after the founding of the Royal Academy of Painting and Sculpture, the Académie de France in Rome was intended to give France's best students access to what were then seen as the indispensable models of antiquity and the Italian Renaissance. Discipline was strict and the teaching program demanding: life drawing, anatomy and perspective, copying from Classical works and early painting, and, for architects, detailed drawings of existing buildings. All the work produced there would go to the king. Until the 19th century the Academy in Rome was a fundamental part of the Beaux-Arts art teaching system. Like the other academies of the Ancien Régime, it was shut down between 1793 and 1795 and only began to function again in 1803, when it was moved to the Villa Medici; prior to this it had been housed in the Mancini Palace, but in 1797 the presence of revolutionary young artists, anticlerical and sometimes confrontational, led to violent clashes culminating in the plundering of the palace. The painter Girodet, then a resident at the Academy, was almost lynched by the local populace.

While much less strict than during the preceding decade, the rules required each artist to create and send to Paris a copy of an old master, three nudes and a historical composition. These *envois* ("parcels") were judged by members of the Institut de France, who checked their fit with official teaching requirements and the antiquity-inflected esthetic that then held sway.

Ingres was uncomfortable in group situations. He did not enjoy mixing with the others and hated the ragging that was part of art school life. He quickly obtained the right to work in a separate pavilion. Initially he was dazed by the sheer extent of the city's artistic heritage: "There are all kinds of beautiful things one on top of the other and seeing them wears you out," he wrote. It was long believed that he made countless drawings of the monuments: he possessed very many drawings of Roman landscapes, most of them unshaded line drawings in a dry style. However, their attribution to him has been challenged, which is also the case for three small, circular, painted landscapes.

As for the landscapes used as backgrounds for his portraits, we now know that they were often the work of assistants. Notable among the latter was Marius Granet, a fellow student during the David years, who lived in Rome and whose features Ingres captured in his sumptuous portrait of 1807.

The Casino of Raphael
1807, oil on panel, 17.5x36.5 cm
Paris, Musée des Arts Décoratifs

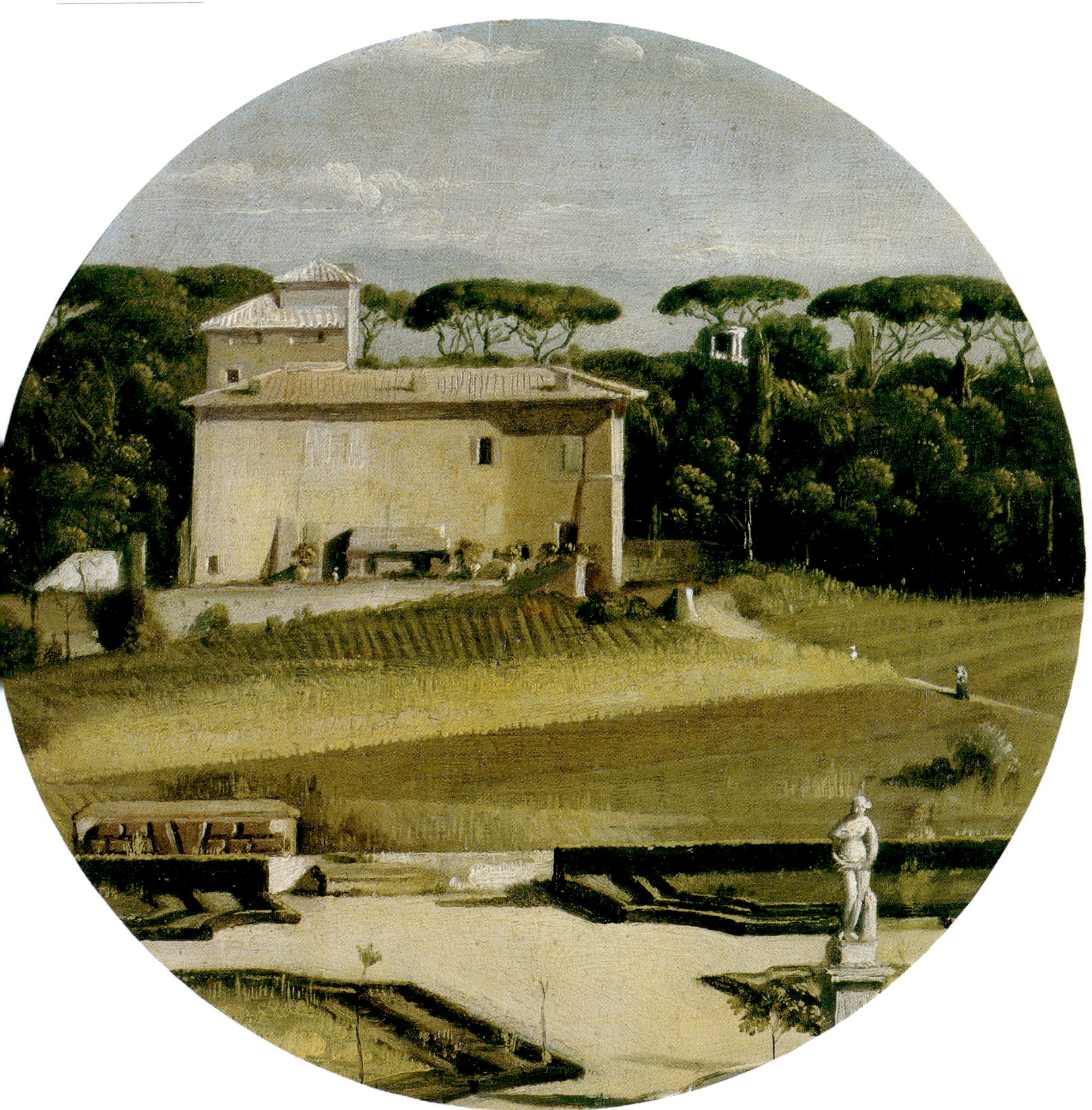

Academic Nudes

The *envois* sent by Academy residents were usually academic male nudes reflecting the ideal Neoclassical esthetic. Male beauty was charged with heroic significance, and a specific pose or the introduction of an accessory could transform a model into a Greek or Roman hero. This is exactly what David, in his time, and then Drouais, Girodet and numerous other boarders had done. Thus the male nude became more than just an exercise, as artists sought to elevate it to the level of history painting. Within the academic teaching system, the study of the human body had the single aim of providing the artist with the skills required by historical compositions; the expression of the "passions" was founded on the language of the body and the face.

Ingres, however, decided to paint a female nude, in back view and singularly lacking in narrative content. His half-length *Bather* of 1807 has its own genealogy – one of its probable sources is an engraving after a Greek vase in the Hamilton Collection – and the subject's frightened, modest pose can be seen as reminiscent of a traditional heroine like Susannah in the Bible, but this is not enough to make the painting historical. Its theme is basically plastic, and can be summed up as the harmony of the golden skin tones with the bluish tinge of the landscape, and of the interplay of anatomical forms set parallel to the picture plane. Its theme is the outline of that too-round eye, that lovingly detailed ear, the deep creases of the neck, the long, curved furrow on the back, the breast oddly set under the arm; with, of course, the subtle counterpoint of the turban or headscarf, which makes its first appearance here.

His second *envoi* was the *Grande Baigneuse* (1808), also known as *La Baigneuse de Valpinçon* after its acquirer. Here there is no suggestion of narrative whatever, and no landscape, gesture, face or gaze. There is no more than a body and drapery: the two essential, self-sufficient elements of the Ingres vocabulary.

Here Ingres develops the aims of the preceding work on a generous scale, revealing a clarity of intention and a calmly total determination in his technical choices that give the work the look of an absolute and definitive affirmation. The lighting of the body is vivid, uniform and, so to speak, abstract, like a limpid pool out of which emerges the flawless structure: a perfect shape defined by its sequence of living curves and a relief without shading that adds to the initial lighting. Once again the figure is seen in back view, so as to avoid any psychological implications likely to compromise its geometrical purity. "Monsieur Ingres draws living beings the way a geometrician describes solid bodies," wrote Théophile Silvestre. The description is an accurate one, but the "geometry" in question is based on a highly developed sensitivity to living form.

In reality, Ingres' stance – somewhere between the observation of nature and the interpretation of early models – remains far from easy to define. He was violently opposed to the Neoclassical notion of "ideal beauty" and the "antiquarian esthetic" it had given rise to. He had an authentic adoration for nature and it was the living model that brought his most potent capacities to the fore. He would endlessly urge his own pupils to copy nature humbly and naively, while never hesitating himself, not to idealize it in the way advocated by Winckelmann, but to interpret it, "rig" it, make it abstract. And thus ultimately to idealize it in his own way. Nature and antiquity are his repeated points of reference, but they are worked on and combined in varying degrees: in the final analysis their relative proportions are a matter of pure intuition and it would be mistaken to look for the secret in any of the theories put forward and taught by the artist.

As for the lessons to be drawn from ancient art, Ingres had a personal perception of things which, apart from possible references to prototypes, looked beyond the letter to the spirit: beauty had to do with a unified conception of the human being, with the idea of a plenitude both spiritual and carnal, and with the total, radiant harmony of a human organism set at the centre of the universe as the measure of all things. Beauty coincides with the rules of a permanent order of which humanity is the guarantor and the living reflection.

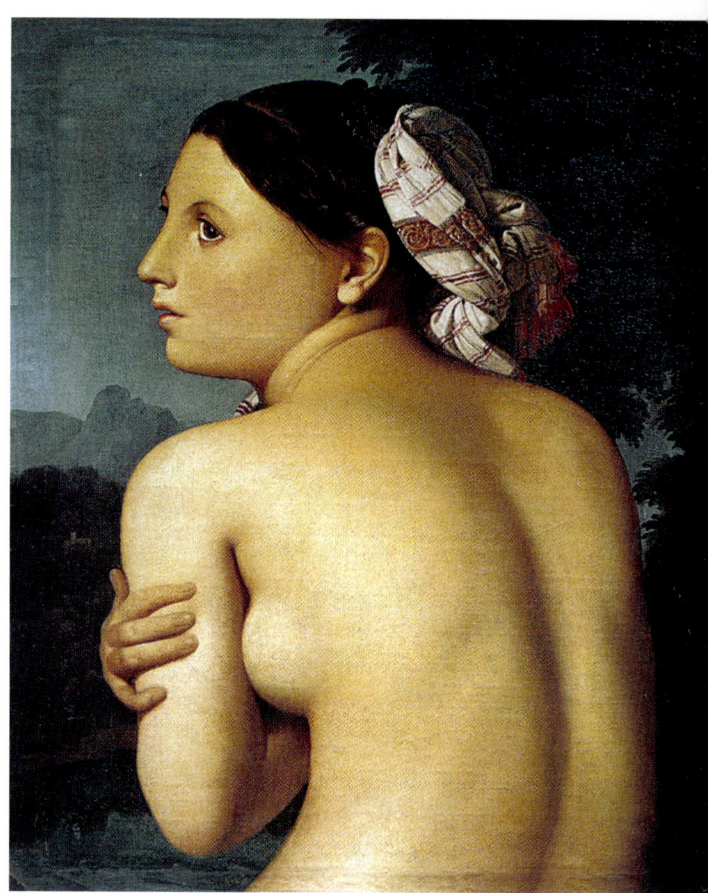

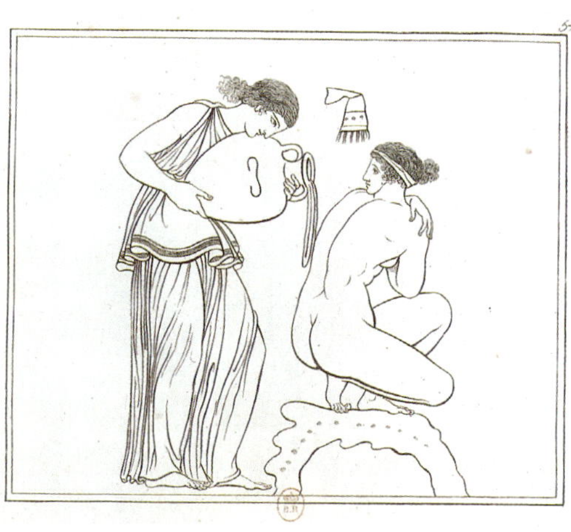

Bather
1807, oil on canvas, 51x42.5 cm
Bayonne, Musée Bonnat

W. Tischbein
Collection of Engravings from Ancient Vases
(vol. I, pl. 57)
1803, Woman Bathing
Paris, Bibliothèque Nationale de France

La Grande Baigneuse, also known as ***La Baigneuse de Valpinçon***
1808, oil on canvas, 146x97 cm
Paris, Musée du Louvre

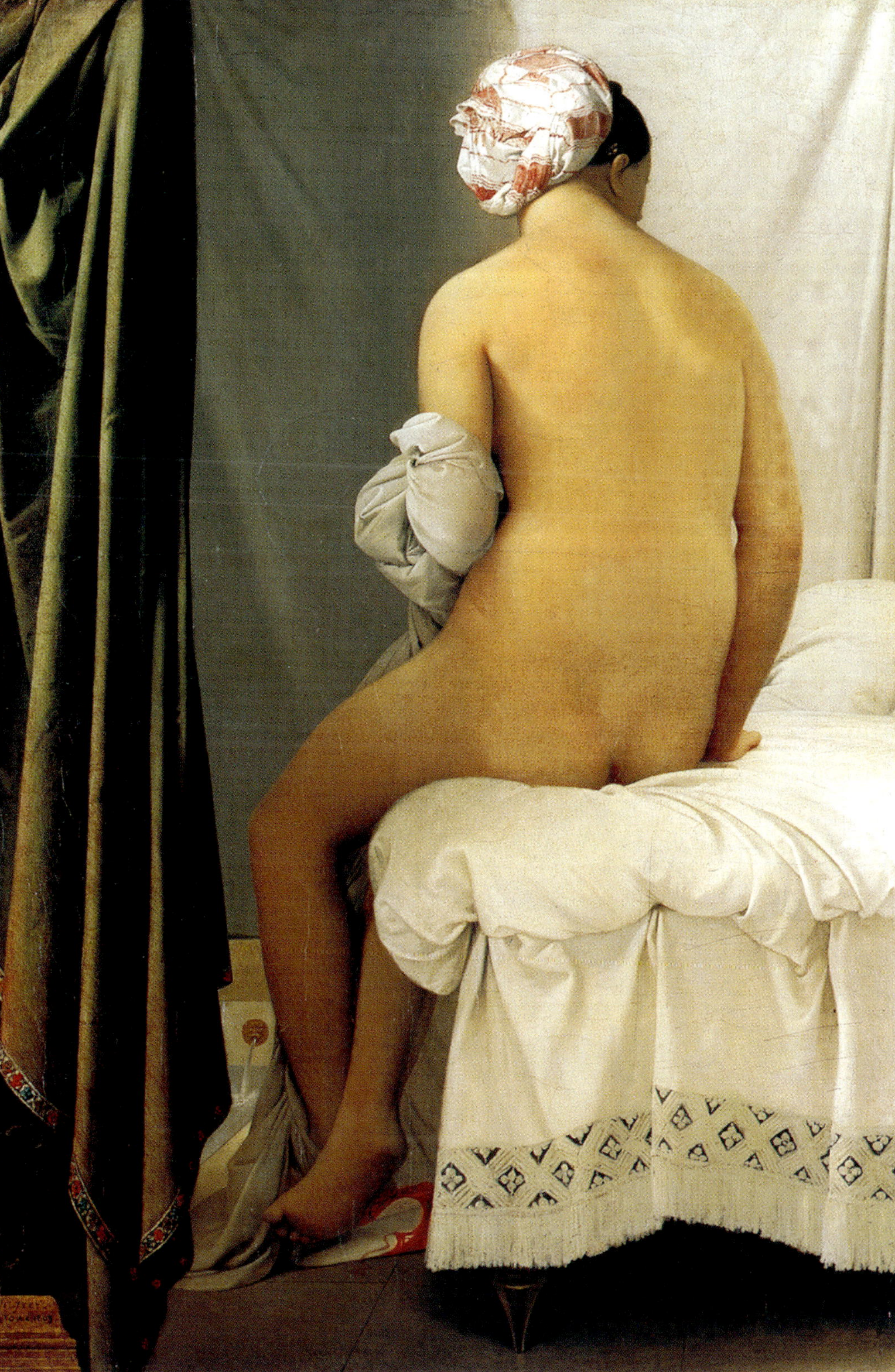

Oedipus and the Sphinx
1808, oil on canvas, 189x144 cm
Paris, Musée du Louvre

It fell to Ingres to make concrete the "pure Greek" dream his master David, a true painter of history – and contemporary history – had pursued in vain. For seizing this dream demanded a grasp of its timelessness, of an abstractness free of historical ties and stripped of all archeological trappings. The dream had to be seized in all its glorious, robust, self-contained nakedness. And this is what Ingres did in his *Grande Baigneuse*, providing – perhaps for the first time since the Renaissance – the exact pictorial equivalent of the greatest Greek statuary.

This was an entirely new idea. For David's disciples the nude was male, heroic, and full of virile virtue. Ingres, by contrast, restored to the female nude all the majesty and artistic dignity it had enjoyed in antiquity.

Oedipus and the Sphinx, the artist's third *envoi*, was a male nude. Initially the figure of Oedipus occupied the entire picture surface: it was only much later, in 1824-27, that Ingres enlarged the canvas, worked up the figure of the Sphinx, and added the bones, the mouth of the cave and the small, terrified figure lower down. Thus he turned a male nude into an authentic history painting. However, the original intention remains clear: the true artistic interest lies in the painting of the human body. Here we have a perfect, magnificently accomplished example of how Ingres saw the notion of nature taken from ancient sources, and its fit with the association of the True and the Beautiful. His inspiration here is a Classical statue of Cincinnatus, but as was his habit, he recreated the figure by drawing it from a model in the required pose. The painting as such was executed from these drawings, the prototype providing a basic outline, a kind of idea imbued with the qualities of nobility, balance and clarity associated with ancient art. Working from the life allowed Ingres to inject a new, carnal reality into this idea. And as we see in the subtle relief of the golden, splendidly textured torso and back, in the vigorous suppleness of the contours, the crucial point is the rendering of living form. Oedipus' skin glows with the warmth of blood and sun. By comparison, other male nudes of the time seem as gray, stony and cold as statues.

At the same time *Oedipus and the Sphinx* demonstrates Ingres' ambiguity, or the complexity of his artistic agenda. Out of a magnificent nude, in which he achieves comprehensive expression of his most powerful artistic "instincts" – spontaneous love of living shapes and the taste for "beautiful" form molded to the imperious demands of style – he produces a fairly average history painting. Bereft of any real dramatic expressiveness, the bones and the gesticulating figure stand exposed for what they are: trivia, mere rhetoric. As we shall see, this contradiction between Ingres' true artistic interests, his most dazzling gifts and the ambition to become a history painter that he pursued with a determination nothing could quell, lies at the core of his oeuvre and would profoundly affect his career.

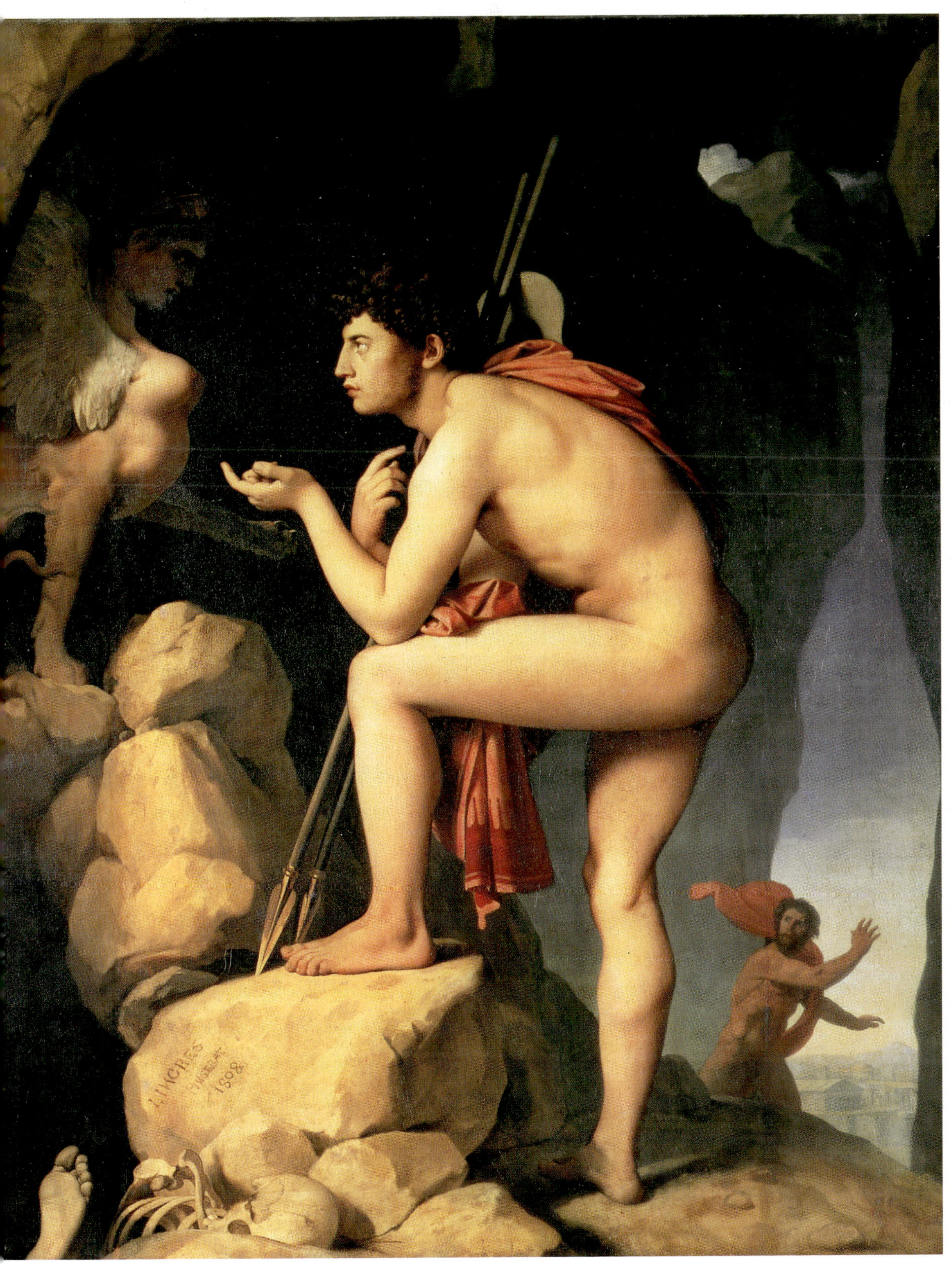
INGRES
1808

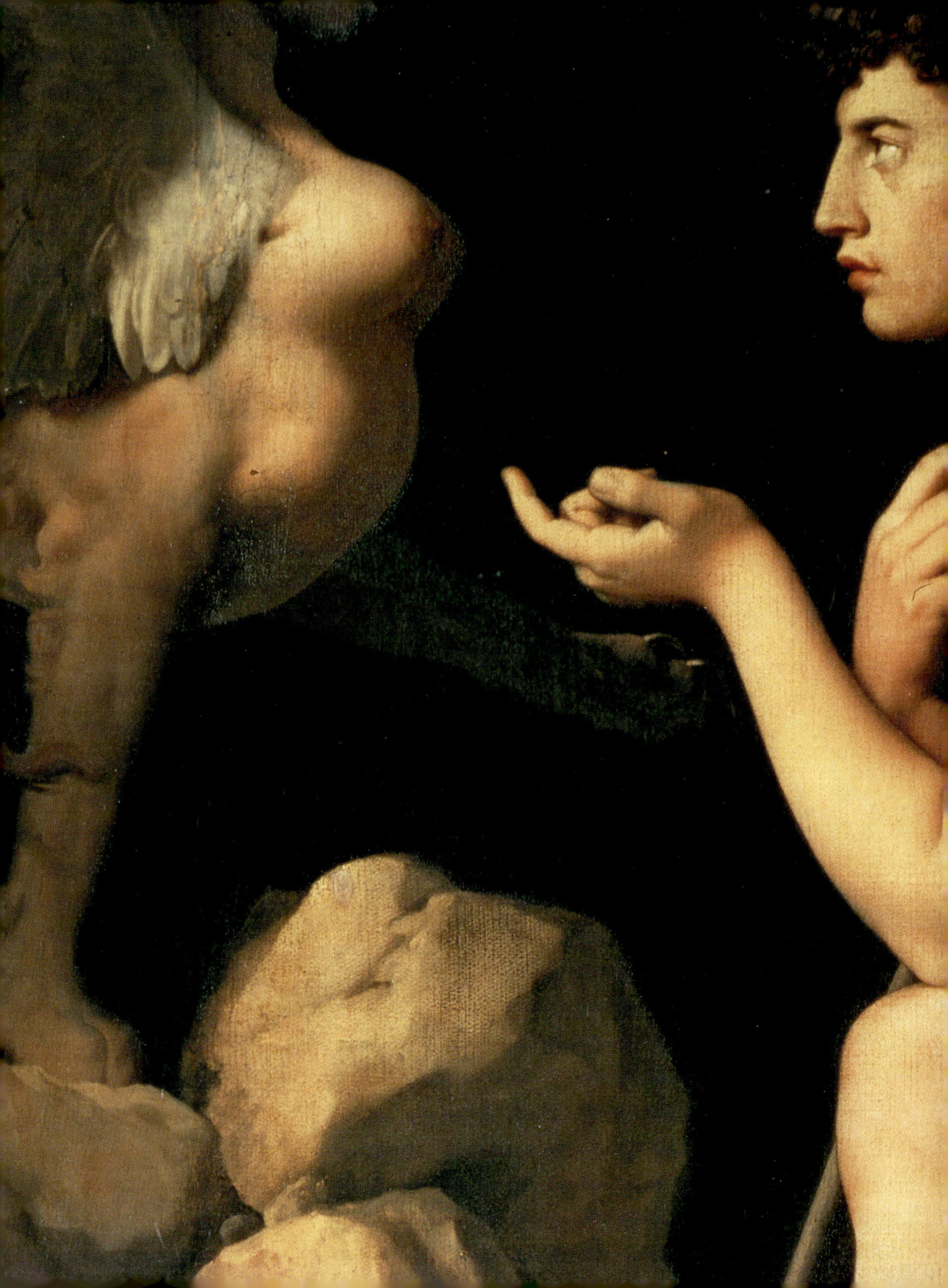

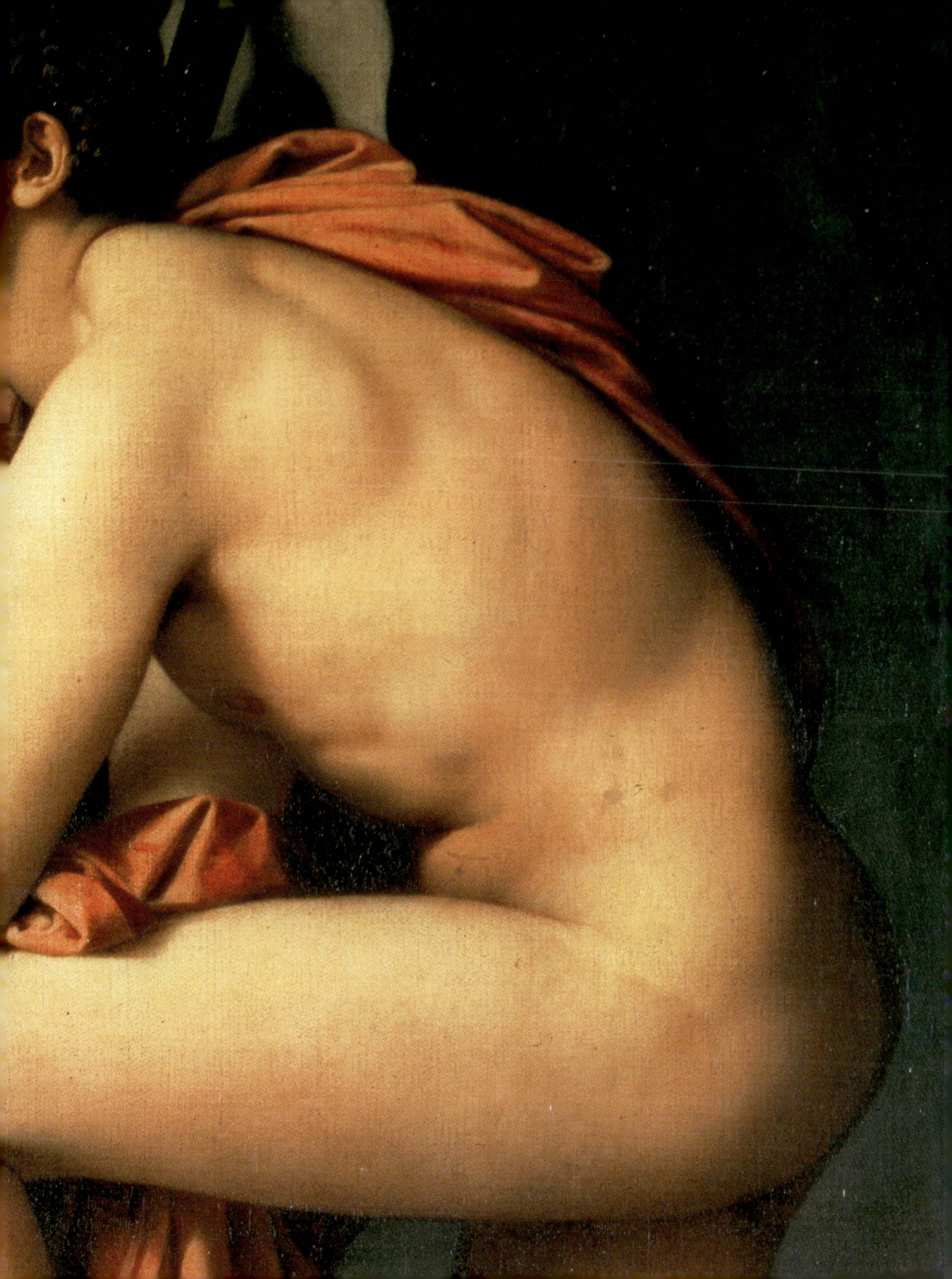

Anomalies

The fusion of the ideal and the real in *Oedipus and the Sphinx* entailed certain distortions. In the right leg, with the foot on the ground, all the anatomical complexity, muscular tension, interplay beneath the skin of muscle, bone and tendon – all the inner workings – are rendered solely by the curves of an exaggeratedly sharp contour, with no recourse to a relief kept extremely minimal in line with the overall notion of a relatively flat, basically linear construction. The result is a somewhat empty, incongruous shape which, after a few seconds' observation resembles not so much a leg as a kind of branch or knotty root. So much so that we find ourselves wondering if, consciously or not, the artist has indicated the answer to the Sphinx's riddle, using this knotty limb to suggest the stick that serves as a third leg for the human animal in the twilight of life.

This kind of distortion – more or less absurd, more or less visible – would become frequent in Ingres' work. We have already noted Ajax's bulging thigh and the displaced breast of the *Bather*, and there were plenty more to come. One of the most startling dates from this period: the foot of the *Grande Baigneuse*, shapeless and swollen – the heat of her bath was to blame, sneered Ingres' contemporaries – to a point that would make a Sunday painter blush. What explains this foot and its total contrast with the mastery shown in the rest of the picture?

Firstly, it should be noted that the foot in no way detracts from the painting as a whole; it can even pass unnoticed. This means that it fits with a certain visual economy. The legs are in a half-light, their form slightly hollow and practically without relief; only the head and back, fully lit, are given the benefit of Ingres' marvelously subtle relief work and its tiny, delectable nuances. This is, in fact, a body that has no need of legs, and even less of a foot: so much so that when he re-used this bather in his *Turkish Bath*, he gave her a different pair of legs, crossed and not separating her from the floor. The Bather's foot, with no active part to play in the overall economy of the picture, and set too far from the incandescent area on which the painter's desire is focused, simply withers like a piece of fruit.

These aberrations merit closer study. Some of them are quite deliberate, but others are more enigmatic: this foot, the incomprehensible stump of a hand in the *Portrait of Delphine Ingres* (1859), and the famous "stain" on the dress in the *Portrait of Inès Moitessier* (1856). What underlies these false "mistakes," these breaks in the weave of an otherwise tight and highly controlled artistic fabric? Art historian Daniel Arasse sees them as Freudian slips, points where the artist's unconscious took over.

"All the Splendid Sumptuousness of Art"

Still in Rome, Ingres chose for his historical composition a subject from the first song of the *Iliad*: the marine divinity Thetis ascends to heaven to beg Zeus/Jupiter to intervene on behalf of her son Achilles. At this time ancient Greece was all the rage and Homer, as part of the literary canon, was a benchmark author for artists. In one of the notebooks [15] he filled with comments on his reading and possible subjects for pictures, the young artist copied the passage that had been his source of inspiration: "So she rose from under the sea and went through great heaven with early morning to Olympus, where she found the mighty son of Saturn sitting all alone upon its topmost ridges. She sat down before him, and with her left hand seized his knees, while with her right she caught him under the chin, and besought him..." At first Zeus does not reply to her supplications, remaining silent on his throne; finally, however, he consents, although complaining of the risk of incurring the jealous wrath of his spouse Juno. Then "the ambrosial locks swayed on his immortal head, till vast Olympus reeled." [16]

Jupiter and Thetis
1811, oil on canvas, 327x260 cm
Aix-en-Provence, Musée Granet

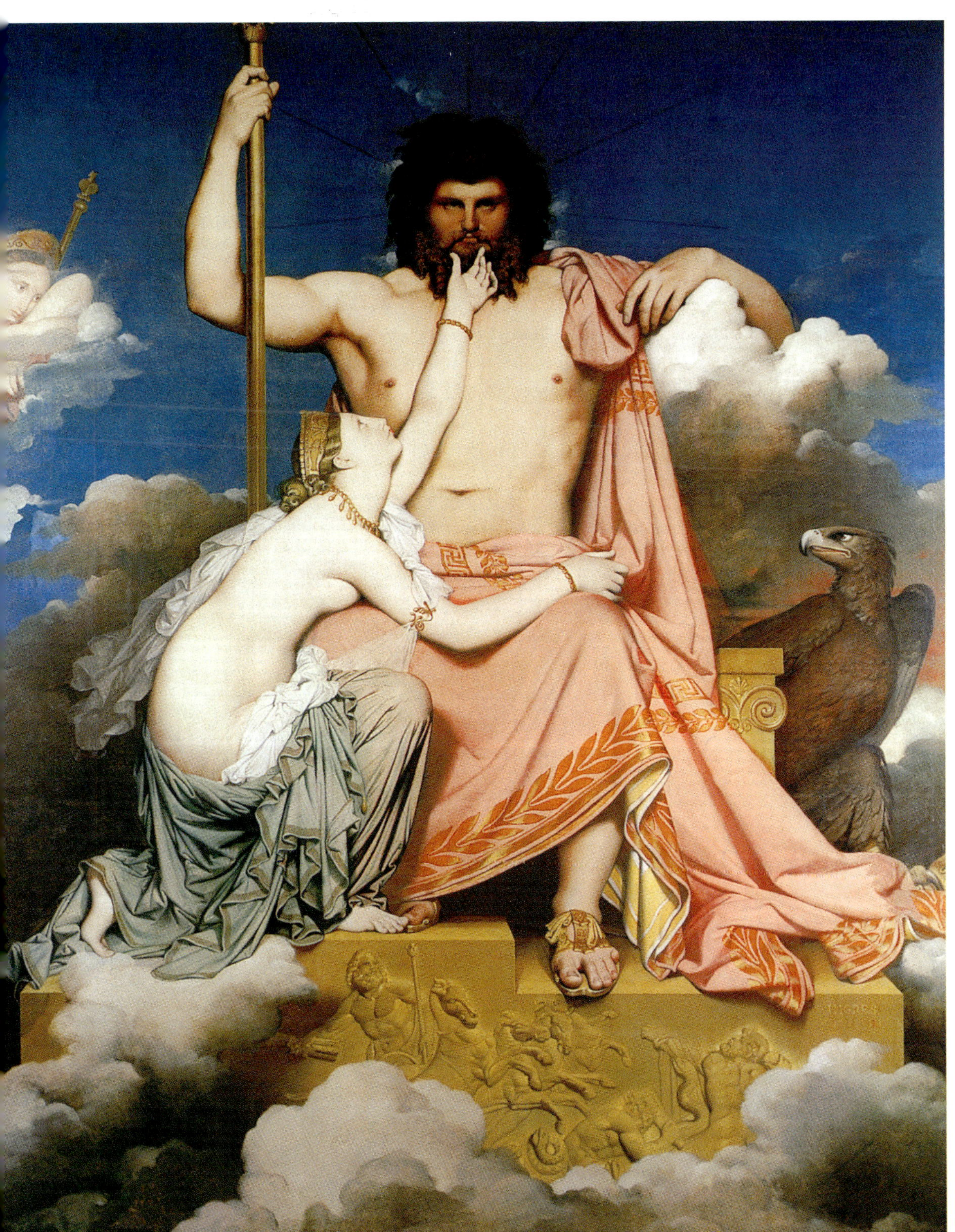

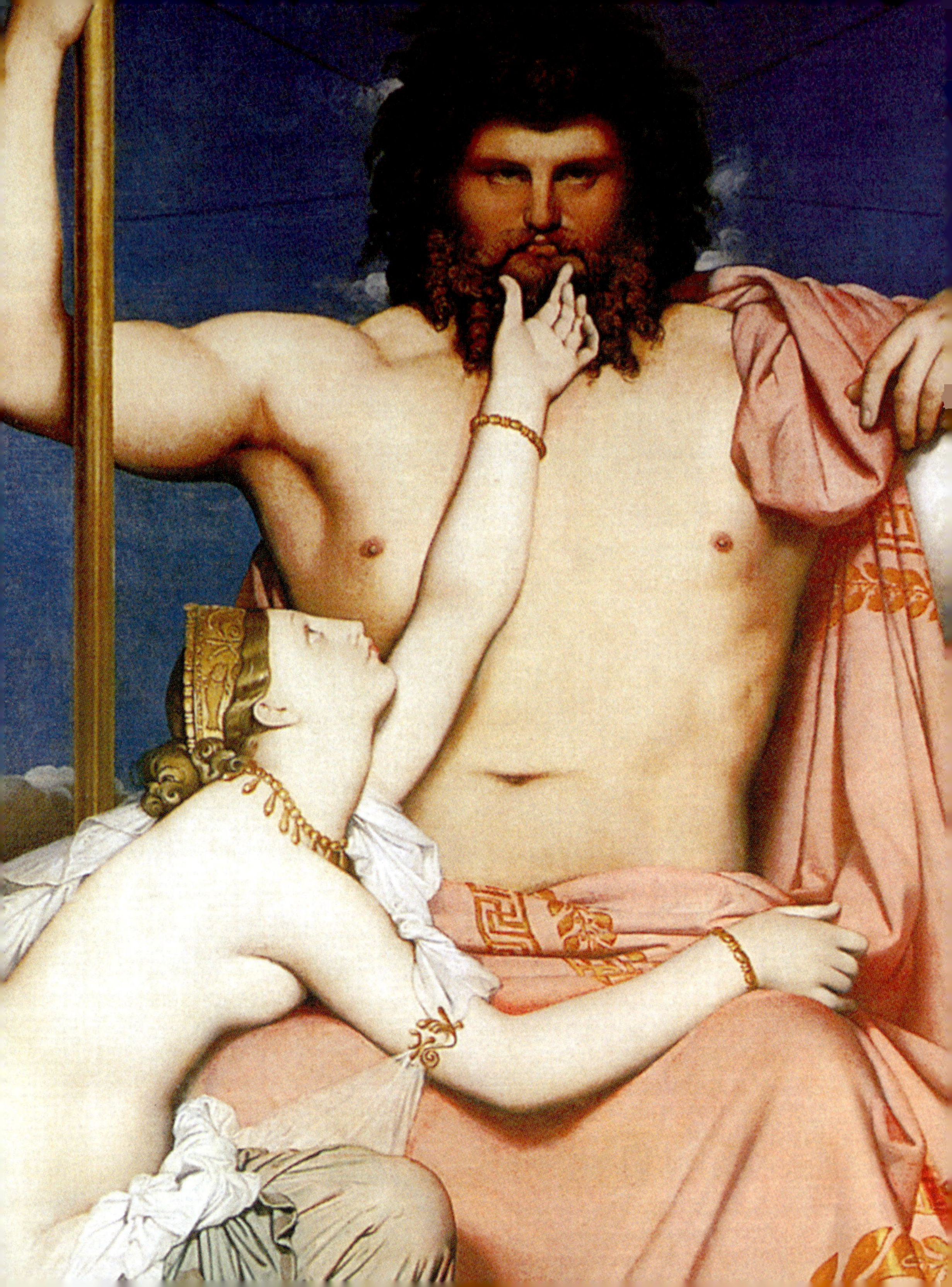

The subject fired imagination of the artist, who intended to bring to it "all the splendid sumptuousness of art." In 1806 – five years before the painting was actually finished – he wrote: "I shall not go into the details of this divine picture, whose ambrosian perfume will carry for a league, nor of the beauty of the figures and of their divine expressions and forms...I have almost composed it in my head and I see it now..." [17]

To the modern eye, this work can seem either the height of Neoclassical kitsch or a masterpiece of anachronism. The painter's contemporaries were totally perplexed. As late as 1862 Théophile Silvestre was able to speak of the picture's "communicative gaiety." So let's have a good laugh – then take a closer look.

What strikes us immediately is the match with the Homeric tone, and with the conception of a deity of truly cosmic magnitude. This dizzying scale is first provided by the colossal size of the god, whose arm rests on distant clouds; then it is reinforced by an intense, vibrant blue suggestive of limitless space. Both Jupiter's proportions and his absurdly fierce, masklike head accord with the idea of the formidable power wielded by the king of the gods. Thetis, with her green robe, the white foam of her veil streaming down her back and thigh, and all the rising vitality of her gesture, truly is the goddess who "rose from under the sea and went through great heaven with early morning to Olympus." Ingres' grasp of Homer's cosmic dimension is such that he succeeds in conveying the impression of the miraculous youthfulness and untrammeled force of the beginnings of the world.

The necessary comparison here is with a work of similar inspiration, by David. The latter, when he saw the painting by his former pupil in Paris, declared that the style suggested "raving madness;" yet his *Mars Disarmed by Venus and the Graces* of 1822-24 shows that he was marked by the Ingres work and that he too had set out to capture the ethereal ambience of the abode of the gods. Despite the unerring control that never lets us forget his greatness as a painter, everything is wrong in a picture that is not unreal, like the Ingres, but simply false: the temple, the flesh, the event, the whole Olympian scene. The real problem is the eroticism, evoked only via simpering affectation that ultimately kills the picture's dignity: this scene of seduction is shot through with a propriety and paltriness worthy of Empire porcelain.

But to return to Ingres. His vast visual apparatus might be absurd, but it throbs with the erotic. Not some superficial, come-hither version, but the true, vital force that gives the forms breadth and resplendence. Ingres offers us a scene of seduction in all its carnality. What else is there but the very image of seduction in the figure of Thetis, imploring, overtly proffered and striving for fusion with the body of Jupiter? Not to mention the sheer eloquence of the hand caressing the chin, the touching of toes, the arm embracing the loins of the god, the other arm pressed to the splendid, vibrant torso. And what are we to say of the association of milky white and golden brown? This may be the perfume of ambrosia: this limpid eroticism dilated to the level of the divine rulers of the universe.

In a secondary register, we note that Thetis derives from the female figures of Roman painting as we find them in the Villa of Mysteries in Pompeii. Flaxman is always mentioned as one of Ingres' likely sources, but no mention ever seems to have been made of the exact match between Thetis and two of the young women shown taking part in the celebration of the Dionysian mysteries in Pompeii: the one bending to take the lash offers the same pear-shaped torso as she leans identically on the knees of a female companion; the second, also kneeling, uncovers the winnowing basket in virtually the same pose, with the arms thrown forward. And what she reveals is not the woven basket itself, but its contents: a giant phallus. We do not know how well Ingres might have been acquainted with the Villa of Mysteries, but we sense in his work the echo of this link between the erotic and the sacred.

We recognize in Thetis, but this time in glory, the undulant, invertebrate female type, somewhere between octopus and algae, already sketched in the figures of Salmacis and the wounded Venus: that supremely influential figure so admirably summed up by Louis Gillet:

"But the true wonder is Thetis. Of all the forms he created, the great discoverer never imagined one more hauntingly delicious. Never did the demon of the arabesque and the despotism of calligraphy lead him to a line more spellbindingly supple, to a volute more serpentine, sinuous and expressive...This is no longer a woman, but a sign, a kind of hieroglyph in feminine form...So as not to break the unity of this melodic figure, he removes its right shoulder, deprives it of all projection, takes it back to the level of absolute profile as imperiously as any Egyptian painter." [18] Gillet goes on to point out the "rigorously horizontal profile," the "exquisite monstrousness" of the neck, and the "adorable chinoiserie" of the hand. And to this list of the "hauntingly delicious" physical attributes of the goddess, let us add the marvelous lengths of flesh formed by her arms.

Thetis is a harmony of interwoven lines, as fluidly alive as the aquatic, feminine context they suggest, and as abstract as a celestial constellation. The surging vitality of the drawing and the beauty of the forms it outlines suffice in themselves to justify this work.

In Paris, Ingres' *envois* were coolly received. The colors were seen as flat and dry and the style was once again dismissed as "Gothic." His approach was deprecated as peculiar and deliberately archaic.

This lack of comprehension was to prove enduring. The artist, who initially had thought of a year at the Villa Medici, spent four years there, then opted to stay in Rome. This was not the moment to return to a hostile Paris.

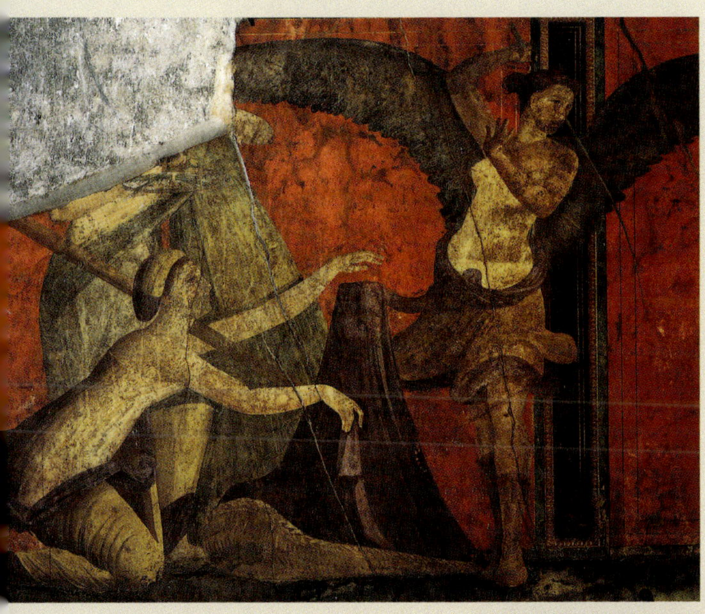

The Unveiling of the Basket
60 BC, fresco,
Pompeii, Villa of Mysteries

Jacques Louis David
Mars Disarmed by Venus and the Three Graces
1824, oil on canvas, 308x265
Brussels, Musées Royaux des Beaux-Arts

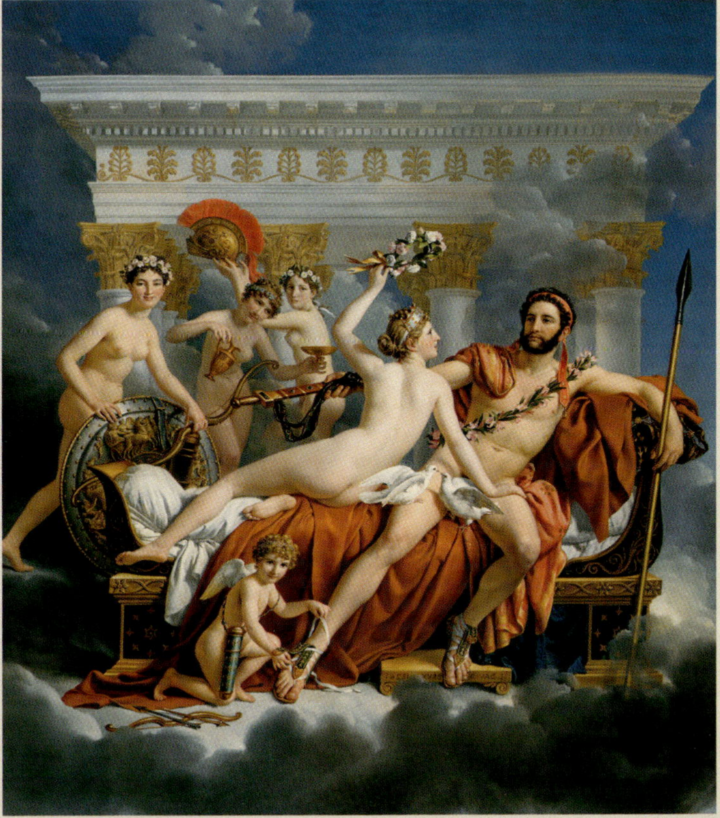

Ossian and Virgil

One of Ingres' protectors was the art patron and collector General Miollis, who had him officially commissioned to paint two large canvases for the Quirinal Palace. A visit to Rome by Napoleon was planned for 1812 and to receive him the general had overseen the renovation of the pontifical palace of Montecavallo, on the Quirinal; the decoration was entrusted to a number of artists, the brief being based on the emperor's tastes. Ingres was commissioned to paint *Romulus as Conqueror of King Acron* for the empress's drawing room and *The Dream of Ossian* for the emperor's bedroom. Napoleon had a special fondness for the *Poems*

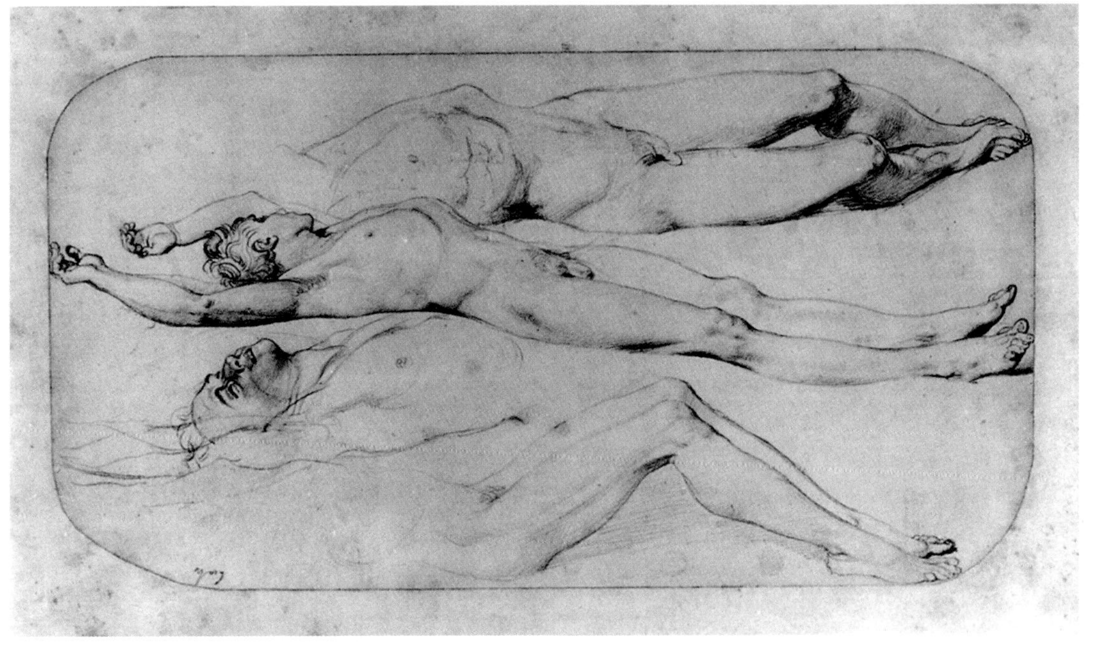

Study for Acron

1811, pencil on paper, 19.7x37.5 cm
New York Metropolitan Museum of Art

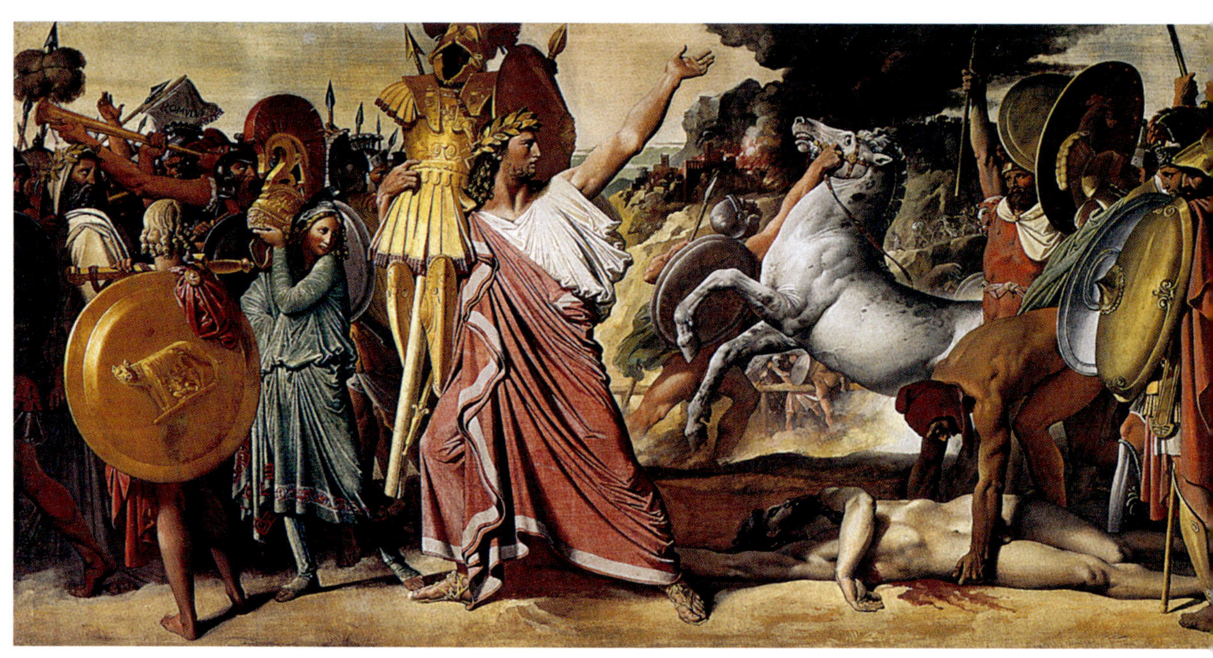

Romulus as Conqueror of King Acron

1811, tempera on canvas, 276x530 cm

Paris, Musée du Louvre

of Ossian, supposedly written by a medieval Gaelic bard and collected by the Scotsman James Macpherson, who published them in 1760-63. The poems were later translated into German – Goethe inserted whole chunks of them into his Werther – and into French in 1777. The poems were in fact pastiches cooked up by Macpherson from old Gaelic legends, but even when the fraud was exposed in 1805, the reputation of the poems continued to grow: the melancholy, warlike songs of the "Homer of the North" fit all too well with the Primitivist aspirations of the period, offering an alternative to the exclusively Greco-Roman material of Neoclassicism and chiming with the pre-Romantic current then sweeping Europe.

Napoleon had already, in 1800, ordered two canvases on the subject from Gérard and Girodet for the Château de Malmaison. Ingres borrowed Gérard's moonlit approach, but gave his picture a much more dreamlike atmosphere. The bard is shown asleep on his harp, as the white shadows of his heroes – Fingal, Oscar, Malvina and the numerous warriors killed in combat, grouped around the King of the Snows – come to him in a dream.

We can only marvel at Ingres' success in a register so different and so distant from his usual concerns. In this exploration of the dreamlike and irrational he gives proof of a typically Romantic sensibility. his "Ossianism" is doubtless a little Homeric – the thronging warriors and lovelorn women represent a minimally transposed Greco-Roman antiquity – and yet the picture, with its snow-covered forms and ghostly aspect, fits perfectly with the Ossianic tone and is far superior to most of the competition. Ingres seems to have had a special gift for appropriating the poetic essence of texts that moved him and coming up with the right pictorial equivalent.

After Homer and Ossian came Virgil. In 1812 *Virgil Reading the Aeneid to Augustus, Octavia and Livia* was commissioned from Ingres for General Miollis' residence at Villa Aldobrandini. The subject was not taken directly from Virgil, but from a commentary on the *Aeneid*. The picture shows the poet recounting Aeneas' descent into the underworld, with its prediction of the death of Octavia's son Marcellus. On hearing the prediction, Octavia faints on Augustus' knees, watched impassively by Livia who is involved in this death foretold and whose own son Tiberias will succeed to the Empire as a result. The painter brings his figures together in a scrupulously exact Pompeian setting lit by a candelabrum. Sticking to a tried and true formula, he halts the action at the critical moment, when the tension is at its height.

Ingres has created here a handsome, reference-filled picture – all the figures are taken from ancient prototypes – that follows the Poussin-inspired Neoclassical model. As in the case of most of his compositions, he produced many versions of this Virgil, but despite the eloquent silence of the figures and the dramatic nocturnal lighting, he does not succeed in generating real emotion.

Nonetheless one of these versions eclipses all the others. This work, now in Belgium, seems unfinished and it has been suggested that it could be a section cut from a larger canvas; this is because Virgil, on whose presence any understanding of the scene hinges, is absent. However, the compact grouping of the three other figures and the bent, rather than extended arm of Augustus, would seem to indicate an autonomous, deliberately created work. This interpretation is favored by the perfection of the picture in the tightness of its focus on Augustus, Octavia and Livia. The work gains in this shift of economy. Against a neutral backdrop Ingres has retained only the central knot of figures, freed from all narrative constraints and existing only for themselves. Limbs and bodies with little relief, overlapping of forms, draperies in dry or acidic shades, a medallion-style profile, a suspended gesture, and lowered eyelids: here emotion is born out of the rich clarity of structured linear rhythms. This mute confrontation centered on an unconscious body becomes permeated with a disquieting mystery – a mystery totally contained in the lowered eyelids of the pure, cold face of Livia.

"A fragment removed from the walls of Pompeii or Herculaneum," was the description offered by Henri Delaborde, one of the artist's first biographers. And indeed, the flat outlining of the figures and the slight dryness of texture are suggestive of mural technique. Ingres had just painted his enormous *Romulus* for the Quirinal, using tempera and keeping to the spirit of the fresco. He regarded the mural as the highest of all pictorial forms; he himself would never be a great decorative painter, but his attentiveness to the simplification called for by mural painting was doubtless a major factor in the development of a style emphasizing ampleness and flatness of form and the highlighting of linear structure.

The Dream of Ossian
1813, oil on canvas, 348x275 cm
Montauban, Musée Ingres

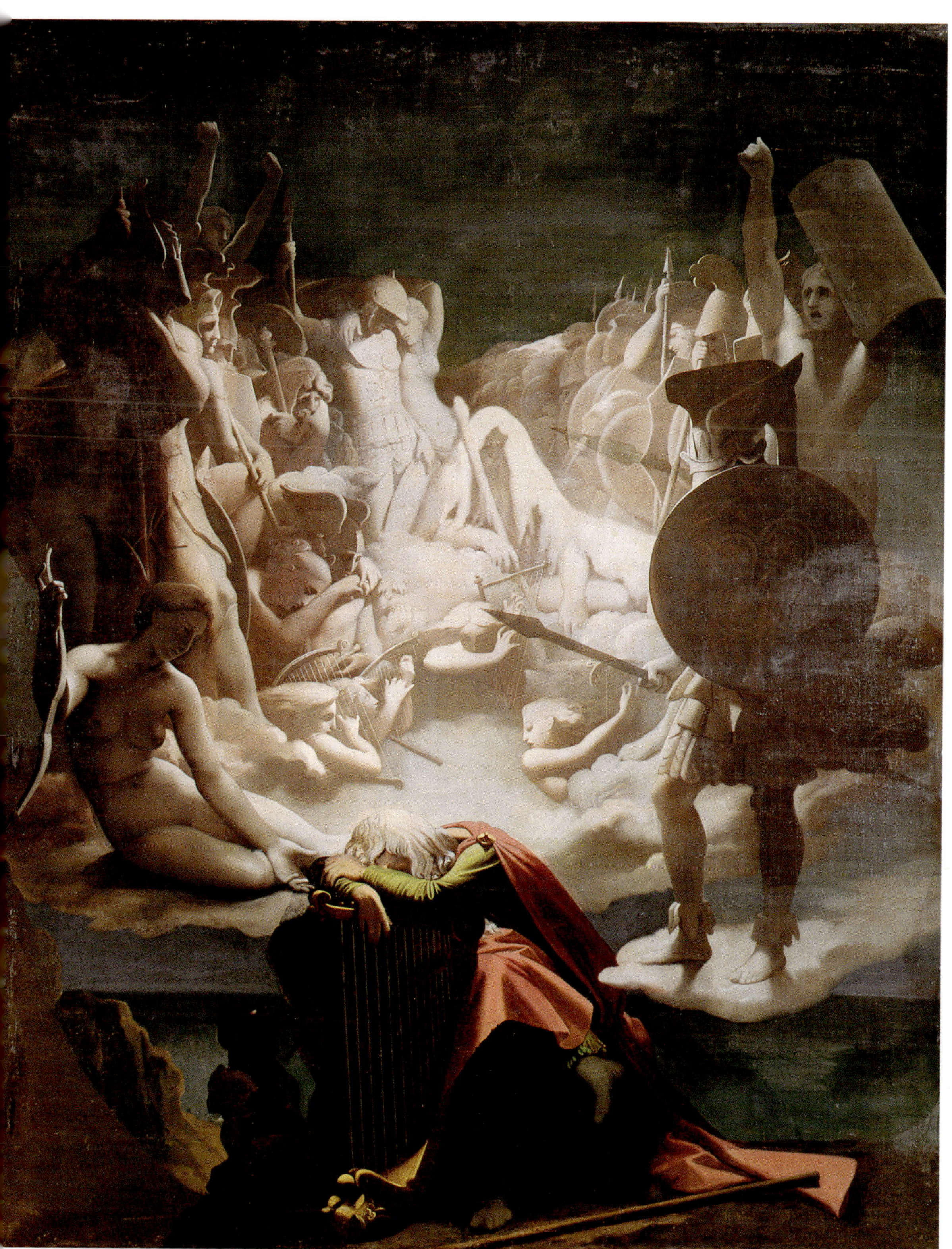

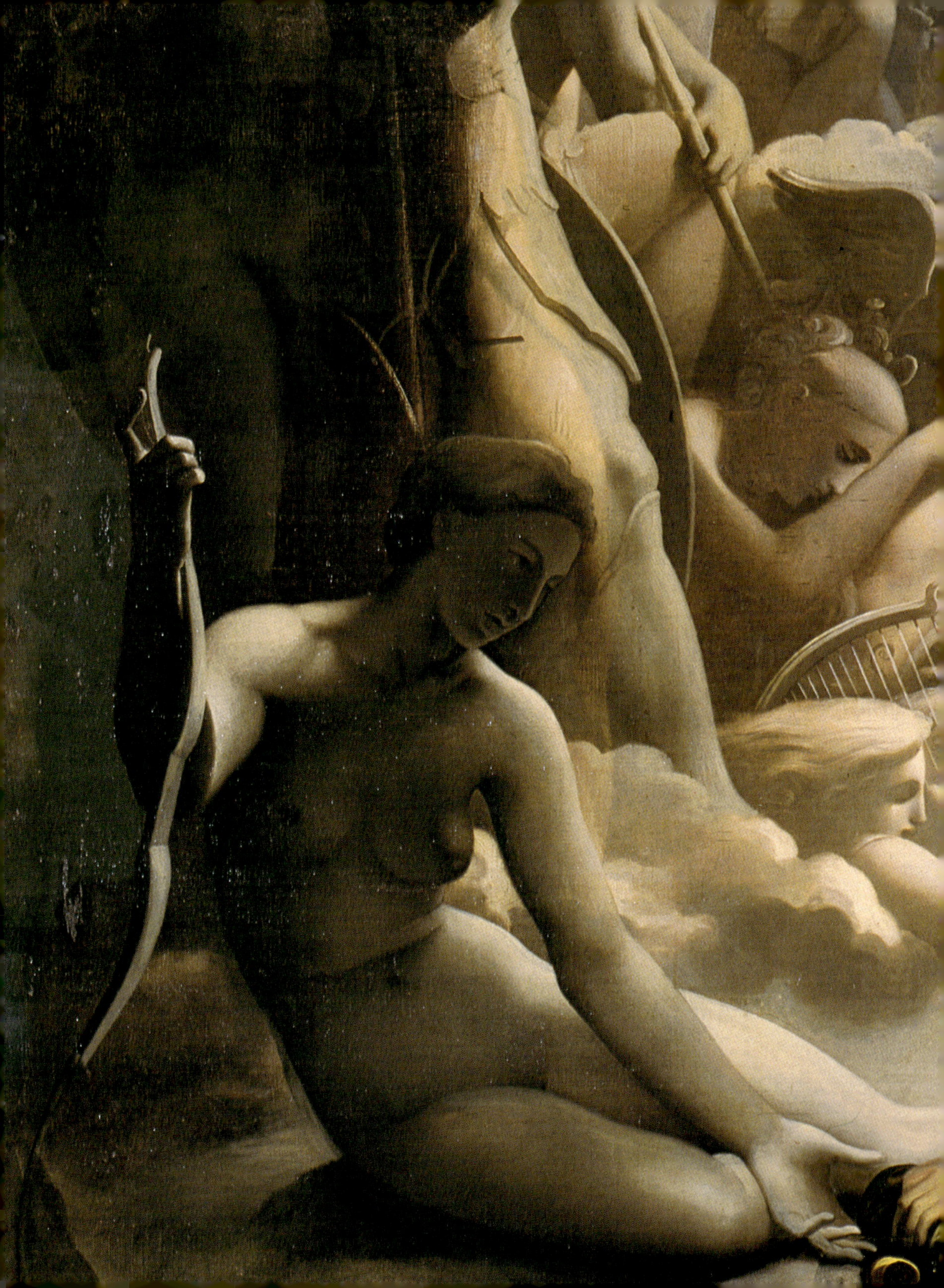

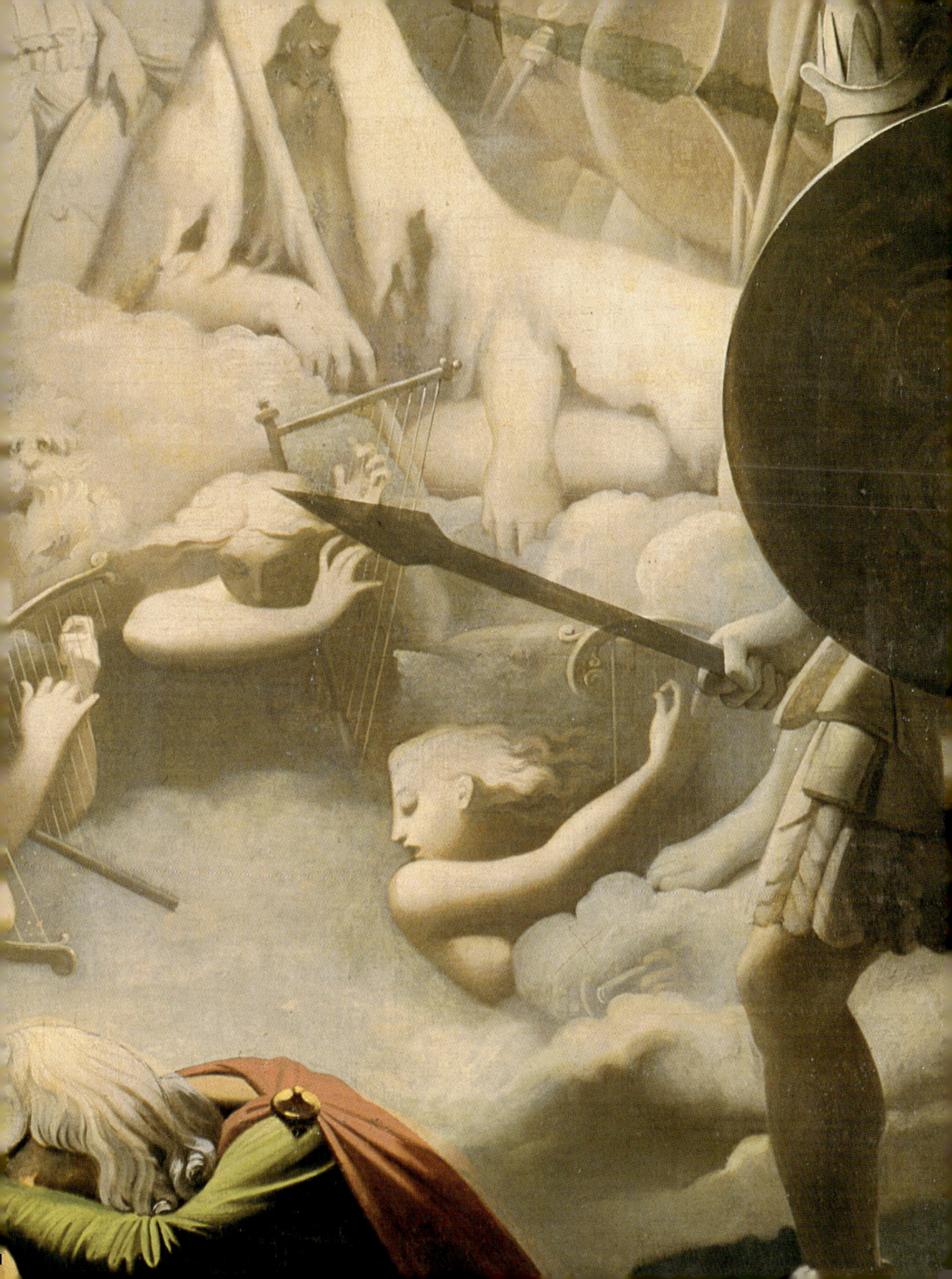

Virgil Reading the Aeneid to Augustus, Octavia and Livia
1819, oil on canvas, 138x142 cm
Brussels, Musées Royaux des Beaux-Arts

Virgil Reading the Aeneid to Augustus, Octavia and Livia, *or* "tu Marcellus eris"
1812, oil on canvas, 302x325 cm
Toulouse, Musées des Augustins

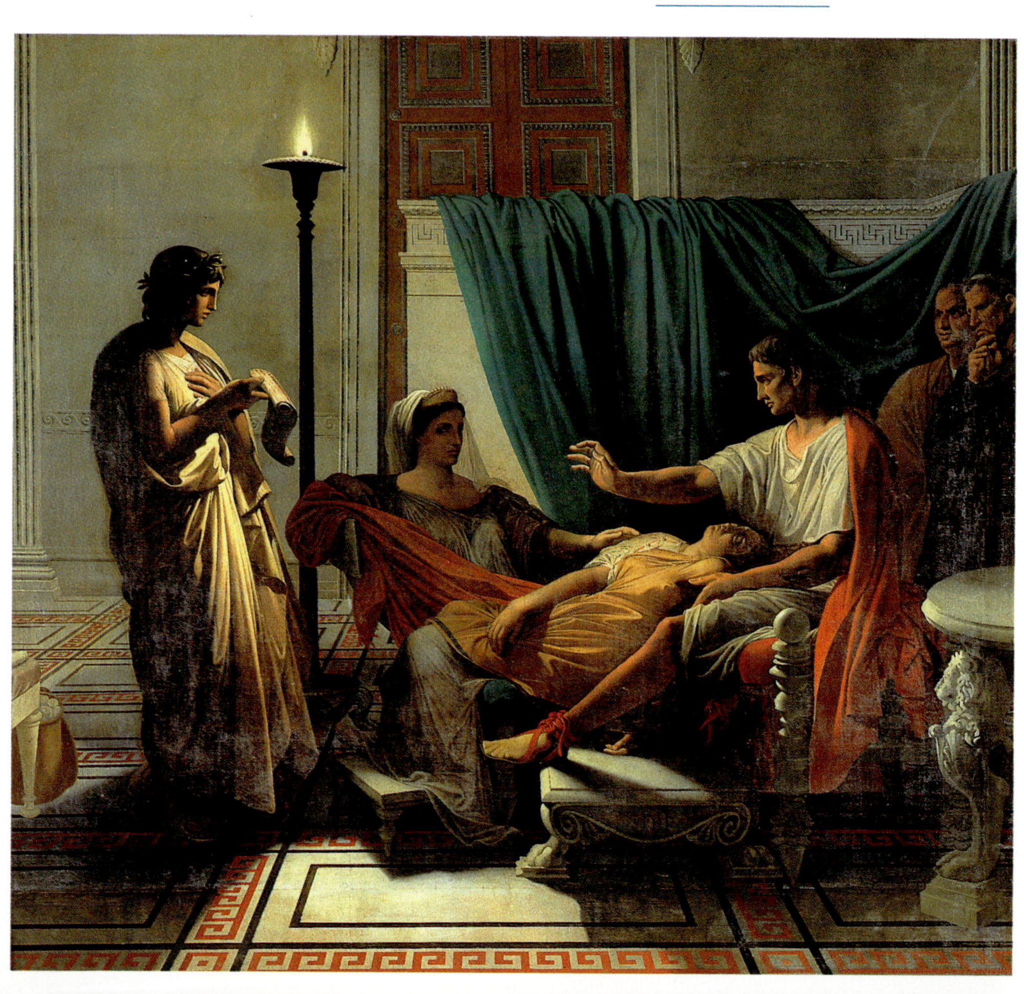

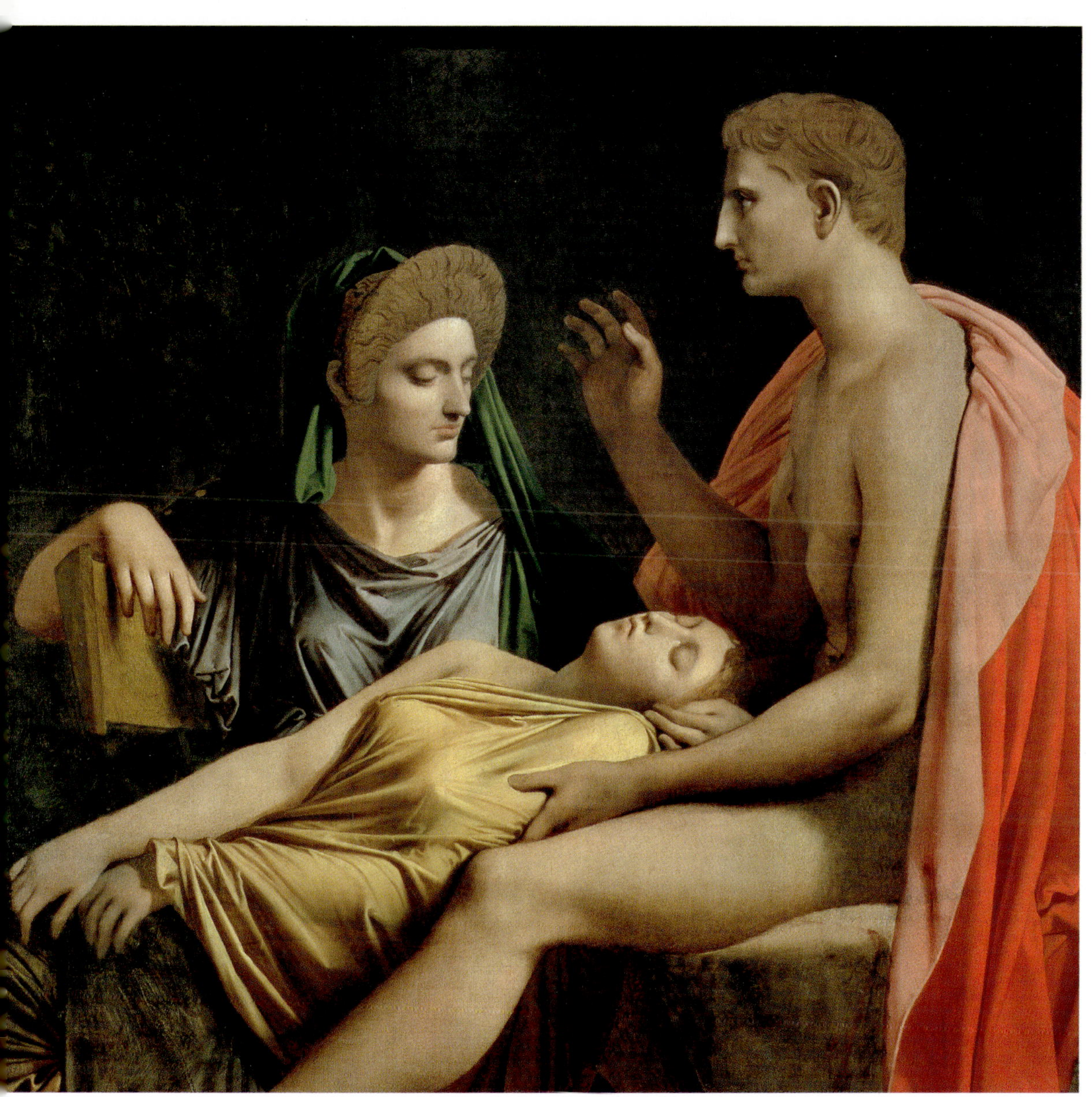

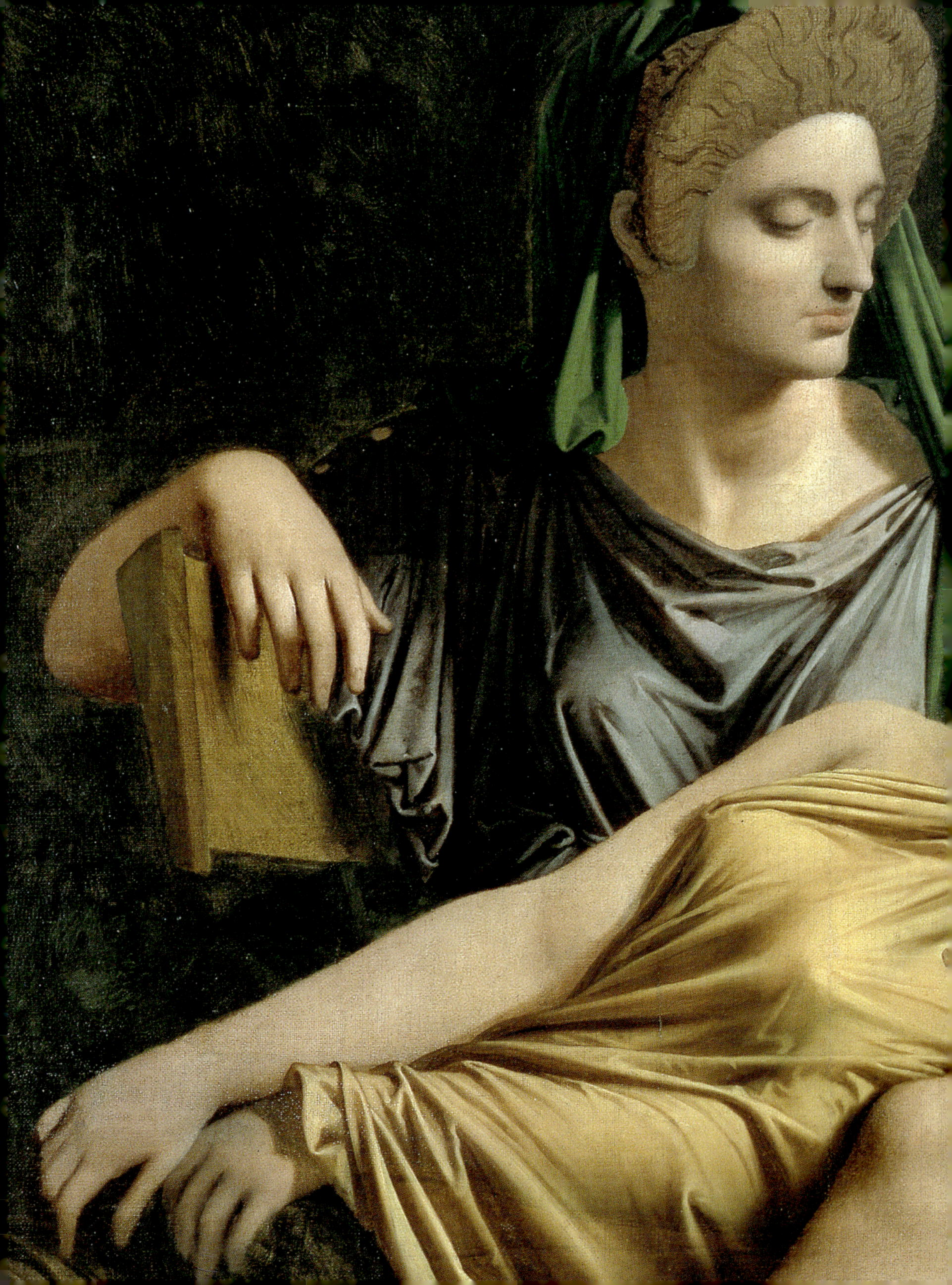

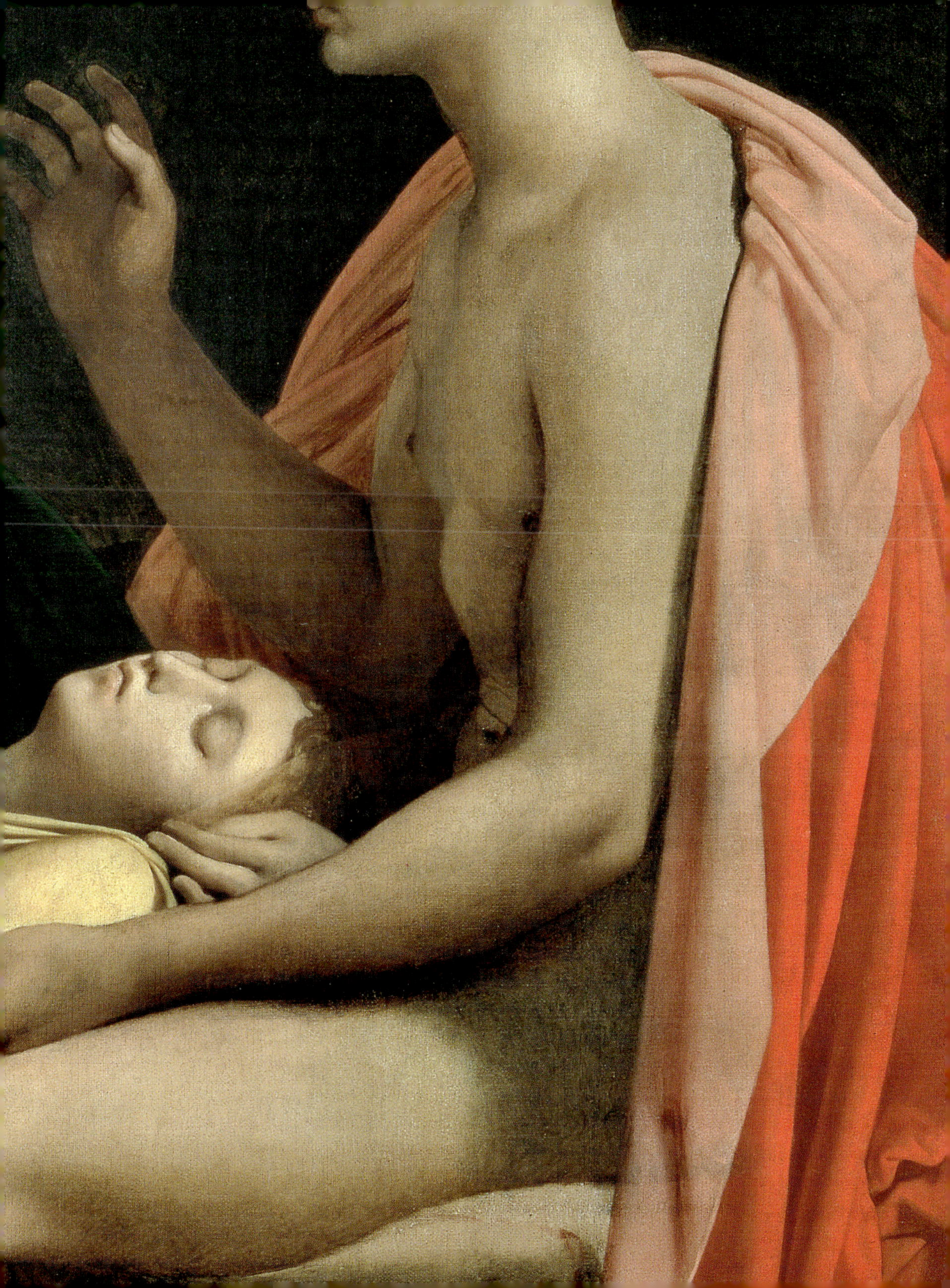

"Never Sufficiently Supple and Long"

Following pages
Sleeping Woman, Nude
1808, oil on canvas, 30x48
London, Victoria & Albert Museum

The period 1810-15 saw one commission after another. Firstly Joachim Murat, King of Naples, and his wife Caroline Bonaparte bought a *Sleeping Woman, Nude*, now lost but known from drawings and a number of variants, including one in the Victoria & Albert Museum in London. This was a full-face nude in a style reminiscent of the Venetian models of the Renaissance, and its contours would be reused later in *Odalisque and Female Slave*. The king then ordered a companion piece – the nude in back view now known as the *Grande Odalisque* – and portraits for which the painter traveled to Naples in 1814. This round of royal commissions closed with the two historical genre works *Raphael and La Fornarina* and *Paolo and Francesca*.

The extraordinarily famous *Grande Odalisque* is now considered one of the icons of Classical painting. Yet each time it was shown during the painter's lifetime it drew critical fire: at the 1819 Salon, for example, art historian Auguste-Hilarion de Kératry found the subject had three vertebrae too many; how he managed to count them on such a perfectly smooth back remains a mystery.

Another critic, Charles Landon, wrote, "The briefest of glances reveals that this figure has no bones, muscles, blood, life or relief, and nothing called for by imitation. The skin is muddy and monotonous and the light is spread so flatly, with so little skill or subtlety, that the areas requiring gradations of shading are as strongly lit as the most prominent ones. It is obvious that the artist has perversely sought to work badly or has set out to revive the pure, primitive manner of the painters of antiquity; but he has chosen to work with a few fragments of some past period and a degenerate technique, and they have led him wildly astray." [19]

Intelligently formulated negative criticism has some interest, for it often highlights the vital aspects of a work much better than the writing of admirers. Ingres' critical legacy is rich in commentary that is both acerbic and illuminating, one of the most frequent reproaches being that a self-indulgent archaism led him to sacrifice accurate imitation of reality for mere stylistic effect. His anatomical liberties were especially outrageous at the time: Ingres knew anatomy well, but could not abide "this frightful science, this horrible thing I cannot think about without disgust." For him anatomy was for surgeons, not painters: our inner workings had the reek of death about them and confined the body to a purely materialist view of nature. Nature itself was an endless source of delight, witness his hundreds of extraordinarily beautiful drawings of nudes, but his personal approach was incompatible with rational knowledge. In his view of things the human figure was, so to speak, the chosen form, and he had no interest in anything – anatomy, violence, pain, ageing, death and even psychology – that tainted its beauty. His art shrinks from the expression of time and the impermanence and fragility of things, just as it shrinks from portraying any dramatic action that might compromise balance of form.

Once again a comparison with a work by David, a nude painted in 1800 and one of the probable sources of Ingres' *Grande Odalisque*, highlights the singularity of his esthetic notions. Set beside the David, the *Grande Odalisque* stands as a rigorous piece of composition, with all the solidity and purity of classical architecture. The subject has nothing to do with a real woman: she is a combination of elements inspired by nature, reworked and fused into a single, seamless form as beautiful as a Greek temple, as rhythmical as a line of classical French poetry. This is where Ingres is undeniably modern: it is perceived form that interests him, not real form.

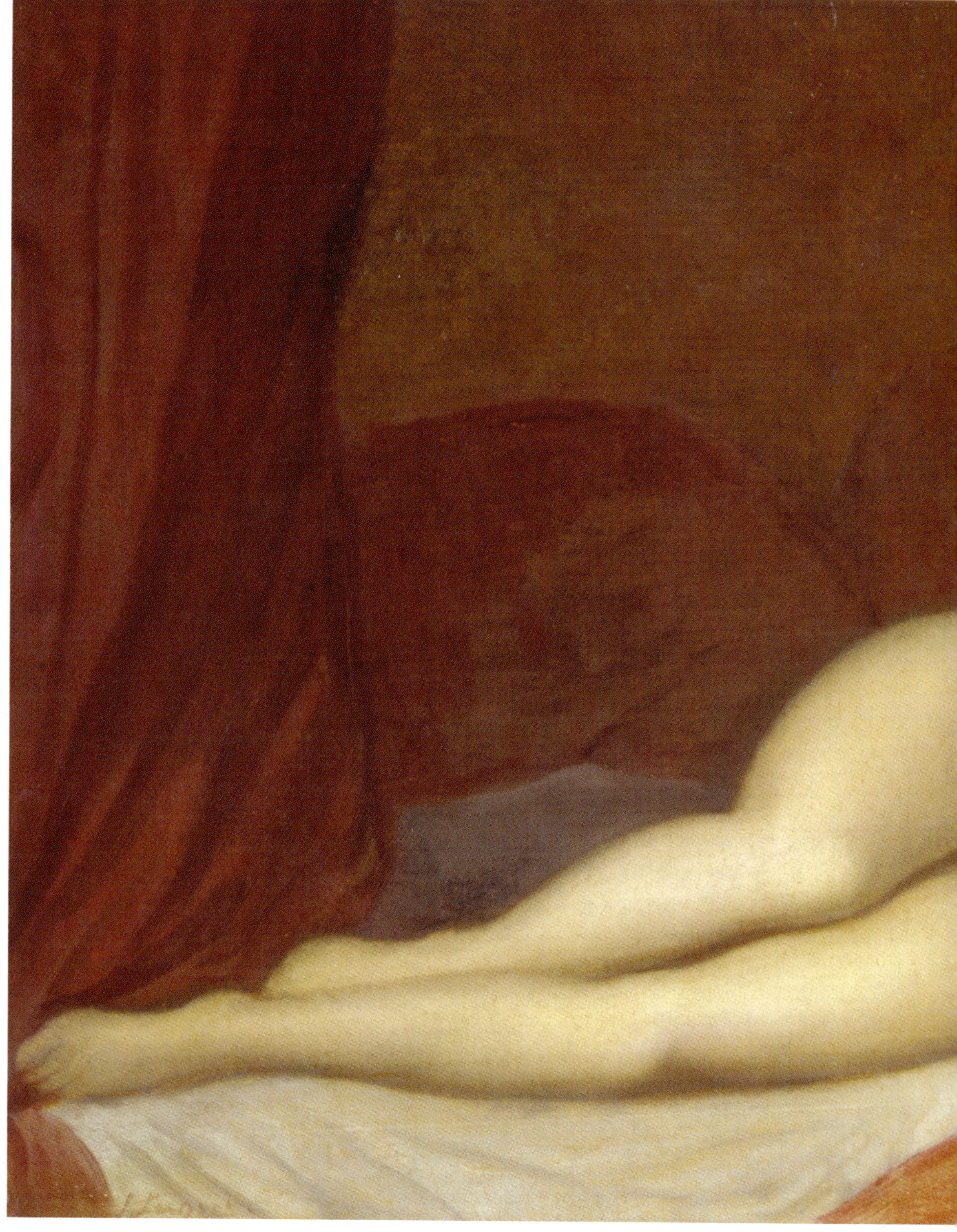

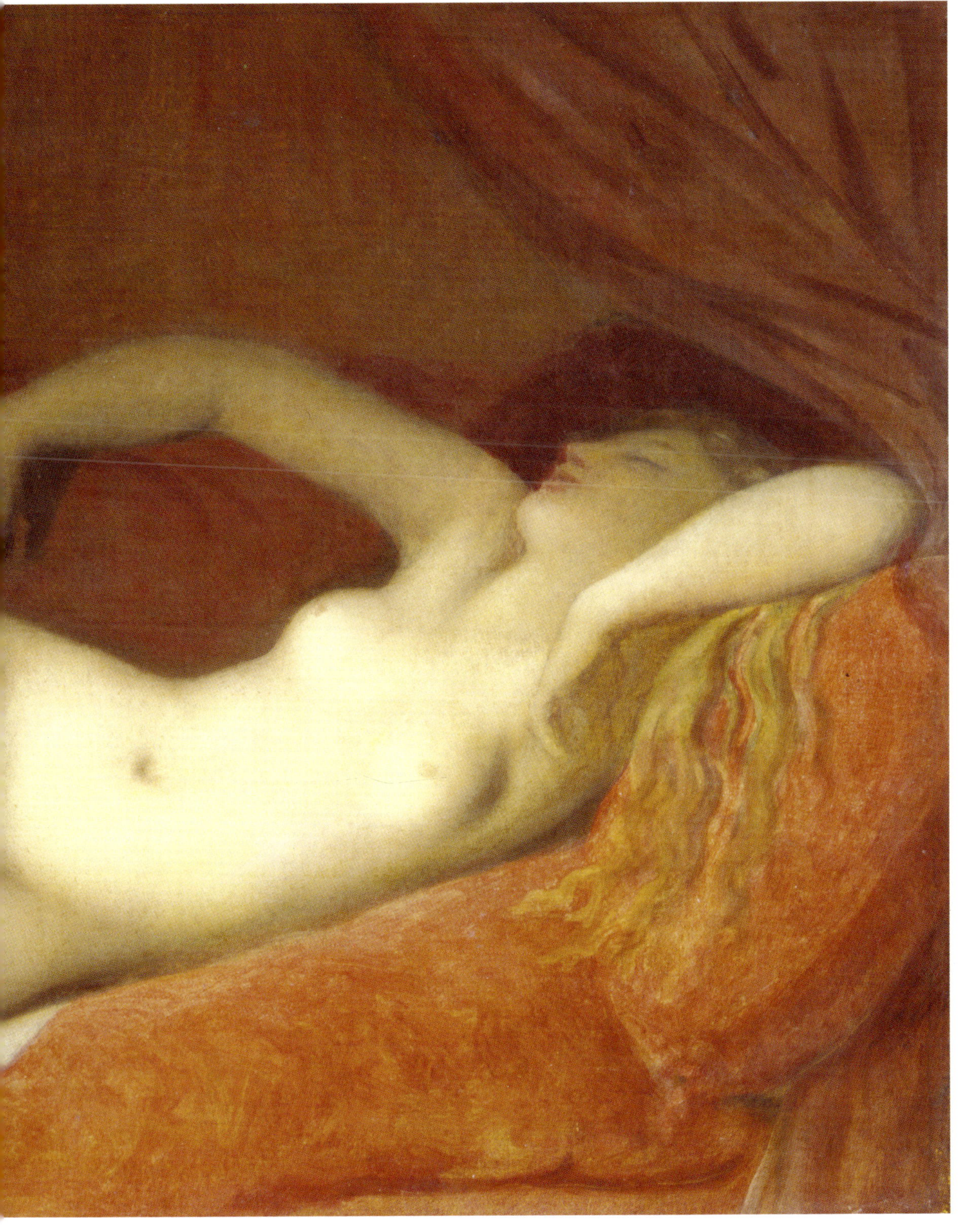

Study for *La Grande Odalisque*
1814, pencil, 25.4x26.5 cm
Paris, Musée du Louvre, Cabinet des dessins

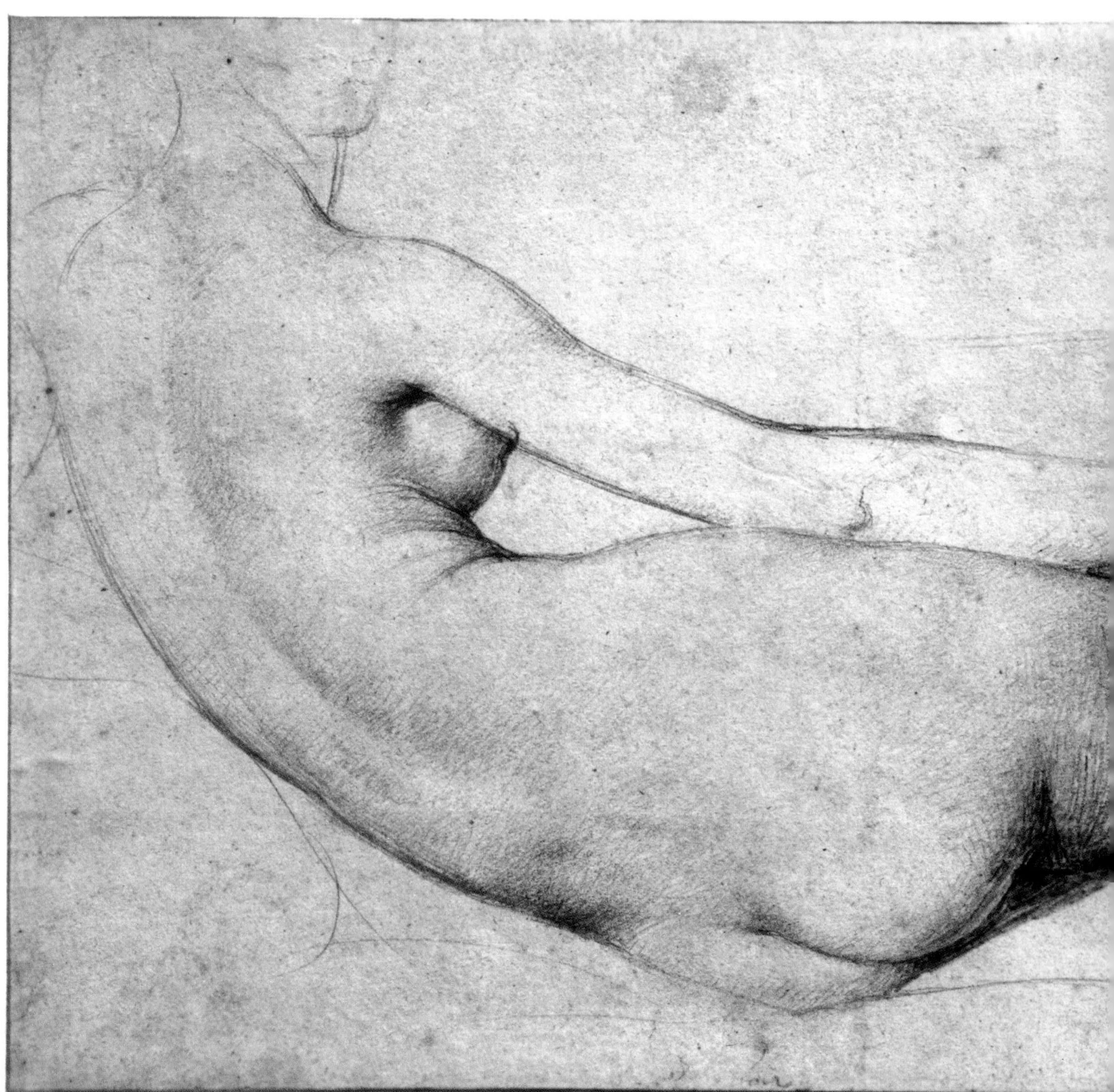

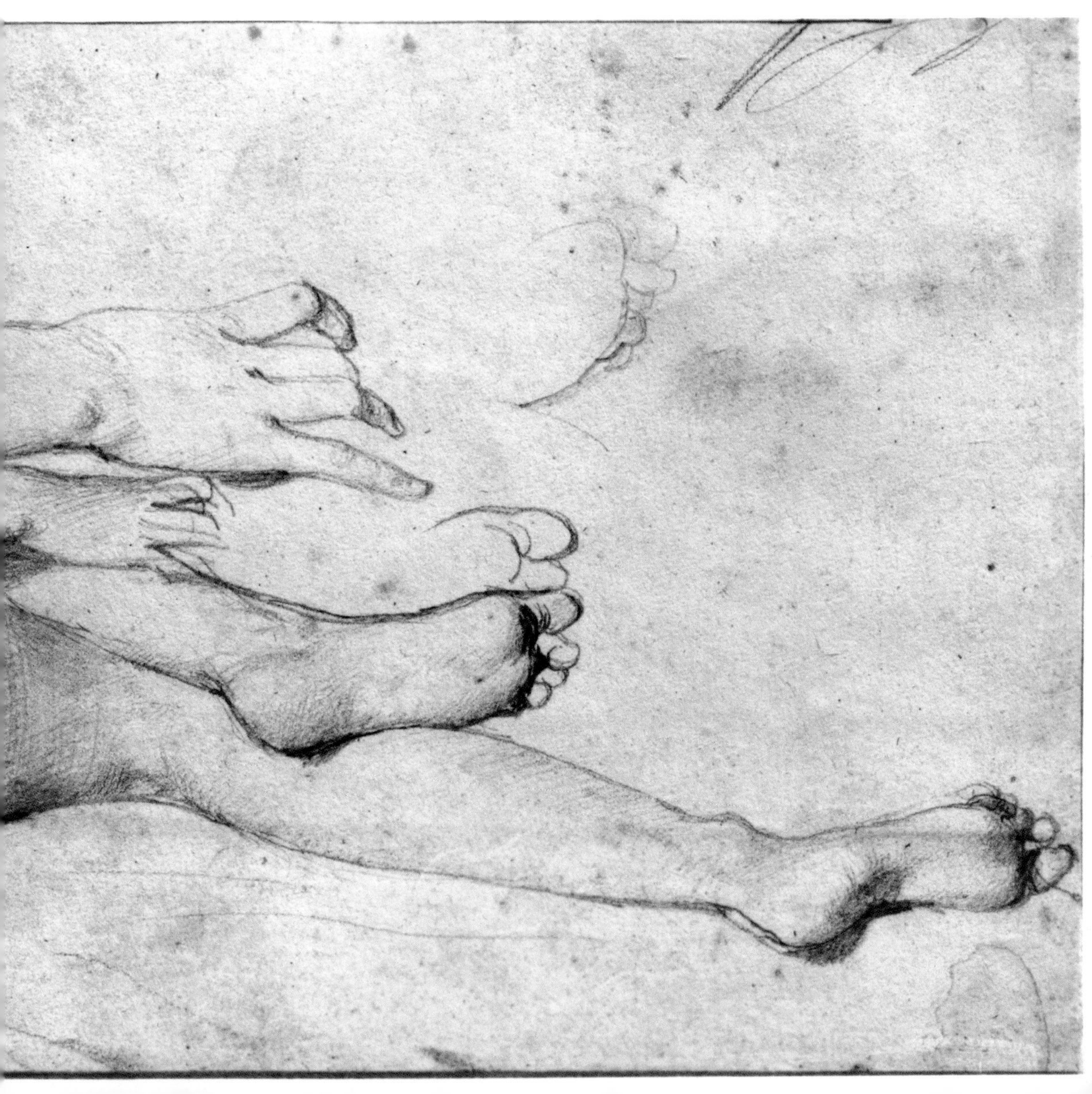

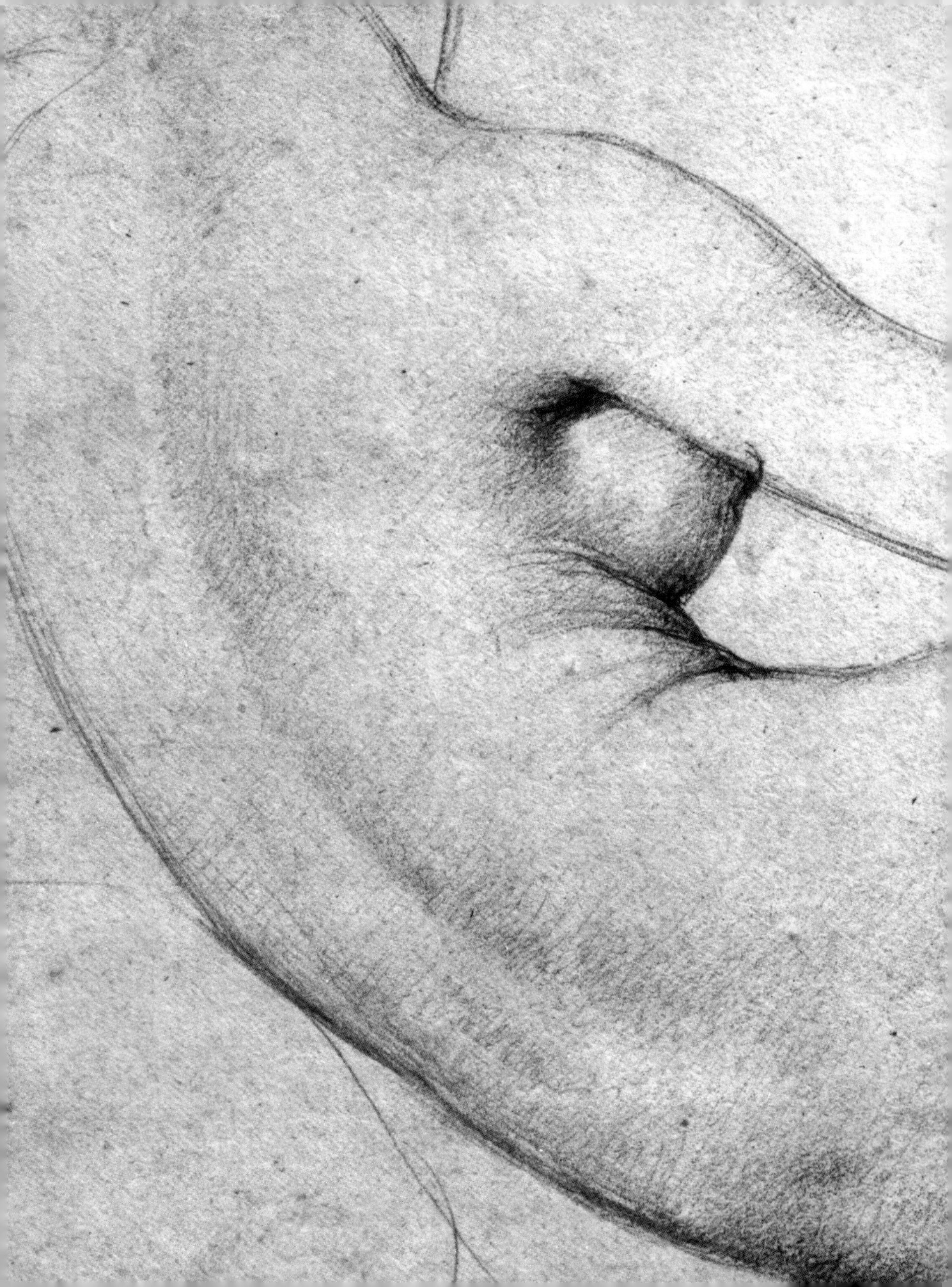

The poets of the time were more sensitive to the originality of this sphinxlike figure than the art critics. "What abandoned elegance in these long limbs, graceful as the stems of flowers in the current of a stream," cried Théophile Gautier. [20] Later, Paul Valéry would write, "The spine can never be sufficiently supple and long, nor the neck sufficiently flexible, the thighs sufficiently smooth, nor all the curves of the body sufficiently accommodating to the gaze that envelops them, touching more than seeing..." [21]

As ever with Ingres, idealization and abstraction of form are associated with the meticulously realistic detail of the setting and the accessories. However we remain very much aware that the point of this realism is not a depiction of reality, but a more beautiful rendering of the image, an enhancement of the illusion via "all the splendid sumptuousness of art," as he had written of *Jupiter and Thetis*.

Following pages
La Grande Odalisque
1814, oil on canvas, 91x162 cm
Paris, Musée du Louvre

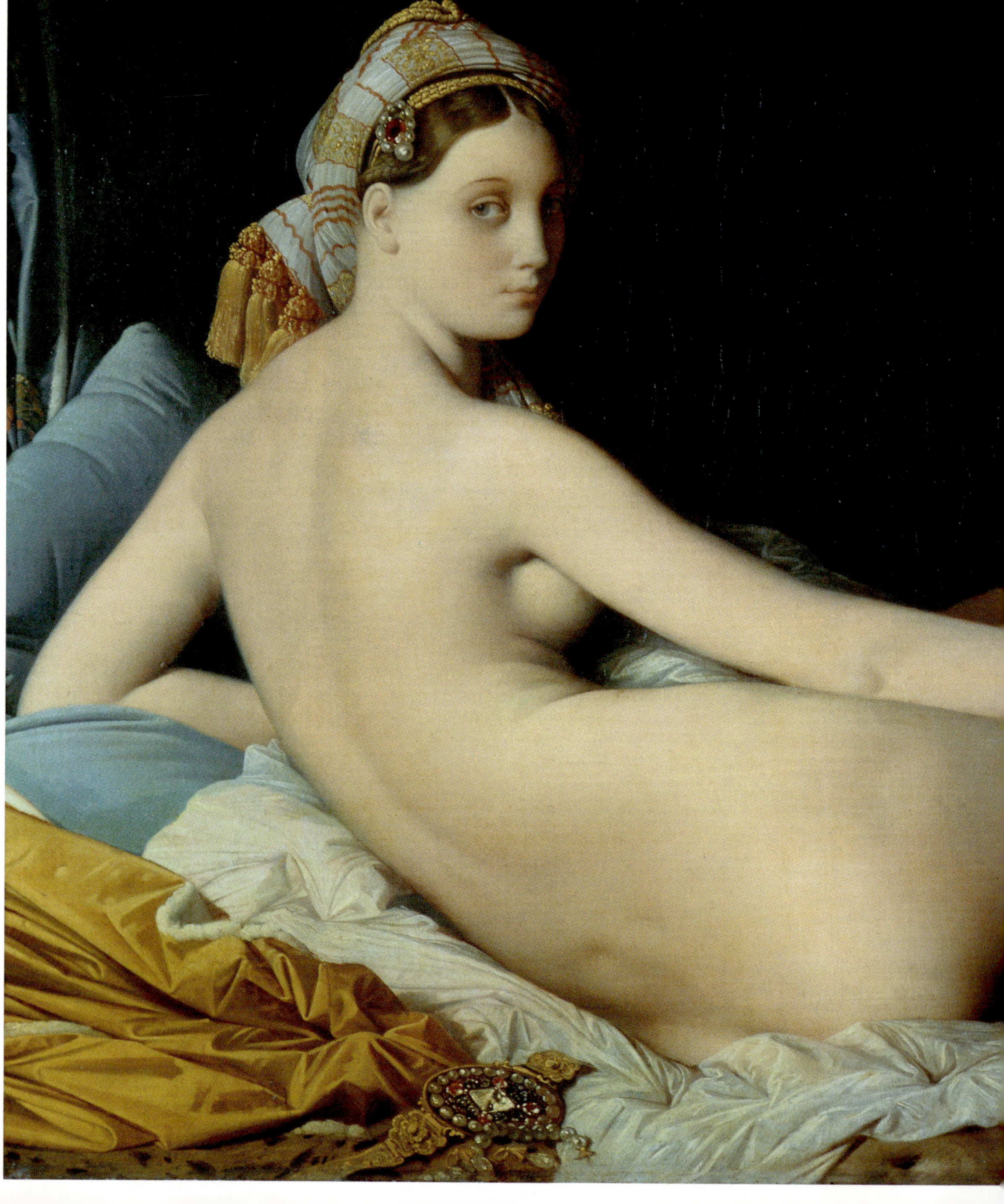

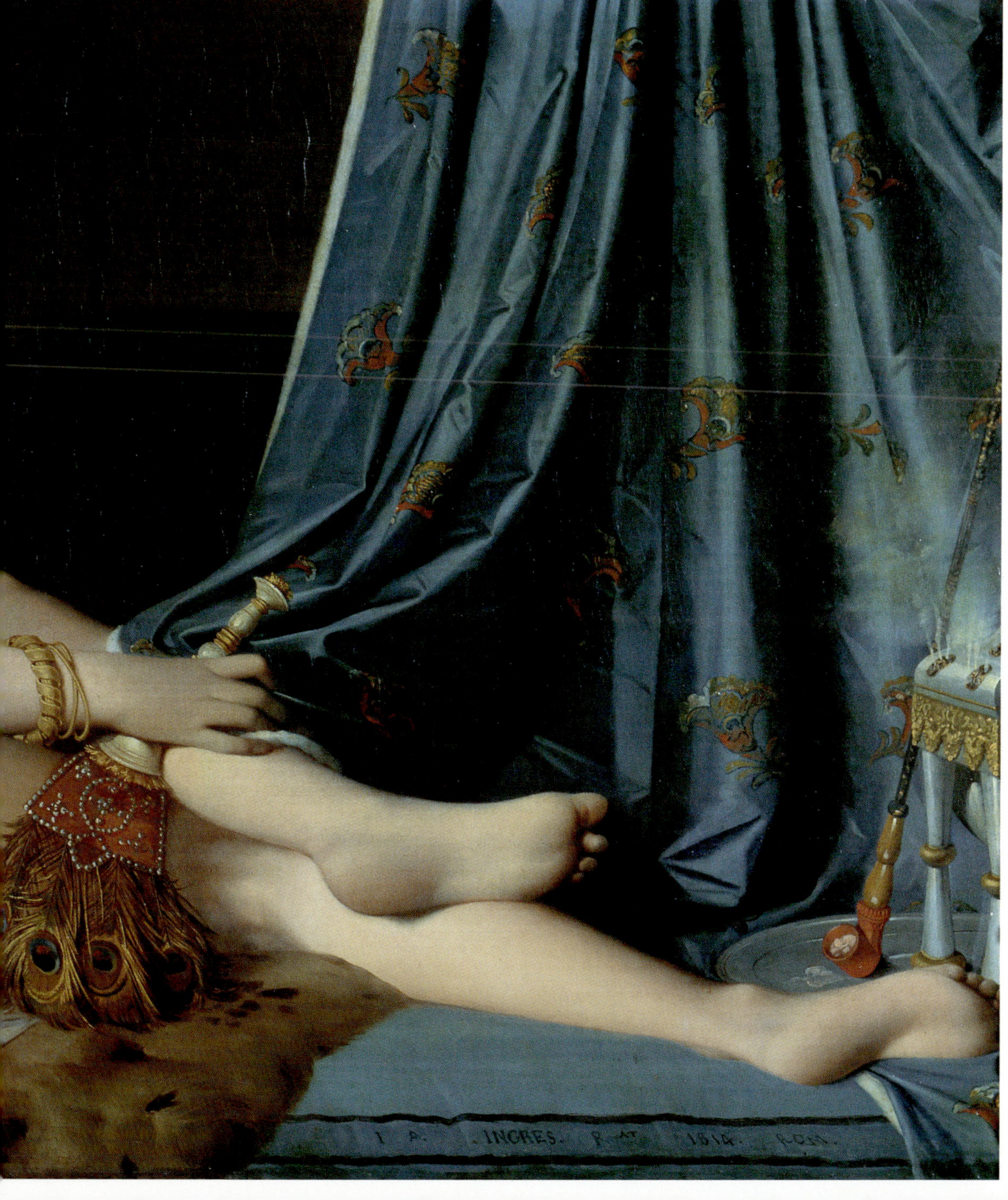
I A. INGRES. 1814.

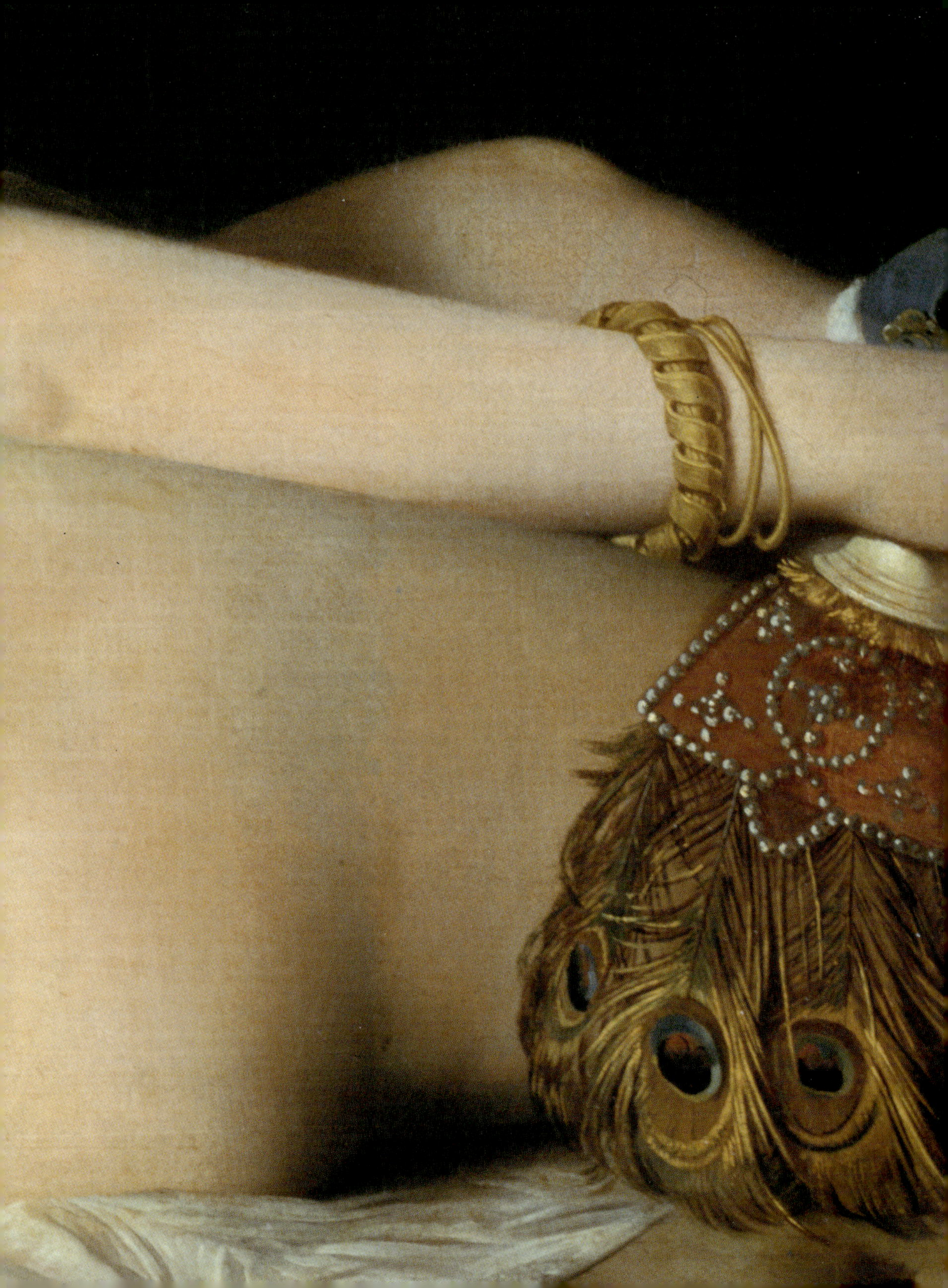

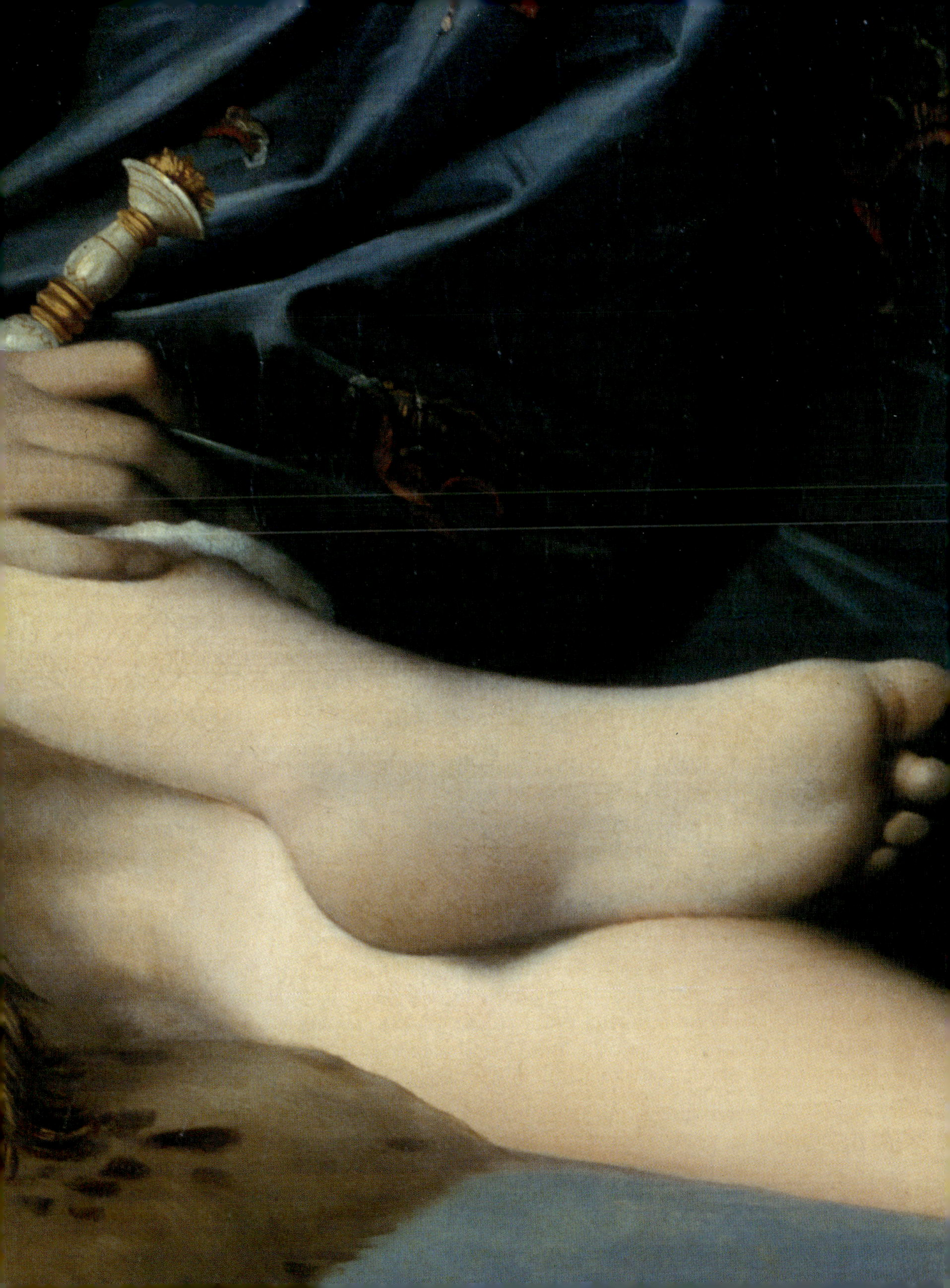

Anecdotal Genre Painting and the Troubadour Style

In the early 1790s the opening of the Museum of French Monuments, showing sculpture saved from Revolutionary vandalism in a medieval setting, contributed to the development of a new pictorial style that would flourish at the beginning of the following decade. A new awareness of medieval and national historical subjects developed within David's atelier. Marius Granet, Jean-Louis Ducis, Fleury-Richard and the Lyon painter Pierre Révoil launched the fashion for small pictures with a historical or literary slant that focused not on the great deeds of famous figures, but on aspects of their everyday or sentimental lives. Related to the "Troubadour" style and then described as "historical" or "anecdotal," this approach fell between genre and history painting, its success depending largely on the picturesqueness and documentary realism of its settings and costumes.

Jean Alaux
The Atelier of Ingres in Rome
1818, oil on canvas, 55.64x53 cm
Montauban, Musée Ingres

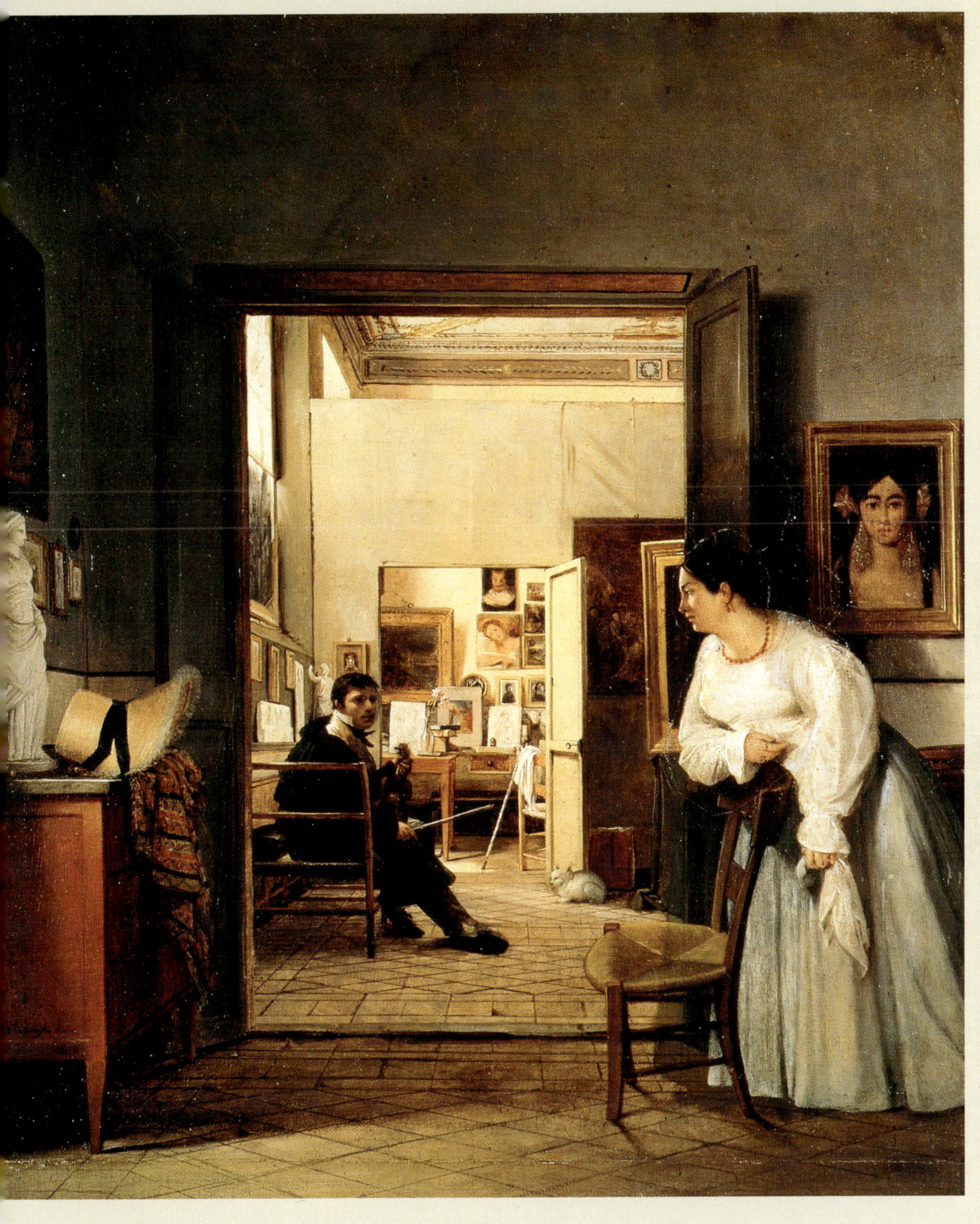

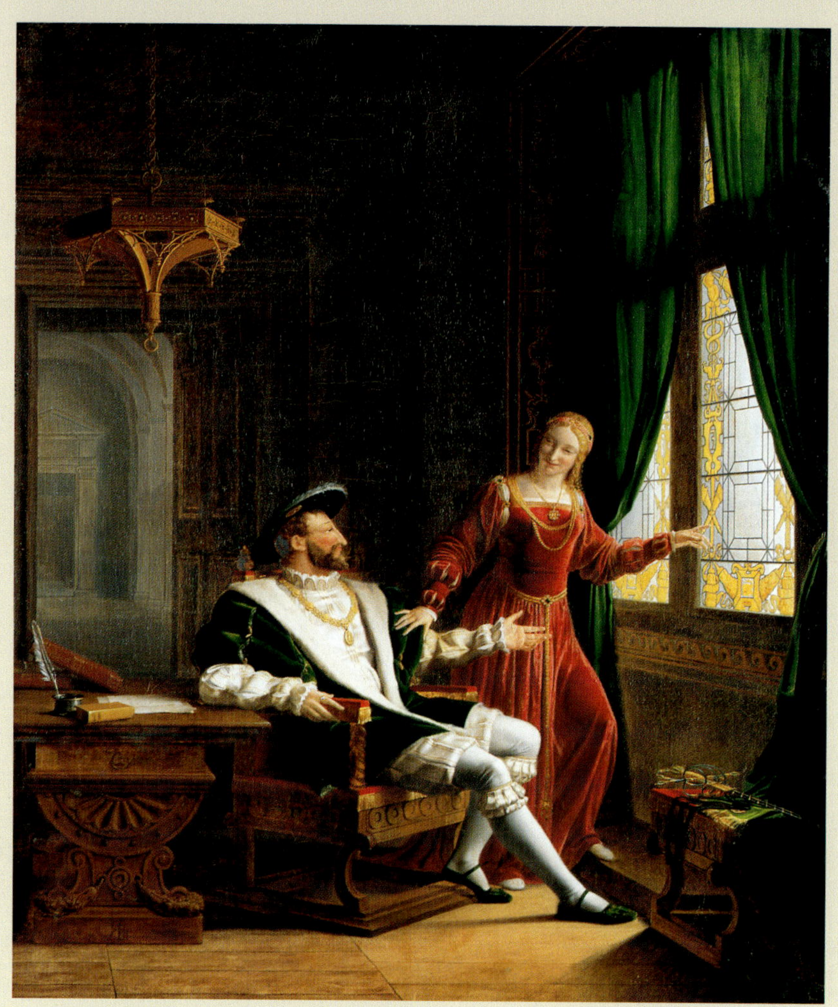

Fleury-Richard
Francis I and the Queen of Navarre
1804, oil on panel, 81x64 cm
Arenenberg, Musée Napoléon

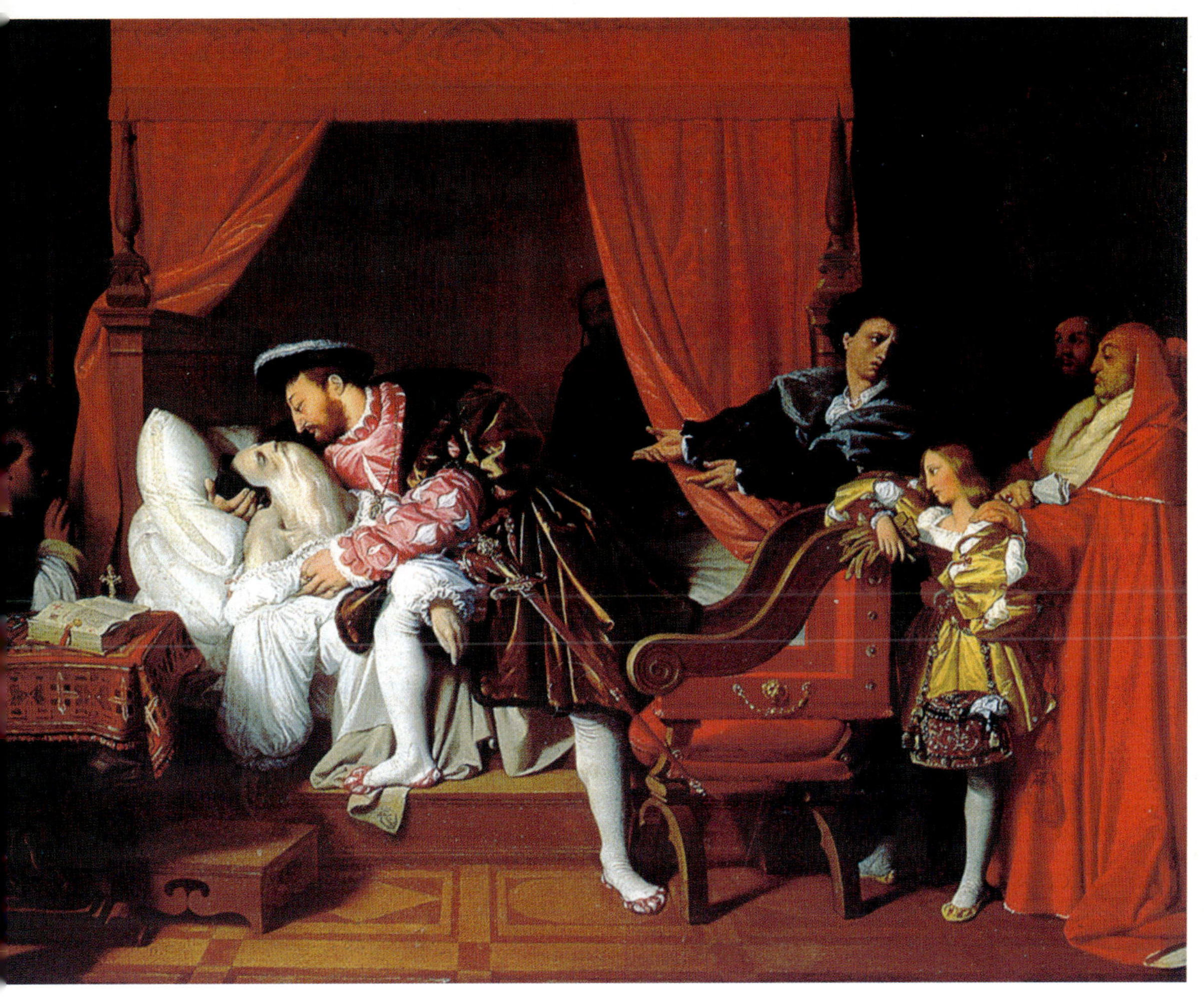

The Death of Leonardo da Vinci
1818, oil on canvas, 40x50 cm
Paris, Musée du Petit Palais

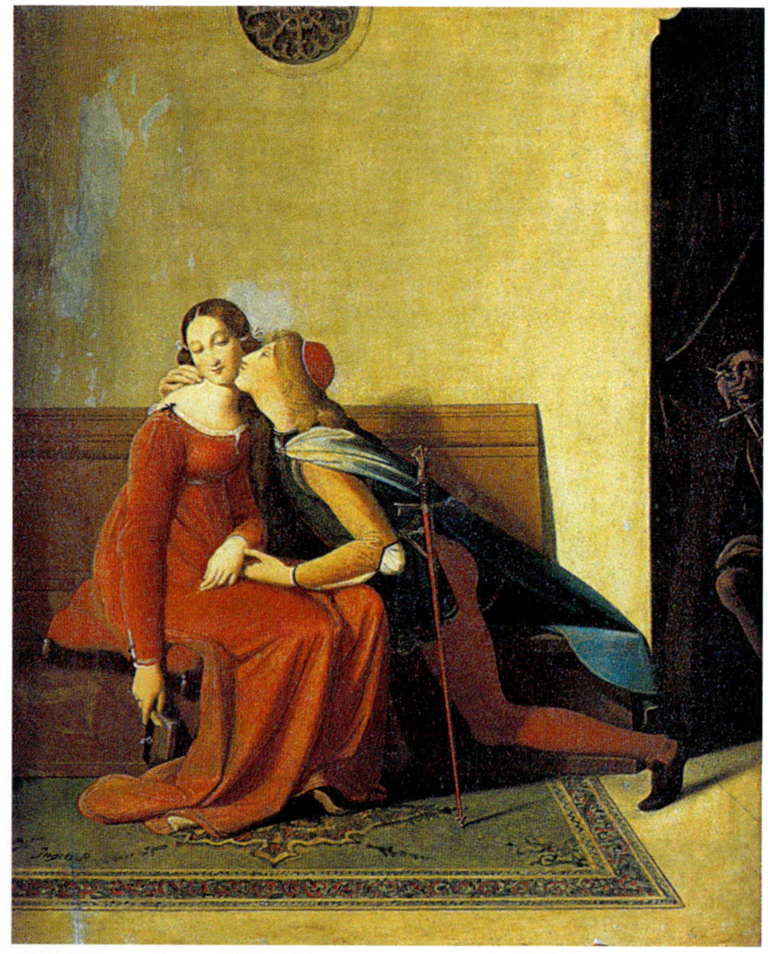

Paolo and Francesca
1814, oil on panel, 35x28 cm
Chantilly, Musée Condé

Paolo and Francesca
1819, oil on canvas, 48x39 cm
Angers, Musée des Beaux-Arts

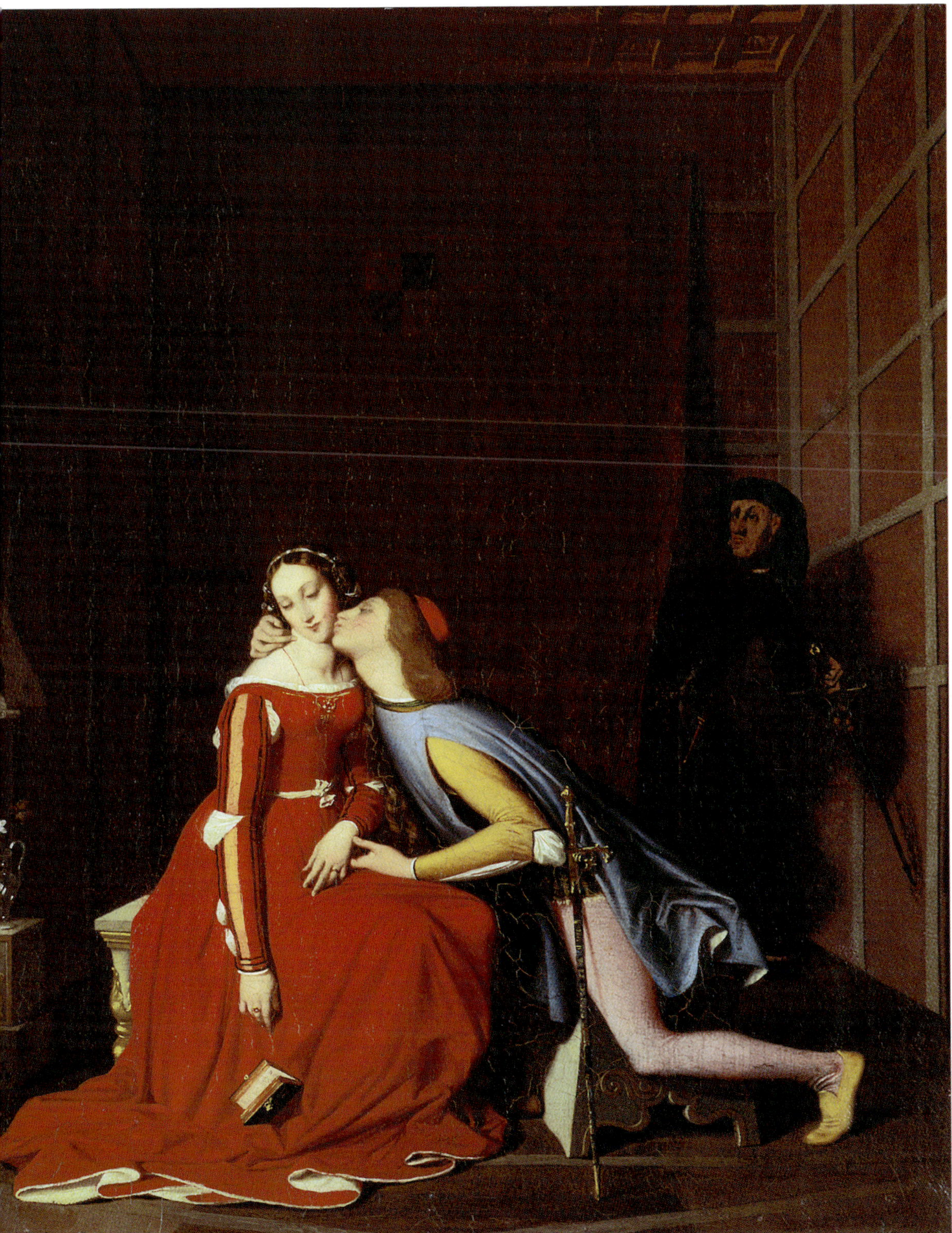

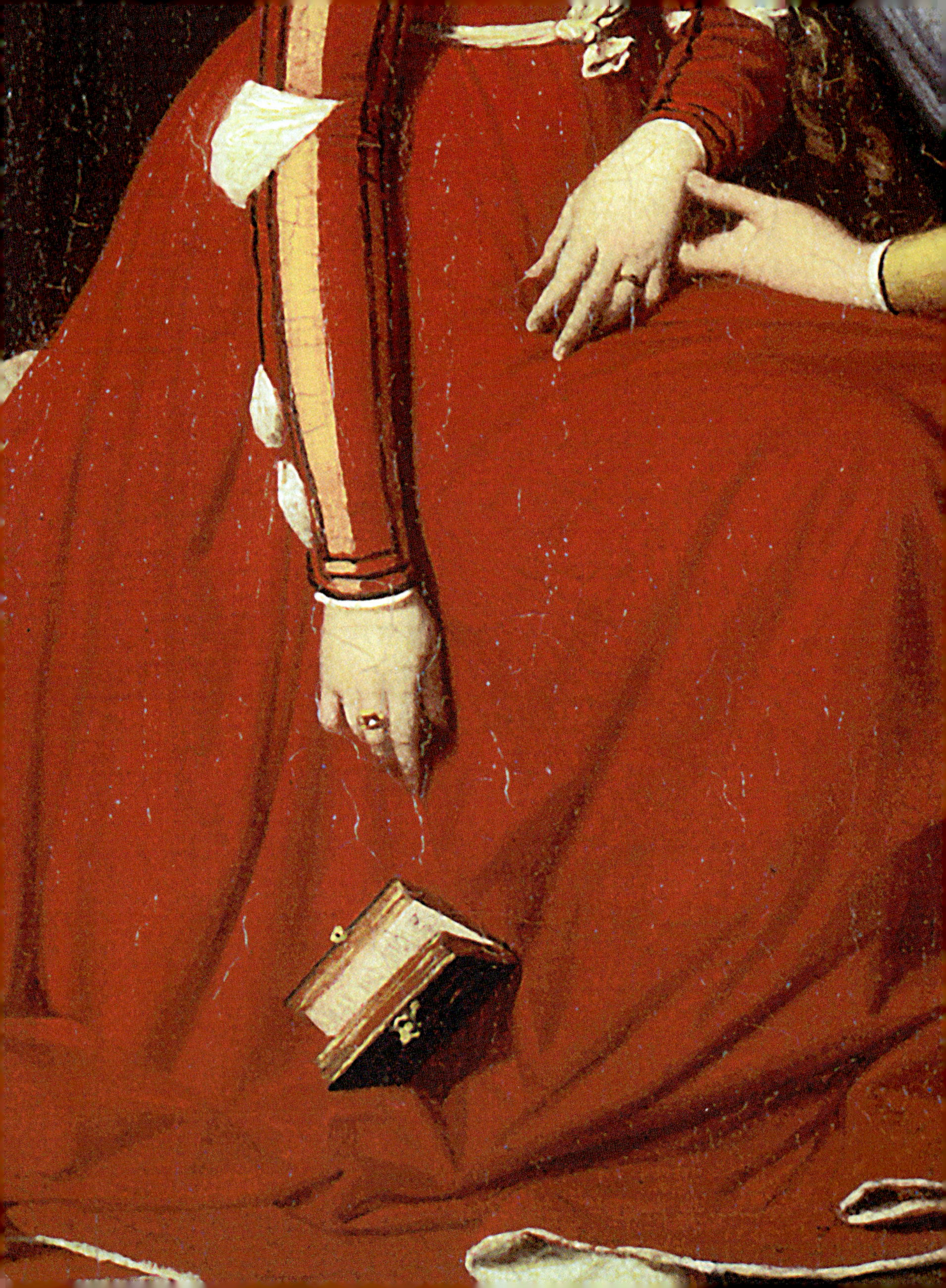

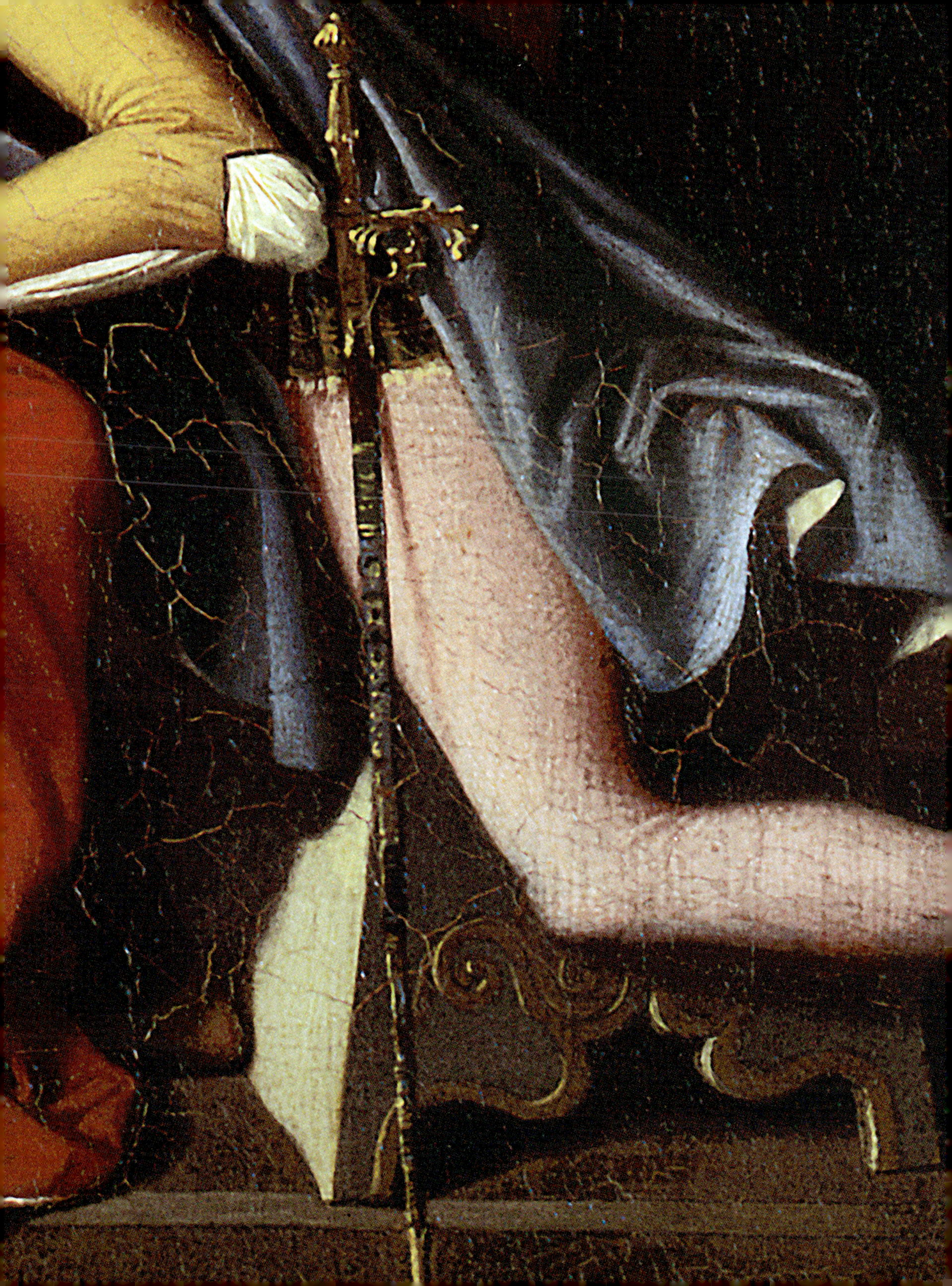

Nude Study for Ruggiero
1819, black chalk on paper, 29.1x23.5 cm
Montauban, Musée Ingres

During his time in Rome Ingres painted a succession of pictures of this kind. Some drew on history as such, celebrating the restoration of the monarchy after the fall of the Empire: *Don Pedro of Toledo Kissing the Rapier of Henry IV* (1814) and *Henry IV Receiving the Ambassador of Spain*. Others illustrated the lives of the artists: *Raphael and La Fornarina* (1813), *Aretino in the Studio of Tintoretto* (1815) and *The Death of Leonardo da Vinci* (1818). Others still found their subject matter in literature.

Like those of his former fellow students, Ingres' pictures used extensive research to optimize the historical veracity of their costumes, settings and accessories – "local color," as this was called at the time. Space reduced to doll-house proportions, a mass of obsessively precise detail and brilliant coloring all played their part in making of these small works kinds of illuminations or miniatures that have been compared to "pages torn from a missal." Indeed, the stress on formal originality was such that some of them have attained the status of masterpieces, despite their triviality and sentimentalism.

Paolo and Francesca illustrates Canto V of *Hell* from Dante's *Divine Comedy*, in which the hapless protagonists are surprised and killed by Francesca's jealous husband just as they are about to express their love. Flaxman's illustrations for the 1802 French edition probably provided Ingres with his starting point. Of the four known versions of the painting, the one now in Angers, France (1819) is unquestionably the most perfect, whether or not it is the prototype for the series. Its naive sentimentality and the burlesque figure of the husband would make the picture a kind of popular cliché had Ingres not invested it with all his personal sumptuousness: the originality of a style that makes equal play with the Quattrocento tradition (the perspective box, large areas of solid color) and Flemish Primitivism (the realism of every detail, right down to the reflection of the window on the vase); and above all the linear beauty of the setting, pressing in on the pair of lovers and seemingly welding them together for eternity. The moment of the kiss seems destined to endure forever: that falling book will never reach the floor. A suspended moment, crystallized in the mirror of painting and as estranged from reality as the souls of Paolo and Francesca are irrevocably cut off from their earthly existence.

It is clear here that the subject is a pretext for a plastic poem in which all that counts is the beauty of language, line and rhyme. We find ourselves thinking of the Parnassian poets, and Théophile Gautier, one of the artist's great admirers.

If its subject, size and intended location – it was commissioned for the throne room at Versailles – put *Ruggiero Frees Angelica* in the "major" history painting category, its style is closer to that of the "anecdotal genre" and Troubadour imagery. This is a small picture given the big treatment. The subject is taken

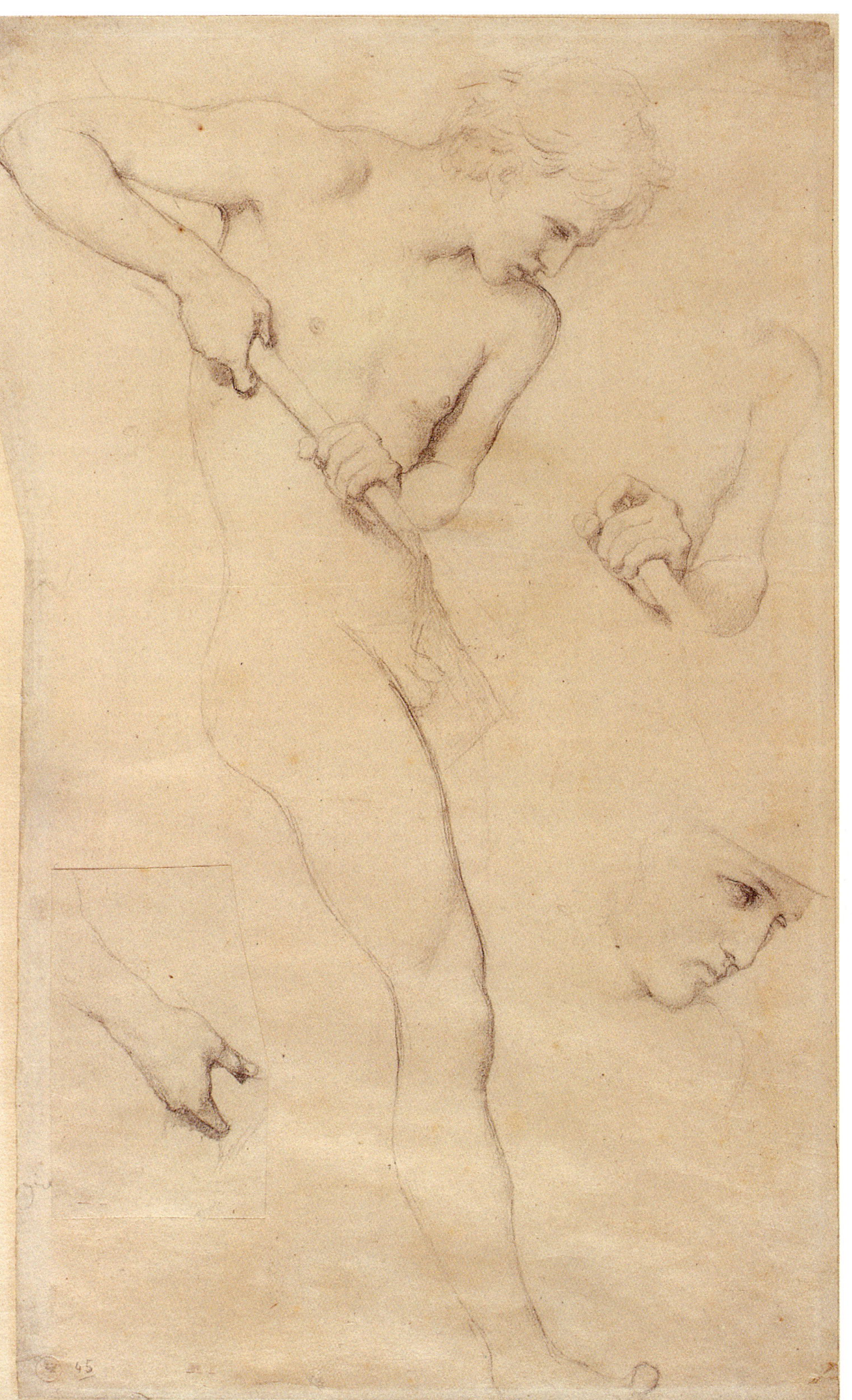

Study for Angelica
1818, oil on canvas, 45.8x36.8 cm
Cambridge, The Fogg Art Museum

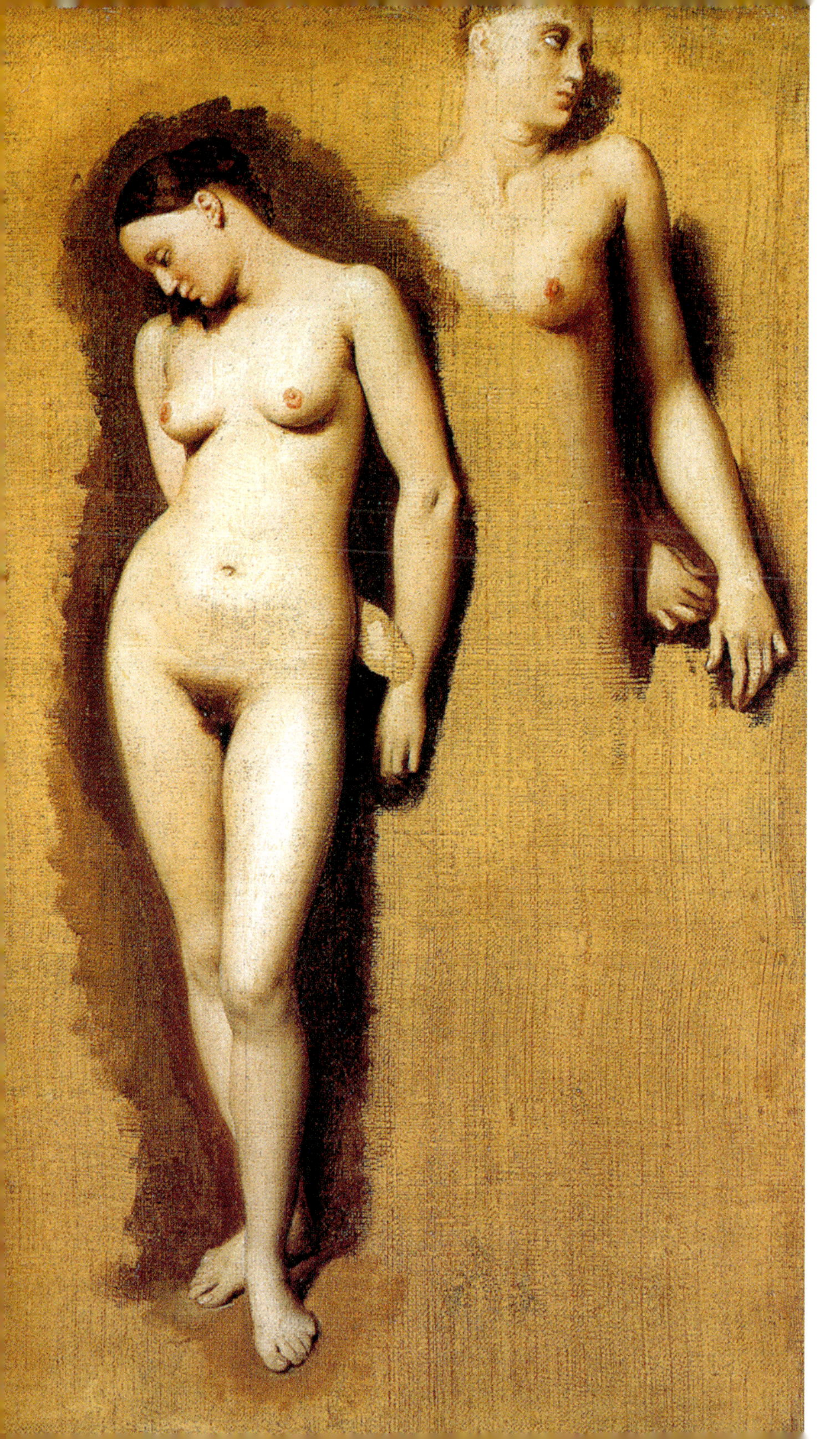

from Ariosto's *Orlando Furioso*: Angelica, queen of Cathay [China], has been abducted by the Ebudians and held in chains on the Island of Complaint as prey for a sea monster, the orc. She is rescued by Ruggiero, a knight in the army of Agramant, king of the Moors. In Ingres' hybrid representation of the scene, Angelica's nakedness belongs to the world of classical mythology and echoes the story of Perseus and Andromeda, while the chivalrous Ruggiero takes us back to the medieval legend of St George and the Dragon. The outcome of this poetic-esthetic mix is weird to say the least, and in a way emphasized by the varying treatment accorded the different areas of the painting: the setting and the monster are dealt with summarily; Ruggiero and his hippogriff are meticulously "hyper-realistic"; and the nude figure has the purity of a Florentine ivory. One quickly realizes, in fact, that only Angelica counts here: the rest is no more than a feeble bit of stage business intended to justify her peculiar, highly sexual pose. Is anyone likely to be fooled by this set, with its cardboard rock, funfair monster and a Ruggiero straight out of an uplifting book for children? The naivety of these figures is fake from start to finish.

Ruggiero and his mount are fused into a single figure as detailed as a piece of goldsmithing, right down to the last bit of chasing on the armor. Yet this is also a dual figure, driven by two conflicting intentions: the first is positive and noble – to kill the orc and rescue the queen; while the second is negative and unavowed but clearly expressed by the hippogriff's claws, so aggressively leveled at Angelica that they look more threatening than the gaping jaws of the monster. From this we can deduce the dual nature of the male protagonist: noble and spiritual on the one hand, bestial and predatory on the other.

The focus of all this more or less conscious passion is also the focus of all the painter's attentions: she is the work's core figure and the only real reason for its existence. We have only to look at the various painted studies for Angelica, especially the one in the Louvre, to realize that she embodies the entire artistic intent of the work. This study, with its mix of realism and stylization, its emphasis on the breasts, belly and thighs, its "Expressionist" distortions of the arms, swollen throat and face, and the remarkable red rectangle as a sincere pointer to the "temperature" of the painter's commitment, is infinitely superior to the finished picture. And this is not at all uncommon in Ingres' oeuvre.

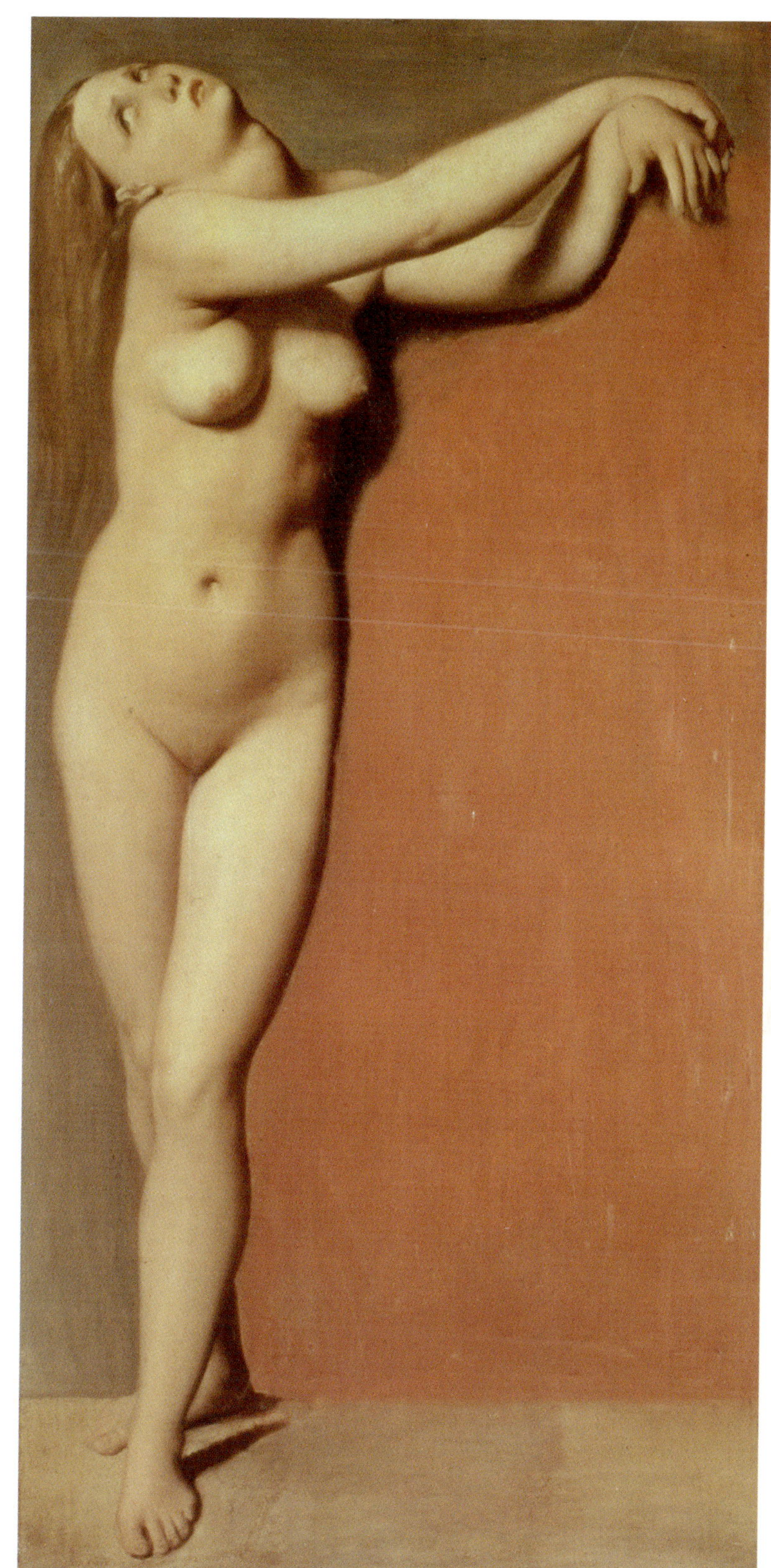

Angelica (study)
1819, oil on canvas, 84.5x42.5 cm
Paris, Musée du Louvre

Following Pages
Ruggiero Frees Angelica
1819, oil on canvas, 147x199 cm
Paris, Musée du Louvre

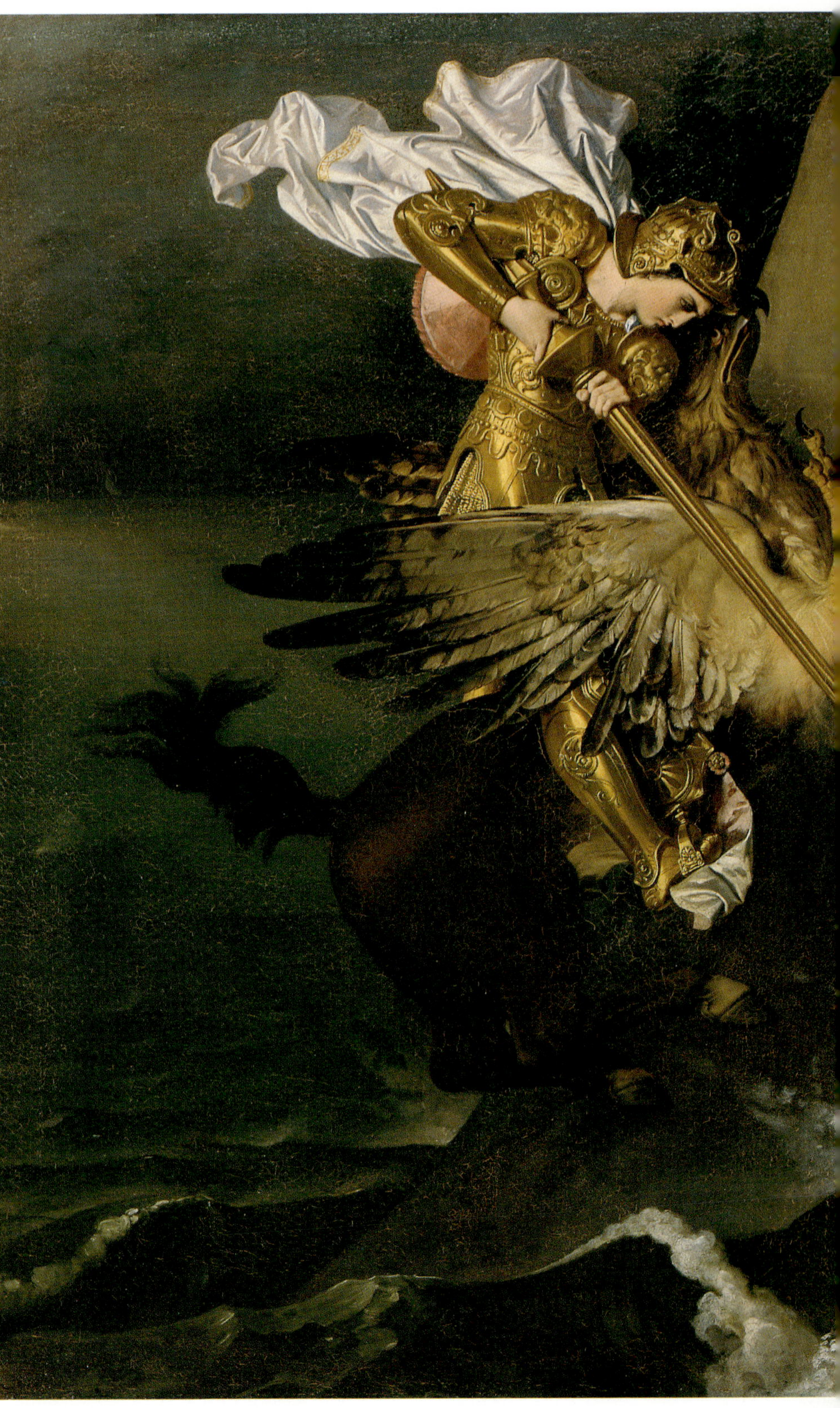

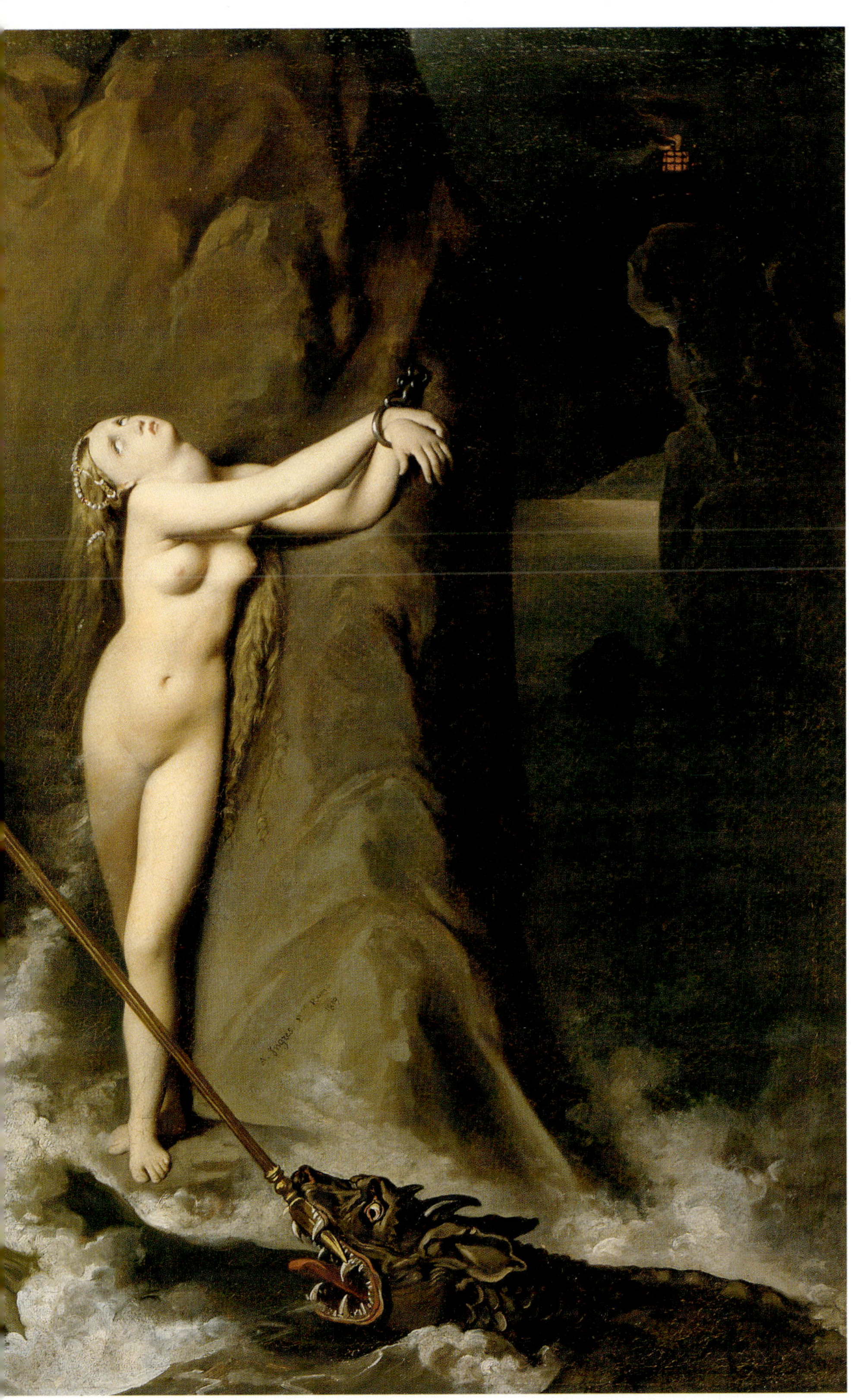

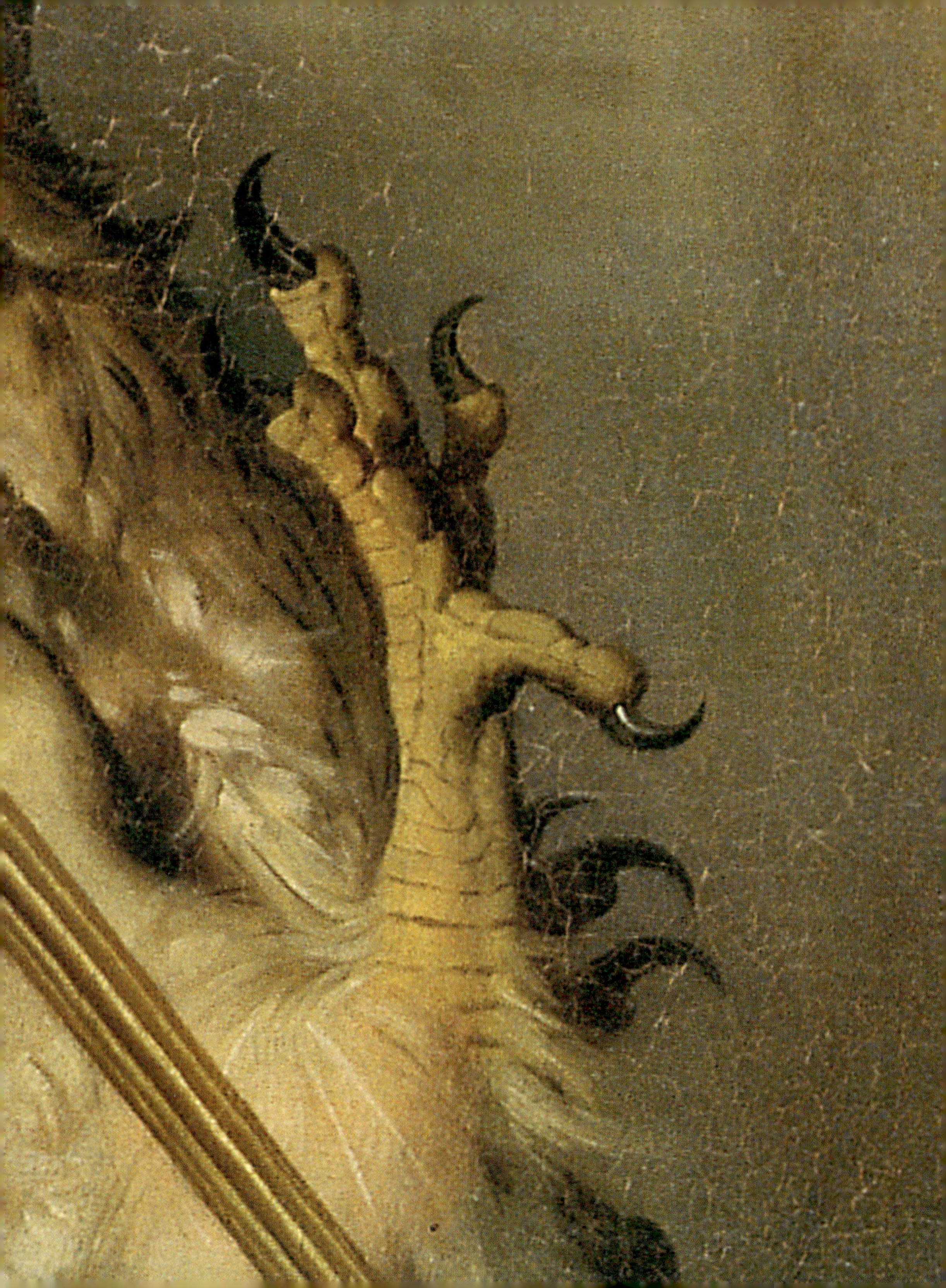

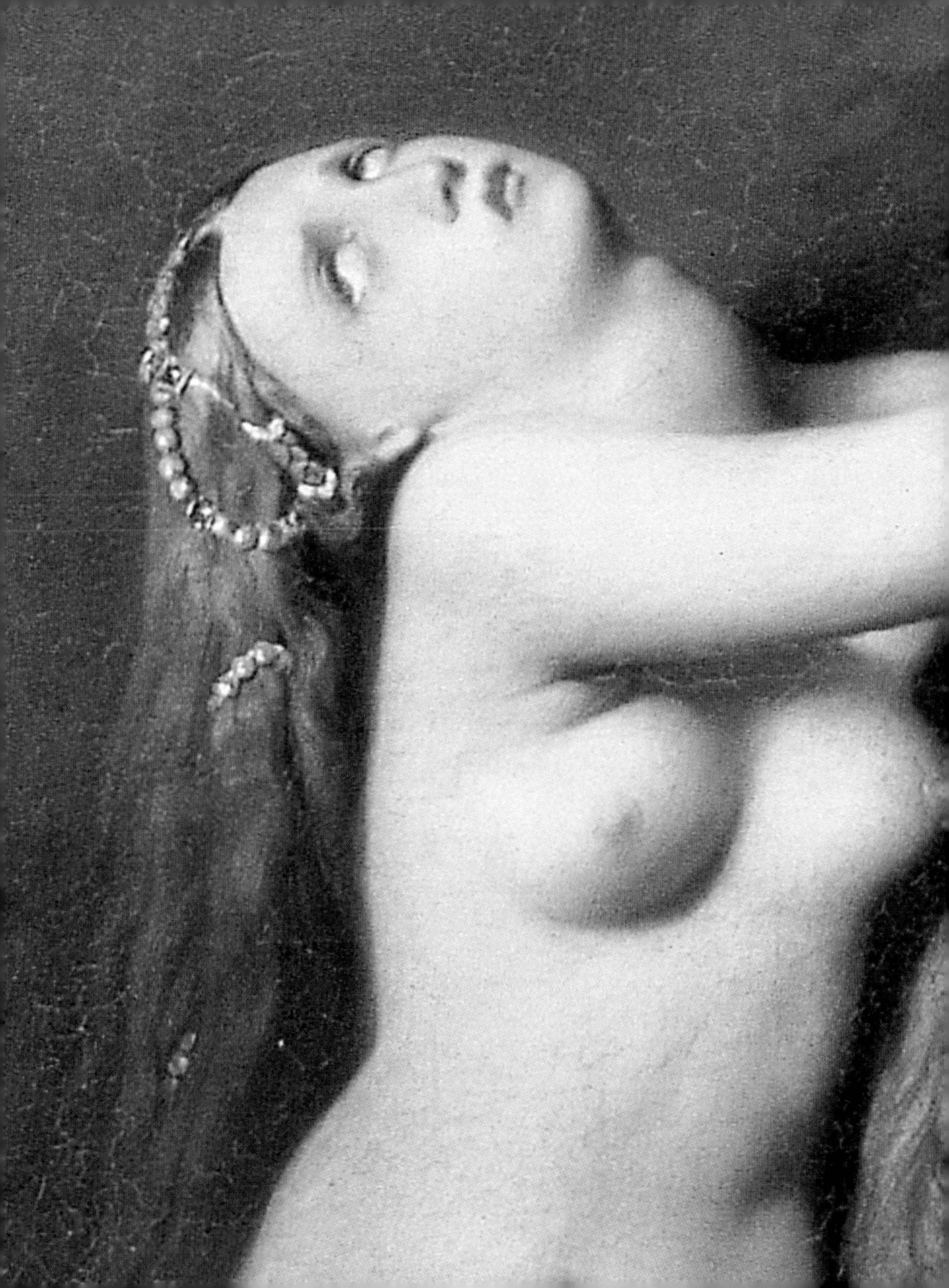

Raphael and La Fornarina's Turban

Looking back to the early days of his training in Toulouse, Ingres mentions his discovery of Raphael as a fundamental event: "A copy of the *Madonna of the Chair* belonging to my master made the scales fall from my eyes. Raphael stood revealed to me. I burst into tears. That first impression decided my vocation and filled my life; Ingres today is what little Ingres was at the age of twelve." [22]

He goes on to speak of a "revelation," and all his life he would worship the master of Urbino, considering him a kind of saint of painting, or a demi-god. The situation had its downside, however: Ingres sometimes took his idol's models too seriously, even if, globally, they were only one source of inspiration among many in his work.

This veneration found expression in specific subjects. Ingres had planned a sequence of pictures illustrating different moments in the master's life, but only two were actually painted, in 1813-14: *The Betrothal of Raphael and the Niece of Cardinal Bibbiena* and *Raphael and La Fornarina*. Curiously Ingres' interest went not to the painter as such, but to his emotional life: "La Fornarina" is the name of the mistress attributed to Raphael by tradition or legend.

Raphael and La Fornarina
1811-12, oil on canvas, 64.7x53.3 cm
Cambridge, The Fogg Art Museum

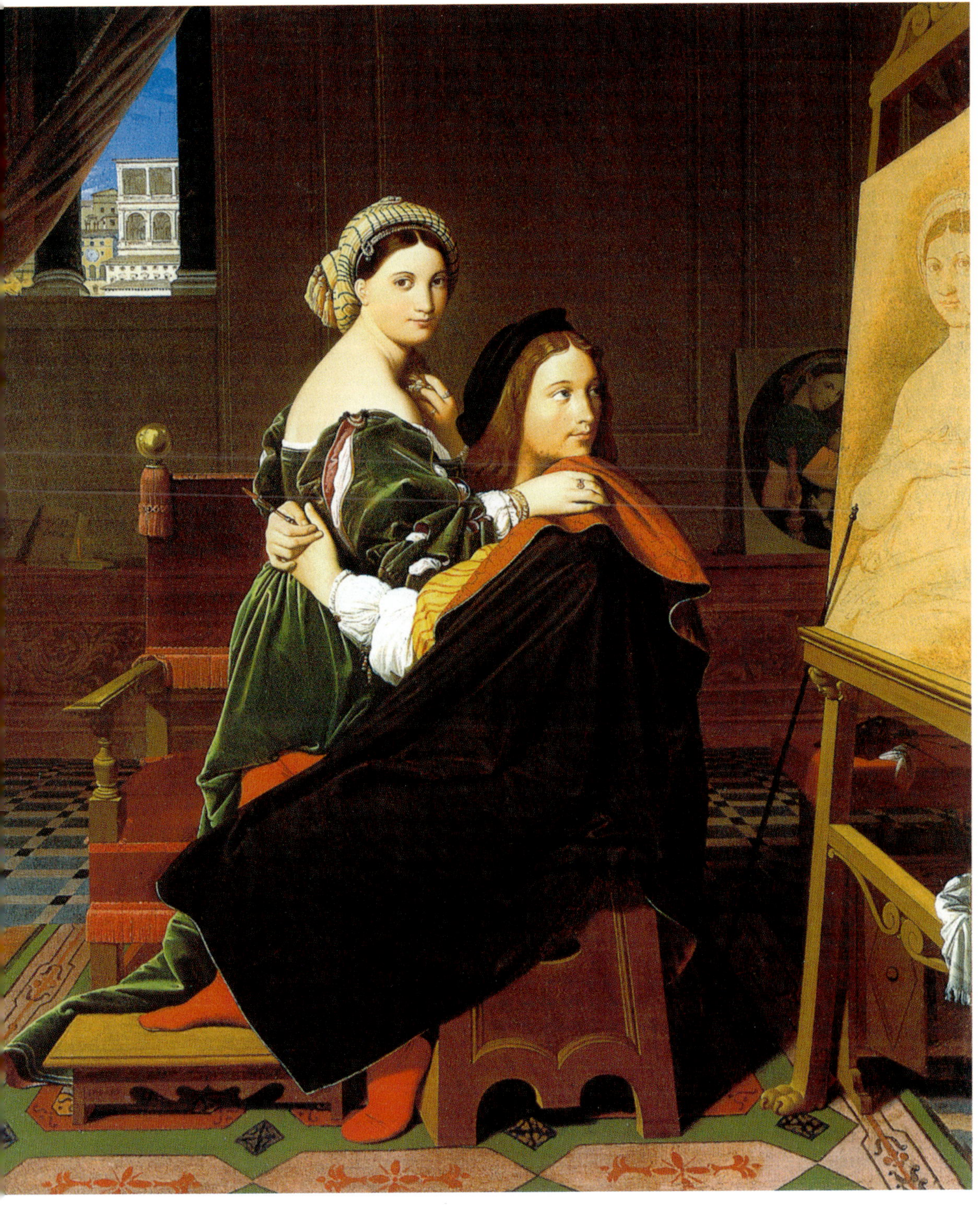

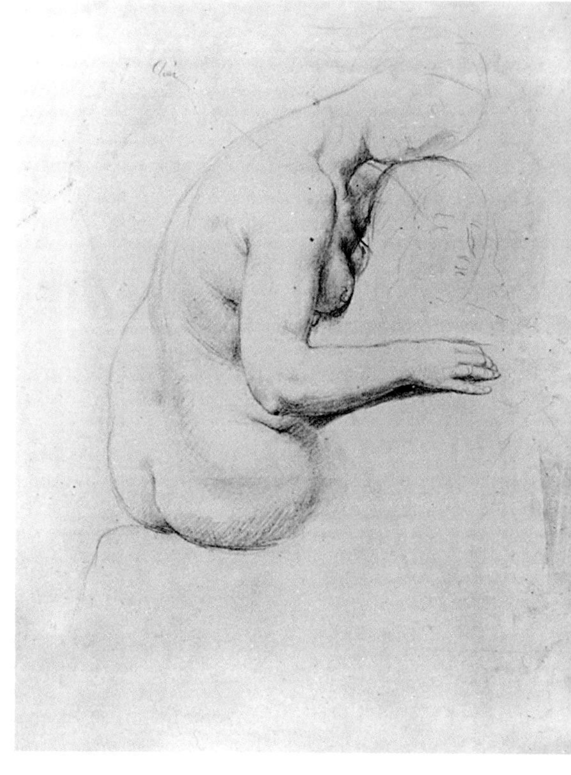

Study for La Fornarina
1811, pencil on papier Japon, 37.6x29.3 cm
Lyon, Musée des Beaux-Arts

However, his admiration also emerged as a remarkable bit of thievery, for Ingres took the *Madonna of the Chair*, the very origin of his "cult of Raphael" and incorporated it into his own oeuvre.

This was done using quotations and discreet homage. The painting is visible in several of his canvases: in the *Portrait of Philibert Rivière*, as an engraving on the table; in *Napoleon as Jupiter Enthroned*, as part of the carpet; in *Henry IV Playing with His Children*, hanging on the wall; and in *Raphael and La Fornarina*, set on the floor against the back wall of the studio.

The *Madonna* also served as a model for one of Ingres' favored poses: a woman seen in profile or three-quarter view, the head upright or more or less bent as she looks at us over her shoulder. This motif is to be found both in the Odalisque of 1814 and La Fornarina; the latter's pose used the position of the Virgin's head and arm, but the arm that originally held the Infant Jesus now embraces the lover. The Raphaelesque origin of the motif is underscored by the physical similarities between the Virgin and Ingres' heroines.

A distinctive feature of the Virgin is her headscarf, or turban, also to be found in another painting by (or at the time attributed to) Raphael: the famous *La Fornarina*, now in the Galleria Nazionale in Rome. In this potently erotic portrait the young woman is shown barebreasted.

In his own picture, Ingres goes along with the idea that Raphael used his mistress as a model for some of his figures, or at least as a source of inspiration. He juxtaposes the "flesh and blood" model – the young woman in the turban, sitting on her lover's knee and looking at us over her shoulder; the barebreasted *La Fornarina* as we know it, on the easel but only just begun; and at the back of the studio, but visually tied to the portrait, the *Madonna of the Chair*. The latter is so placed, however, as to exclude the Infant Jesus: we see only Mary, as if Ingres is pointing up the relationship of the two works with the "flesh and blood model."

Ingres painted five versions of his picture, each successively showing the young woman leaning her head more and more on her lover's shoulder, in an increasingly amorous pose. Raphael, however, both embraces his mistress and turns away from her to look at his picture on the easel. The underlying idea, perhaps, is that beauty is firstly discovered and *loved* in nature, then transposed into the world of art, where it becomes something enduring.

Raphael and La Fornarina allows us to monitor this process of transformation of a loved, living form – the actual body of the lover – into ideal artistic forms: firstly those of the erotic portrait, still marked by the artist's affective and sensual attachments, then those of the purified religious image. Certainly, our eye is summoned to follow this triple cycle of sublimation, but it is also led back to the point of departure, to the "living" young woman and the opposite message: all sublimation has its source in the experience of love.

In the image of the Virgin at the back of the studio, only the turban signals the identity of the model and the painter's carnal interests. But it is precisely this "flow" of the turban, from reality to art and from the profane to the religious, that seems to interest Ingres. It is the second subject of the picture, we might say.

In the 19th century the turban signified the Orient. It orientalized the woman wearing it, and in the thinking of the time the Oriental woman, especially unclad, was an odalisque or a slave: a sexual object.

The presence of the turban even in Ingres' most chaste pictures – and in a way they are all extremely chaste – is a discreet sexual allusion. It made its first appearance in the *Bather* of 1807, then wrapped around the hair of the *Baigneuse de Valpinçon*, the *Grande Odalisque*, the *Small Bather, Interior of Harem* and the slave of the 1839 *Odalisque*. Finally, in *The Turkish Bath*, it is accompanied by all sorts of voluptuous head coverings. In this way an iconic object allows the reintroduction, into representations markedly idealized by their nobility of drawing and form, of a truth – the concretely carnal side of nature – which, consciously or otherwise, keeps on resurfacing.

Like the Raphael of his imagination, Ingres strives vainly to concentrate on an artistic and moral ideal whose realization demands the chastisement of nature: for nothing can prevent nature from signaling to us, via details as eloquent as a simple turban.

Portraits II

For a relative unknown like Ingres, there would never be enough official and private commissions to ensure a living. He had to paint portraits as well. Since the invasion by Napoleon's troops in 1808, and its subsequent incorporation into France, Rome was more than half French. The legions of state officials who poured in, with their wives and mistresses, made up most of the painter's clientele.

In turn Forestry Commissioner Charles Marcotte, police chief Jacques Marquet de Monbreton de Norvins, postal service director Joseph Antoine Moltedo, and Charles Laurent Cordier of the Registration Department sat for Ingres, probably without suspecting that they were obtaining masterpieces. The princely authority, haughtiness and moral energy of the male portraits was matched by the languid, sensual grace of the female ones: Antonia Duvauçay, Cécile Panckouke – and Marie de Senonnes who, with one arm too long, her tapering fingers, the near-perfect oval of her face, and the slightly slumping posture that bespeaks so eloquently the weight of her breasts, seems a profane sister of Thetis. As Gaétan Picon has insightfully remarked, the clothing and finery of the women in Ingres' portraits are like a natural extension of their bodies. The endless

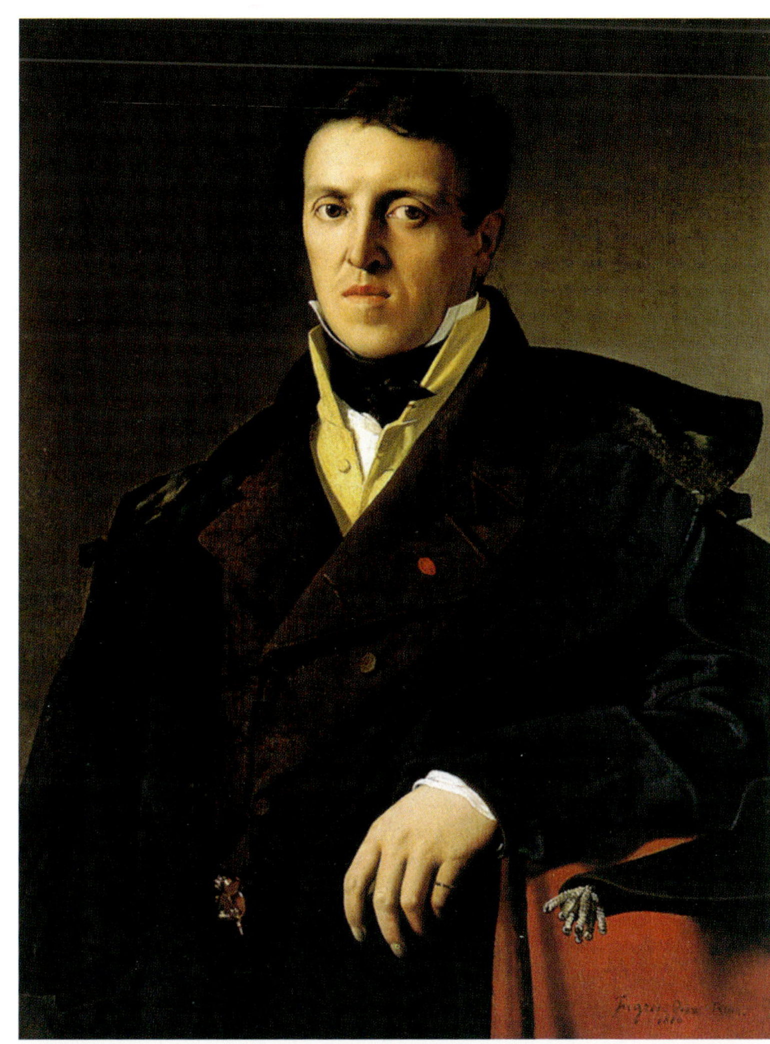

Portrait de Charles Marcotte
1810, oil on canvas, 93.7x69.4 cm
Washington, National Gallery of Art

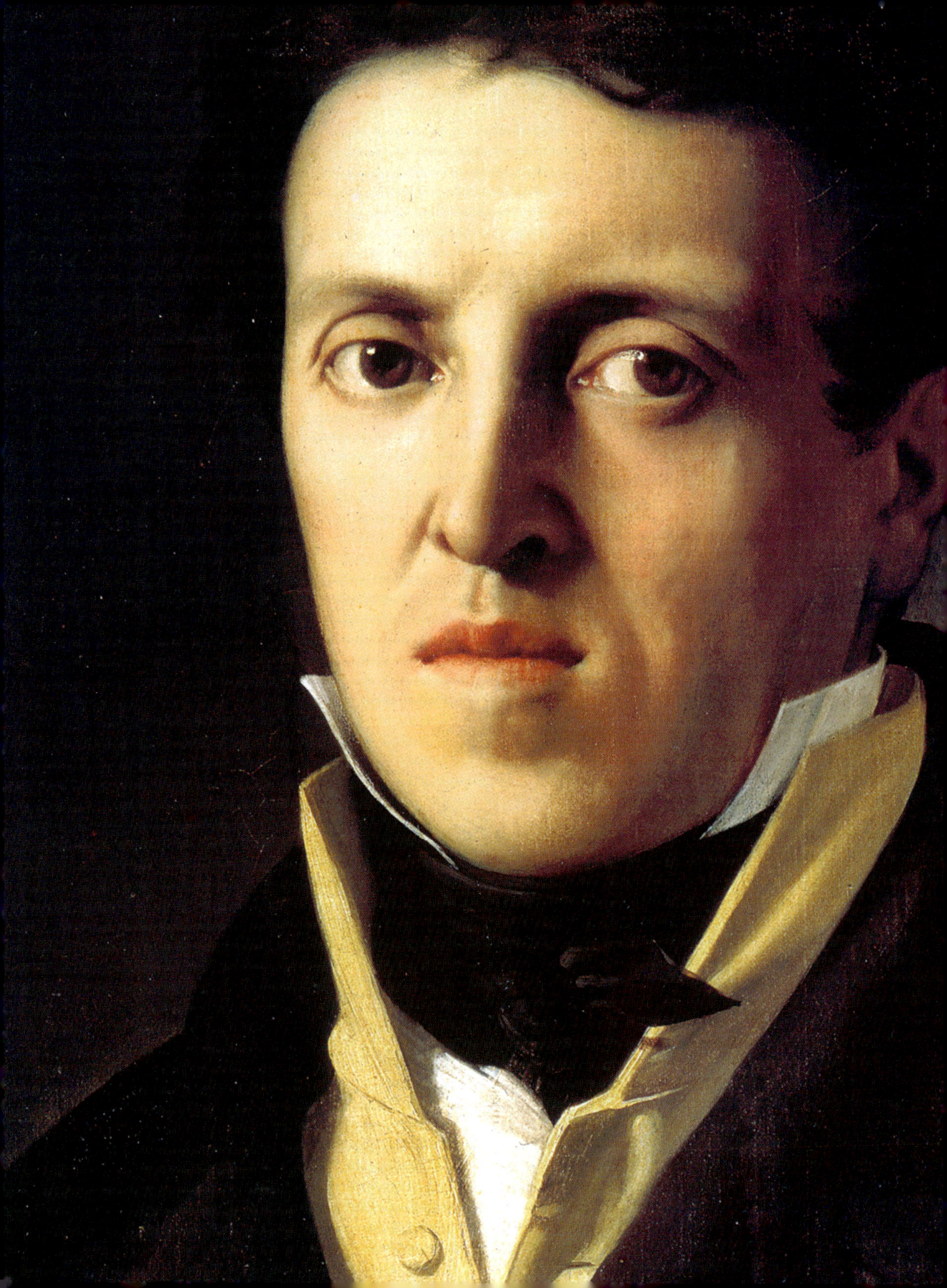

rings and ribbons, and the shimmering folds of satin, silk and velvet are less ornaments than complements to nudity.

After Napoleon's defeat and the departure of the French administration in 1814, portrait commissions were rare, and Ingres found himself in a precarious situation. He reacted by boosting his output of the handsome pencil portraits he had been making since the beginning of his career. Apart from friends and relations, his customers were mainly foreigners, and notably traveling English people. These countless portraits – there exist some 500 of them, according to Ingres specialist Hans Naef – are regarded by some as the most dubious part of the entire oeuvre, but they reveal impressive virtuosity in the capturing of character and appearance. Their beauty lies in the artist's magical capacity to tell all with incredibly precise variation of line: quick and spirited for the folds of garments, gentle and light for the contour of a cheek – and unfailingly accurate. The values are minimal and shadow almost entirely eliminated: rather than standing out against the white of the paper, the figures are set in its light, as if cut into silver plate. This is what gives these drawings their incomparable clearness. Many of them are masterpieces, especially the portraits of friends, relatives and other artists, like his wife Madeleine, and musicians like Paganini and, later, Liszt.

Taken together, what characterizes these works is a remarkable photographic quality. We sometimes have the impression that Ingres worked as photographers later did, giving his customers what they wanted – the closest possible likeness – with absolute precision. And yet nothing could be less mechanical than this realism: neither the painter's virtuosity nor his exceptional visual acuity explain the powerful sense of truth they convey. What is involved here is looking beyond appearances to the truth of the individual, an enterprise presenting difficulties of quite another order than mere reproduction of facial features. These difficulties could be appalling, as Ingres' lamentations make clear in the account by his pupil Amaury-Duval: "'Ah, my friend,' he cried, 'don't talk to me about it...it's very bad. I've forgotten how to draw...I don't know anything anymore...The portrait of a woman! There's nothing in the world more difficult, it can't be done...I'll try again tomorrow, when I go back to it...It's enough to make you weep.' And tears really did spring to his eyes." [23]

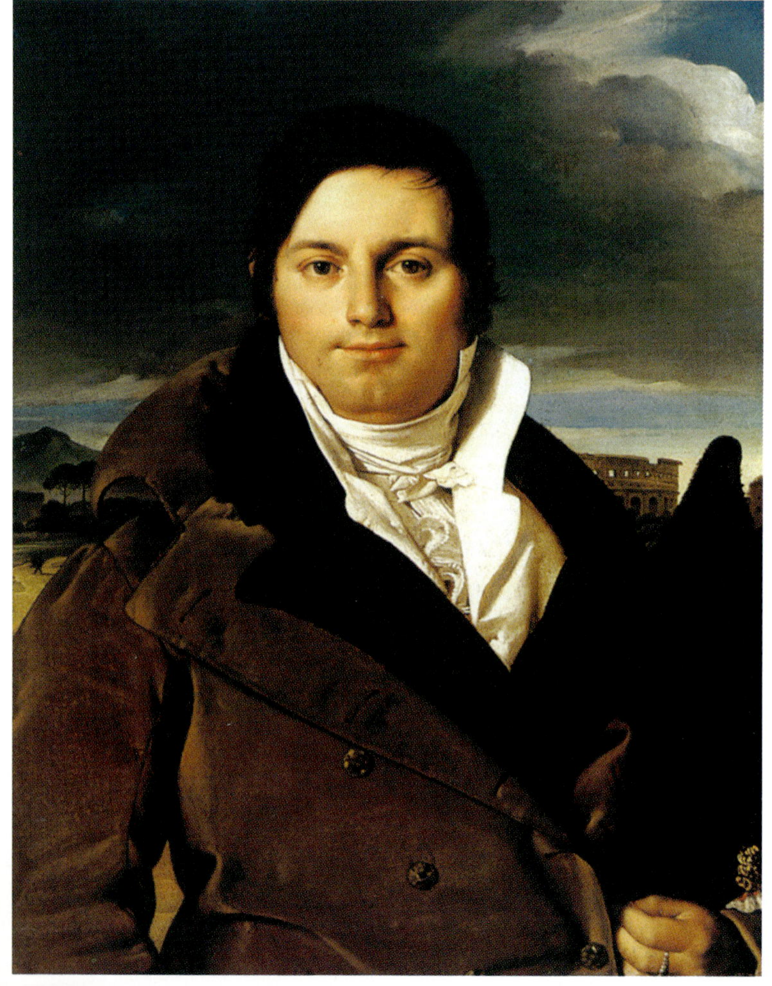

Portrait of Joseph-Antoine Moltedo
1810, oil on canvas, 75.3x58.1 cm
New York , Metropolitan Museum of Art

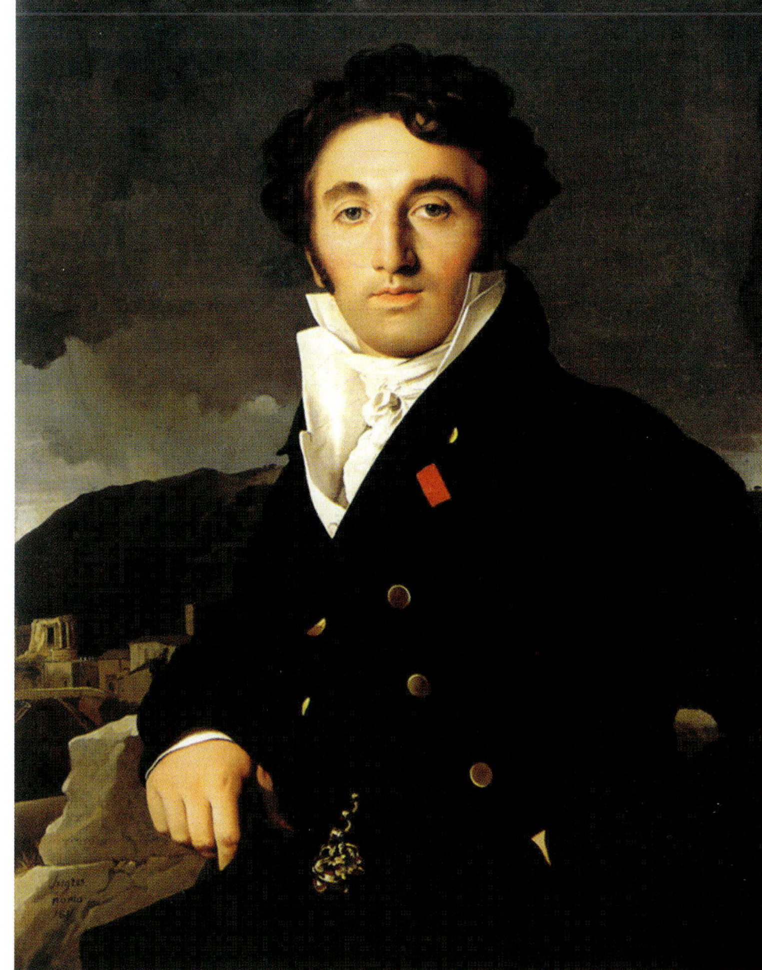

Portrait of Charles-Laurent Cordier
1811, oil on canvas, 90x69.5 cm
Paris, Musée du Louvre

Portrait de Jacques Marquet,
Baron de Monbreton de Norvins
1813, oil on canvas, 97x79 cm
London, National Gallery

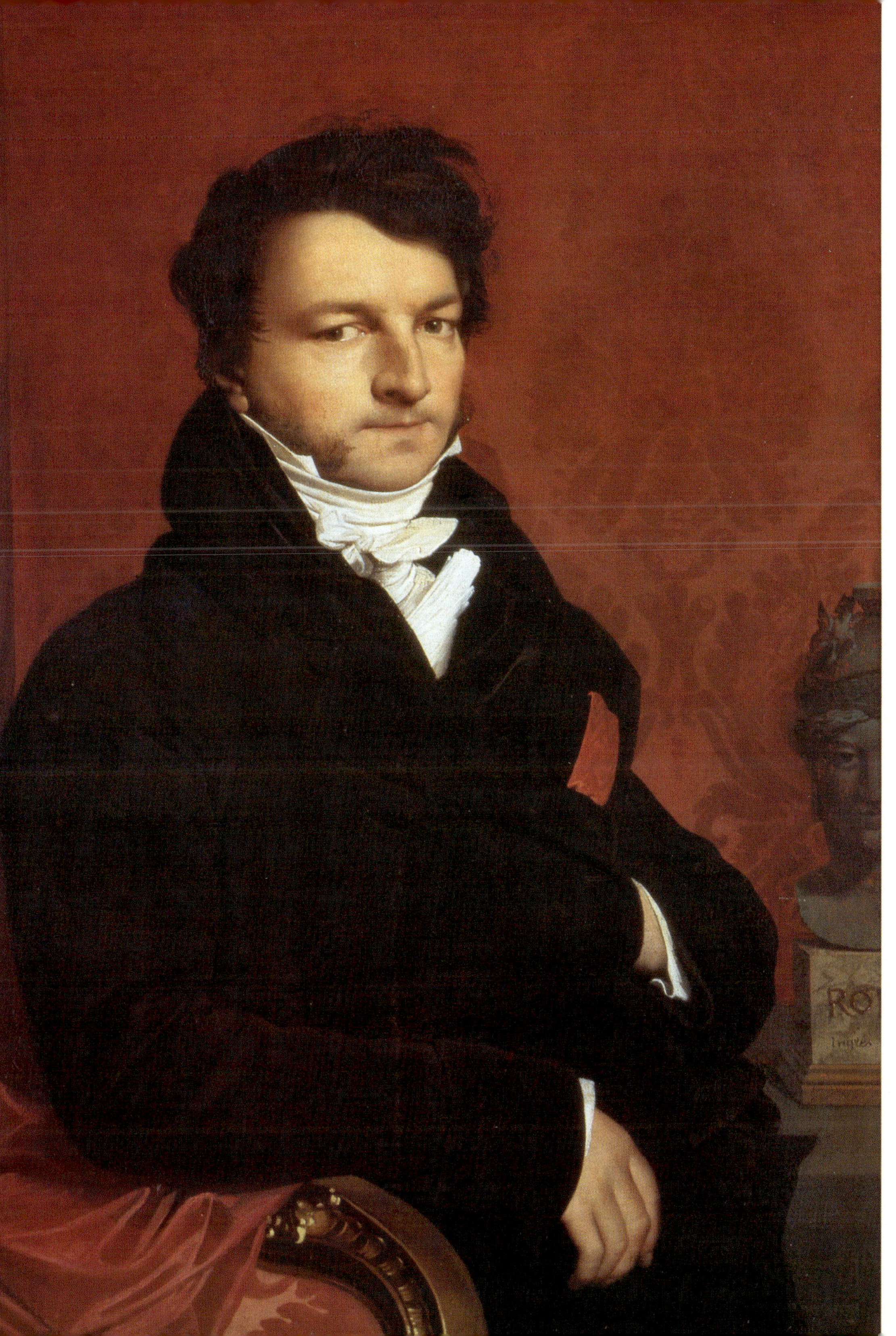

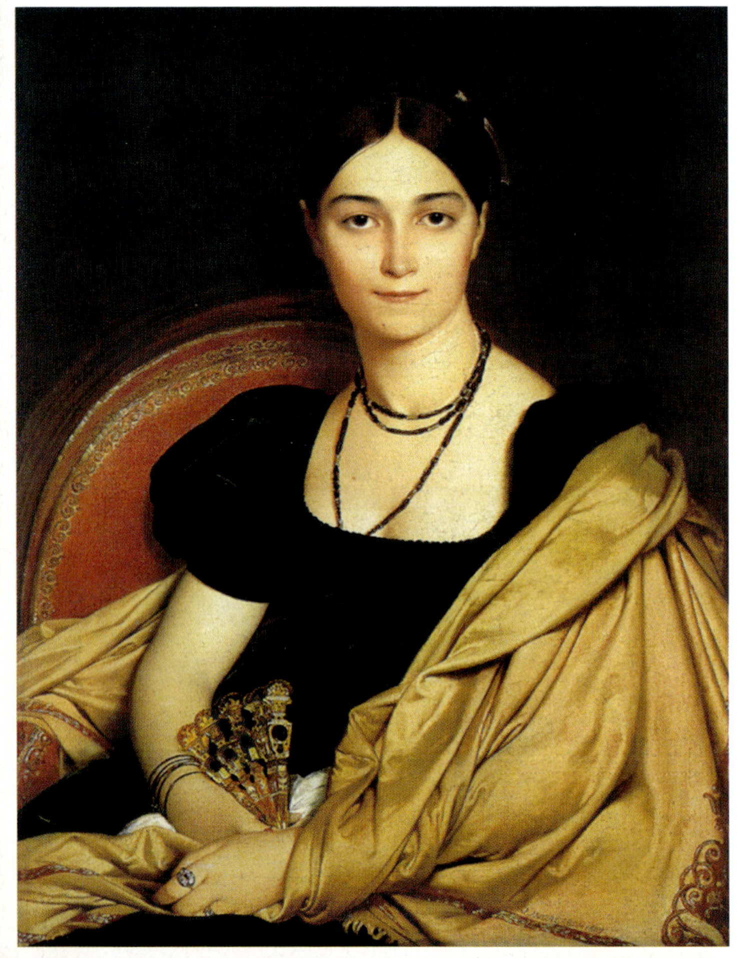

Portrait of Antonia Duvauçay
1807, oil on canvas, 76x59 cm
Chantilly, Musée Condé

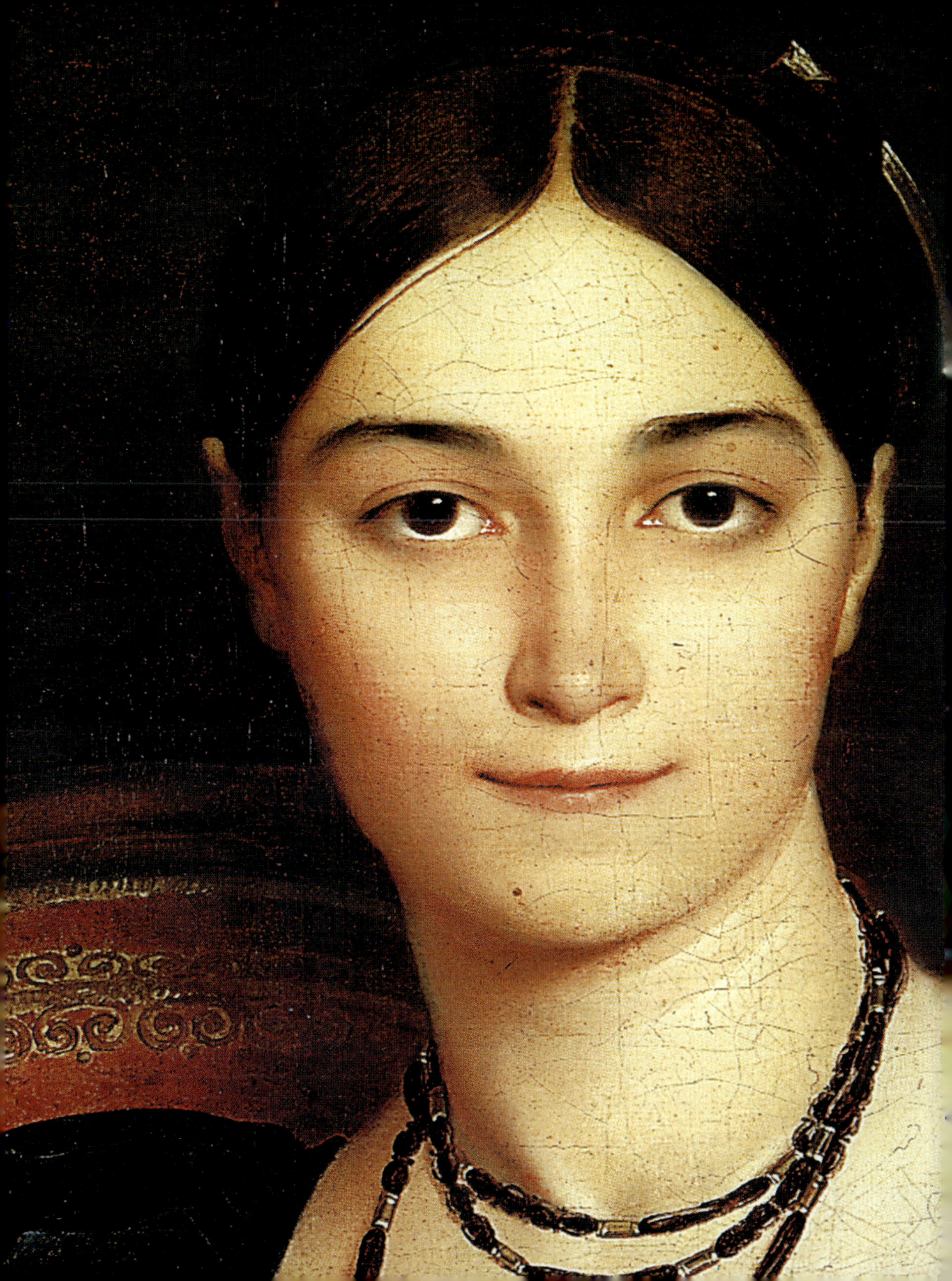

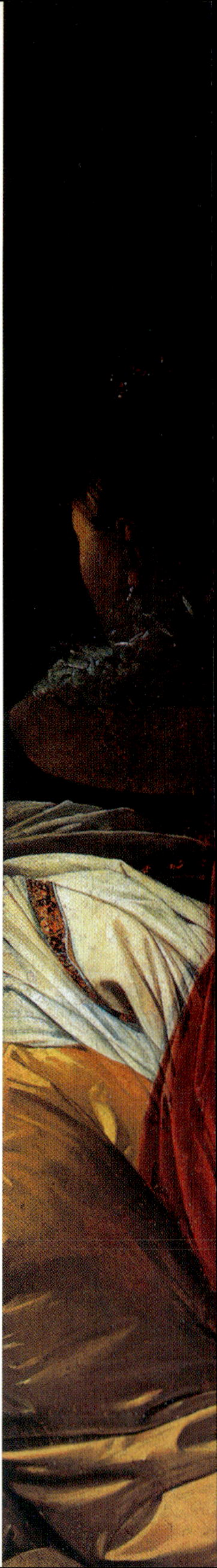

Portrait of Marie Marcoz, later Vicomtesse de Senonnes
1814–16, oil on canvas, 106x84 cm
Nantes, Musée des Beaux-Arts

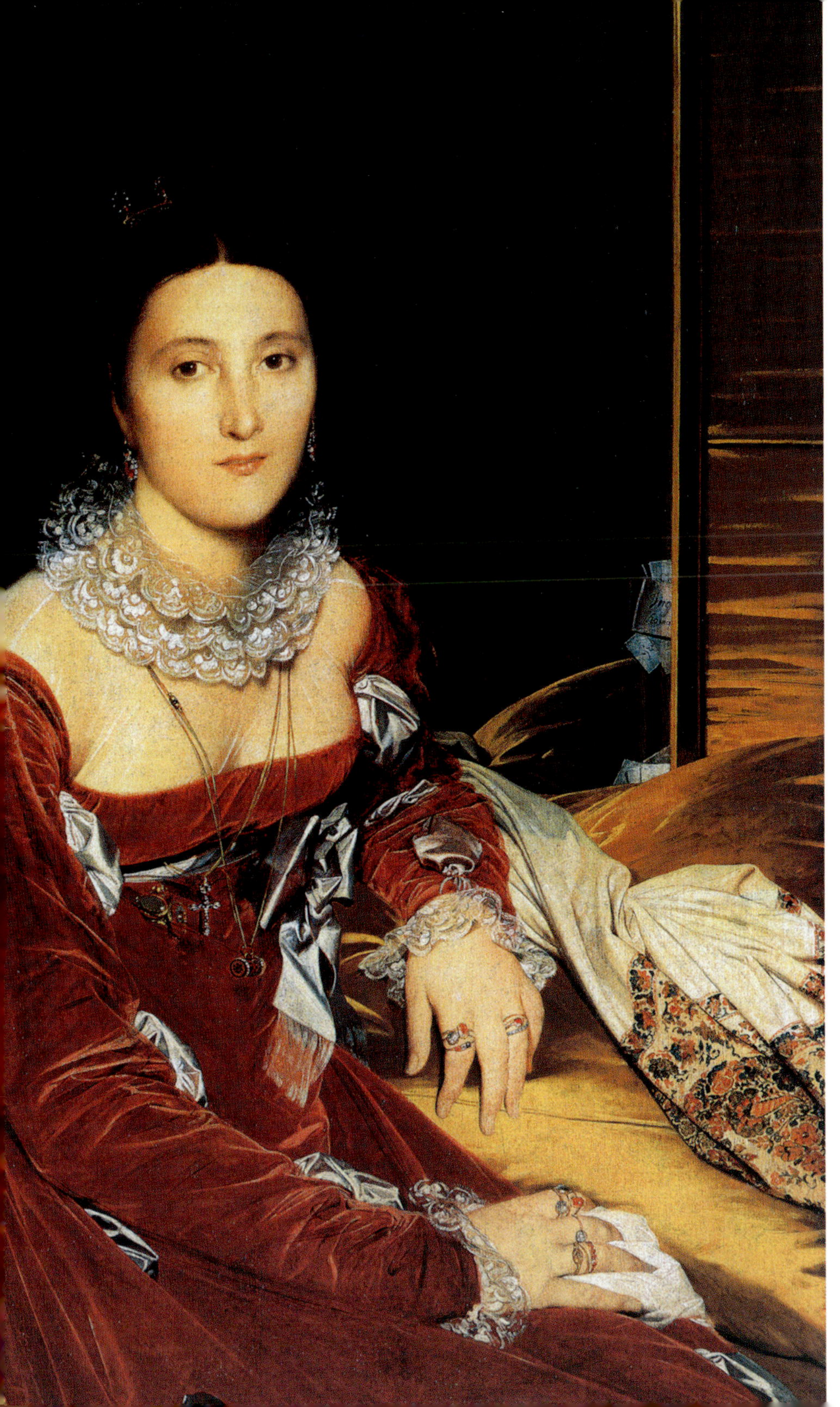

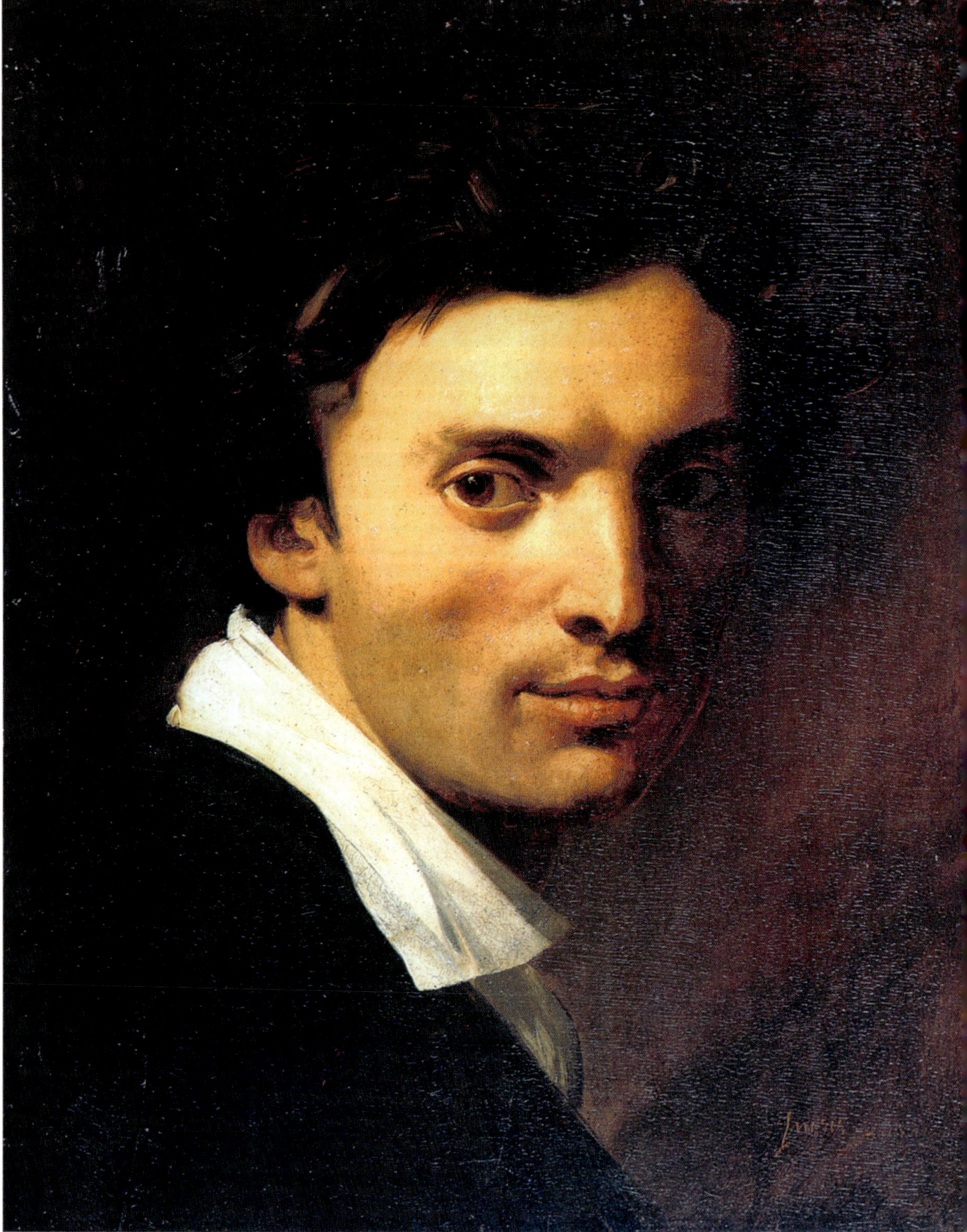

Portrait of Jean-Pierre Cortot
1815, oil on panel, 42x33 cm
Paris, Musée du Louvre

Portrait of Jean-Baptiste Desdéban
1810, oil on canvas, 63x49 cm
Besançon, Musée des Beaux-Arts et d'Archéologie

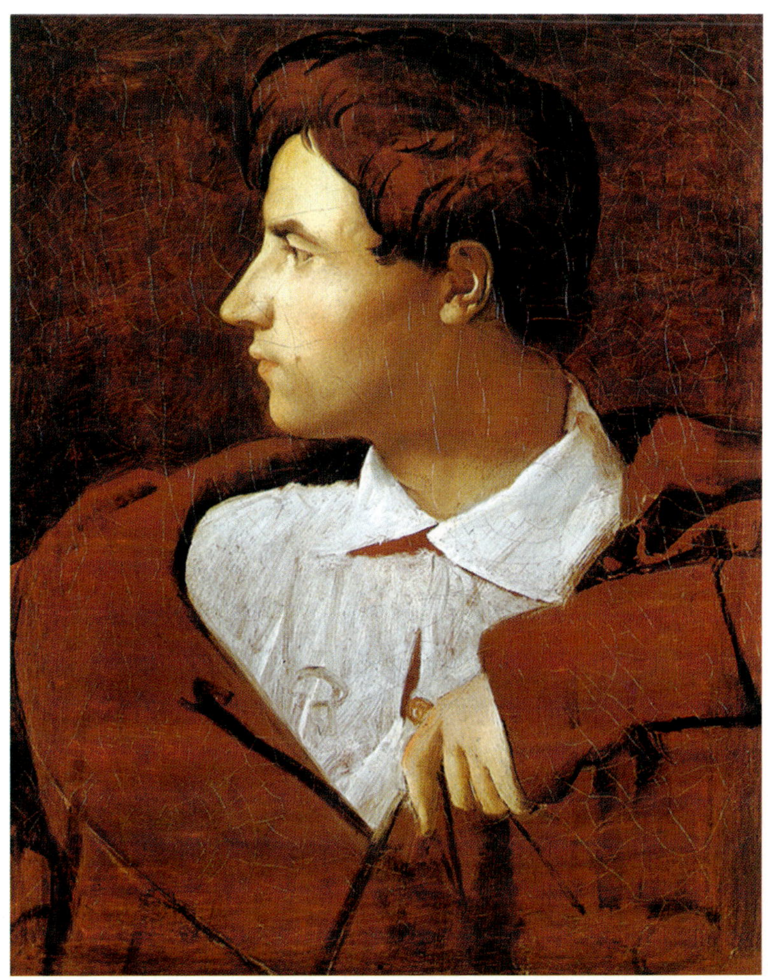

Madeleine Ingres
1835, pencil on white paper, 30x22 cm
Montauban, Musée Ingres

Lady Harriet Mary Montagu and Lady Catherine Caroline Montagu
1815, pencil, 32x25.5 cm
Private collection

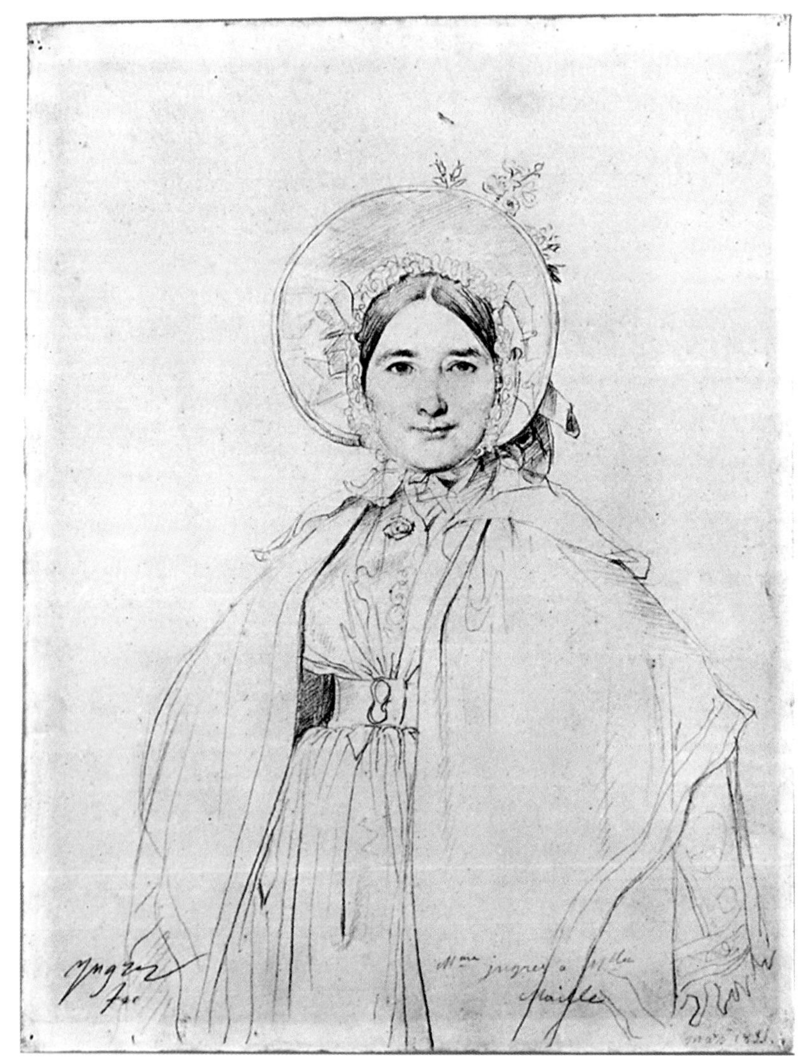

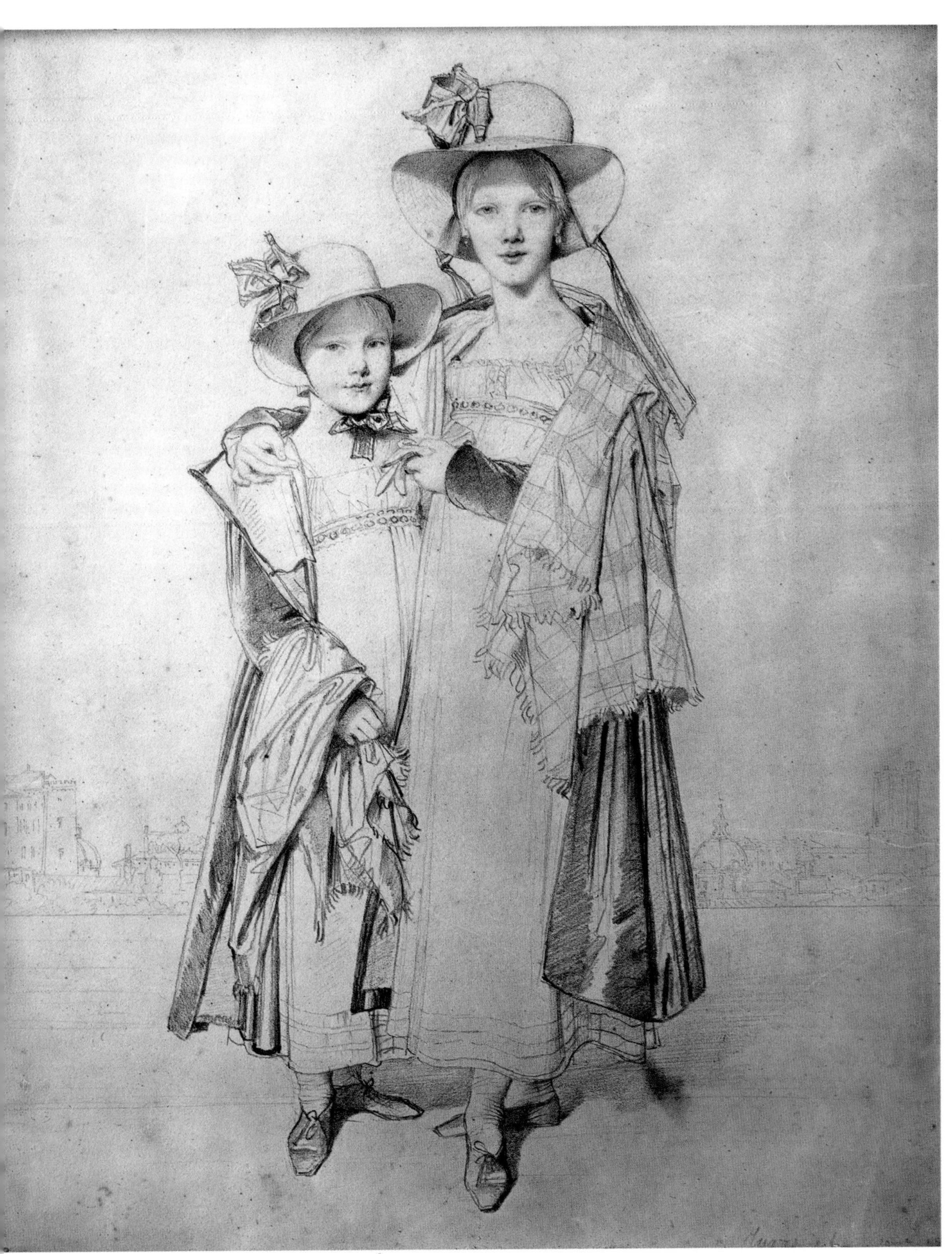

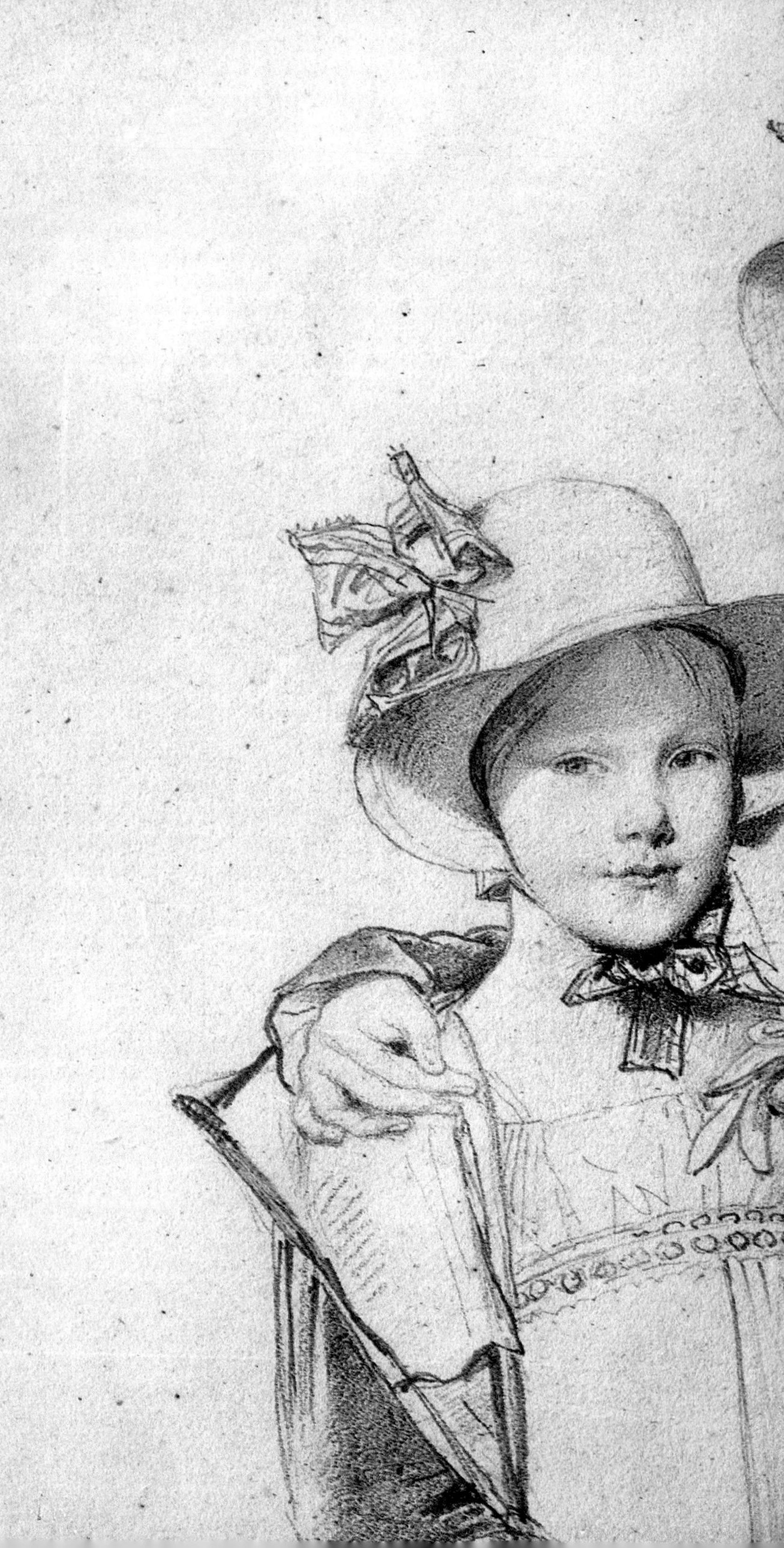

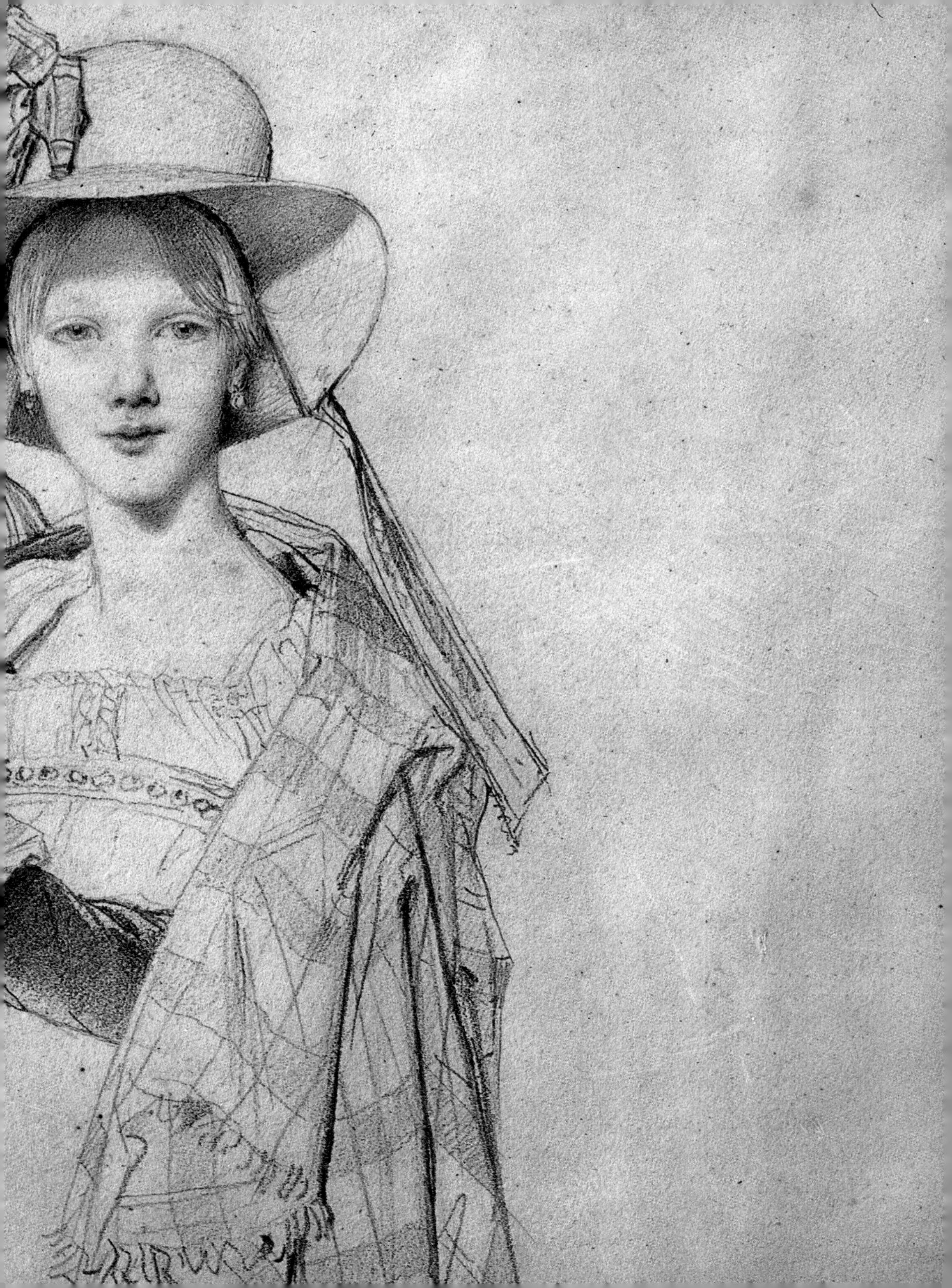

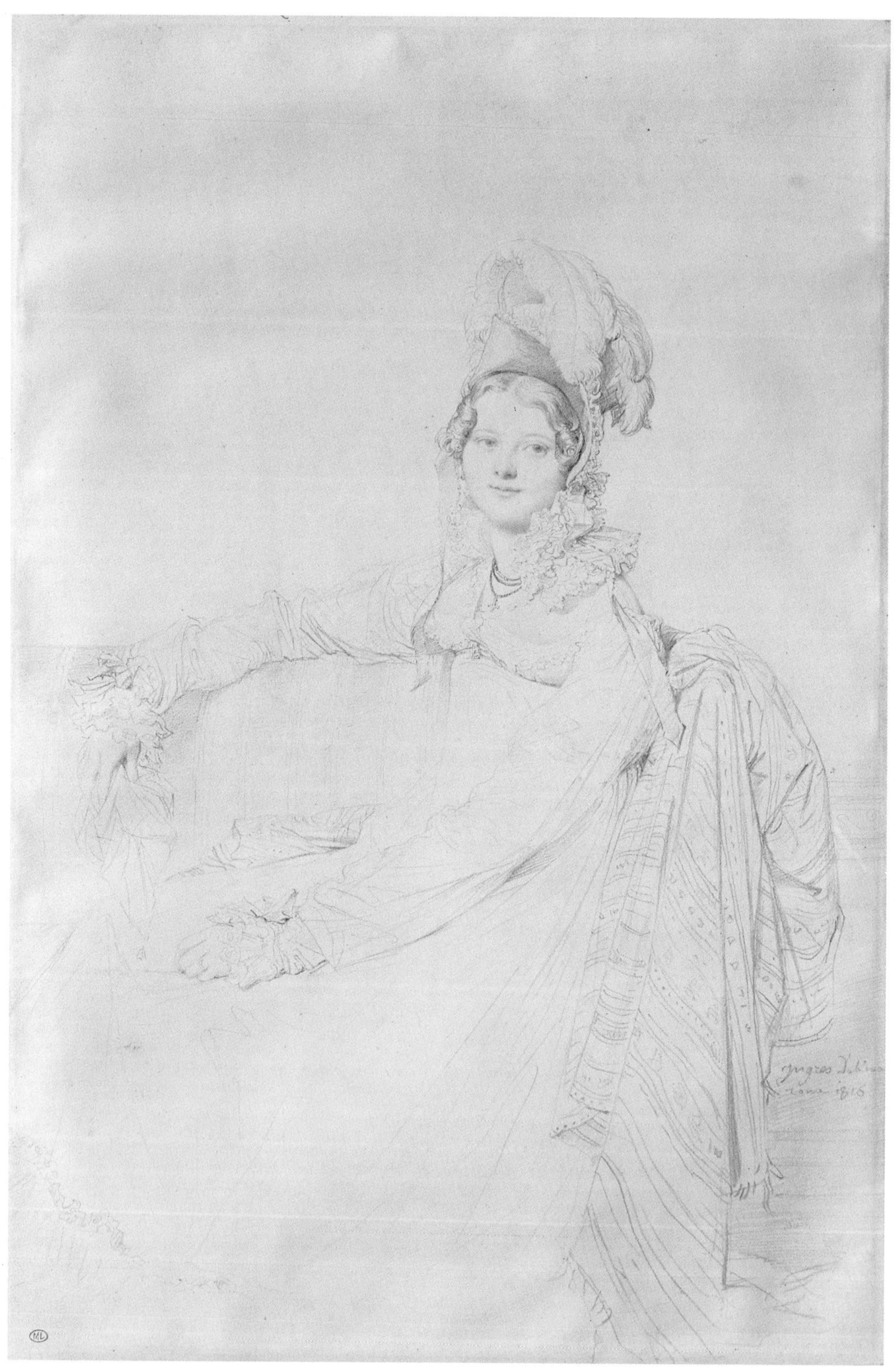

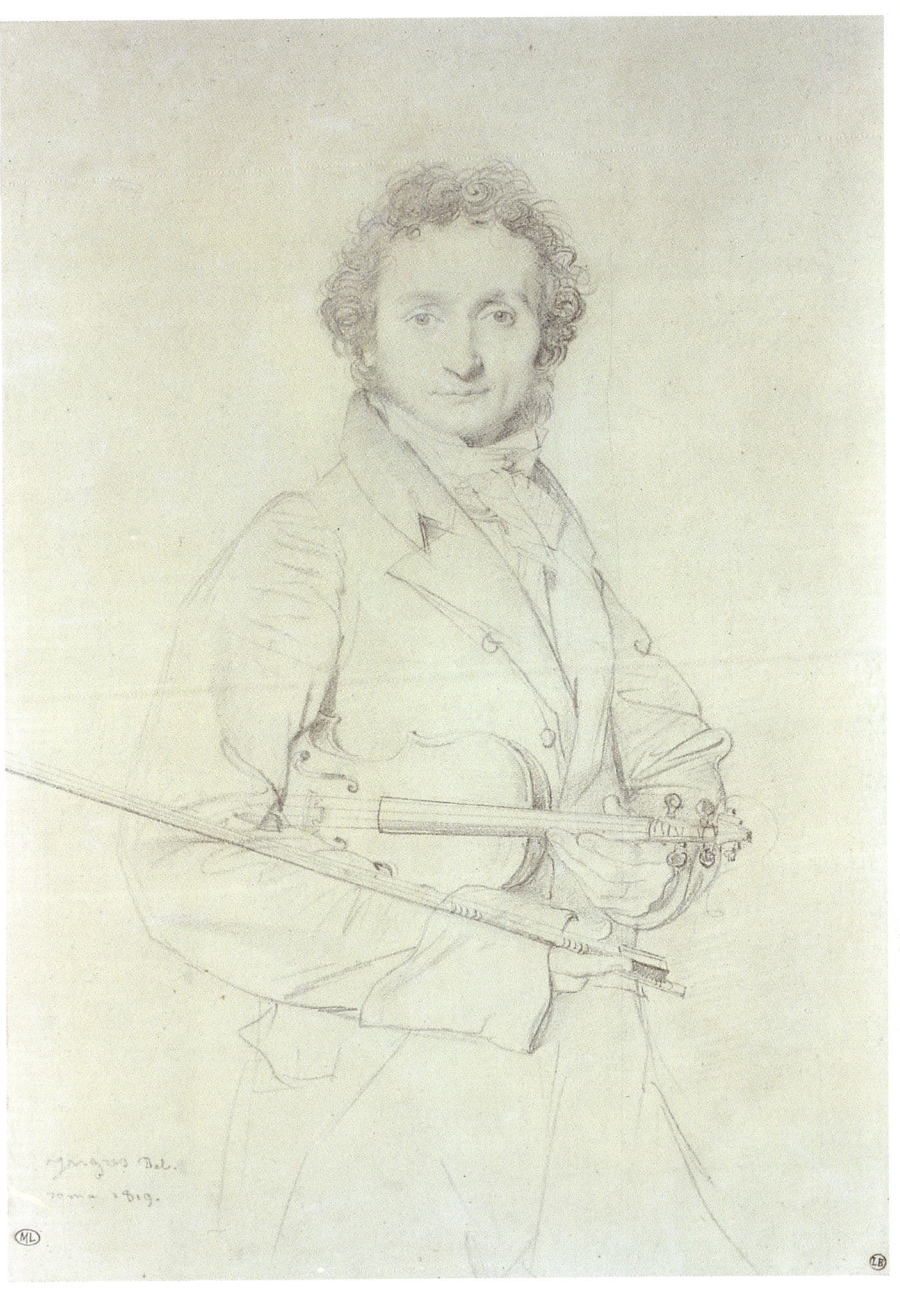

Portrait of Madame Louis-Nicolas-Marie Destouches

1816, pencil, 39.5x28 cm

Paris, Musée du Louvre, Cabinet des Dessins

Portrait of Niccolo Paganini

1819, pencil, 29.5x21.6 cm

Paris, Musée du Louvre, Cabinet des Dessins

The Stamaty Family
1818, pencil, 45x36.5 cm
Paris, Musée du Louvre, Cabinet des Dessins

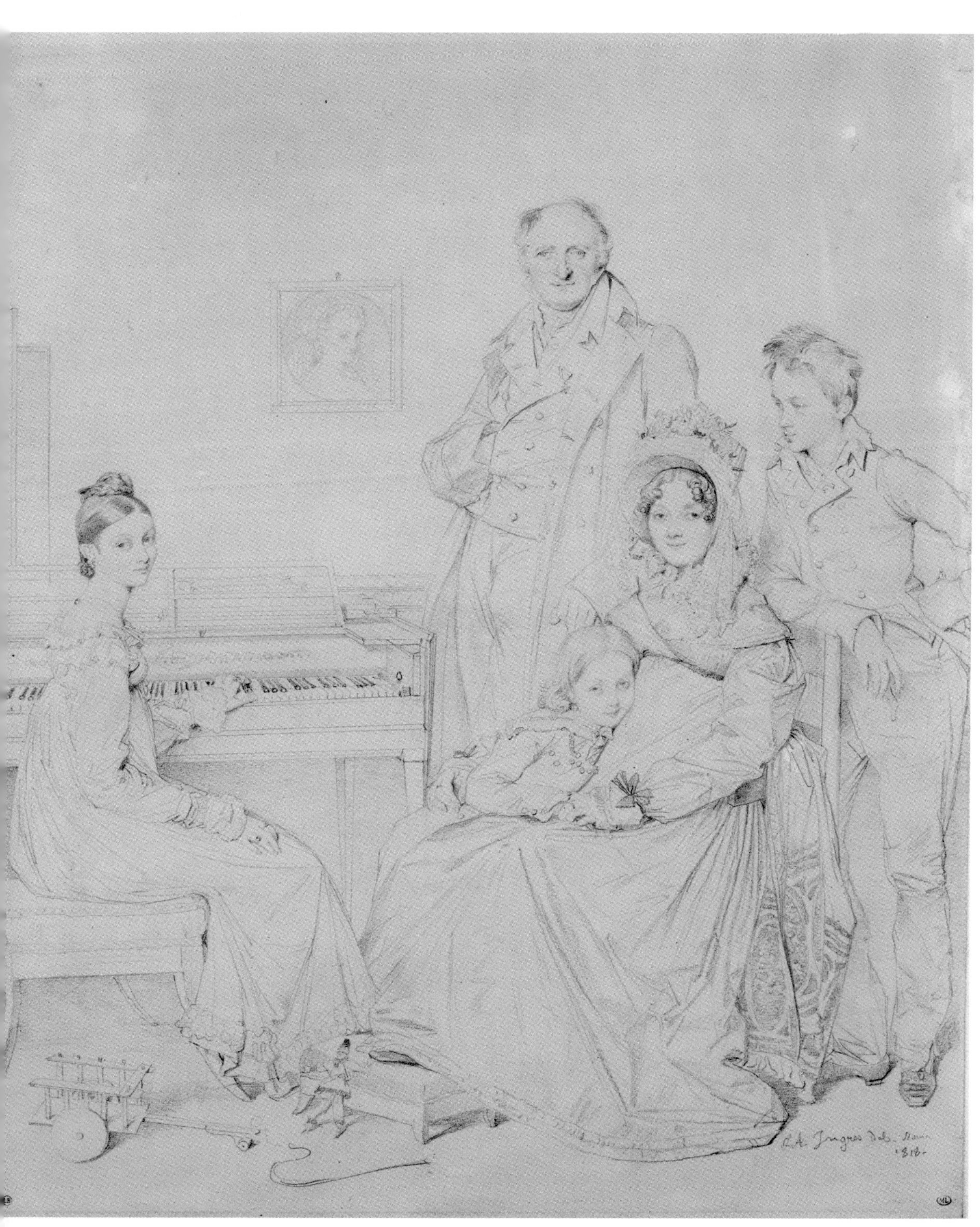
Ingres Del.

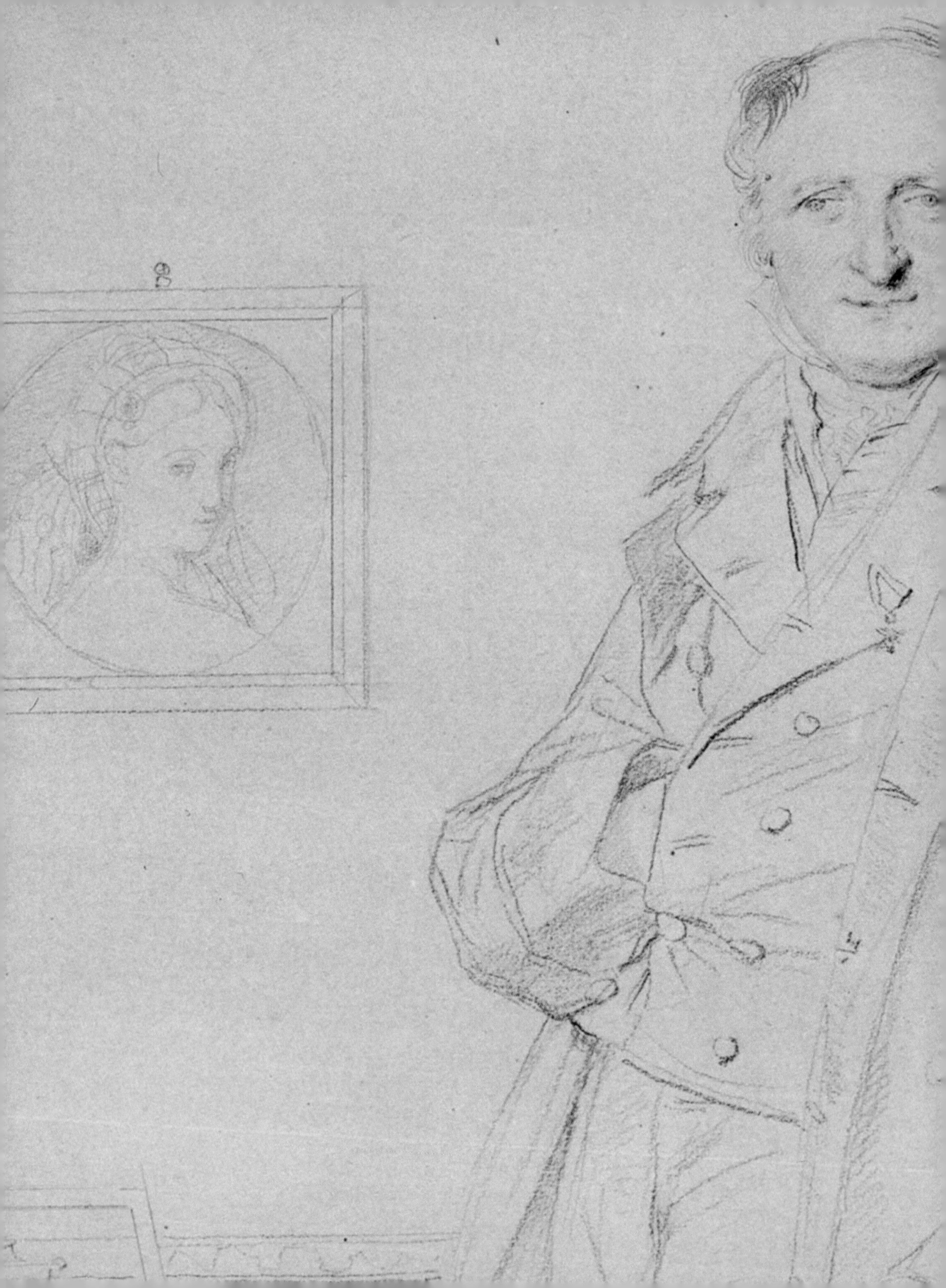

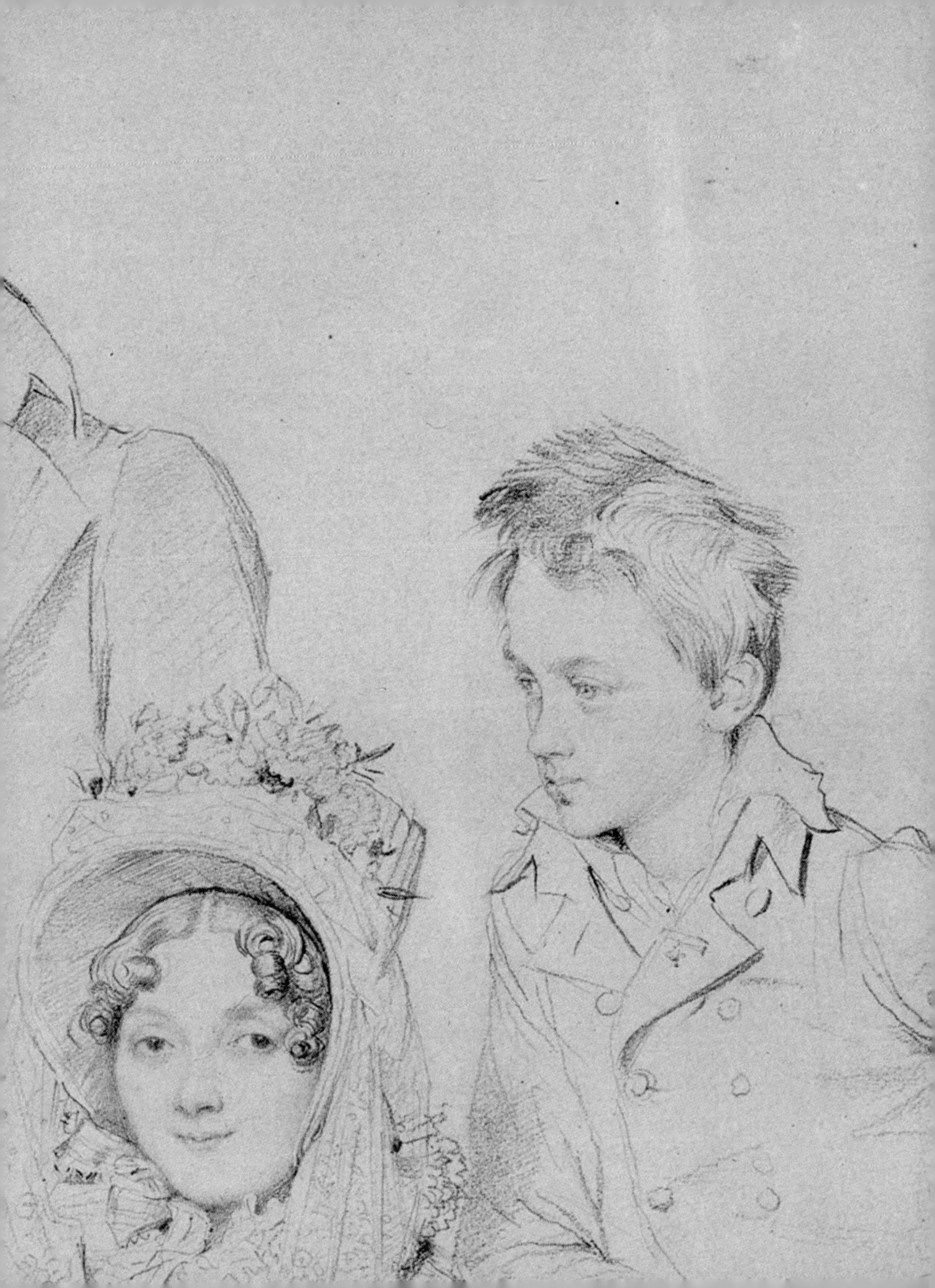

Religious Subjects

The return of the monarchy in France brought with it a wave of crusading religious fervor. Already, in 1814, Ingres had painted *The Sistine Chapel*, a curious scene of ecclesiastical life imbued with his admiration for the splendors of the Church in Rome and their close association with the greatest works of the Renaissance. The vast swathes of frescoes by Michelangelo, Botticelli and Perugino featured in the canvas are as important as the ceremony itself. The work is probably intended to express the notion of a close and necessary dependence between art and religion; just as the series of small pictures painted in the years 1814-21 – representations of the French Kings Charles V, Henri IV and François I – were tokens offered to the Catholic monarchy.

Through the good offices of the Count of Blacas, appointed French Ambassador in Rome, the painter received a commission for a work for the Trinità dei Monti church. *Christ Giving Peter the Keys of Paradise* is Ingres' first religious work and marks a shift towards the great Classical tradition of Raphael and Poussin.

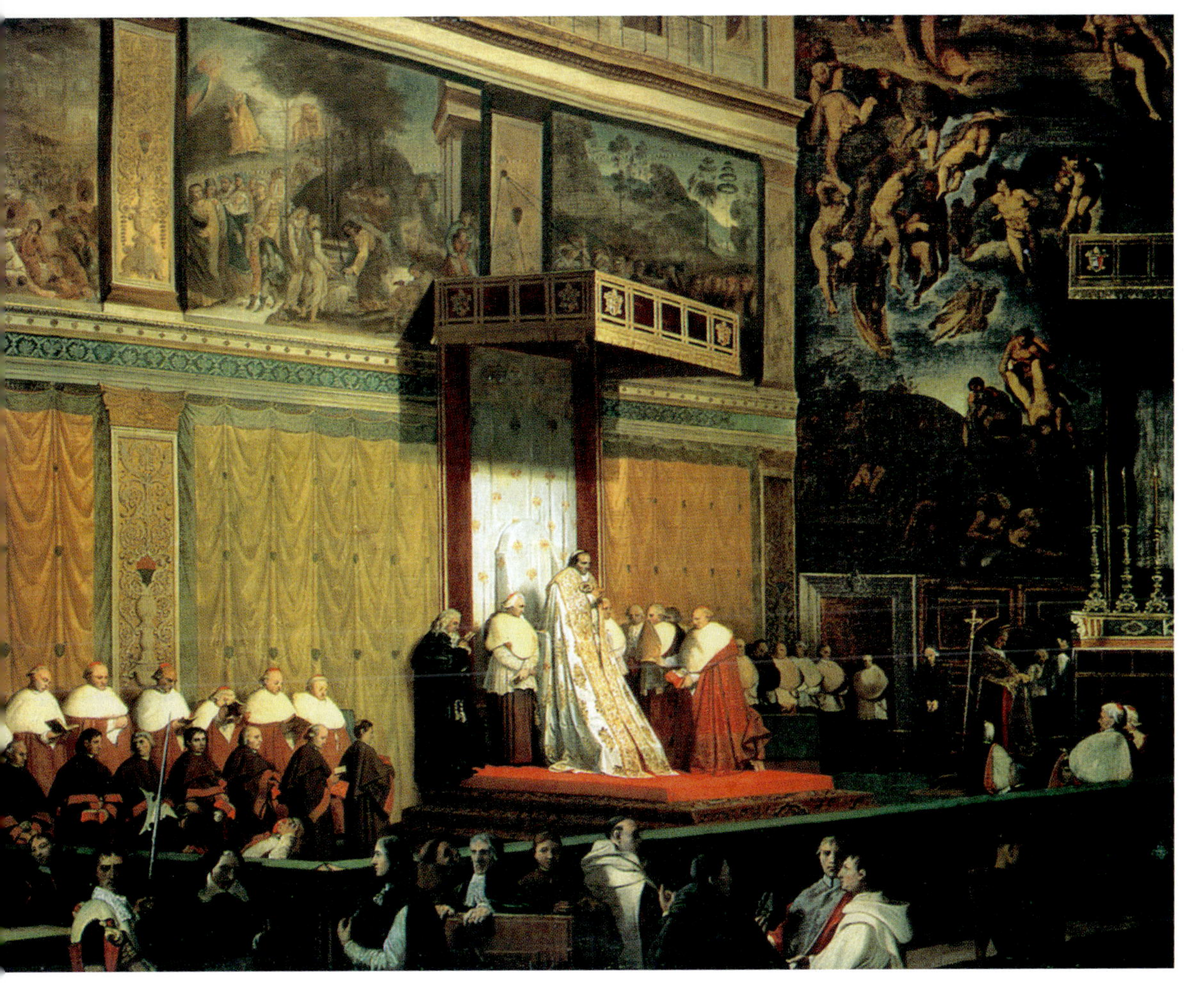

The Sistine Chapel

1814, oil on canvas, 74.5x92.7 cm
Washington, National Gallery of Art

Raphael
Christ Giving Peter the Keys of Paradise
1514–15, 319x399 cm
London, Victoria & Albert Museum

Christ Giving Peter the Keys of Paradise
1820, oil on canvas, 280x217 cm
Montauban, Musée Ingres

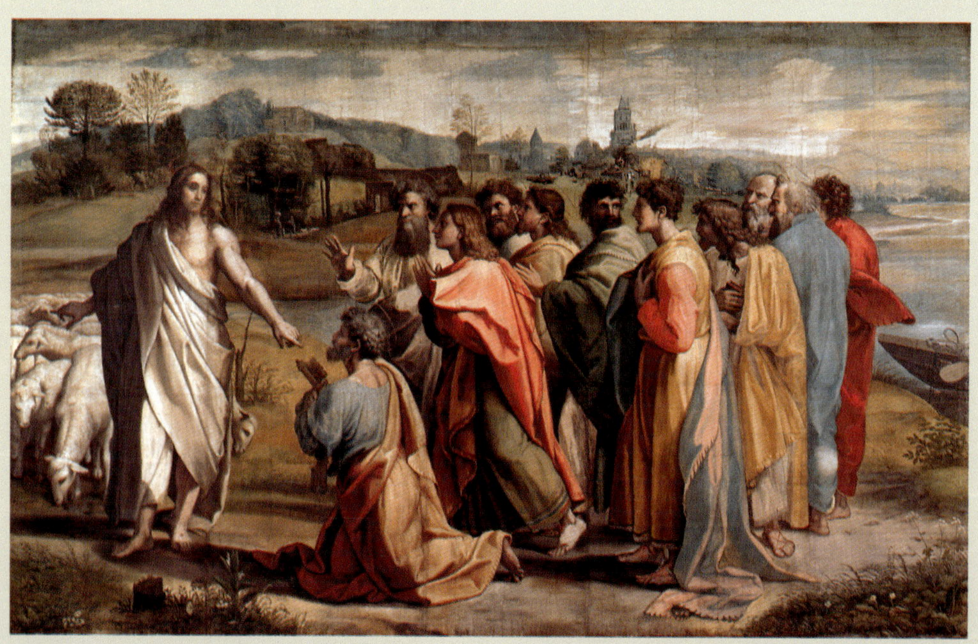

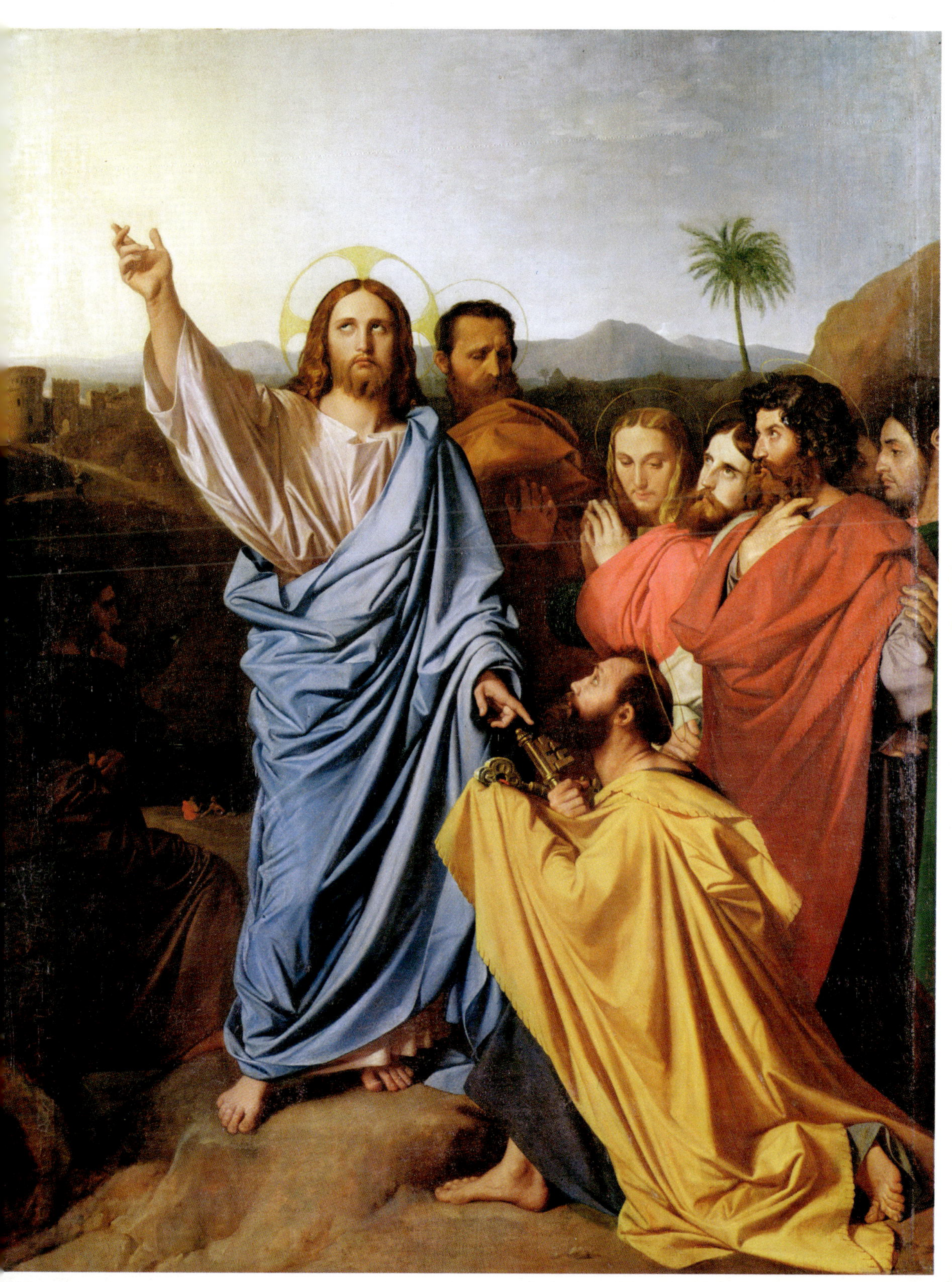

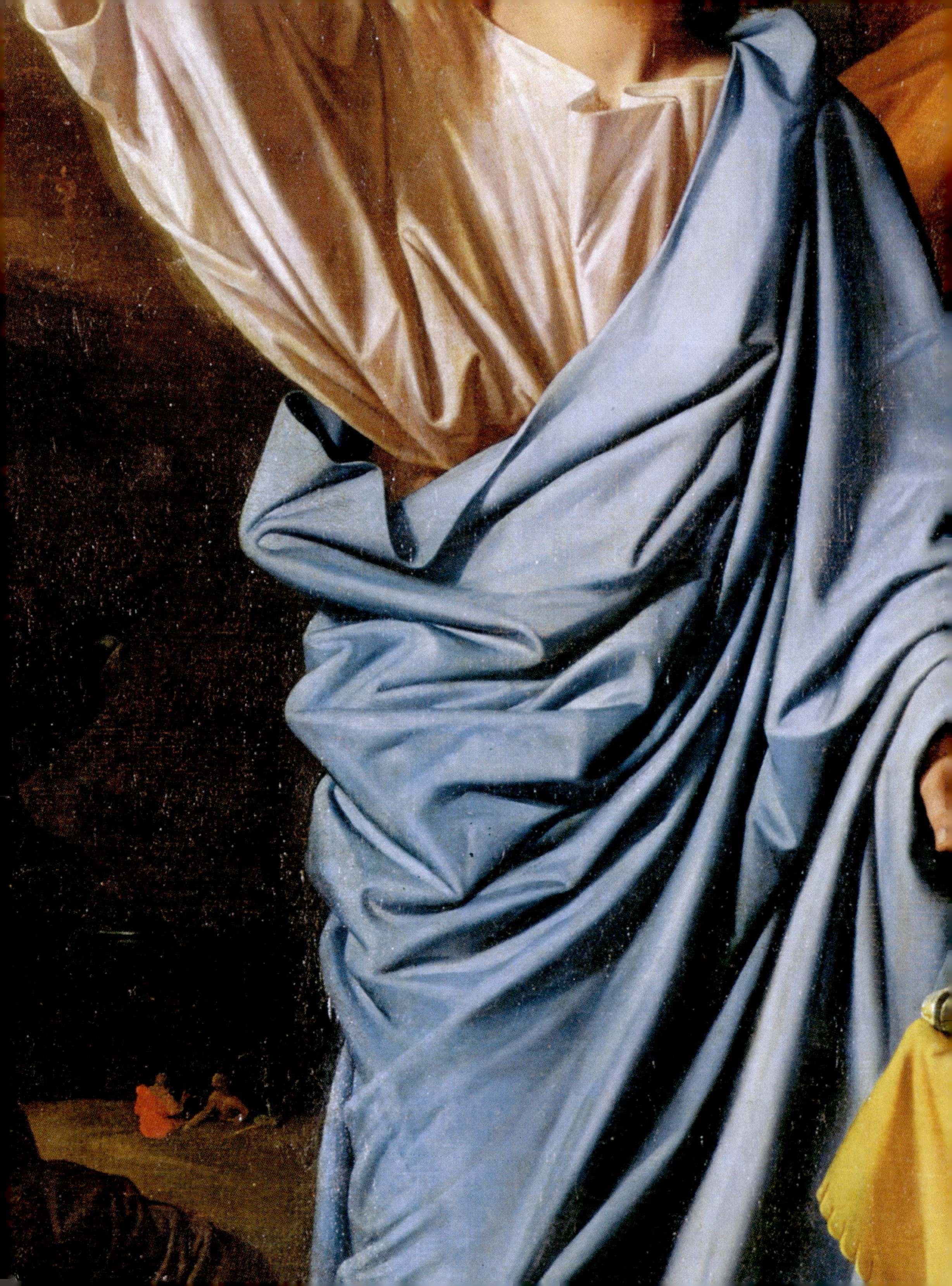

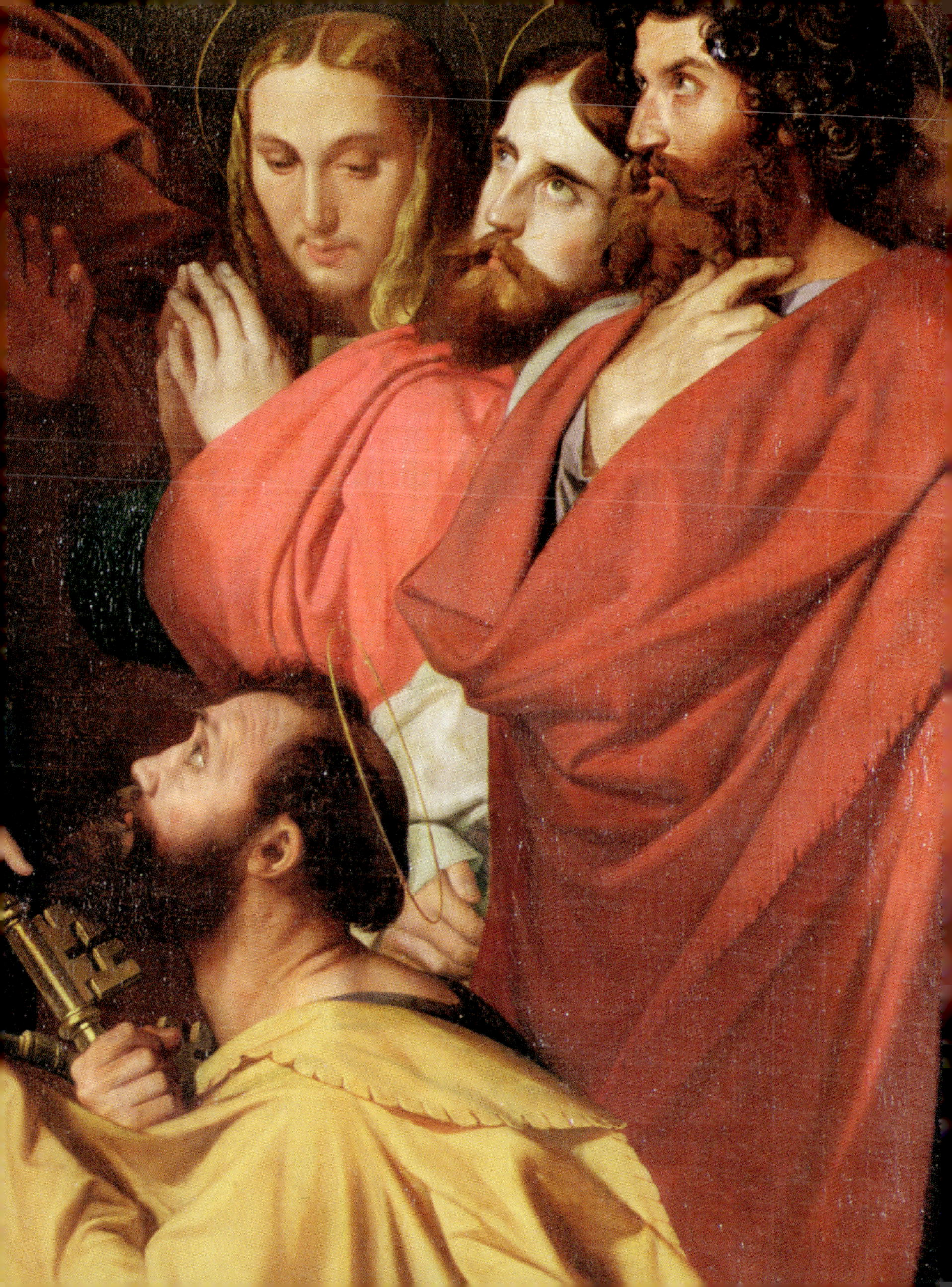

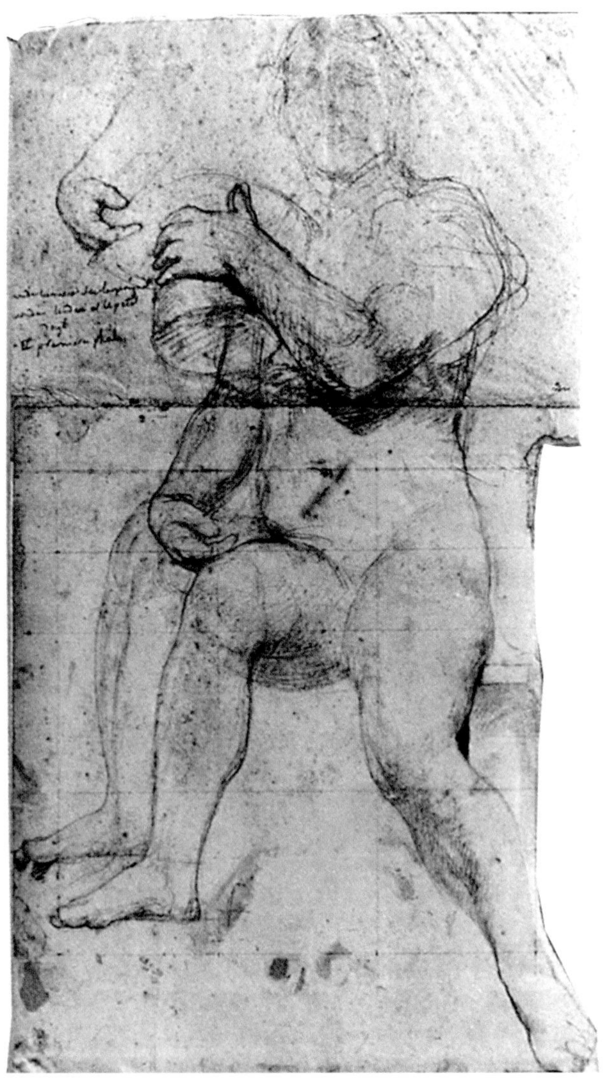

Abraham Constantin
Ingres Posing for the Figure of the Virgin in *The Vow of Louis XIII*
1842, pencil on two sheets of paper, 42.5x23 cm
Montauban, Musée Ingres

Study for the Angels in *The Vow of Louis XIII*
1824, pencil, 23x17.5 cm
Lille, Musée des Beaux-Arts

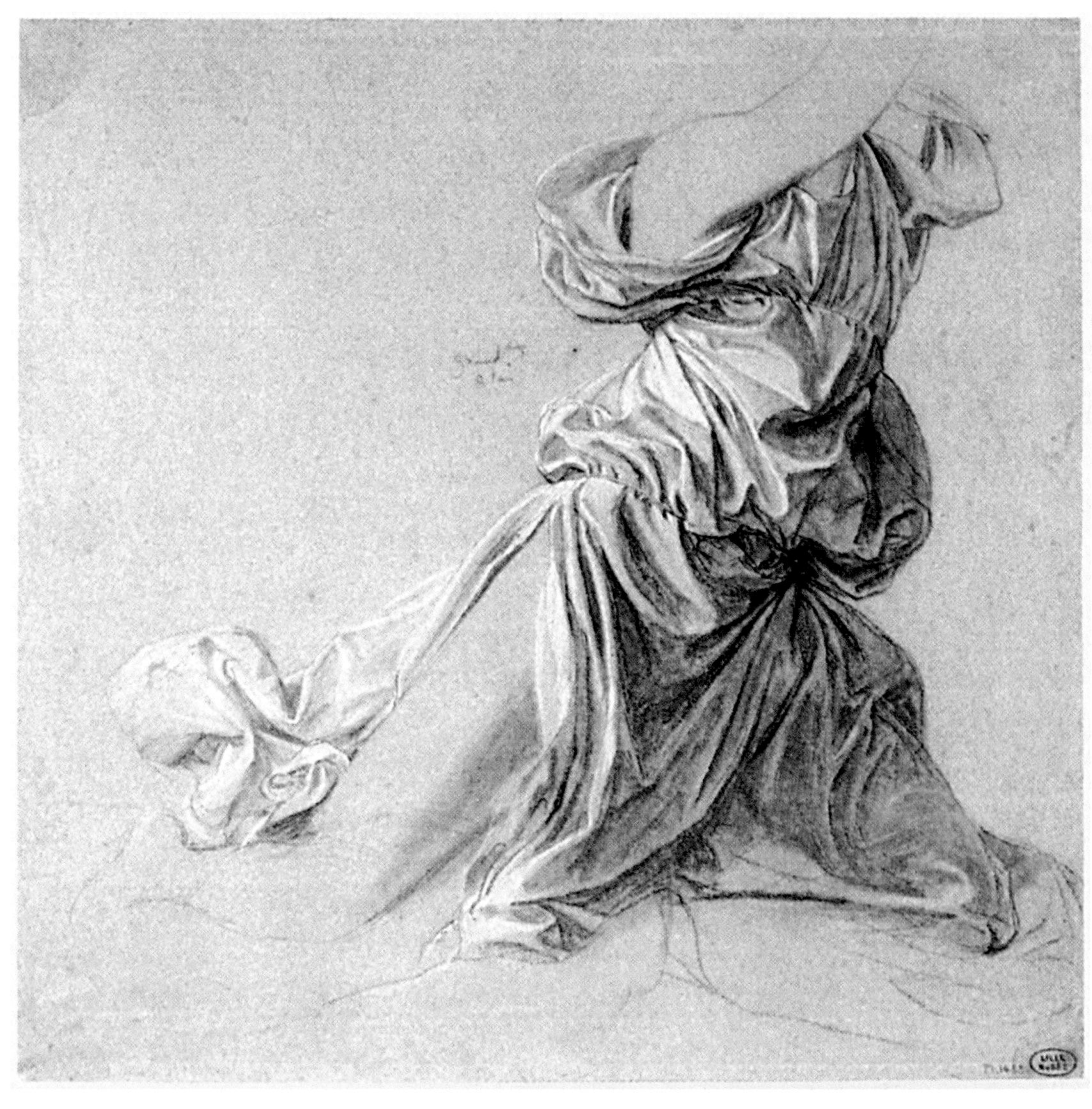

The Vow of Louis XIII
1824, oil on canvas, 421x262 cm
Montauban, Notre-Dame Cathédrale

Everything here meets Classical standards: the sharpness of composition, the static equilibrium of the forms, the perfect legibility of the narrative content and symbolism provided by aptness of pose, gesture and facial expression, and the appropriateness of each element to the subject matter. All this skill, however, cannot compensate for the crying lack of religious sentiment or spirituality of any kind, and the picture boils down to the plastic impact of its draperies, underscored by the acidity of the colors. This remarkable piece of work monopolizes the eye, while what should be its core is relegated to the second rank. Eclipsed by the flashy beauty of the garments, the faces of the apostles and even of the totally stereotyped Christ lack all spiritual depth and seem almost as superfluous as the slender little palm tree supposed to signal the Oriental context of the scene.

But the picture was well received. Naturally, for it had been purged of all the archaisms, all the formal and graphic inventions, that had drawn such critical fire and given Ingres' painting its specific flavor. In addition, the massively direct reference to Raphael set the work within the reassuring confines of the most orthodox Classicism.

This success, of which the news reached Paris, did not stop the artist from leaving Rome, where his future remained uncertain. In 1820, at the invitation of his friend Bartolini and in the hope of expanding his clientele, he moved to Florence. Disillusion was not slow to come: the Florence of the time was highly conservative, with an academy holding fast to the same Neoclassical Parisian models he had rejected from the outset. Furthermore, the locally established artists fought bitterly for a small clientele. "No one knows me here; I have works that no one comes to see, and even less to buy," he wrote to his friend Gilibert.[24] The few portraits he painted were as sumptuous as ever: Bartolini the banker, Jacques-Louis Leblanc and his wife, and the Russian Ambassador Count Gouriev. He made a copy of Titian's *Venus*, a light-drenched model that would have its influence on his own future nudes. but none of this was getting his career anywhere.

In 1820, at the instigation of the director of the Académie de France in Rome, Ingres was commissioned by the Minister for the Interior to paint a large picture for the cathedral in Montauban. The subject, chosen by the mayor of that city, fit with the monarchy's determination to restore the broken bonds between the State and religion: Louis XIII consecrating his country to the Virgin Mary in 1638. In that year Philippe de Champaigne had painted a picture for the high altar of Notre Dame de Paris: the kneeling king offering scepter and crown to a Virgin holding her dead Son in her arms. Ingres was to portray the same event, but with the Virgin in Assumption.

Initially disconcerted by the association of the two

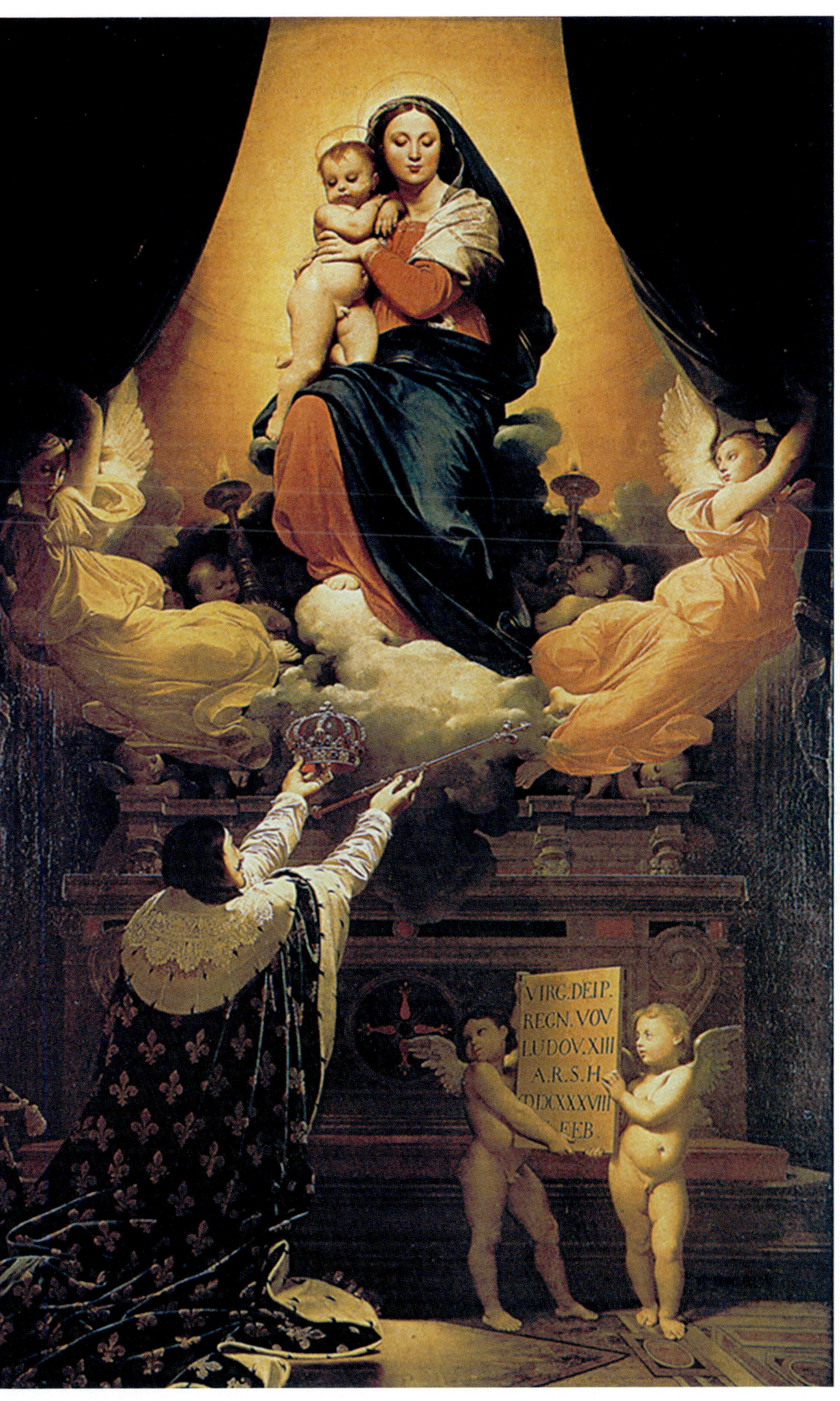
VIRG. DEI P.
REGN. VOV
LUDOV. XIII
A.R.S.H
CXXXVIII
FEB.

Studies of Female Nudes for the Angels in *The Vow of Louis XIII*
1823-24, pencil on blue paper, 23.8x32.8 cm
Montauban, Musée Ingres

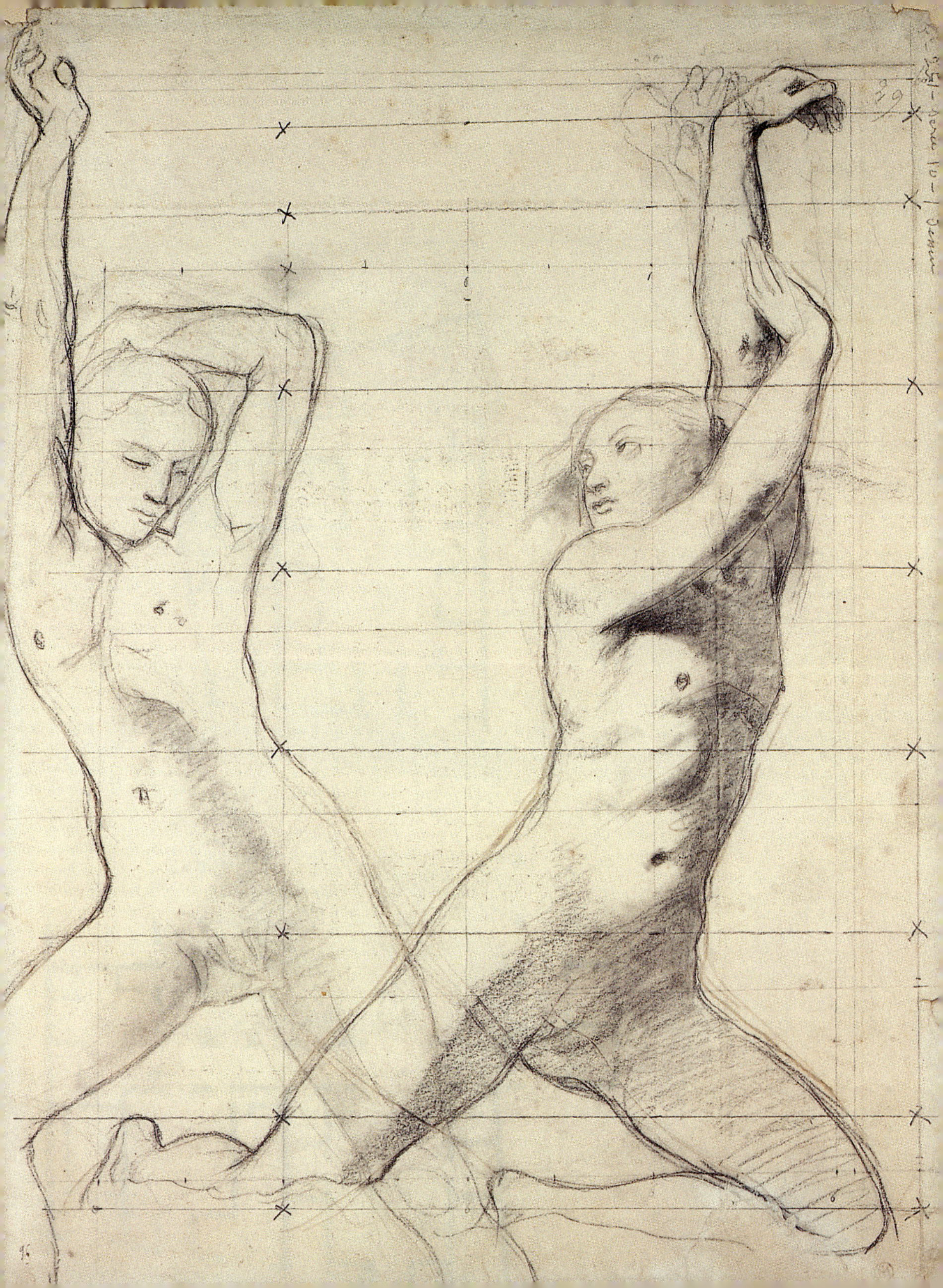

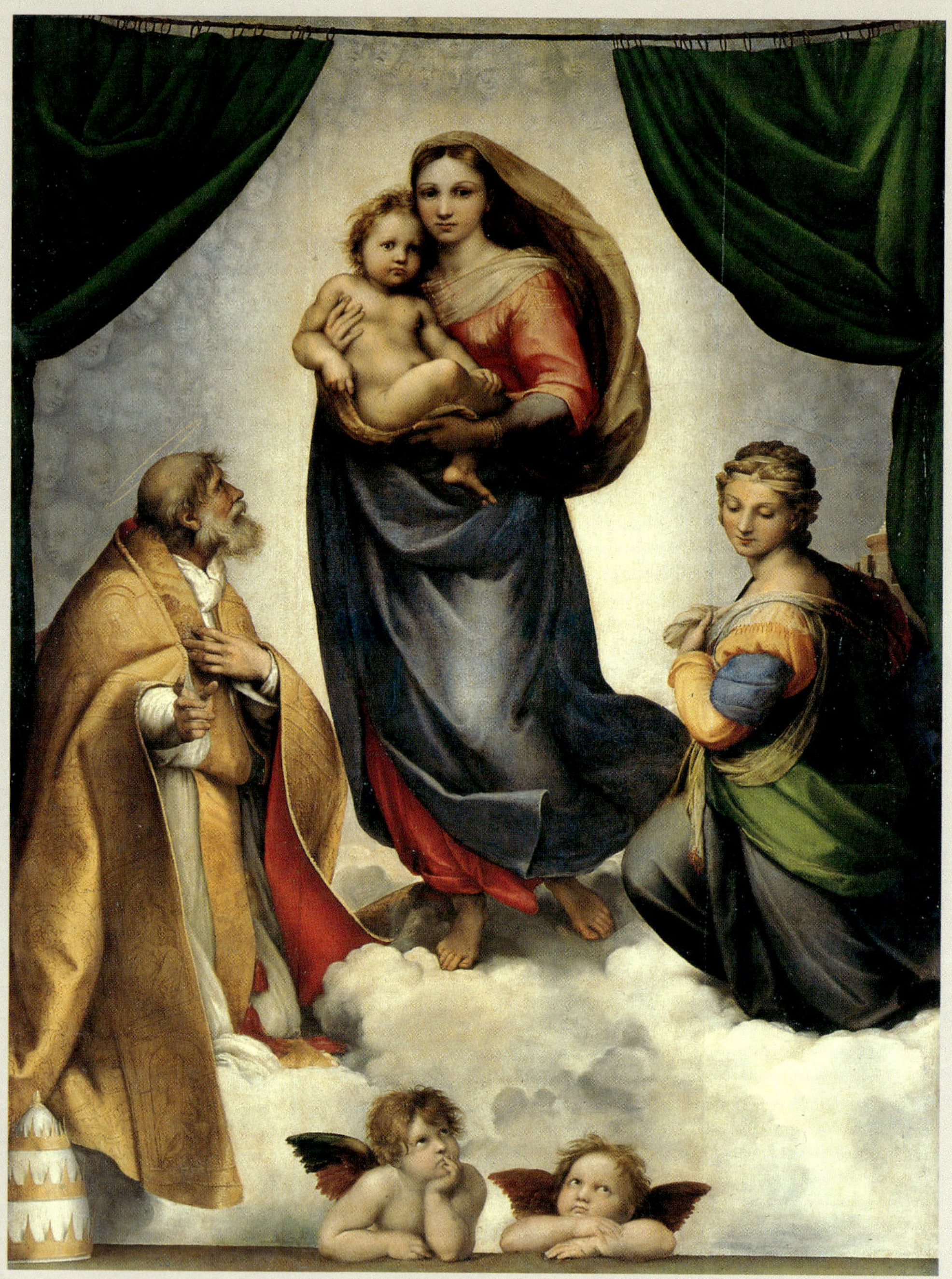

Raphael
The Sistine Madonna
1513, oil on canvas, 265x196 cm
Dresde, Gemaldegalerie

subjects – the act performed by the king and the Assumption of the Virgin – Ingres opted for replacing the Assumption with a Virgin and Child in glory on the altar. Once again he gave in totally to his admiration for Raphael. With its marked symmetry, the dignity of its figures and the perfect balance of its generous, prominent forms, the style is strongly reminiscent of that of the Italian master; indeed, the Madonna and the two cherubs holding the plaque are almost direct quotations. As we have seen, Ingres had always drawn on the models of the past, interpreting and revivifying them with his work from the life model. This time, however, the imitation is almost literal, the Madonna above all being a conventional figure owing nothing to nature. We know that she was posed – but by the artist himself, as deliciously recounted by Charles Blanc: unable to find a female model, Ingres had asked his painter friend Abraham Constantin, but Constantin could not provide the required pose; so "Ingres undressed, climbed onto the altar and posed while Constantin sketched, in place of the Virgin, this squat little man clutching the bundle of clothes that represented the Infant Jesus." [25]

The drawing has survived, and shows us what Ingres was looking for: the superlative, almost arrogant majesty that makes this Virgin utterly inhuman. Ingres had long been waiting for the right moment to return to Paris, and now the time seemed ripe. With this picture, he hoped to make a place for himself on the Paris scene.

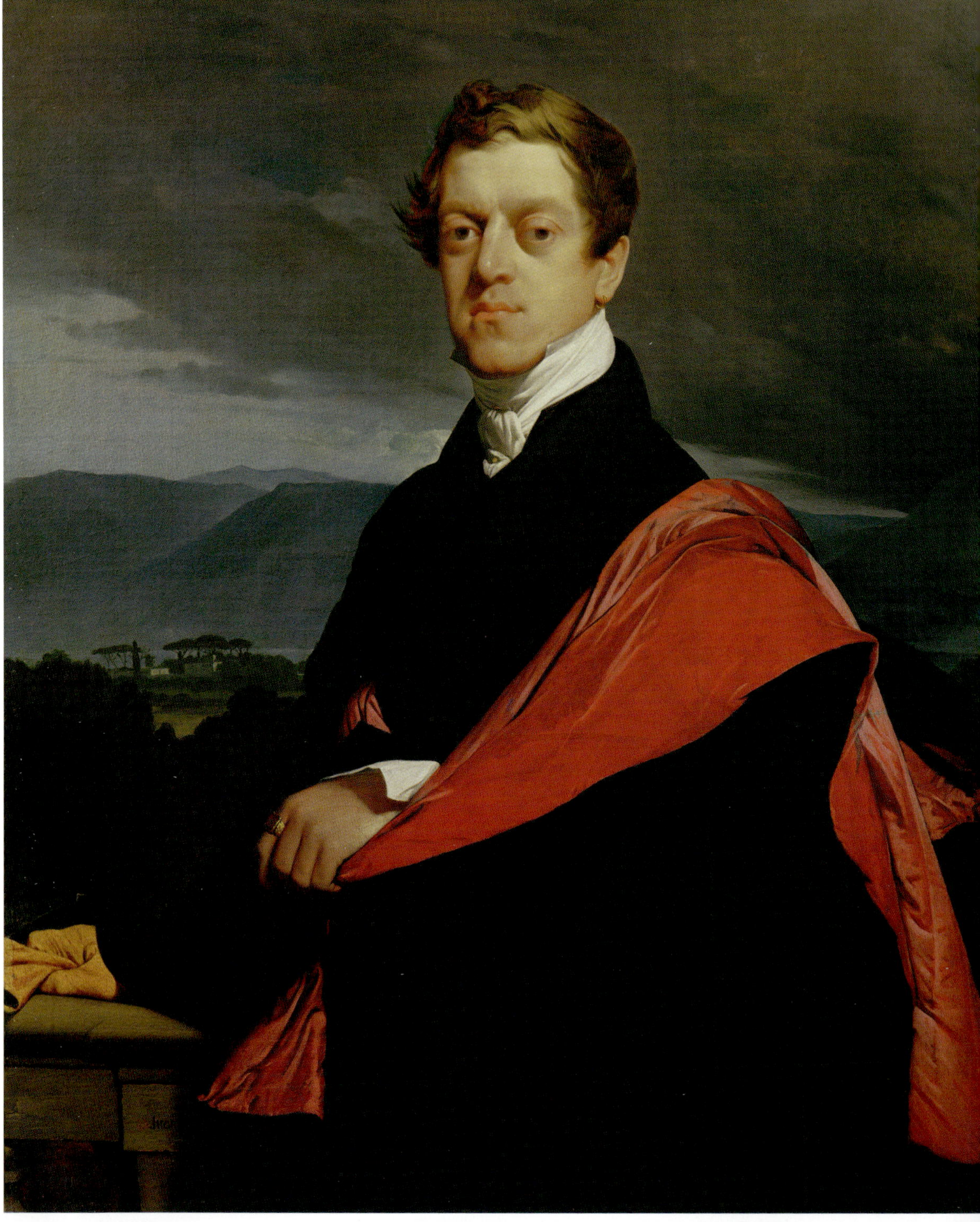

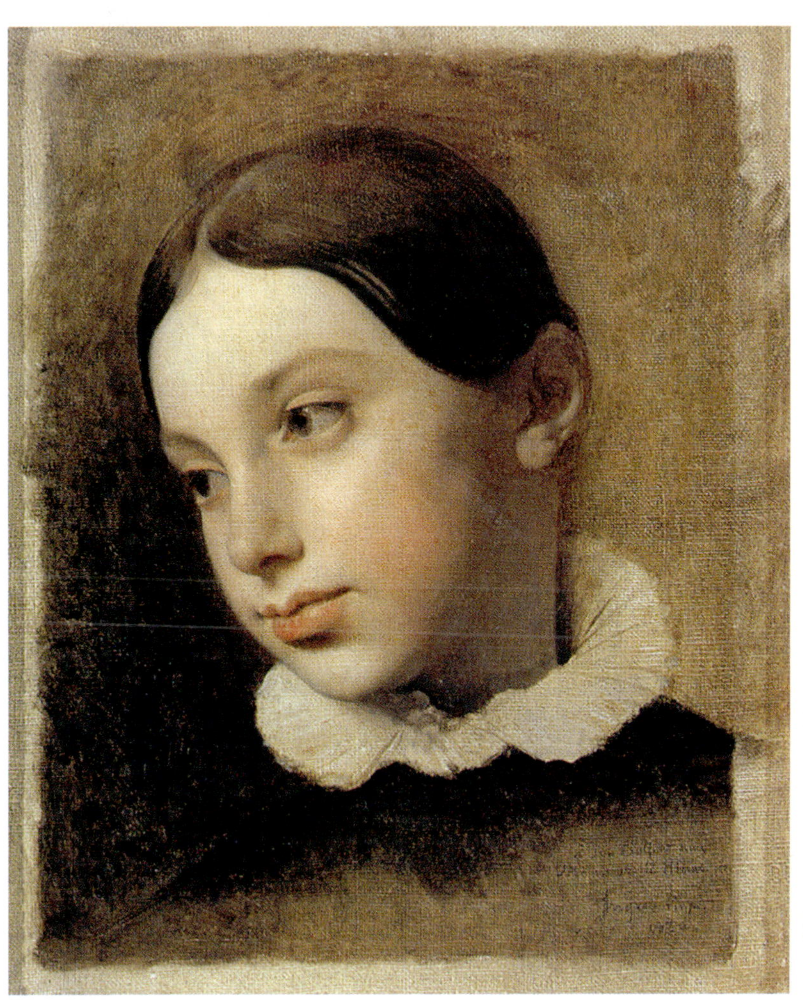

Portrait of Françoise Leblanc
1823, oil on canvas, 119x92.7 cm
New York Metropolitan Museum of Art

Portrait of Count Nikolai Gouriev
1821, oil on canvas, 107x86 cm
St Petersburg, Hermitage Museum

III
The Paris

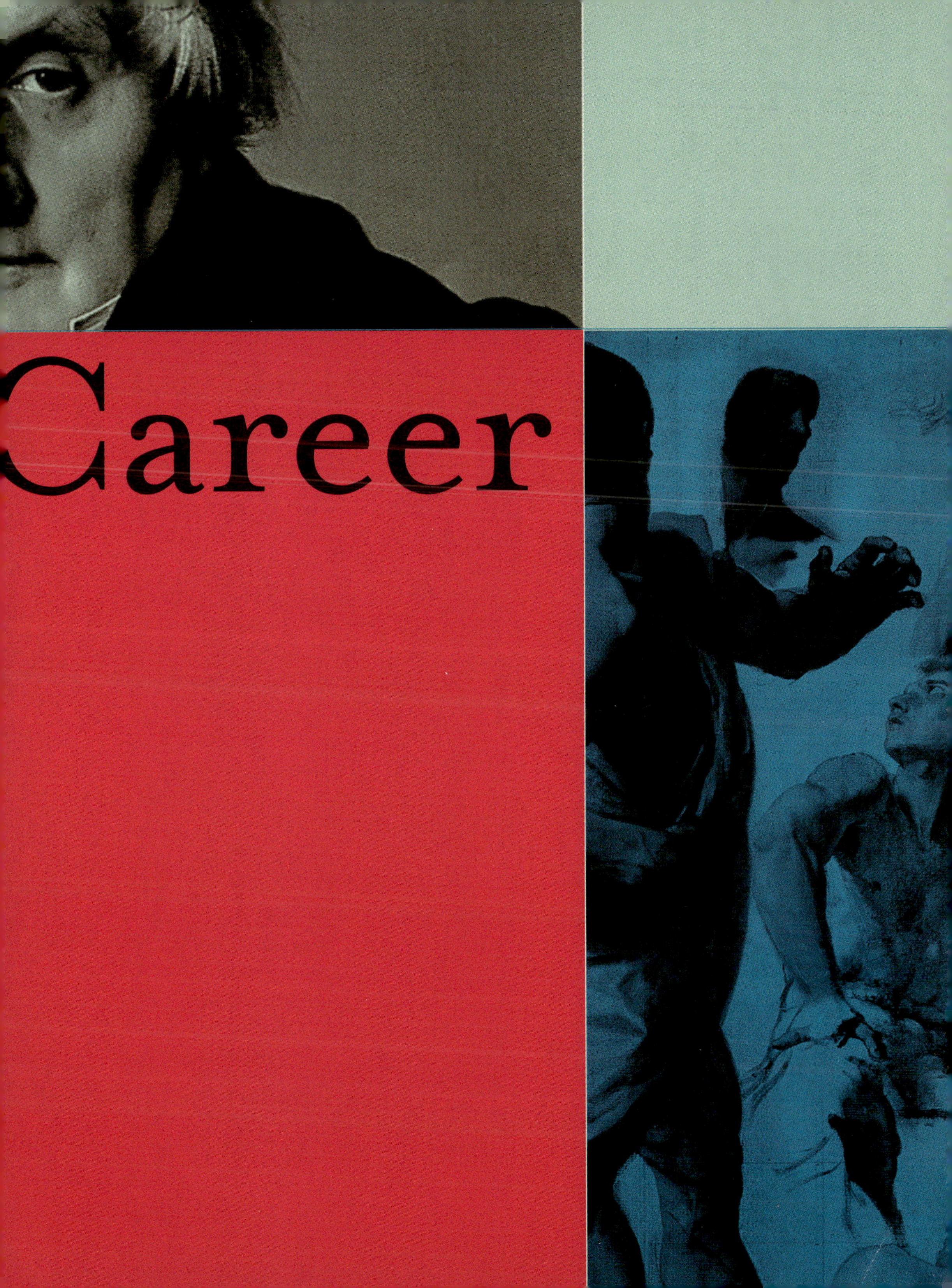
Career

The 1824 Salon

The Vow of Louis XIII enjoyed enormous success at the 1824 Salon. Apart from a few reservations – Stendhal denounced this "kind of material beauty that excludes the idea of divinity" and was disappointed by "this failing, which is one of feeling, not of skill" – critical acclaim was unanimous. Ingres thus became one of the many innovators hailed by the critic (and future minister) Adolphe Thiers: "The cry for independence has reached the ears of the artists. Each has taken his own path. One loves the handsome form of *Romulus* and of *Leonidas*, or the grandeur and profundity of the paintings of the 16th century; another prefers our everyday lives and does not scorn our customs; and each, following his personal inclinations, indulges his own taste, offering us different styles and genres...Nothing is more pleasing that the variety that characterizes the present-day school." [26]

Indeed, the 1824 Salon was a fine sample of the variety that followed the long reign of the Neoclassical esthetics and its decay in the mediocre output of David's last pupils. With the fall of the Empire and the master's exile, the Greco-Roman subjects the public had wearied of had been supplanted by others. New trends had worked a shift in public taste.

The painters of the younger generation, like Horace Vernet, Ary Scheffer and Paul Delaroche, were interested in historical subjects from the distant or recent past. With his *Raft of the Medusa*, shown at the Salon in 1819, Géricault had given new breadth to the portrayal of a dramatic contemporary event. And in 1824 the discovery of the work of Constable was to have a considerable effect on French art to come.

Eugène Delacroix
The Massacre of Chios
1824, oil on canvas, 419x354 cm
Paris, Musée du Louvre

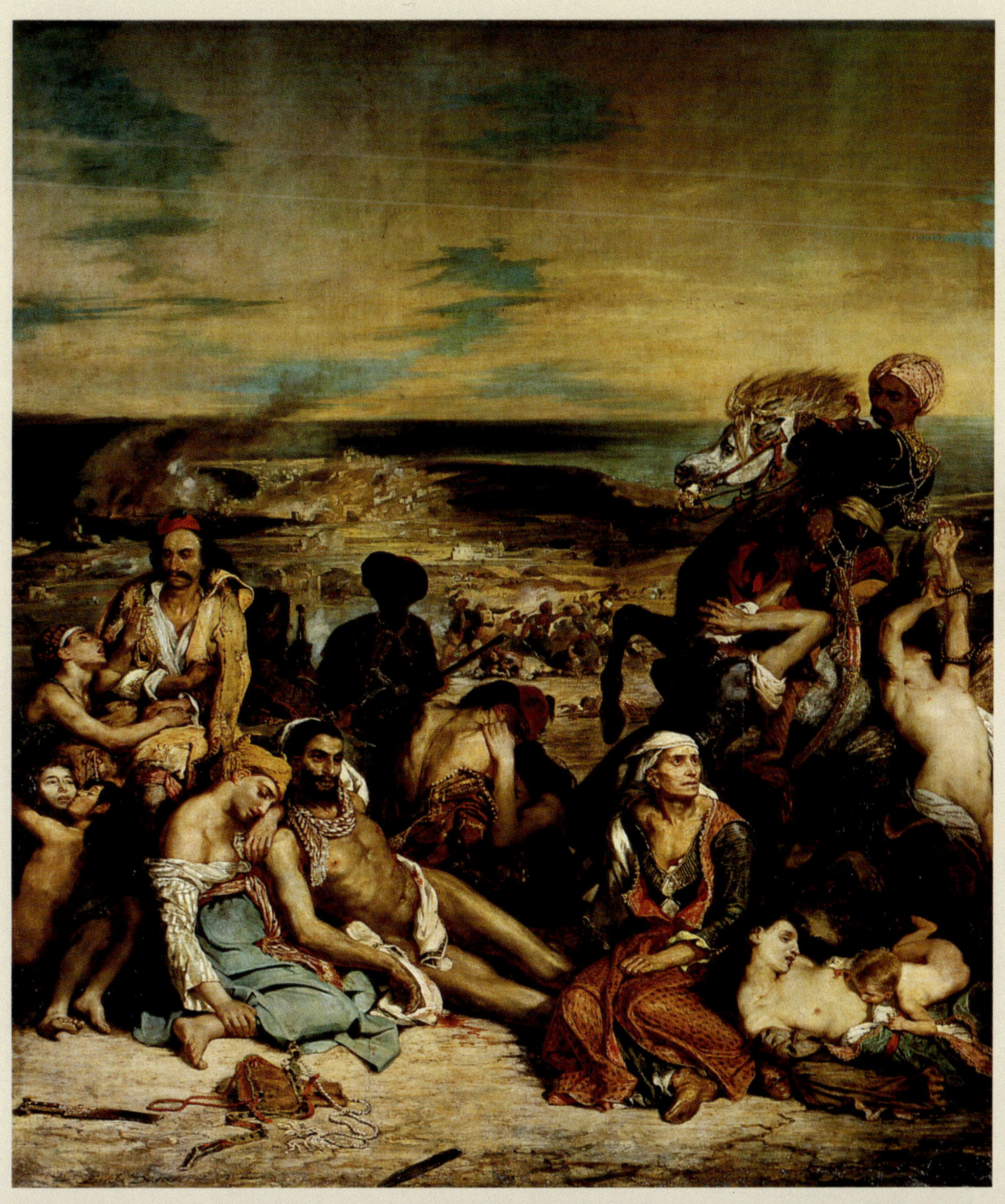

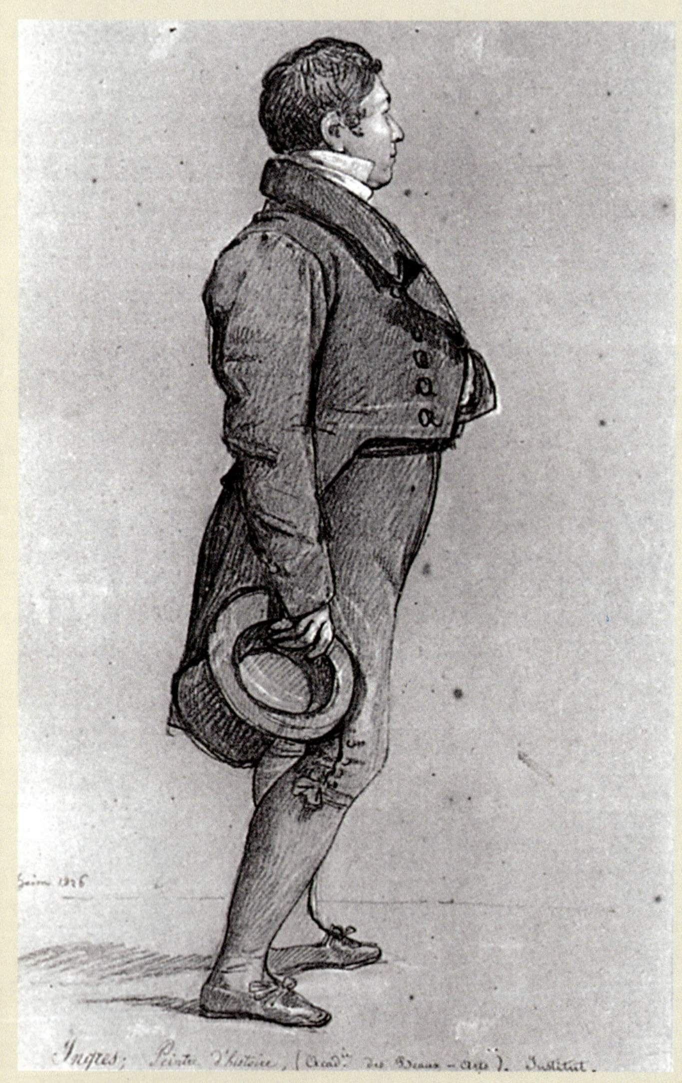

François-Joseph Heim
Ingres
1826, black chalk and white highlights on paper, 40x24.2 cm
Paris, Musée du Louvre, Cabinet des Dessins

A new cultural trend had taken shape that would soon be described as "Romantic". Its main artistic representative was the 26-year-old painter Eugène Delacroix, who in 1824 showed his large *Massacre of Chios*; and Ingres realized that he would now have to face an art exactly, and aggressively, opposed to his own.

The Delacroix took a modern subject, an episode from the Greek war of independence, and brought to it a boldly original technique full of references to non-Classical traditions: the Venetians, Rubens and the English landscape painters. The Ingres offered a national subject serving the new political order, whose esthetic was founded on skilled interpretation of the most wisely accepted Classical models. It was precisely for these reasons that *The Vow of Louis XIII* was admired and its creator considered the new, gifted representative of that tradition.

Ingres would come to see himself as invested with the mission of saving art: by confining it to a sort of eternal Classicism with its roots in the ancient Greeks and Raphael; and by protecting it against the onslaughts of the "barbarians" – all those who did not subscribe to this doctrine. His first Paris success was the major turning point in his career, and he himself would refer to it as a "coup d'état." The hitherto marginal figure would rapidly become the leader of a school, and the wielder of steadily increasing power: at the close of the 1824 Salon he was awarded the Cross of the Legion of Honor and given a seat at the Académie des Beaux-Arts. The atelier he opened shortly afterwards would become the most important of its time, and Ingres was made a teacher at the Écoles des Beaux-Arts. Henceforth honors and commissions flowed in.

The Ingres-Delacroix dichotomy came vigorously to the fore in a number of exhibitions. At the 1827 Salon Ingres' *Apotheosis of Homer* was placed close to *The Death of Sardanapalus*, one of Delacroix's most furiously Romantic works. Another confrontation between the two masters came at the Bazar de Bonne-Nouvelle exhibition in 1846 and, most vehemently, at the 1855 Universal Exhibition. Fuelled by all sorts of anecdotes and exacerbated by the critics, their differences became a commonplace of the art history of the first half of the 19th century; but they were very real, being founded on the clear antagonism between their conceptions of art.

Moreover, the flames were constantly fanned by Ingres' hatred of the man he called "the apostle of the ugly"– he could not see Delacroix in the street without losing his temper. His hatred was deliberate and dogmatic: Ingres confided to the painter Robert-Fleury that he respected Delacroix's "talent, honorable character and distinguished mind," but added that "he has tendencies I consider dangerous and which I must put an end to."

A Painting Manifesto

If *The Vow of Louis XIII* was a "coup d'état," *The Apotheosis of Homer* was the manifesto par excellence: it could even be described as the direct illustration of an esthetic doctrine. It was commissioned in 1826 for the ceiling of a room in the Charles X museum in the Louvre, but instead of the usual view from below used for ceiling paintings, Ingres opted for a frontal approach, a strictly symmetrical frieze whose composition was taken straight from the Raphael frescoes *The School of Athens* and *Parnassus*, in the Vatican. The Italian master had provided an imaginary assembly of the great men of history around two philosophers symbolizing two great worldviews – Aristotle and Plato – and around the arts' tutelary divinities: Apollo and the Muses. At the centre of the Ingres pantheon is a single figure, Homer, presented as the father and source of all the arts.

Seated on a pedestal in front of the temple dedicated to him, the poet receives a crown from the hands of a Winged Victory. At his feet are personifications of the *Iliad* (in red) and the *Odyssey* (in green). On each side of the central group, a crowd of great men, mainly artists, poets and philosophers, pay tribute to Homer. The upper part of the group, except for a chosen few including Raphael (with Apellus holding his hand), comprises figures from antiquity. The "moderns," shown half-length, are at the bottom of the steps: on the right we can identify Molière, Racine and Boileau, and on the left Corneille and Poussin. Poussin is the spokesman for the entire picture, pointing to Homer to underscore its already clear message: the only true source of beauty is Greece – the Greece of the early, Homeric era. Homer is considered "the principle and the model for all beauty in the arts as in literature." And the greatest artists, the only ones who count (for Ingres) are those who have maintained, through imitation, the great models of antiquity.

The classical theory of imitation, with its advocacy of the consecrated models of the past, is at the heart of Ingres' doctrine: "I think I can be original by imitating. After all, who among the great ones has not imitated? Nothing can be made out of nothing and it is by making others' discoveries known that we make our own. Those who cultivate literature and the arts are all children of Homer."

Ingres never ceased applying this doctrine, eclectically and with varying degrees of success. But *The Apotheosis of Homer* is not the illustration of a dogma. Almost all the figures come from ancient models, with, in parallel, each anatomical fragment taken from the life model in endless drawn and painted studies – magnificent heads, torsos, hands and feet – testifying to that passionate attention to detail. The finished painting is a painstaking assemblage of all this fine work, but one lacking any overall, unifying sense of form. Once again the failing is one not of "skill" but of "feeling," and the error lies in the confusion of esthetic belief and ideology. Nothing can be more certain than that Ingres raised this academic pantheon in response to the violent innovations of Romantic painting: it is as if he was grouping his troops for battle. Confronting Delacroix's tumultuous *Death of Sardanapalus* at the Salon in 1827, the *Apotheosis* was intended to rise like the rampart of the eternal values. But a feeble little rampart, in fact, and one that a touch of humor could bring low: as Stendhal said, "It's the opposite of *farce*." [27]

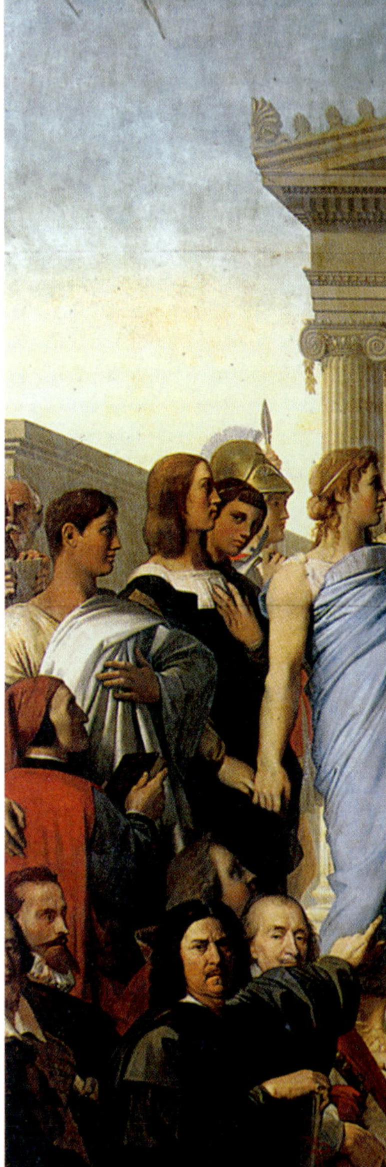

The Apotheosis of Homer
1827, oil on canvas, 152x203 cm
Paris, Musée du Louvre

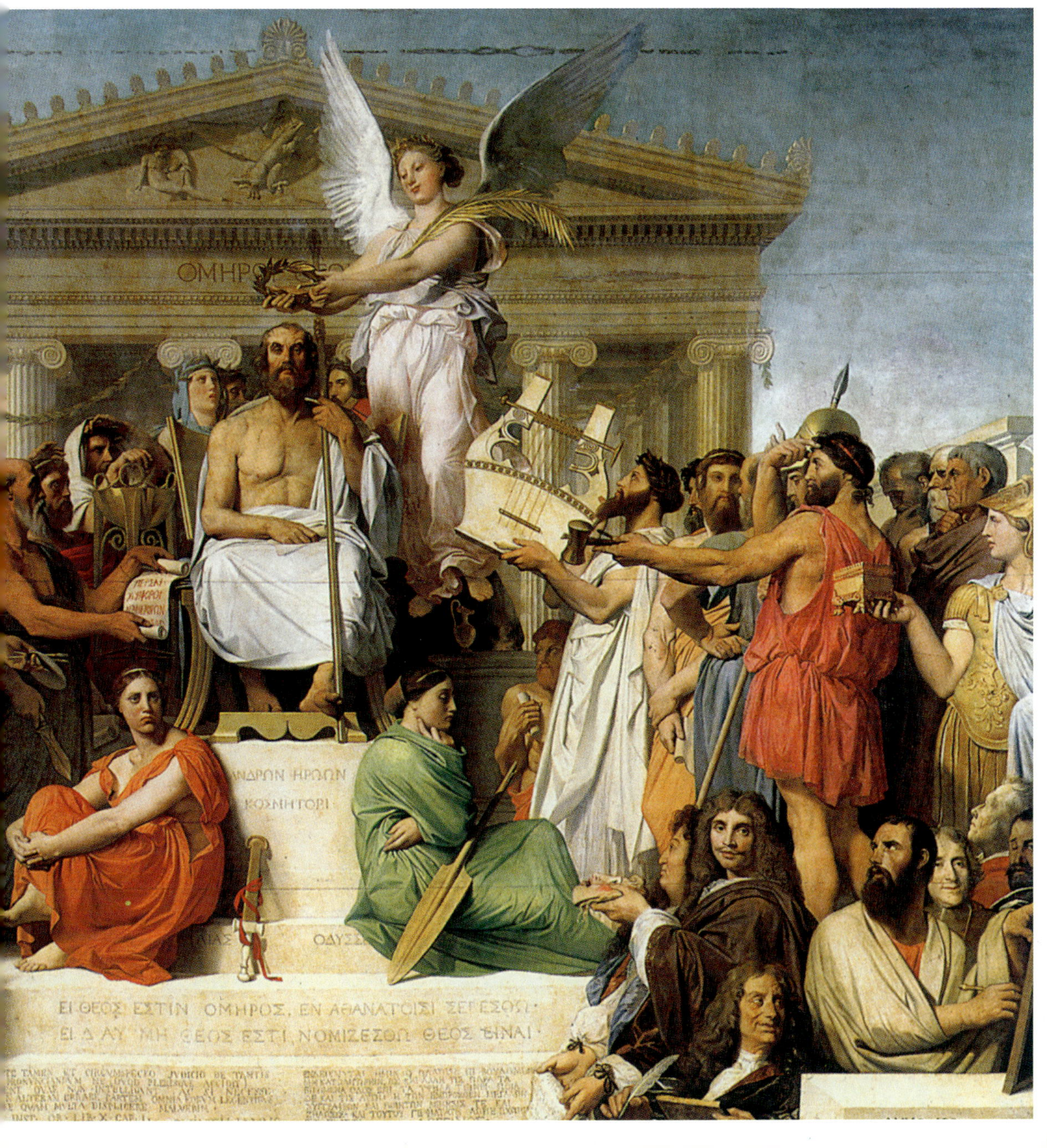
ΑΝΔΡΩΝ ΗΡΩΩΝ
ΚΟΣΜΗΤΟΡΙ
ΕΙ ΘΕΟΣ ΕΣΤΙΝ ΟΜΗΡΟΣ, ΕΝ ΑΘΑΝΑΤΟΙΣΙ ΣΕΒΕΣΘΩ·
ΕΙ Δ ΑΥ ΜΗ ΘΕΟΣ ΕΣΤΙ ΝΟΜΙΖΕΣΘΩ ΘΕΟΣ ΕΙΝΑΙ·

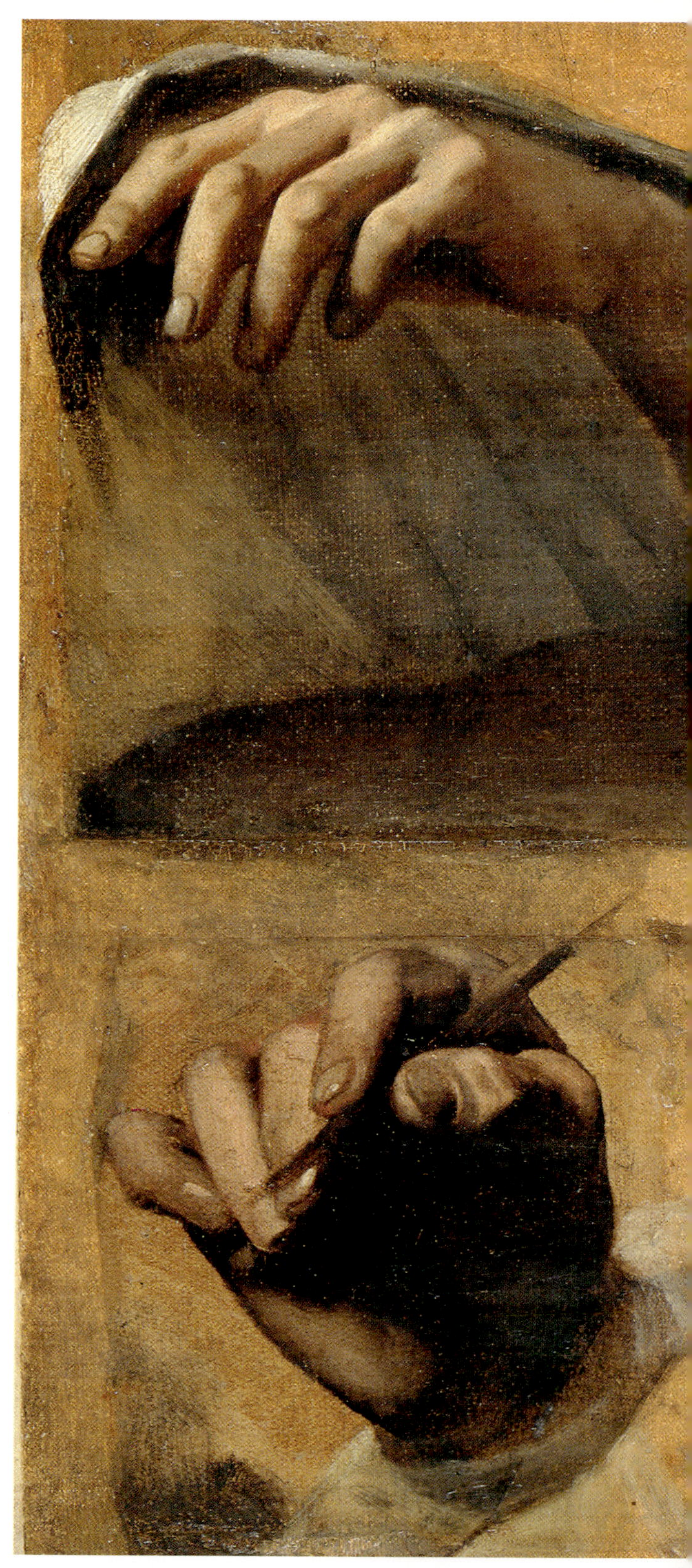

Study of Hands for
The Apotheosis of Homer
1827, oil on canvas mounted on panel, 32x36.5 cm
Lyon, Musée des Beaux-Arts

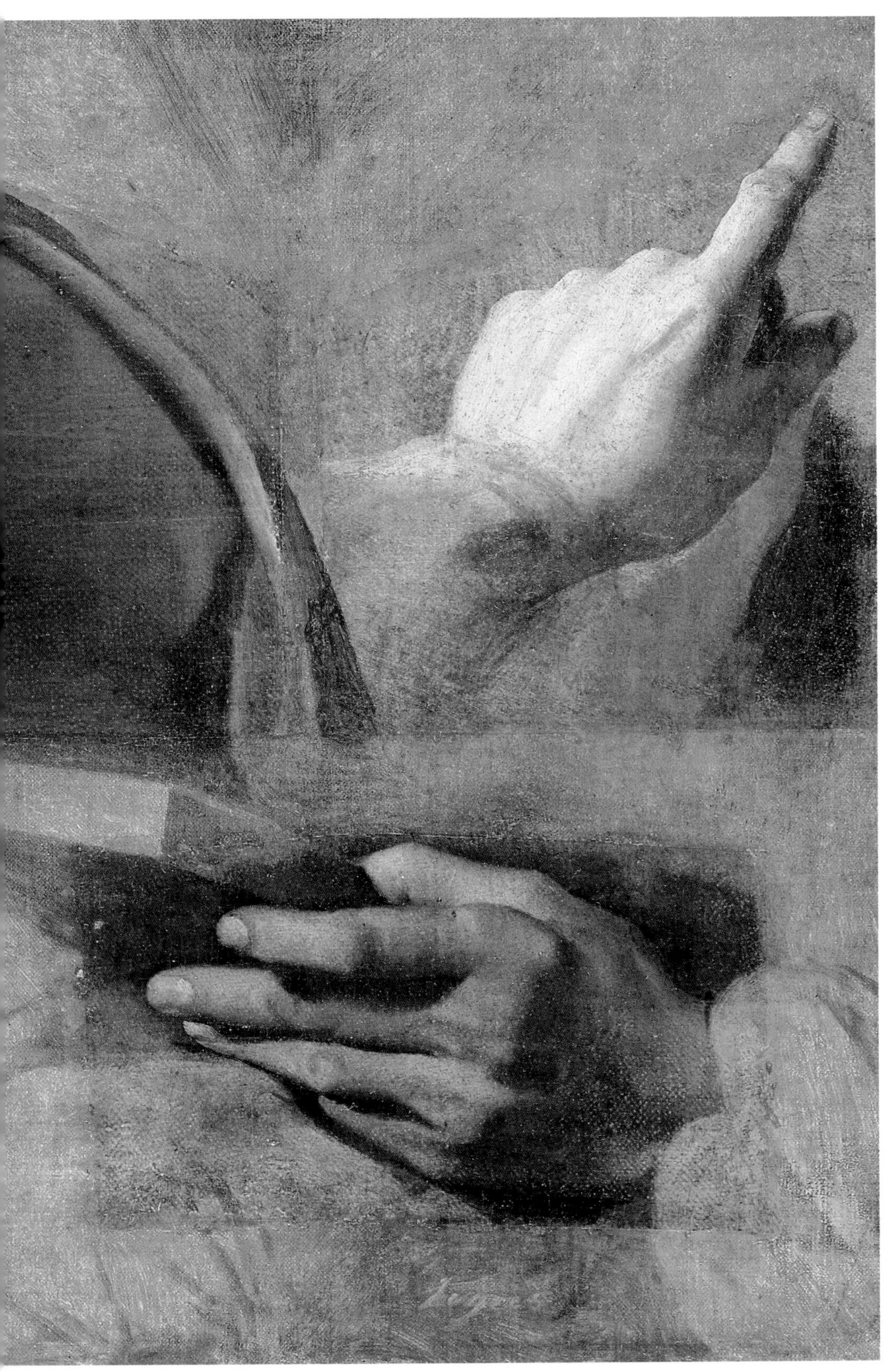

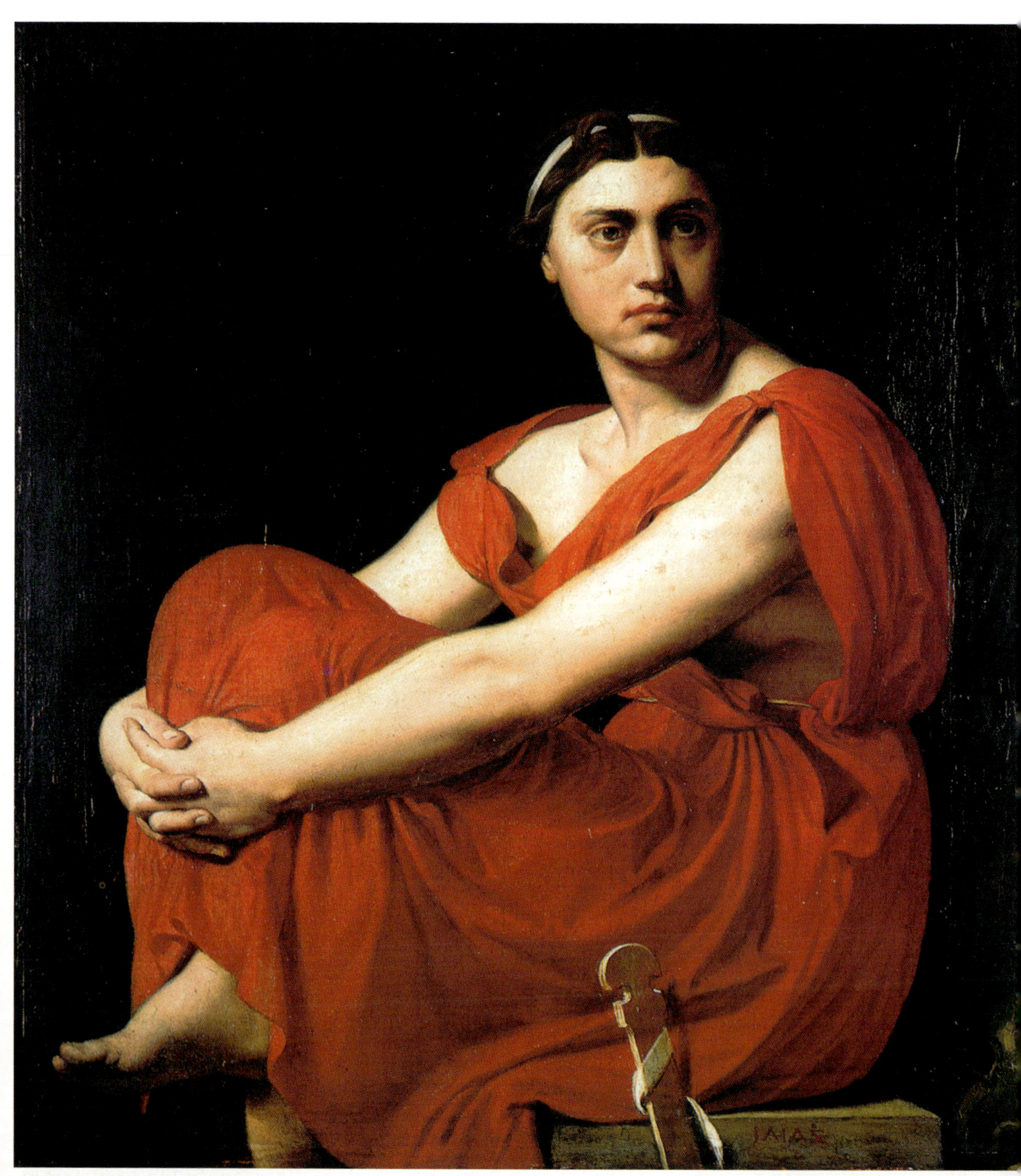

The Iliad
1827, oil on canvas, 59.5x53.5 cm
Private collection

The Odyssey
1827, oil on canvas, 61x55 cm
Lyon, Musée des Beaux-Arts

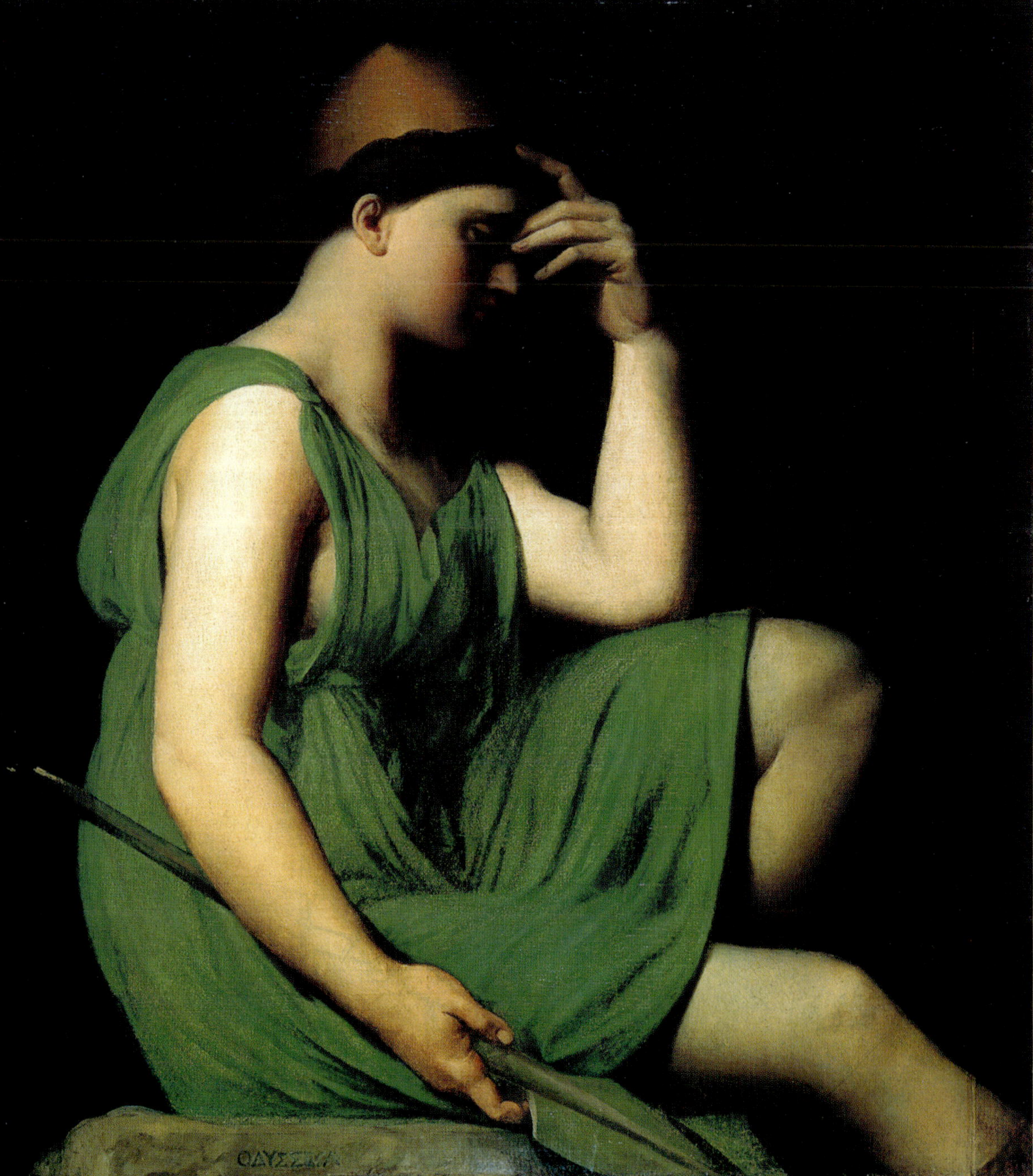

Painting in Pieces

Study for *The Martyrdom of St. Symphorian*
1824–34, oil on canvas, 60.9x46.5 cm
Cambridge, The Fogg Art Museum

Ingres' worst mistake was to identify with the dogma he was defending, to the point of sacrificing his most precious artistic capacities. This is true, at least, of his most ambitious compositions, the big history pictures. Some years after *The Apotheosis of Homer* he was given a major commission for the cathedral at Autun. *The Martyrdom of St. Symphorian* (1834) shows the moment when the young Christian is dragged out of the city towards a pagan temple, where he must sacrifice to the gods or die. With a gesture combining a last goodbye and acceptance of the supreme sacrifice, he turns to look back at his mother who, from the city wall, is exhorting him not to betray his faith. This is a genuinely spectacular picture, not

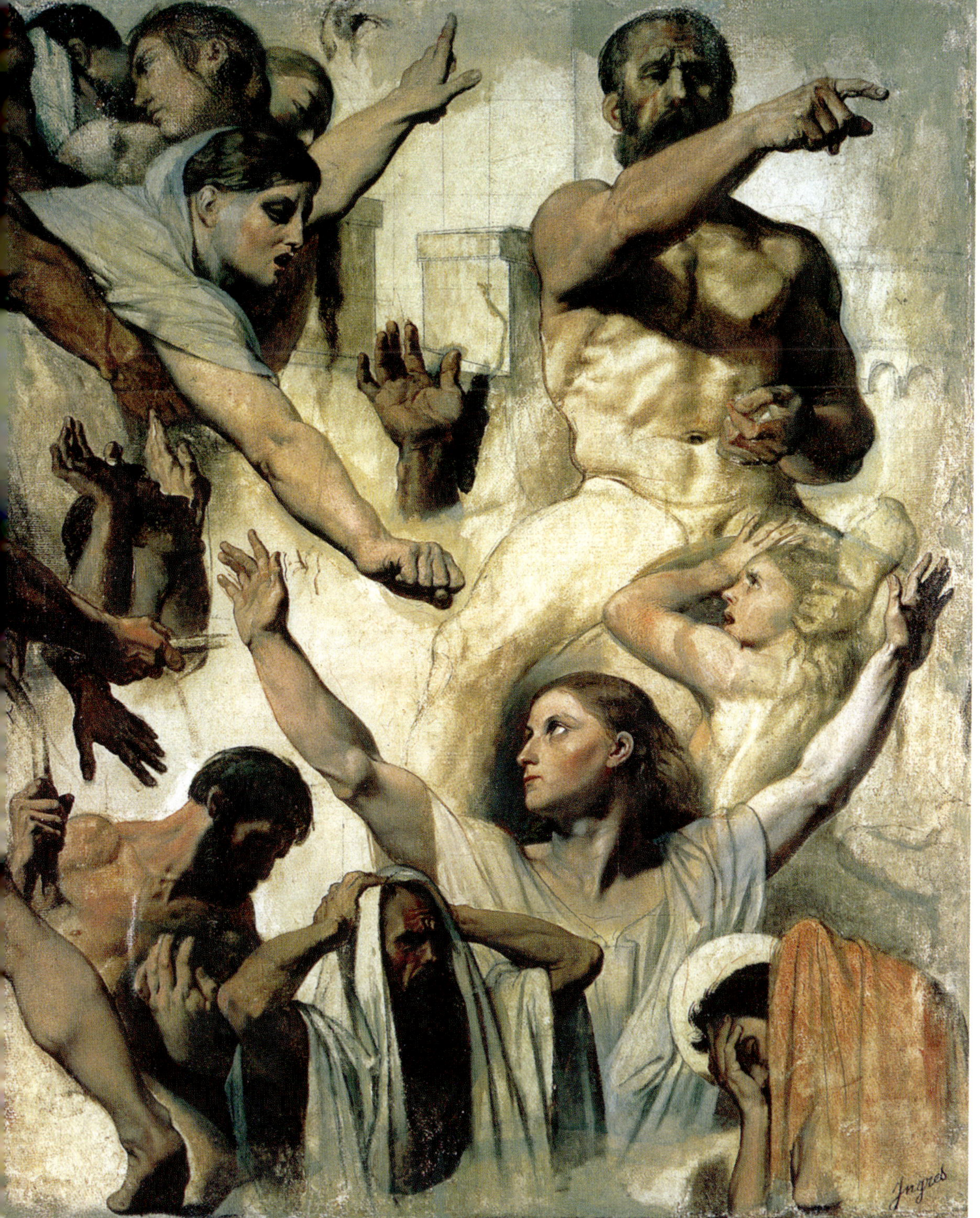
Ingres

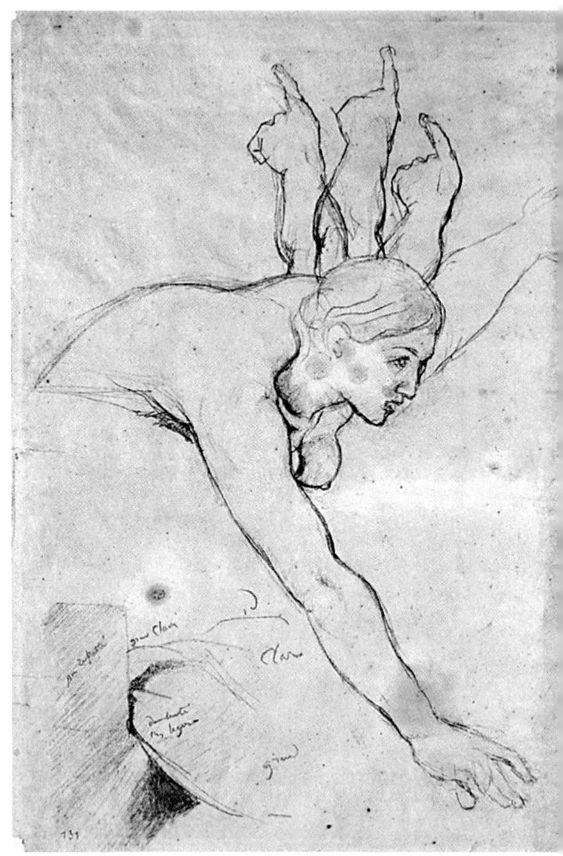

Study for the Mother of St. Symphorian
1824–34, pencil and black chalk on paper, 36.6x25 cm
Montauban, Musée Ingres

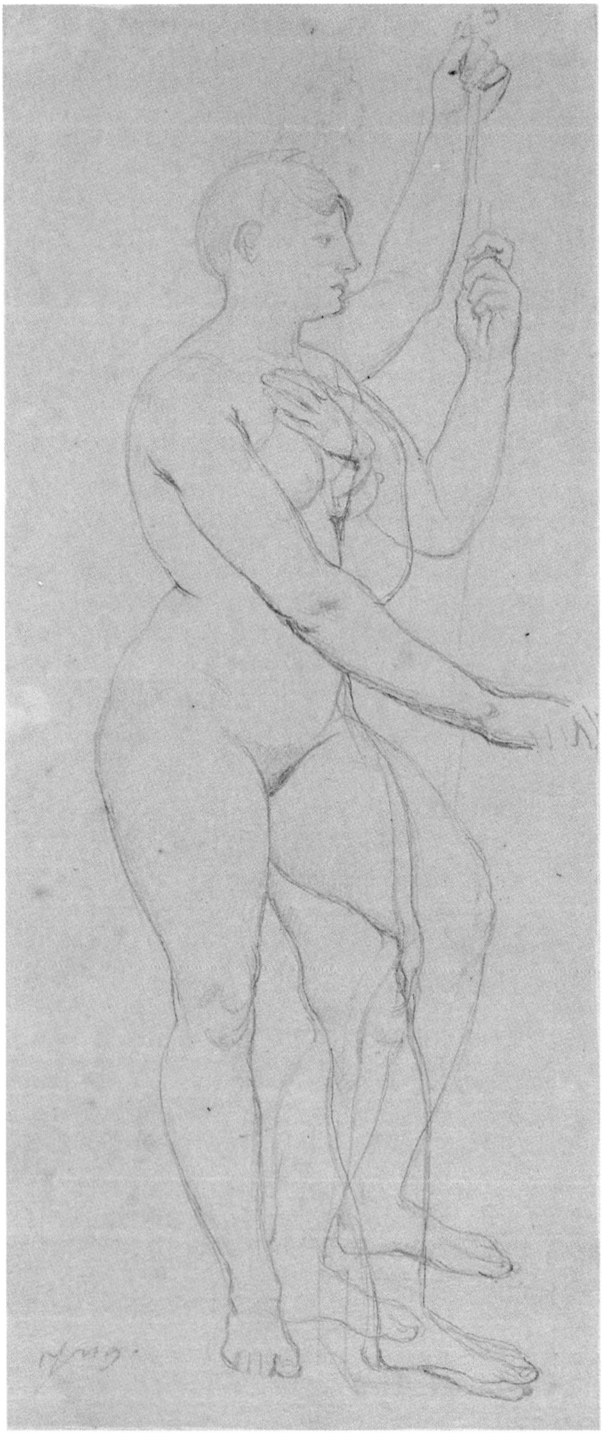

Study for France
pencil on paper, 25.7x10.5 cm
Montauban, Musée Ingres

through the effect it was meant to produce – and even if the gestures of the saint, his mother, and the proconsul on horseback, effectively sum up the event and the meaning of the work – but through its incredible hurly-burly, its inextricable accumulation of figures and details. Not even the most cluttered 16th-century Mannerist compositions – which the artist doubtless had on his mind at the time – achieve this degree of sheer visual confusion.

Even more than its predecessor, this work betrays Ingres' weakness in handling large numbers of figures and his inability, when dealing with a large-scale event, to provide it with the overall feeling, the poetically expressive dimension that alone can touch the viewer. He is, as ever, too attached to the physical beauty of each body, and even of each limb.

And it is the limbs that stand out here: the veined, muscular arms of the two executioners, the massive arms of the woman clutching her child, the plumply energetic arms of the saint's mother, and the incredibly twisted arms of Symphorian himself, already seemingly dislocated by torture and forming a cross that announces the imminent Christian sacrifice. Legs and feet too: cut off by the lower right edge of the picture, a handsome, thoroughly living foot leads the way in echo of the pointing index finger of the proconsul. Totally incongruous, this isolated foot serves as a kind of leitmotif, as the module or base cell of the picture's proliferation: arms, forearms, thighs, calves, shoulders, living fragments the artist cannot make up his mind to get rid of. And for good reason: for it is in the hundreds of drawings and the dozens of painted studies which, as usual with Ingres, preceded the work itself, that he finds his pleasure. Facing the model, his pencil and brush bring astounding accuracy and sobriety to the structure of living forms – but he cannot stop himself from putting all those forms into the finished work. As his pupil Louis Lacuria wrote, "In this picture, each hand, each fragment is an entire painting."

Critic Daniel Arasse has pointed out that Ingres' flagrant dilemma – how to bring his fragments together in a united whole – is symptomatic of a period in which classical composition, bound to the narrative demands of history painting, was breaking down in the face of more organic notions of the picture and of painting.

In line with Alberti's theories of the 15th century, concern with "true" representation and scrupulous imitation of nature required that different parts of the composition be studied and worked up separately, then assembled to form a harmonious, intelligible whole. However, this process should not be visible in itself. Each component, placed as required by the rationale of the *storia* (the story told by the picture), should melt into a space unified by the rules of perspective and anatomy and by a "transparent" execution that left no trace of its own passing. And everything should contribute to the creation of a single, dominant impression, to the conveying of the principal idea.

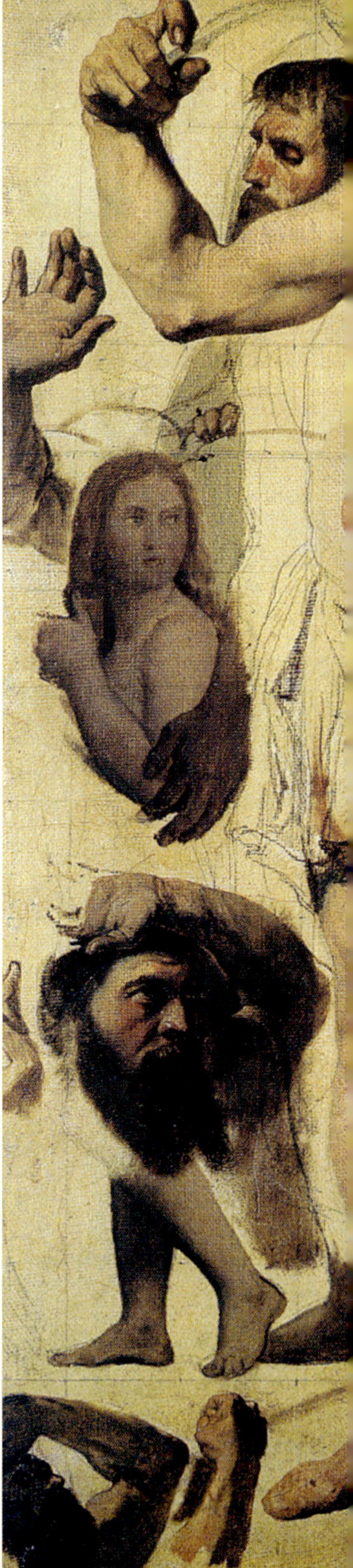

Study for *The Martyrdom of St. Symphorian*
1824–34, oil on canvas, 61x50
Montauban, Musée Ingres

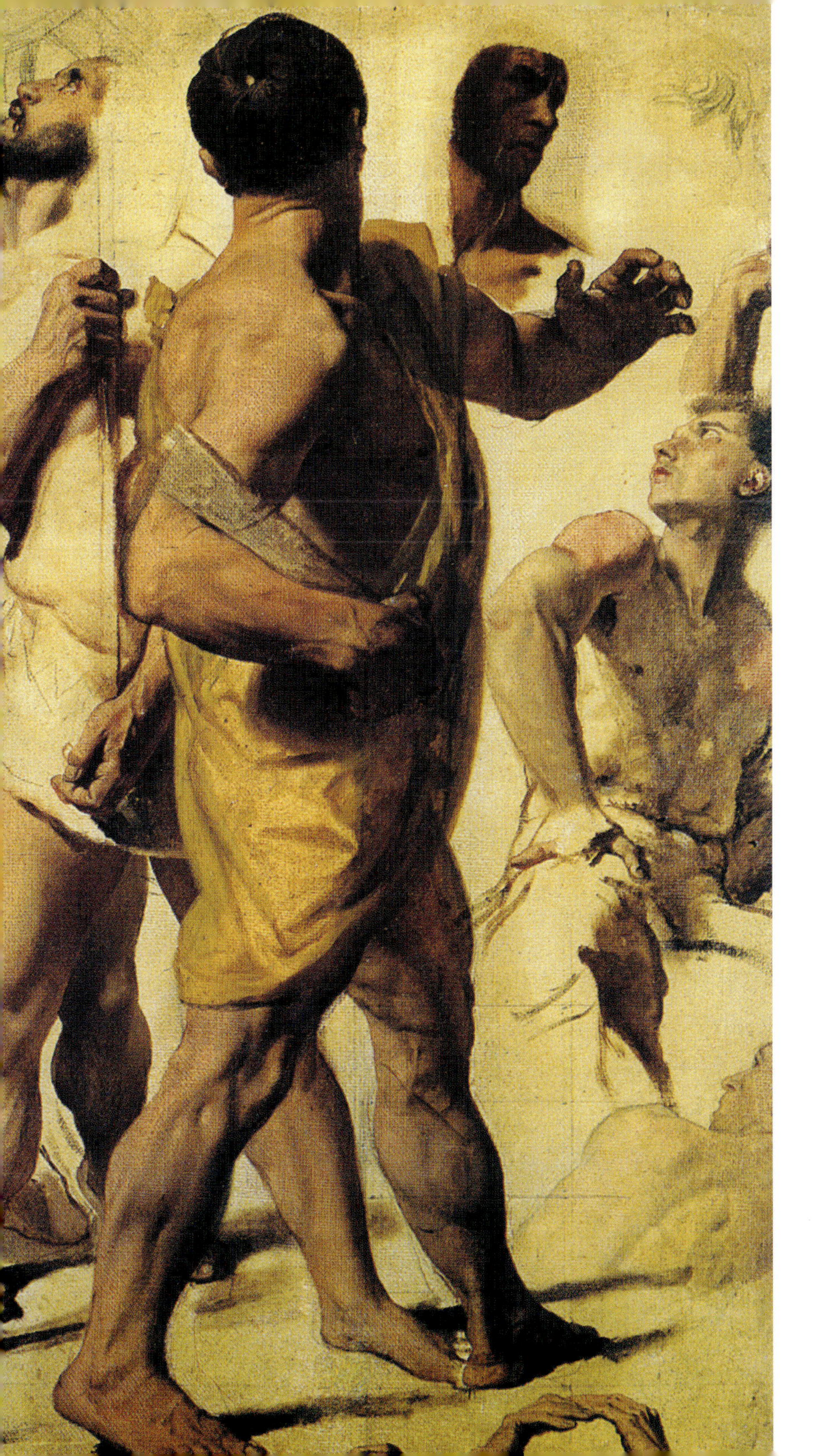

This Classical approach to the construction and the reading of pictures still held sway in the 19th century. But in the Romantic era, as the traditional hierarchy of the genres was undermined, as new expressive issues began to upset the strictly organized "discourse" of the work, and as other ways of painting – freer, more allusive, more founded on the magic of color than on the descriptive function of drawing – gained acceptance, this view of things suffered major losses in terms of its necessity and inner logic. In Ingres' lifetime it became no more than an anachronistic system doomed to an early death. And with the assembling of the various parts and the insertion of multiple details no longer justified by a valid approach, the picture "machine" started to seize up.

Made up of hundreds of small components laboriously fitted together, Ingres' *St. Symphorian* is the perfect illustration of the system's breakdown; and of its creator's immense, painful effort to "stick back together" the pieces of a crumbling tradition.

The Martyrdom of St. Symphorian
1834, oil on canvas, 407x339 cm
Autun, Cathedral of Saint-Lazare

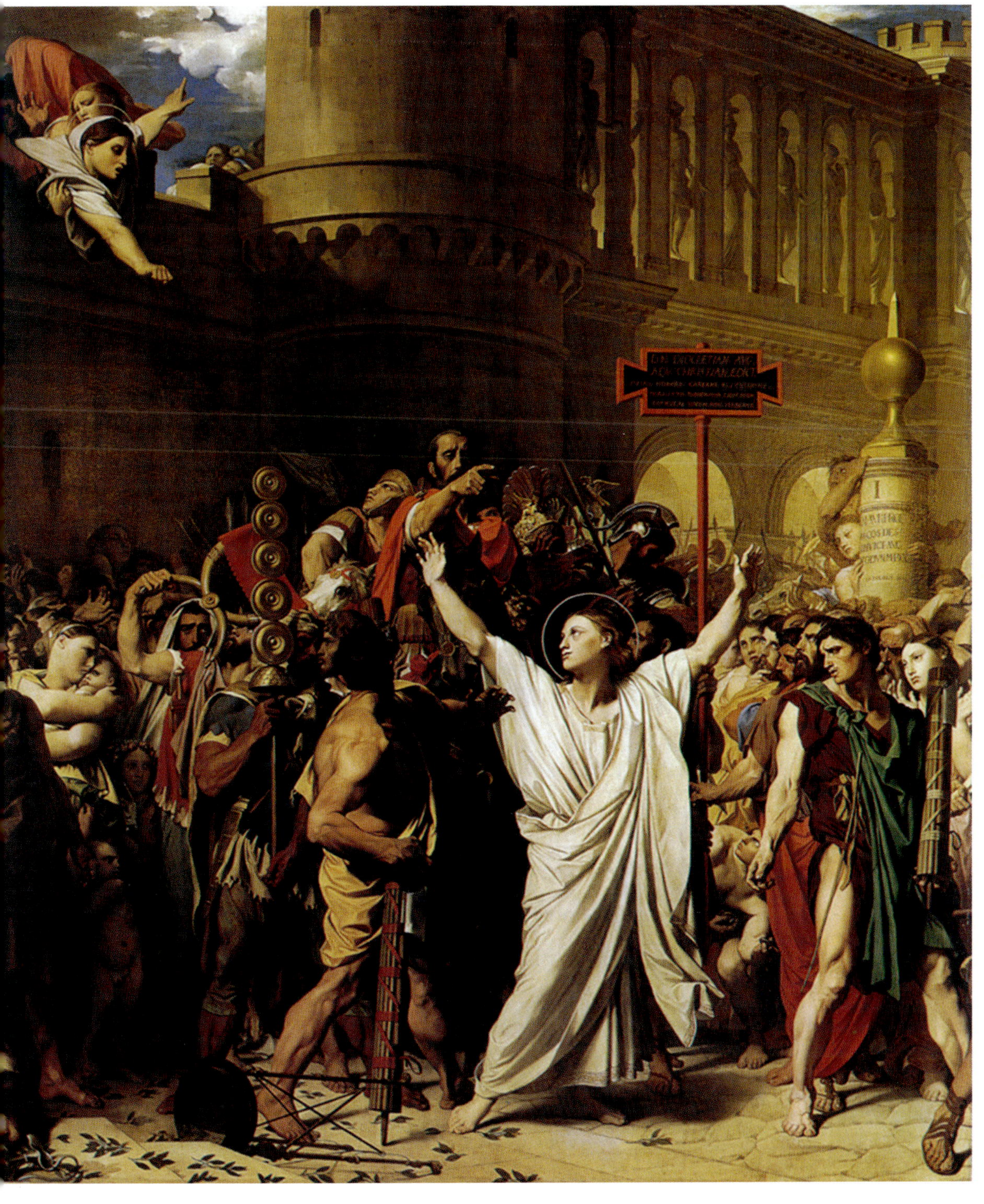

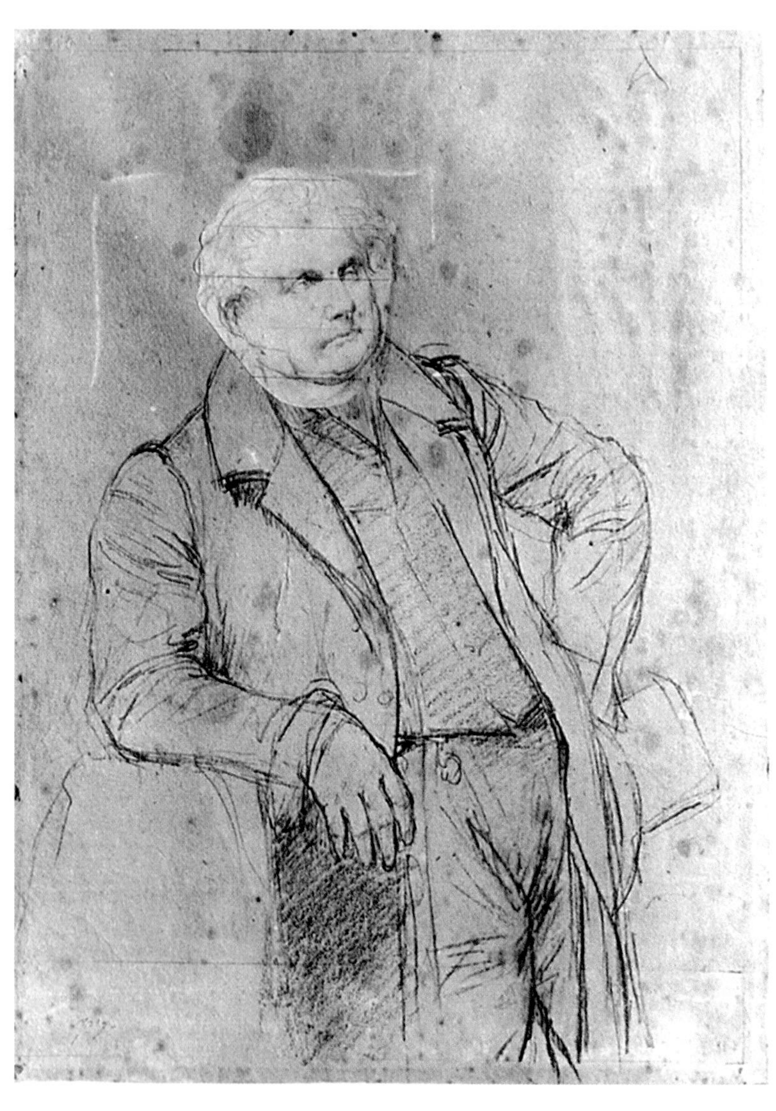

Study for the *Portrait of Louis-François Bertin*
1833, black chalk and pencil on paper,
37.6x26.7 cm
Montauban, Musée Ingres

Monsieur Bertin, or the Portrait of an Epoch

This effort was also devoted to the acquisition of new qualities: a formal power, relief and energy that might have seemed to go counter to Ingres' sensibility had he not, just before *St. Symphorian*, painted the staggering *Portrait of Louis-François Bertin*.

Ingres complained endlessly about having to paint portraits. A lifelong burden – initially out of necessity and then as a result of his success – they represented "a considerable waste of time, and of efforts rendered fruitless by the dryness of the genre, which is utterly anti-beautiful and picturesque..." The "genre" was "dry" because it revolved around the imitation of a model lacking in grandeur: "The history painter shows the species in general; while the portrait painter represents only the specific individual – a model often ordinary and full of shortcomings." In fact Ingres never stuck strictly to the limitations of the genre or to mere likeness. As we have seen, from the very beginning his portraits embodied innovative, sophisticated stylistic experiments, as the artist set out to capture the truth of his subjects. The creation of a portrait was sometimes a very long – up to several years – process, and one full of difficulties. And this because Ingres was just as artistically demanding here as in his other work.

Louis François Bertin was a publisher. In 1800 he and his brother Bertin de Veaux had founded the *Journal des Débats*, which advocated a constitutional monarchy. The Empire brought him endless difficulties – prison, exile, confiscation of his publication – and he only got his paper back with the Restoration, when it became the voice of the upper-middle business classes under Louis-Philippe.

Bertin was also a collector – he owned *The Burial of Atala*, a major work by Girodet – and appreciated the company of artists, often inviting Victor Hugo, Berlioz, and the painter Victor Orsel to his home. His son Edouard, a painter who studied in Ingres' atelier, was the intermediary between the painter and his model.

Ingres had begun with a first version showing Bertin standing, as in the Montauban drawing, firstly full face and then in three-quarter view. But he was not satisfied and Amaury-Duval has left us a precious account of the genesis of the final work:

One day Monsieur Ingres told me of the countless difficulties he had experienced with this portrait. "It was impossible...I had no ideas...what I did was bad...I could not finish it as things stood. But I had the good fortune to find myself dealing with the best and most intelligent of men. Monsieur Bertin came from Bièvres expressly to pose for me. He had already granted me a large number of sittings and there I was forced to tell him it was all for nothing. I was mortified, but I had the courage to do it...And do you know what he replied? 'My dear Ingres, don't worry about me, and above all stop torturing yourself. You want to start from the beginning again? As you wish. You will never wear me out and for as long as you need me I shall be at your command.' That really brightened me up...I asked him to take a break, as I intended to do, and later it came right...and I painted the portrait you have seen.' Monsieur Bertin himself...spoke to me of the pain Ingres' despair caused him during the sittings. 'He wept...and I spent my time consoling him. Finally we agreed to start over. One day Ingres had dined here and, just as we are doing today, we were drinking coffee on this very spot. I was chatting with a friend and, it seems, I had taken the pose of the portrait. Ingres got to his feet, came over and, almost whispering, said: 'Come and pose tomorrow, your portrait's done.' So I began the sittings again the next day...and in less than a month the portrait was finished."[28]

The effect of the work is one of "total" physical and psychological realism. Formally the ingredients are a skilful dose of extreme realism in the purest Flemish tradition – the pitiless description of the face, and the reflection of the window both on the chair-back and on the spectacles hanging from the belt echo Van Eyck – plus a stylization worthy of the Renaissance masters: a pyramidal sketch; a clarity of composition and color from which only the basic essentials emerge; and an emphasis on contour that makes the silhouette stand out against its neutral backdrop. All these factors combine to highlight the picture's principal idea: the force and eloquence of a moment seized as it occurred. We have the impression that Bertin is about to reply to his interlocutor, yet at the same time there is nothing fleeting about this lifelikeness: seemingly absolutely sure of the arguments he is going to put, Bertin is the very image of certainty. Balanced by the arms arching out over the thighs, his substantial body is as immovable as the determination we read in his face. This is a portrait of willpower. The artist's contemporaries understood and acclaimed the "moral" realism of the work, and in 1846 Baudelaire, for whom Ingres was "the only man in France who really makes portraits," would write: "The portraits of Monsieur Bertin, Monsieur Molé and Madame d'Haussonville are true portraits, that is to say the ideal reconstruction of individuals." [29]

He would later produce a definition that seems made for Ingres: "A good portrait always looks to me like a dramatized biography." [30]

Charles Blanc resumed in a few words the masterly summary Ingres had achieved here: "With what force does this individual, caught down to the last detail, represent the upper middle class he belongs to and whose general features he typifies!" [31] Edouard Manet saw Bertin as a symbol: "Monsieur Ingres chose old Bertin to stylize a whole era: he made him the Buddha of the affluent bourgeoisie, sated and triumphant." [32]

Far from accepting any inherent "destiny," which would have made the portrait the narrow representation of "one person in particular," the artist has created a human type, and even a social archetype: in other words, he has expressed "the species in general." As a perceptive commentator put it in 1833, "Monsieur Ingres is a portraitist in the manner of the masters, who composed their portraits as history paintings." We may feel that, better than in his sweeping compositions, it was with portraits like this one that Ingres attained to the epic grandeur of history painting. But he himself did not see things this way.

Portrait of Louis-François Bertin
1833, oil on canvas, 116x95 cm
Paris, Musée du Louvre

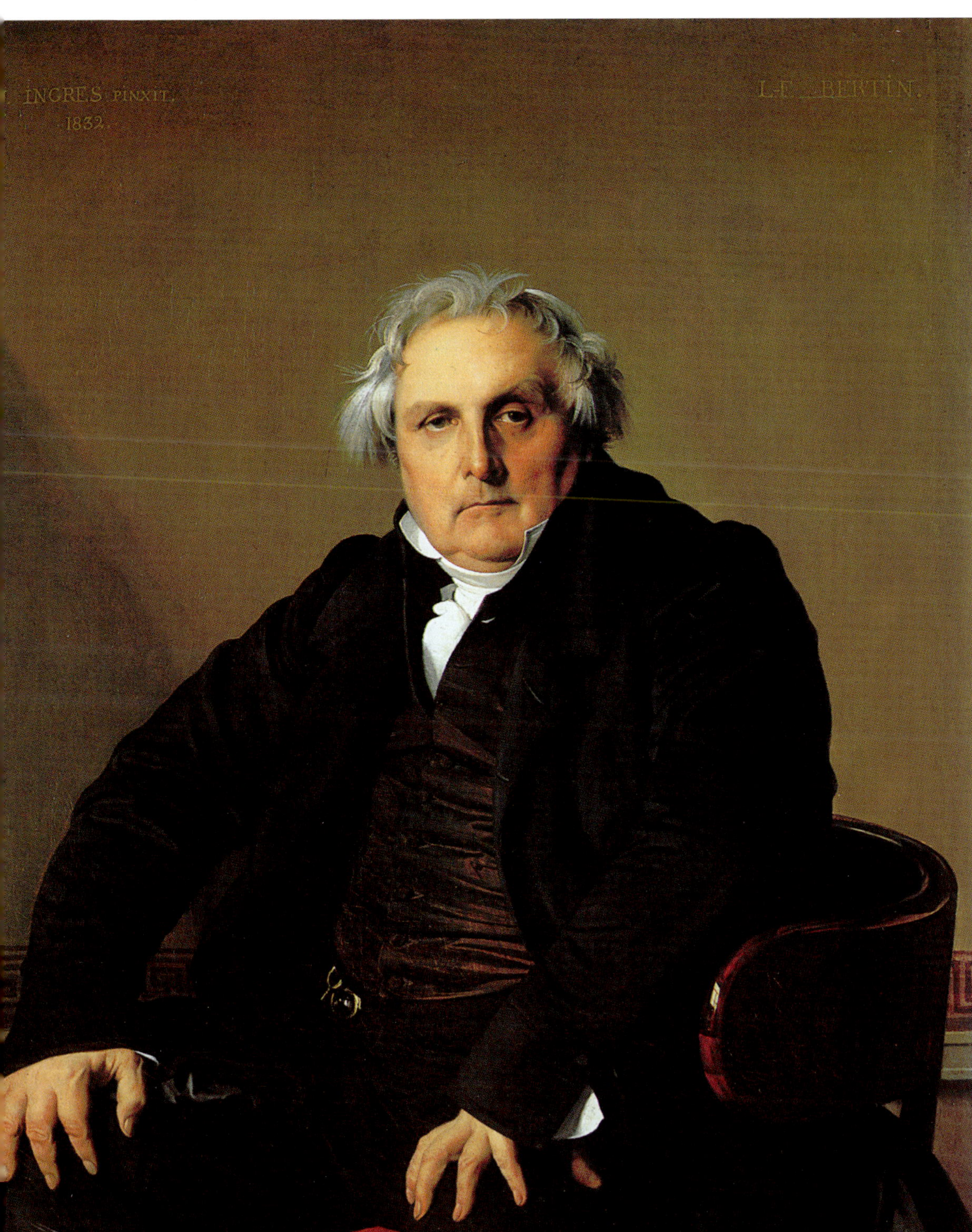
INGRES PINXIT
1832
L.F. BERTIN

Return to the Villa Medici

The failure of *St. Symphorian* at the 1834 Salon was intolerable to Ingres. He had pinned his highest ambitions on the picture and at fifty-four he put up with the critics no better than in his youth. He swore never to show again at the Salon, asked for and was given the directorship of the Académie de France in Rome, and left Paris. This new "retirement" would last six years.

The bubbling social scene the Villa Medici had known under his predecessor Horace Vernet thus gave way to an era of austerity. Amaury-Duval speaks of evenings when all was dark and mournful: "A lamp in each corner of this immense room...a lamp on the table, and by the table, Madame Ingres holding her knitting; and in the middle of a group, Monsieur Ingres speaking earnestly. But no shadow of another woman, black clothing only, and nothing to give pleasure to the eye. And the students had something stilted and ill at ease about them, as we always did in the master's presence..." [33]

Fortunately music played a major part in the life of the Villa. Ingres had the soul of a musician, and used a musical metaphor when explaining the way a painter should react to nature: "If I could turn you all into musicians, you would become better painters. In nature all is harmony: too much or too little upsets the scale and creates a false note. You must learn to sing true with the pencil or the brush, just as with the voice. Forms require accurate pitch just as sounds do."

Curiously, this lover of the Greeks and Raphael was open to modern music. He loved Beethoven, liked Weber and Berlioz, invited Franz Liszt and Fanny Mendelssohn. Charles Gounod, then a resident, wrote, "He was mad about music; he loved Haydn, Mozart and Beethoven passionately, and Gluck above all...For a long time I lived on familiar terms with him and I can state that he was someone simple, direct, open, full of candor and drive and an enthusiasm that sometimes rendered him eloquent. He had the affections of a child and the indignations of an apostle..." [34]

The indignations could be total. One day when Stendhal was visiting and imprudently ventured a criticism of Beethoven, Ingres turned his back and said to the porter, "I shall never be at home to this gentleman." Intolerant and fanatical, he was intransigent where his sacred values were concerned. And art was his true religion.

"I admire Monsieur Ingres," wrote the critic Auguste Jal, "and I shall tell you why: because, in this century of doubt and indifference he has a faith, a burning faith incapable of compromise." [35] True, this faith was founded on an ever-acute sensibility, on the fervor and candor of esthetic emotion, and on the sincerity of total commitment – all of which helped ensure the freshness of his oeuvre. But that same faith ossified into the authoritarian, intellectually limited doctrine that marked his teaching. Through this teaching, dispensed in his Paris atelier from 1825 onwards, then at the Beaux-Arts and the Villa Medici, and through the power he enjoyed as a member of the Institut de France, Ingres had an enormous influence. Like David before him he truly was the leader of a school; it was not for nothing that the movement he generated became known as "Ingrism."

The fundamentals of his teaching approach were studies from the life model, the art of antiquity, and the Renaissance masters, above all Raphael: "Students will divide their time between the study of nature and of the masters, with the main emphases on Phidias, the low reliefs of the Parthenon and ancient sculpture in general; on the Roman and Florentine painters, and the engravings of Muretus." At the Louvre he advised his pupils to put on "blinkers, as for horses," so as not to see what he considered harmful: Rubens, for instance, and more generally anything that strayed from the Classical path. His precepts, as we find them in his notebooks or those of his students, were often contradictory: they can be justified in terms of his own work and personal experimentation, but as a teaching program they are rigid and doctrinaire.

Drawing was traditionally the basis of art studies, but Ingres made it a fundamental, quasi-exclusive principle of painting. Here are some of his best-known maxims:

— Drawing is the integrity of art.

— To draw is not simply to reproduce contours. Drawing does not lie simply in line: drawing is expression, inner form, plane and relief. What more is there apart from that? Drawing includes more than three quarters of what makes up painting. If I had to put a sign over my door, I would write: School of Drawing, and I am sure I would turn out good painters.

— Drawing includes everything, except color.

— You must draw all the time, with your eyes when you cannot draw with a pencil. As long as you fail to combine observation and practise, you will produce nothing good.

— Not a single day without drawing a line, said Appellus. By that he meant, and I repeat it: line is drawing, it's everything.

He was unstoppable when you got him onto drawing and form. Color, on the other hand, seemed to him all but superfluous:

— Color adds ornamentation to painting, but it is only painting's lady in waiting, for all it does is make art's true perfections more agreable.

— Rubens and Van Dyck may please the eye, but they deceive it; they are from a bad school of color, the school of the lie.

— No color too fiery: it's anti-historical. Fall victim to the gray rather than the fiery.

This is an extremely impoverished conception of color. Being a great artist, Ingres remained an original colorist in his own way; but his excessively docile pupils could not avoid "falling victim to the gray."

The Institut de France was not slow to reproach him with unduly influencing his pupils, whose *envois* were showing "systematic tendencies" more notably still, in 1838, there were complaints of "culpable negligence concerning the knowledge of the truth and power of color and an understanding of the different effects of light. A drab opacity characterizes the shading of all these pictures, whose ambience seems rigorously twilit."

Baudelaire would confirm this diagnosis: "Monsieur Ingres' pupils have quite pointlessly retained a semblance of color. They believe – or pretend to believe – that they are practicing painting." [36]

"Ingrism" did indeed take on a crepuscular character. One has the feeling that the master had expelled the last of the sap, and gathered in the last rays of sunlight of the great Classical tradition, leaving behind only a bloodless corpse, an empty shell to be shared out among pupils and uncritical followers. The doctrine Ingres had shaped to meet his own needs was balanced out in his work by sheer artistic instinct, but it became a straitjacket for pupils sitting piously at their master's knee. And despite the successful careers that awaited some of them, despite the historical recognition they are currently reaping for their revival of the mural and religious art under the Second Empire, their art suffers from chronic anemia, or worse. One has the impression that they were castrated by the man who loved to call them his "children." Only Théodore Chassériau became a truly great artist, but because he wasted no time in getting free of Ingres' influence and – the ultimate betrayal – opting for Delacroix. "Never speak to me of that child again," Ingres is reported to have said.

Ingrism reflected badly on Ingres to the extent that he could be held responsible for the academicism of his camp-followers. Nonetheless, these latter make excellent foils: we have only to compare Amaury-Duval's *Birth of Venus* with Ingres' version of the same subject, to see how the pitiful imitativeness of the former sets off the latter in all its radiant plenitude.

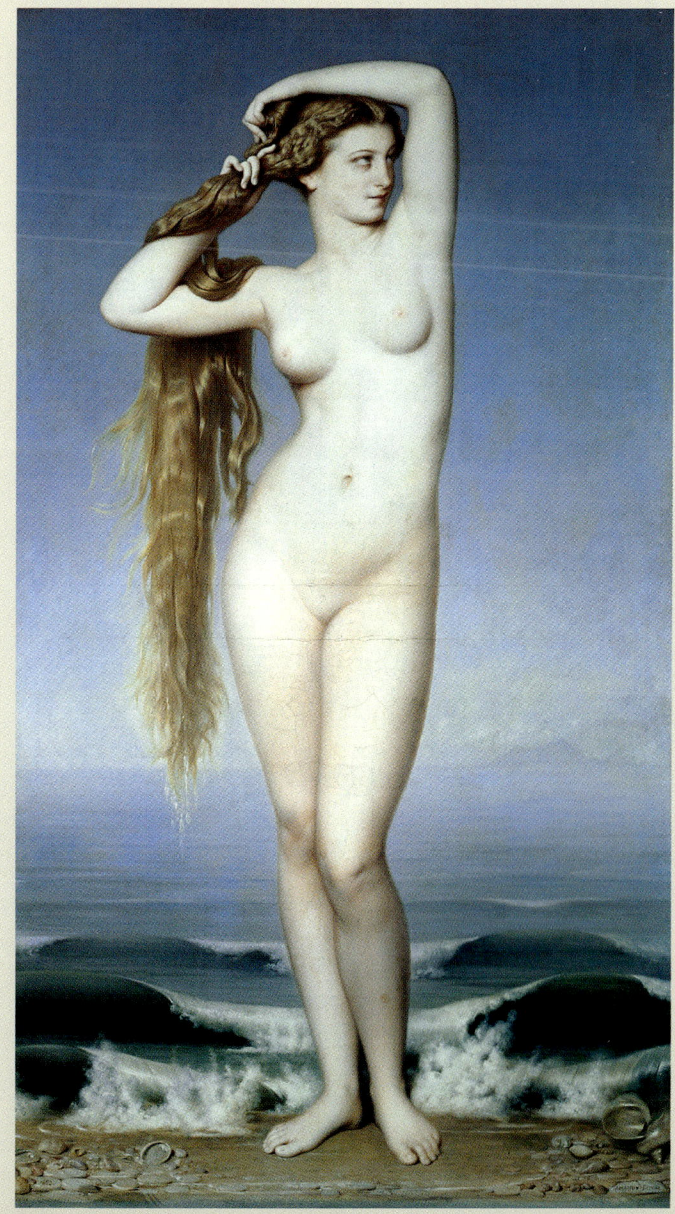

Eugène Emmanuel Amaury-Duval
The Birth of Venus
1850, oil on canvas, 210x92 cm
Lille, Musée des Beaux-Arts

The Most Beautiful Human Flower

"We see a young, blonde woman worn down by the wearying langorousness of the seraglio, her head leaning back on her crossed arms and the rippling waves of her hair. Her semi-nude body is twisted in a spasm of *ennui*. Perhaps some unappeased desire, some surging aspiration towards freedom is at work within this beautiful creature entombed in the harem, making her writhe on the mats and mosaics...All the details of costume and furnishings have that scrupulous accuracy that is one of Monsieur Ingres' qualities. There could be no better rendering of the mystery and suffocating silence of the seraglio: not a ray of sunlight, not a patch of blue sky, not a breath of wind in this cushioned cocoon, with its heady perfumes of tombac, amber and benjamin, where, far from all eyes, the most beautiful human flower is fading." [37]

Thus Théophile Gautier on *Odalisque with Female Slave*, one of the few paintings dating from Ingres' second stay in Rome.

The germ of the idea may have been Delacroix's *Women of Algiers in Their Apartment*, shown at the Salon in 1834, when Orientalism was the fashion, especially in the Romantic camp. Ingres' Orient, however,

Following pages
Odalisque with Female Slave
1839, oil on canvas, 72.4x100 cm
Cambridge, The Fogg Art Museum

has nothing exotic about it: it is simply an ideal imaginary setting for a favorite subject, that of the woman alone, in seclusion, and offered for the viewer's contemplation.

That Orient can also be an esthetic point of reference: for some of his contemporaries Ingres' work was informed by the principles attributed to the arts of the East. At the 1846 Salon the journalist and art critic Théophile Thoré declared that, "Monsieur Ingres' pictures are closer than we might think to the primitive paintings of the Oriental peoples, which are a kind of colored sculpture. Where does art begin for the Indians, the Chinese, the Egyptians and the Etruscans? With the low relief, to which color is applied. Then the relief is eliminated and only the external curve remains: the stroke, the line. Apply color to the interior of this elementary drawing and you have painting; but without air or space."

Odalisque with Female Slave derives from a highly sophisticated esthetic. Inspired by Persian miniatures, its space is built up like a kind of inlay whose countless details suggest the haunting modulations of Eastern music. Into this precious setting Ingres has placed one of his most beautiful nudes.

While taken from the great 16th-century models – Titian and Giorgione – this nude has no equivalent in the history of art. The torsion of the body, with a suppleness both animal and vegetal; the flesh, vacillating in tone between mother of pearl and skin of fruit; the pink profile curled beneath the arch of the arms: *Odalisque with Female Slave* offers a total, perfect image of voluptuousness. Only Matisse has ever achieved the musically replete sensuality of these arabesques.

What Ingres has done is to adapt the sinuous drawing of *Sleeping Woman, Nude*, also visible in various figures in *The Turkish Bath*. His entire oeuvre is built on the "migration" of the same motifs, from one work to another and from one end of his career to the other. Some commentators have seen a lack of imagination here, but in fact this creative "economy" is the sign of the painter's obsessiveness: this clinging to motifs systematically tied to female nudity is clearly part of a concern with the erotic. Throughout, Ingres' formal explorations, centered first and foremost on the human body, are quickened by the erotic instinct; and the fact that this instinct has been pared down, reflected on, broadened, and raised to the status of supreme form makes no difference whatever. This love of the human body, so immoderate, emotional and naive – "primal", we might say – brings form to life, makes it moving. This is what the "Ingrists" failed to grasp, lacking the courage to fire with a personal flame their pale, sexless nudes. On the other hand, many were those who used Orientalism as a pretext for ventures into the overtly erotic; appealing to the viewer's voyeurism, they too were light years away from Ingres' dazzling gravity.

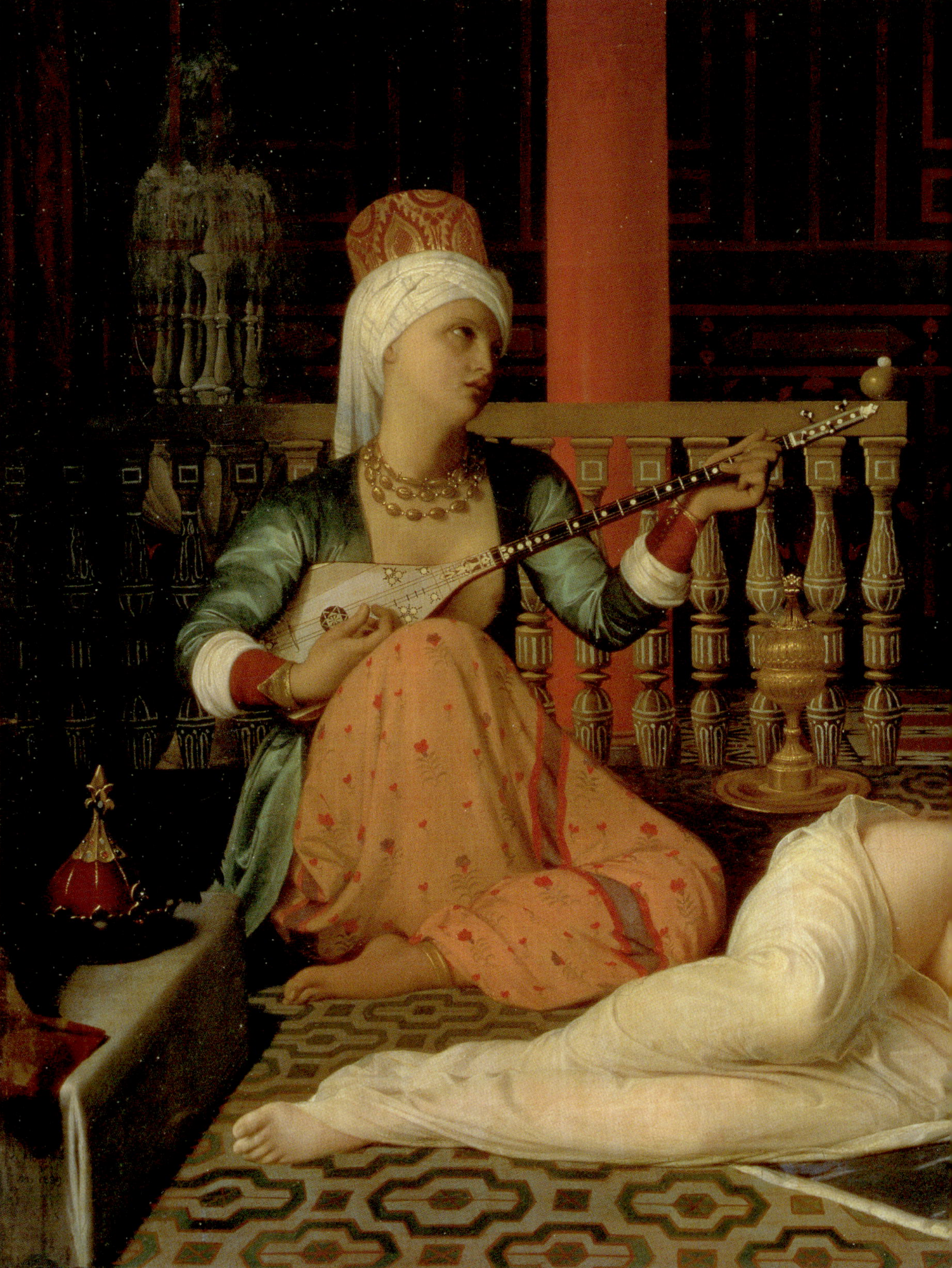

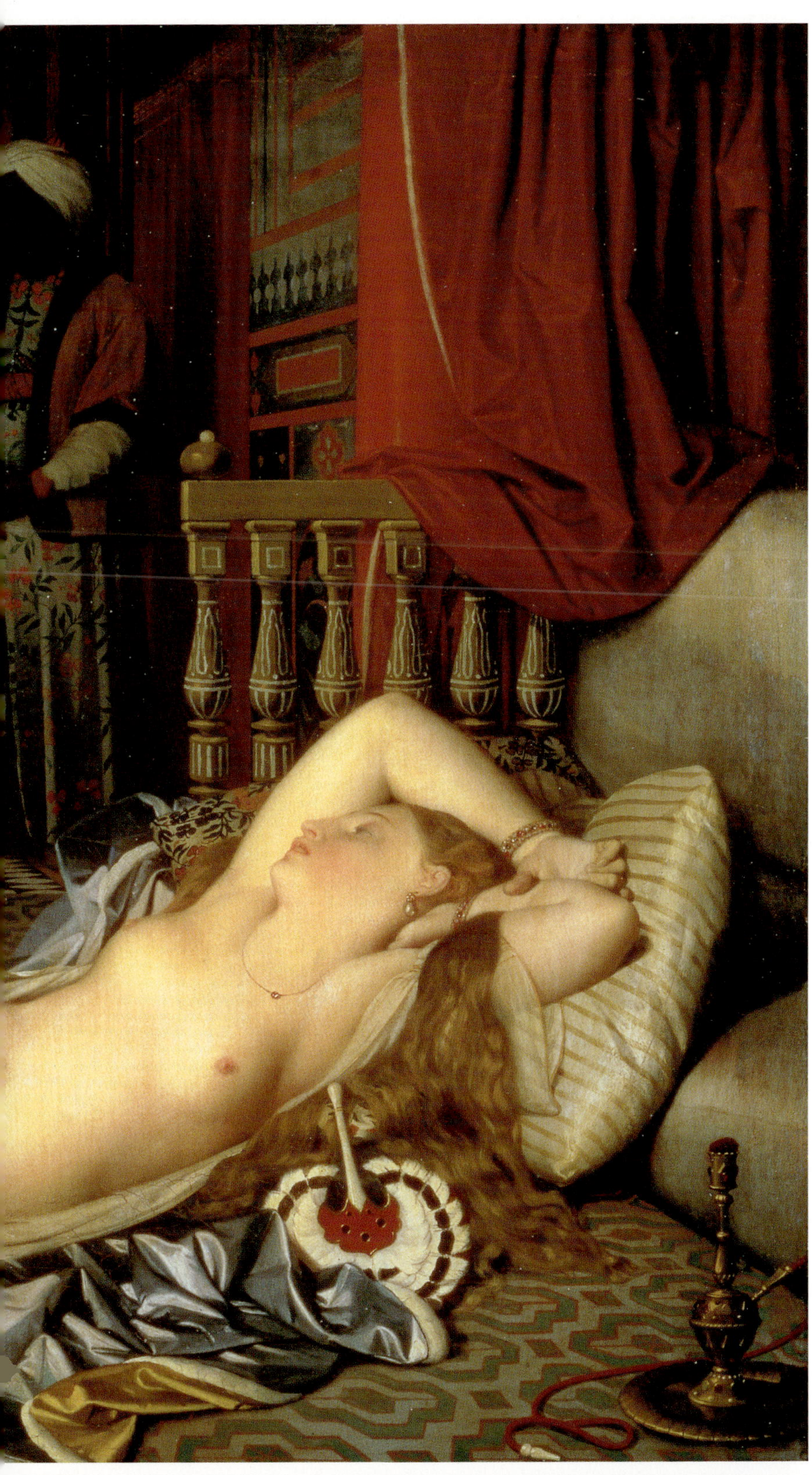

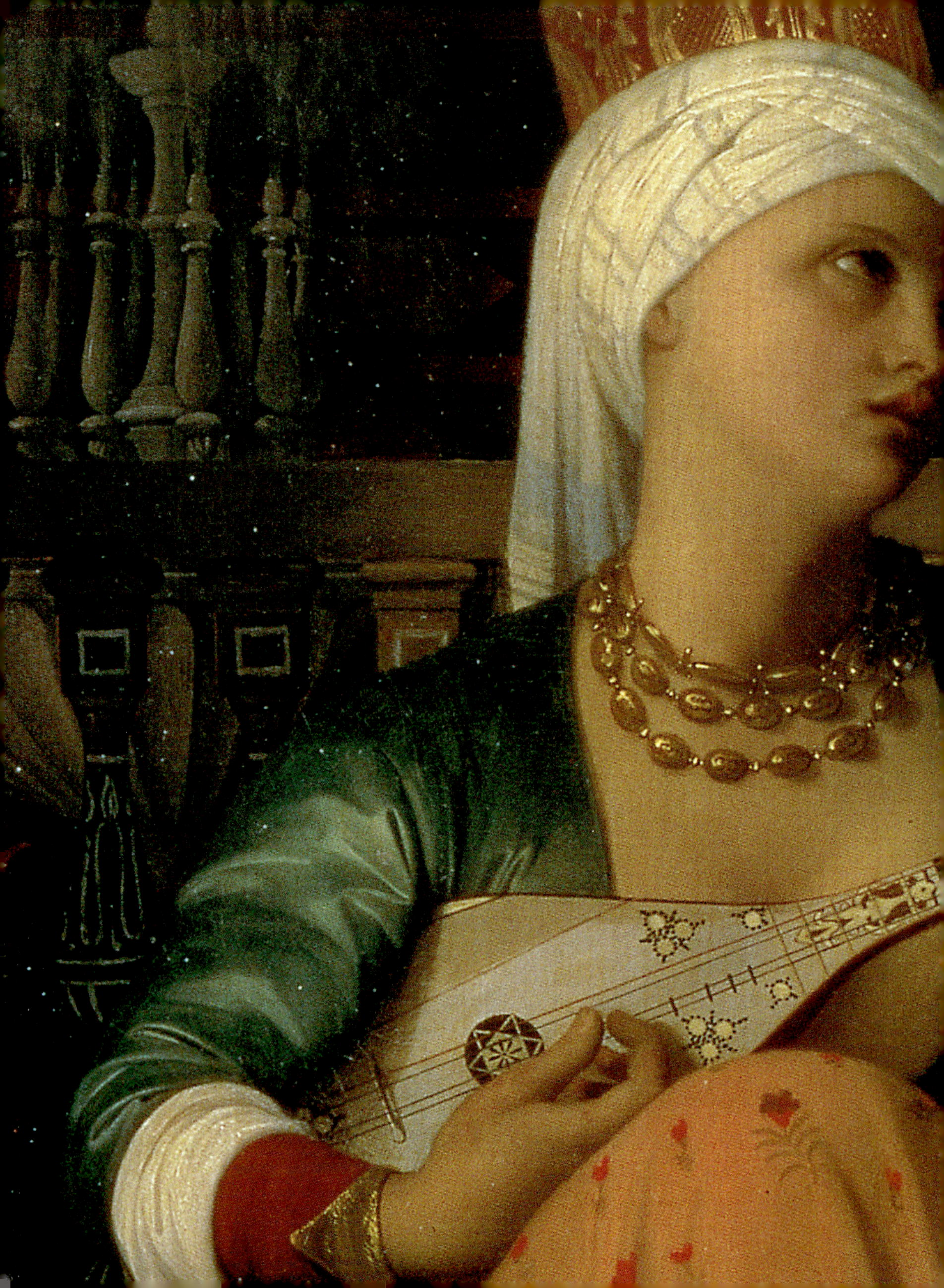

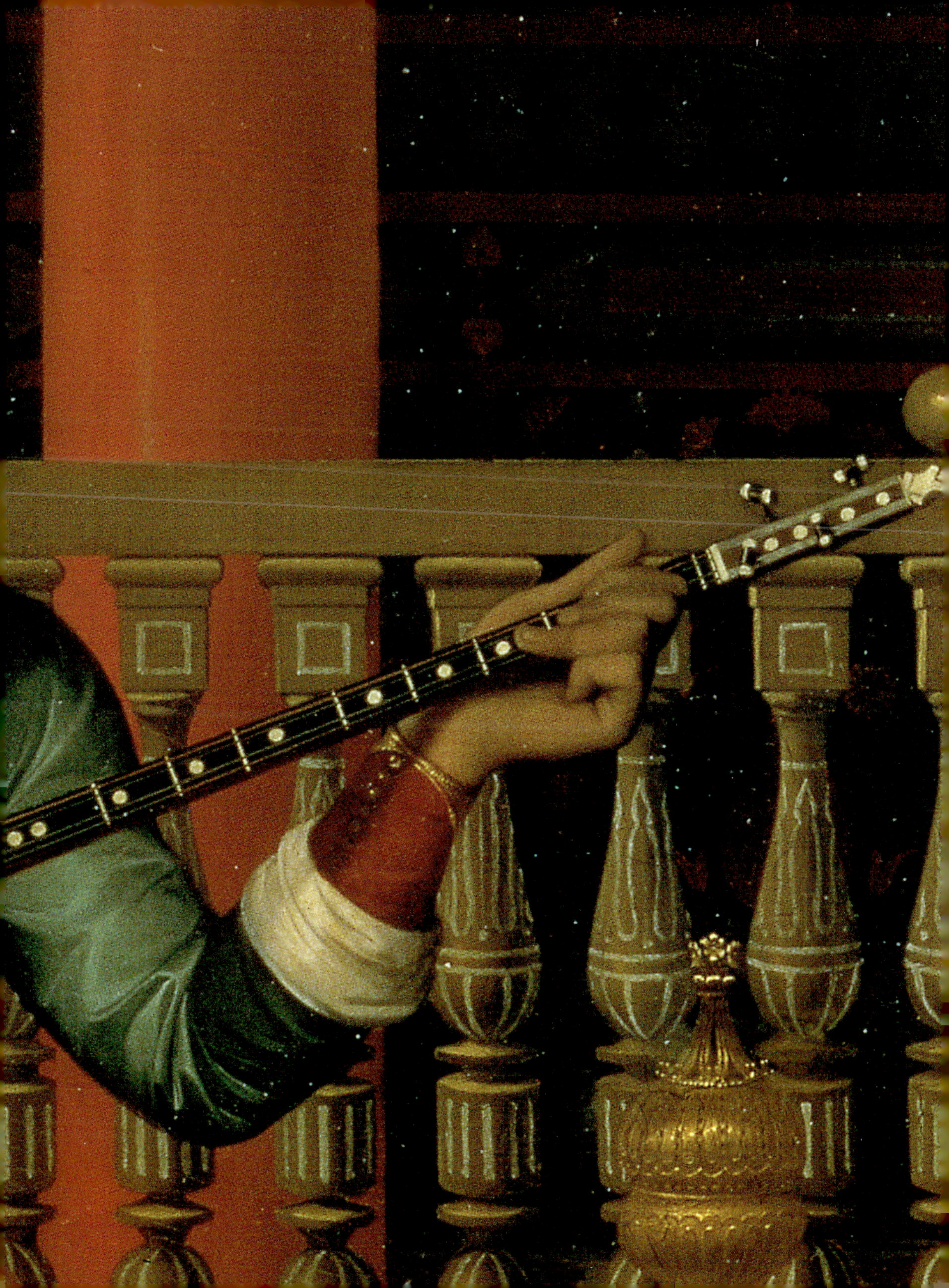

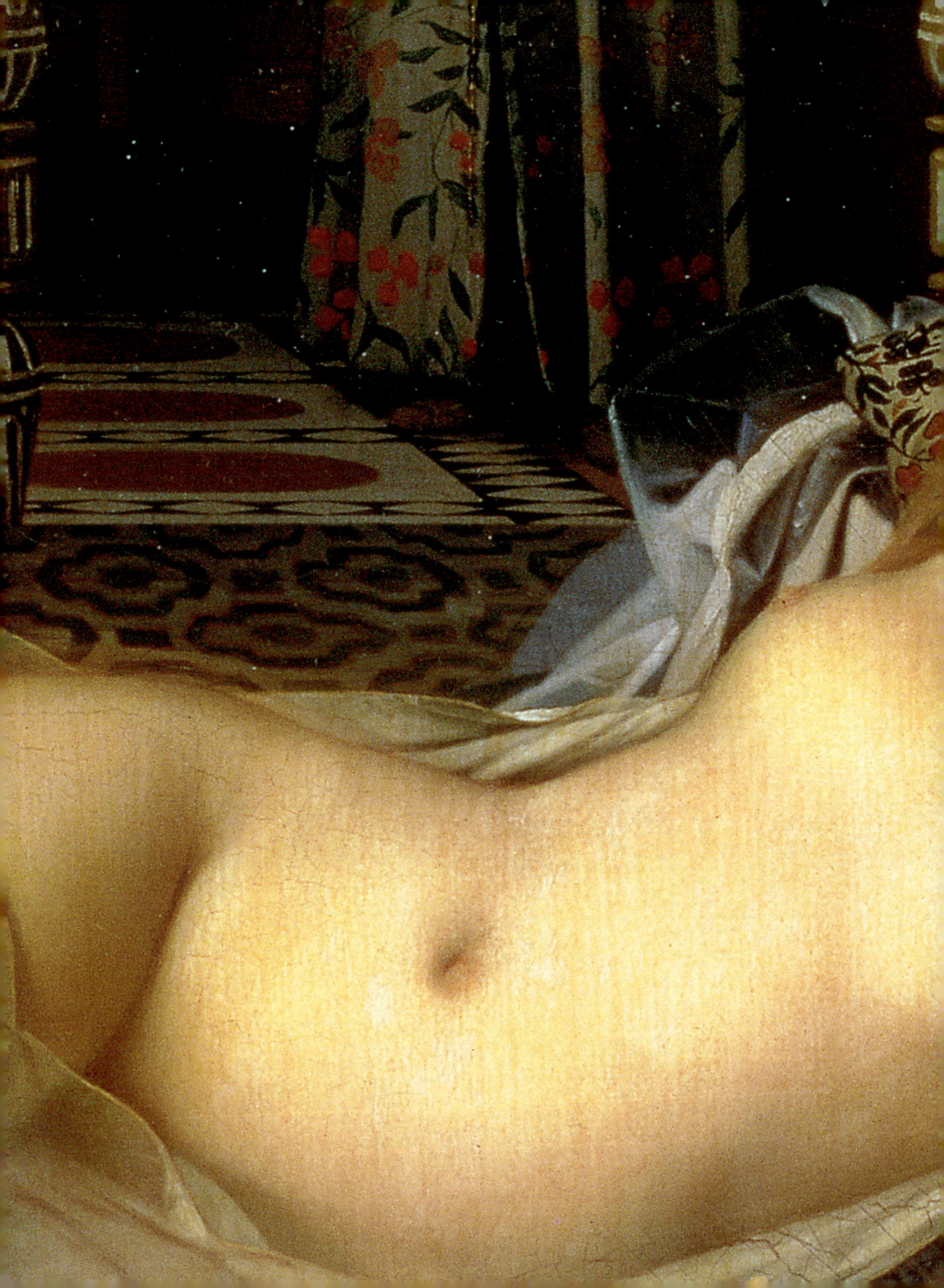

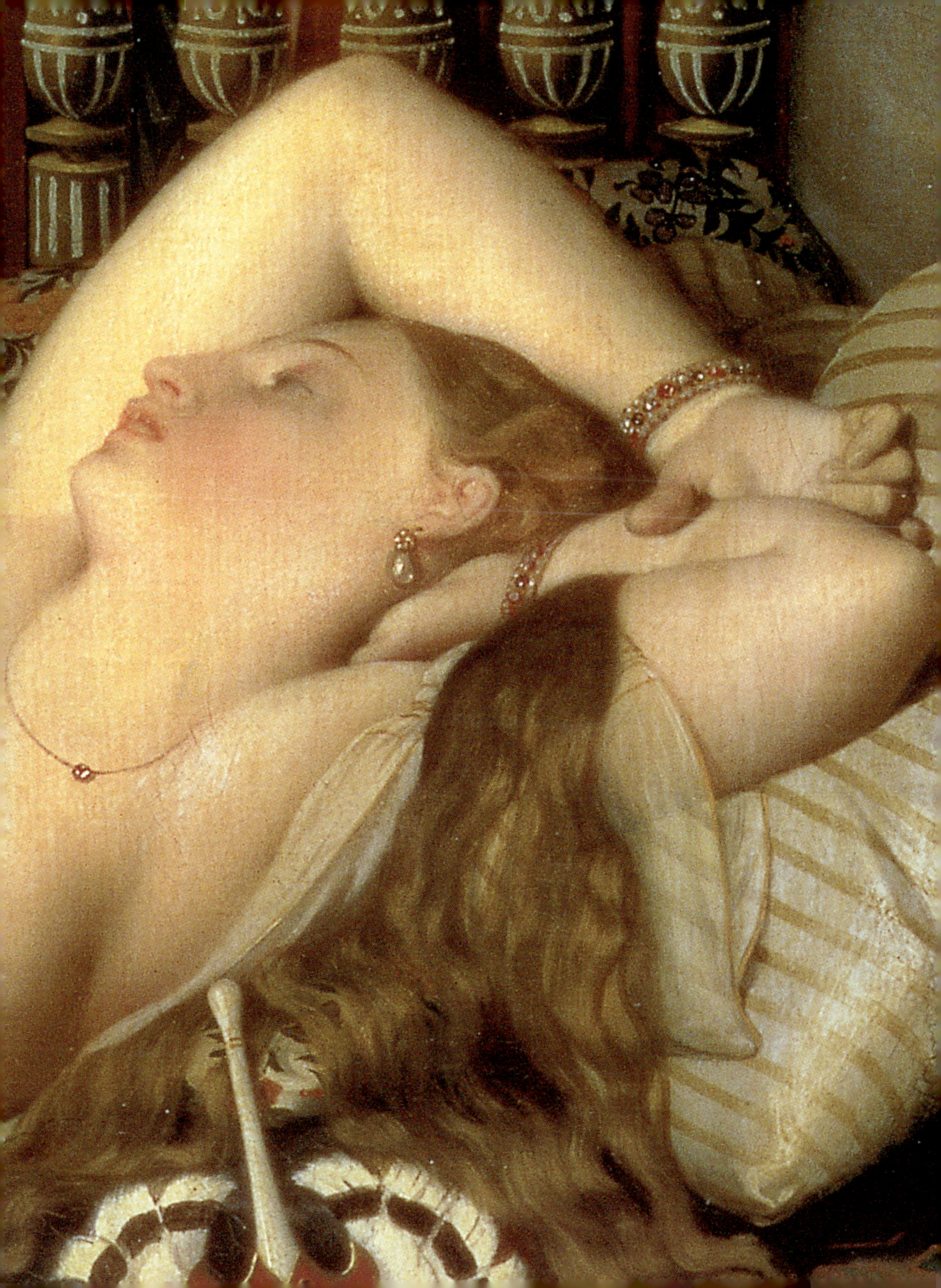

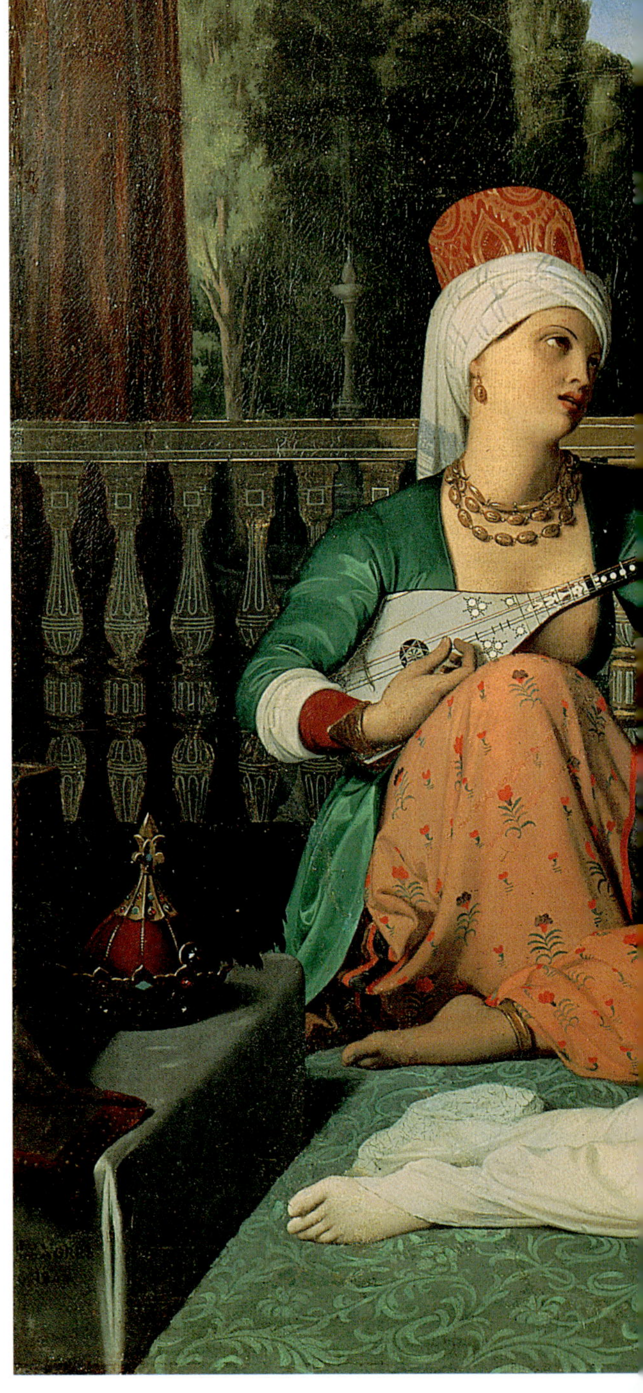

Jean Auguste Dominique Ingres,
Paul and Hippolyte Flandrin
Odalisque with Female Slave
1842, oil on canvas, 76x105 cm
Baltimore, The Walters Art Gallery

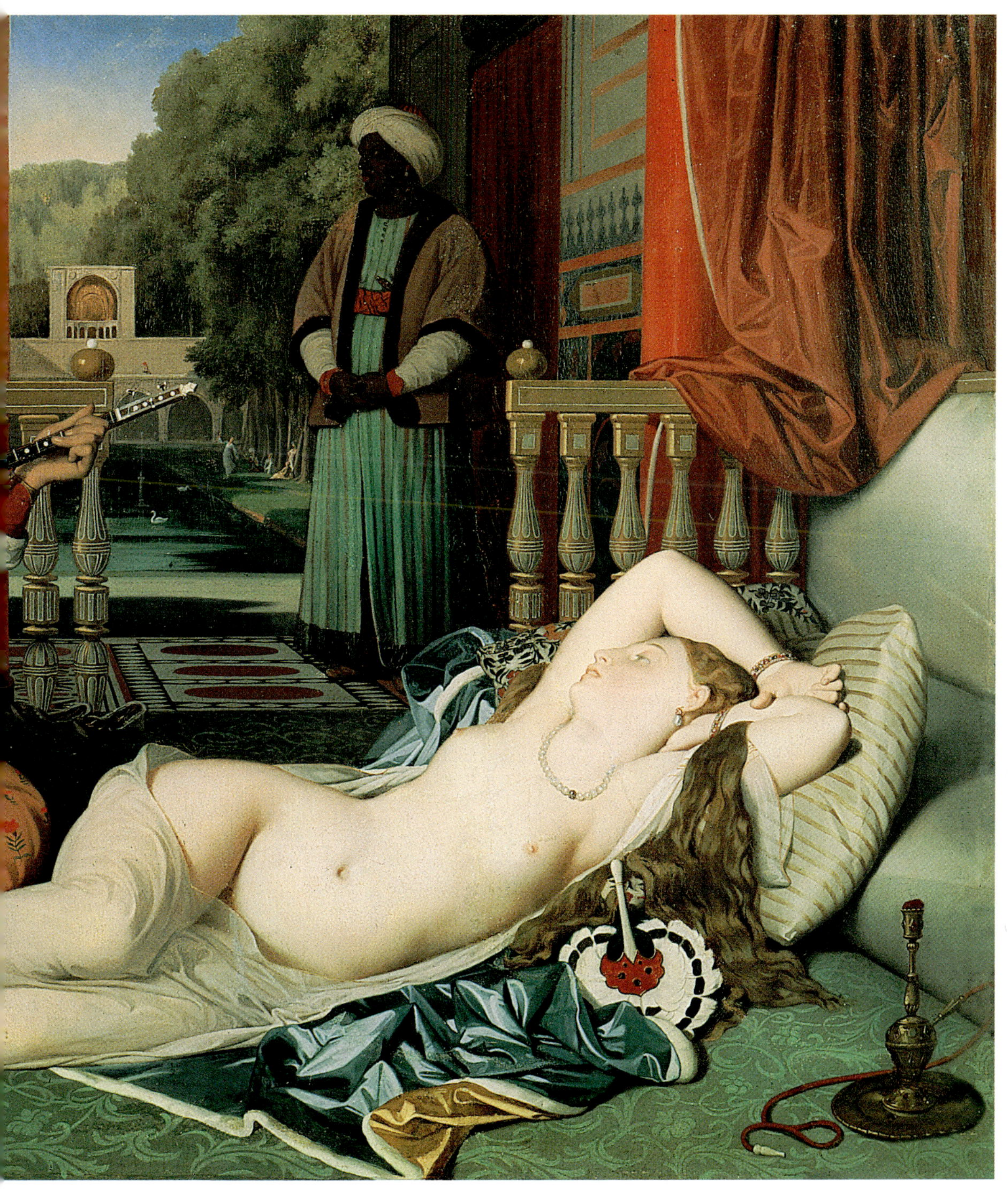

A Historical Miniature

Antiochus, son of Seleucis, king of Syria, is mortally ill. His physician Erasistratus discovers the source of his illness – love – on seeing him swoon at the sight of Stratonice, his youthful stepmother; and to save him, the king will relinquish his wife to his son. Taken from Plutarch, the subject exemplifies paternal magnanimity and abnegation.

Ingres himself described *Antiochus and Stratonice* as a "large historical miniature" and it is hard to imagine a better description for what looks like a painting of an interior, with the setting designed by a specialist (architect Victor Baltard), its pompous architectural realism and its dramatic action all reduced to delicious pantomime.

Antiochus and Stratonice and *Odalisque with Female Slave* were painted over the same period and derive from the same miniaturist style. But while the latter charms and convinces like a melodious love song, the former disappoints with a kind of expressive stinginess and insignificance. The painting is exquisite, the poses delightful and the draperies matchless; but it is all too pretty and slight for a subject of this weight.

For, even sanctioned by Plutarch, the subject remains tricky: a son sexually desires his father's wife, and the father gives her up to him. In the 19th century this story smacking of incest was inevitably perceived differently than in antiquity, morals having changed considerably over the centuries.

Given that the basic essentials of the scene take place in a bed, and that this bed is the picture's dominant visual element, and given that the crux of the story is possession of a woman firstly by the father and then by the son, it has to be said that this exemplary story could be a source of reprehensible ideas. Which means that the painting, openly adopting the noble style of classical tragedy, looks suspiciously proper. And indeed, this is the stumbling block: a story of sexual possession and mortal passion is approached in the chastely moralizing mode of the history painting. Once again we could say, "It's the opposite of farce." Knowing at the same time that extremes meet.

Antiochus and Stratonice
1840, oil on canvas, 57x98 cm
Chantilly, Musée Condé

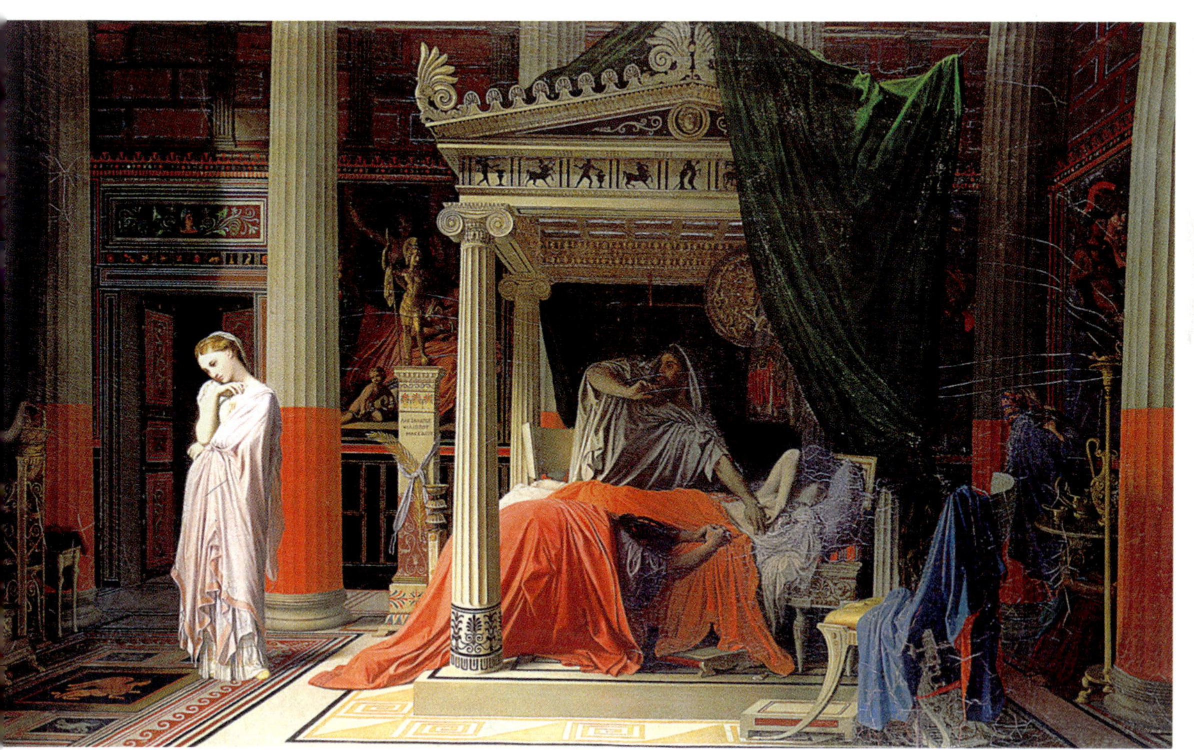

This Absurd Use of Color

Throughout the 19th century Ingres' drawing was widely appreciated and his use of color deprecated.

It was Delacroix, with his pitiless perspicacity, who summed up his limits in this field: "He confuses coloring-in, with color...Have you noticed in *Antiochus and Stratonice* that there's any amount of ingenious color work – very elegant, very shimmery – that leaves no color effect whatever? There's a floor mosaic that would drive a teacher of perspective to distraction; in all maybe a thousand little pieces with all the lines of flight exactly right. But that doesn't stop the mosaic from standing up as straight as a wall..." He goes on to attack "the light drawn with ruler and compass. You have the feeling it's there forever and that Monsieur Ingres' sun will never move in relation to the earth...The only thing he's forgotten is the reflections. Oh yes, the reflections. He's never heard of them. He has no idea that in nature everything is reflection and that all of color is an exchange of reflections." Ingres applies color "the way you sprinkle decoration on a well-cooked cake." Like something superfluous, Delacroix means. And his tones "remain crude, unrelated, cold, shrill." [38]

An all too accurate assessment.

Théophile Silvestre was just as lucid: "As the falseness of tone clashes with the precision of line, the figures advance or withdraw in an unnatural way, and the image is so implausible that all the viewer can do is give up. The various planes are marked out – in vain; the figures have been given linear perspective – in vain; for this absurd use of color ruins everything, emptying what should be full, filling what should be empty, destroying distance, eliminating atmosphere, stacking the figures and then flattening them against each other like a pack of cards." [39]

Baudelaire was cutting too, but subtler: "It is generally agreed that Monsieur Ingres' painting is gray. Open your eyes, nation of idiots: have you ever seen painting brighter and more garish – and a more determined exploration of tone?" [40]

"Monsieur Ingres adores color the way a milliner does. It gives one both pain and pleasure to observe the effort he puts into choosing and combining his tones. The result, not always discordant, but bitter and violent, often appeals to corrupt poets..." [41]

These criticisms are hardly surprising, given that Ingres himself made no secret of the secondary role he gave to color. But to condemn him as a poor colorist, as so often happens, is unjustified. That he had never thought color through, as Delacroix had, is obvious, but we only have to look at the oeuvre to be aware that the role of color is a significant – if different – one. It does not have the expressive function assigned to it by Delacroix, but rather a decorative value often independent of the subject.

Color for Ingres can involve mere "coloring-in," the most extreme subtlety, or a daring unique in his time. Color is put at the service of drawing and form, sustaining them on the picture surface and thus enhancing the abstract organization of the picture. What seemed to Delacroix and the rest of the 19th century a primal approach to color – "primitivist" would be a better description, given Ingres' closeness in this respect to the Italian primitives, or to Oriental painting – would come to be seen in the 20th century as a pre-Modernist approach. "Emptying what should be full, filling what should be empty," of flattening the figures "like a pack of cards," and preferring frontal representation to the tradition of spatial depth: this much-denigrated method would be exactly what attracted the Moderns.

IV The Golden

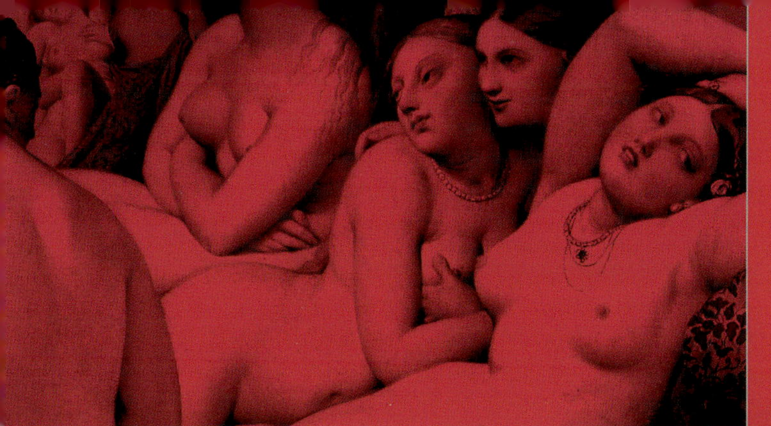

Fruit

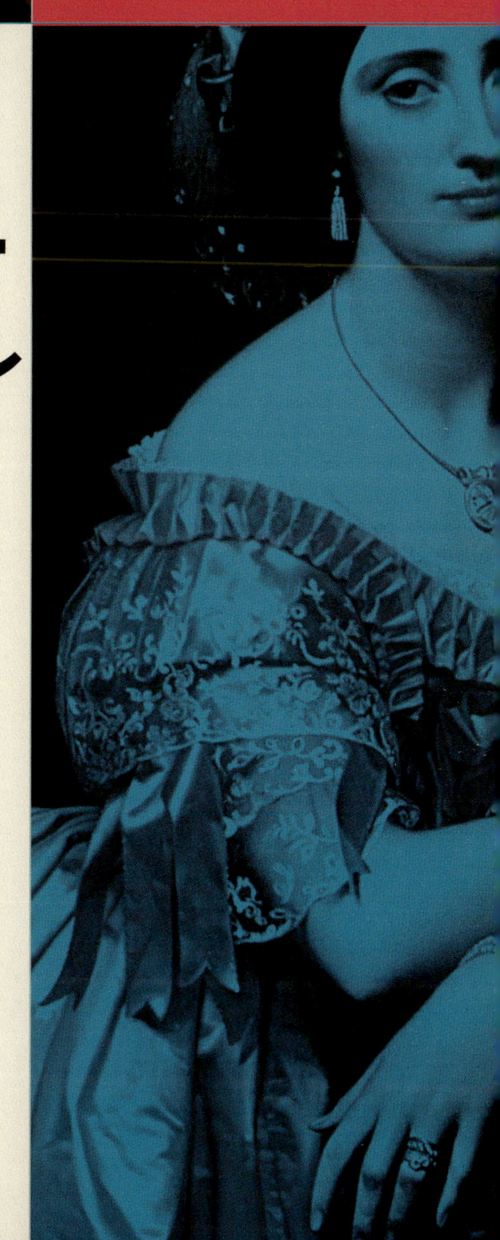

"Nudes, and Nothing but Nudes!"

Portrait of Duke Ferdinand-Philippe of Orléans
1842, oil on canvas, 158x131 cm
Private collection

On his return to France in 1841, Ingres was welcomed as a "national treasure." The Marquis of Pastoret, whose portrait he had painted in 1826, organized a colossal banquet; Louis-Philippe received him at Versailles; and in 1845 he was made a Commander of the Legion of Honor. Painted only months before the accidental death of its subject, his *Portrait of Duke Ferdinand-Philippe of Orléans* (1842) was known everywhere via a host of copies and became a sort of national icon.

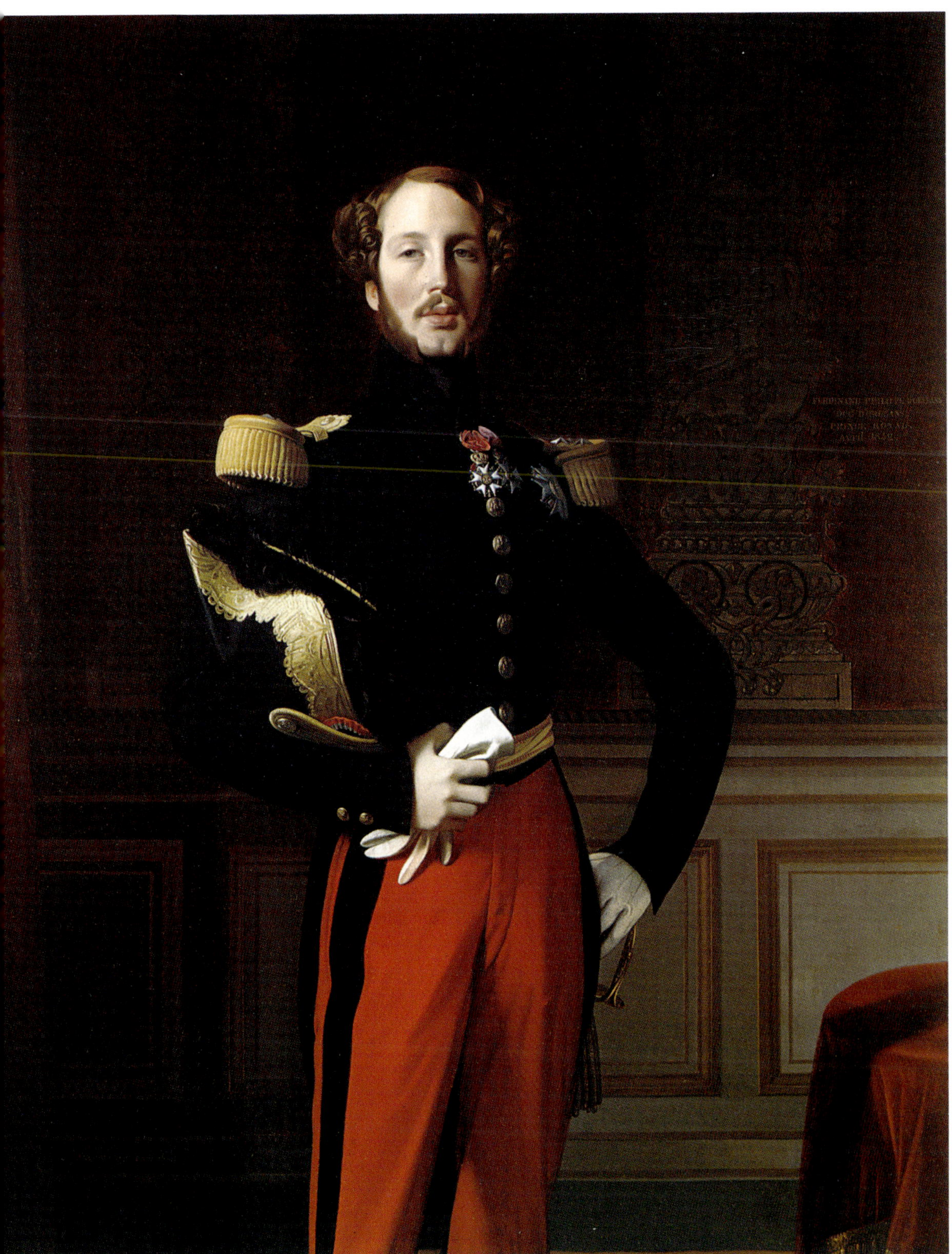

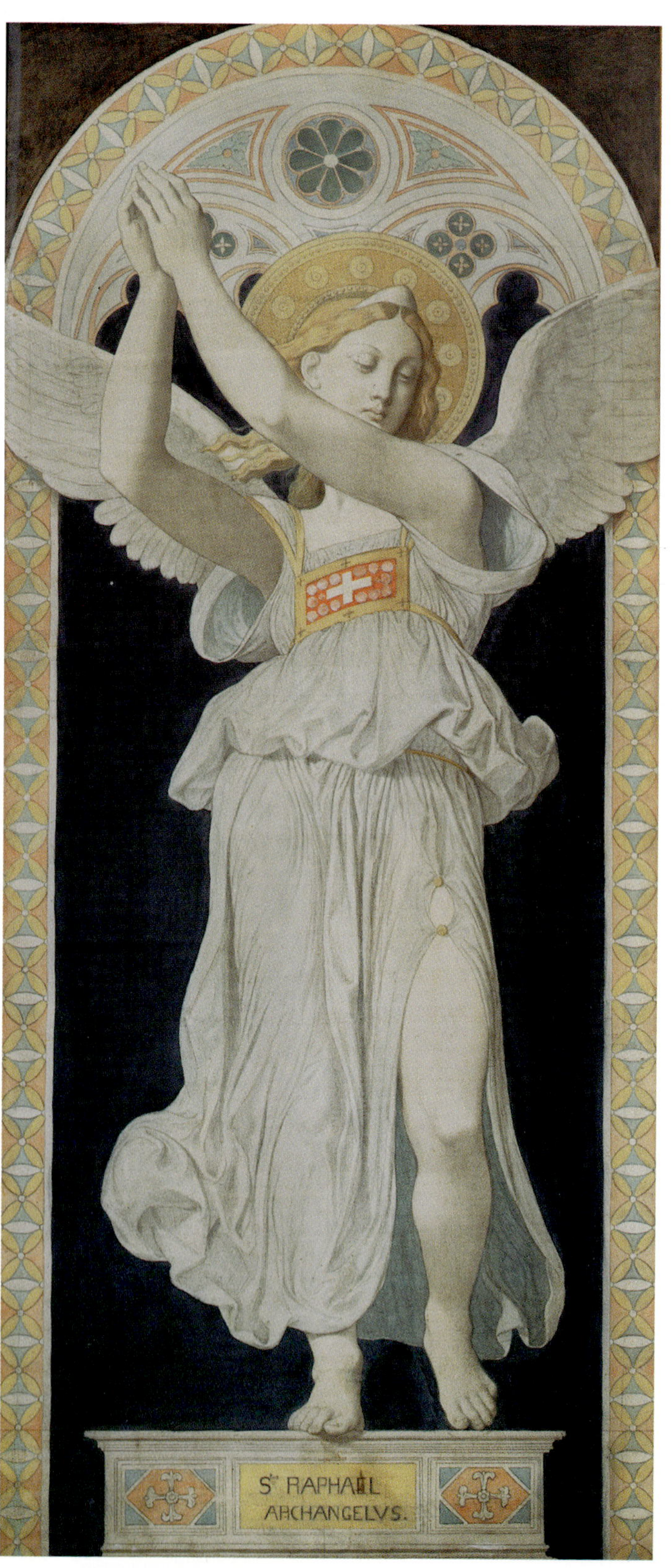

The Archangel Raphael
1842, oil on canvas, 210x92 cm
Paris, Musée du Louvre

A chapel to Our Lady of Mercy was to be built on the site of the accident and the king commissioned from Ingres a set of seventeen stained-glass windows representing the Virtues and the patron saints of the royal family. He responded with a gallery of hieratic figures to whom he gave the features of members of the royal family, in a style that mingled Gothic, oriental and Byzantine influences. For the splendid *St. Raphael* he took his inspiration from the Italian master.

Now endowed with the status of official painter, Ingres enjoyed fame, influence and the support of a court that heaped him with prestigious commissions. However he regularly refused the largest ones: the Galerie des Batailles at Versailles (1834), the interior of the church of La Madeleine in Paris (1835), the throne room in the Chambre des Pairs at the Palais du Luxembourg in Paris (1840), and the church of St. Vincent de Paul (1845).

Why? Because of his legendary slowness, which would have tied him down too long? For fear of appearing, in the field of large-scale decoration, inferior to other artists: his own pupils – Hippolyte Flandrin, Ziegler, Amaury-Duval – or his rival Delacroix, who had triumphed with his work at Versailles, the Palais Bourbon and the Palais du Luxembourg? Whatever the explanation, Ingres felt himself out of phase with current taste: the failure of the Martyrdom of St. Symphorian, for him the embodiment of his conception of the noble, "elevated" style called for by large-scale decoration, showed just how real and enduring was the discrepancy between his esthetic ambitions and what the public wanted.

But there was something else, too. His first love was the nude, and the official and religious commissions of the time left little scope for this. Significantly, he did accept a commission – a private one – that gave him a free hand with nude figures.

In 1839 the Duke of Luynes had asked Ingres to decorate a gallery in his Château at Dampierre, in the Chevreuse Valley, near Paris. The work involved two enormous semicircles that were part of a painted and gilded setting created by the architect Félix Duban and several sculptors. In terms of style and subject matter the focus was to be ancient Greece, and Ingres met the client's requirements with projects for the *Golden Age* and the *Bronze Age*: these were Classical themes par excellence, with their references to the mythic ages of humanity, the establishment of the fundamental values, and the chaos that marked the beginnings of History.

In an Arcadian setting reminiscent of late Poussin historical landscapes, the *Golden Age* presents "a just and virtuous people". On the left the goddess Astraea is "speaking of love, justice and virtue"; in the centre – the "religious part"– is "an altar set on a rocky outcrop," which is being heaped with flowers and fruit, with the Seasons dancing around it. On the right we see a meal of fruit and milk being eaten. The painting includes some fifty figures, all of them naked, with the exception of the goddess.

"Nudes, and nothing but nudes!" rejoiced the painter, who envisaged himself creating, in his own words, "a mass of beautiful idlers." Apart from the picture's instructive content, such was the program he set himself.

Ingres then devoted some ten years to what was his biggest venture ever. But with the death of his wife in 1849 and the incomprehension of the Duke at the sight of all these nude figures, despondency set in and he abandoned the project. The *Golden Age* was well advanced, but still unfinished, and of the *Bronze Age*, only the architectural section was painted.

It is not easy to imagine what a completed *Golden Age* would have looked like, especially since a colossal statue of Minerva now blocks our view of the central area. As it stands, the work offers admirable sections in the form of pleasing intertwinings of bodies and groups of men, women and children. However its size, the number of figures, a new medium (oil on plaster, a compromise between fresco and oils), and the involvement of a large number of assistants (for the landscape in its entirety, for example), must have made the undertaking particularly difficult for someone whose forte was easel painting showing a limited number of figures in a combined space.

Like all his large compositions, this one was preceded by a profusion of marvelous preparatory drawings – over five hundred in all – that reveal just what the painter had on his mind. These drawings leave us with an impression of inexhaustible, ever-fresh inspiration; it is here, rather than in the ghostly decor of Dampierre, that we should seek the true *Golden Age*.

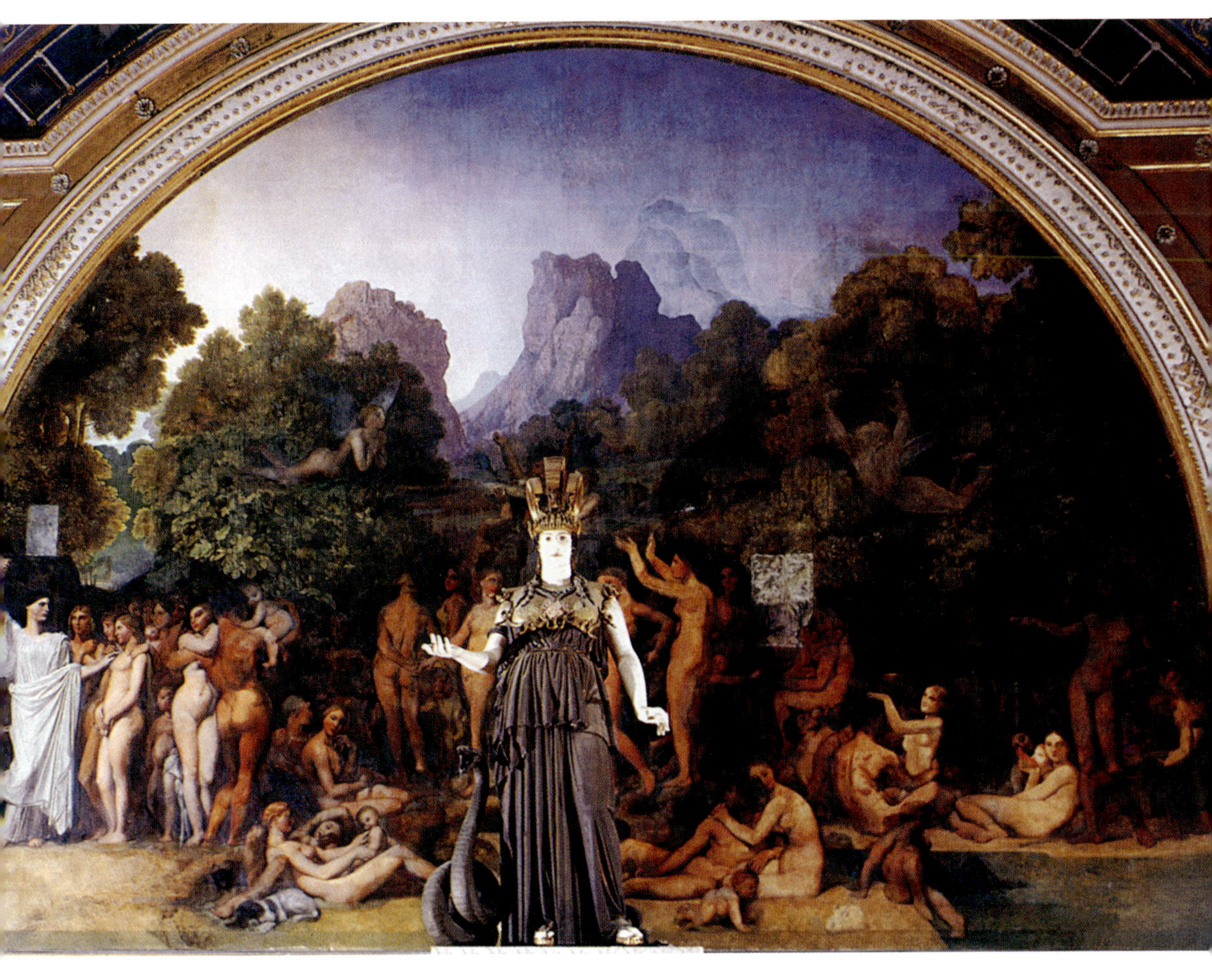

The Golden Age

1842–1847, oil on plaster, 480x660 cm

Château de Dampierre

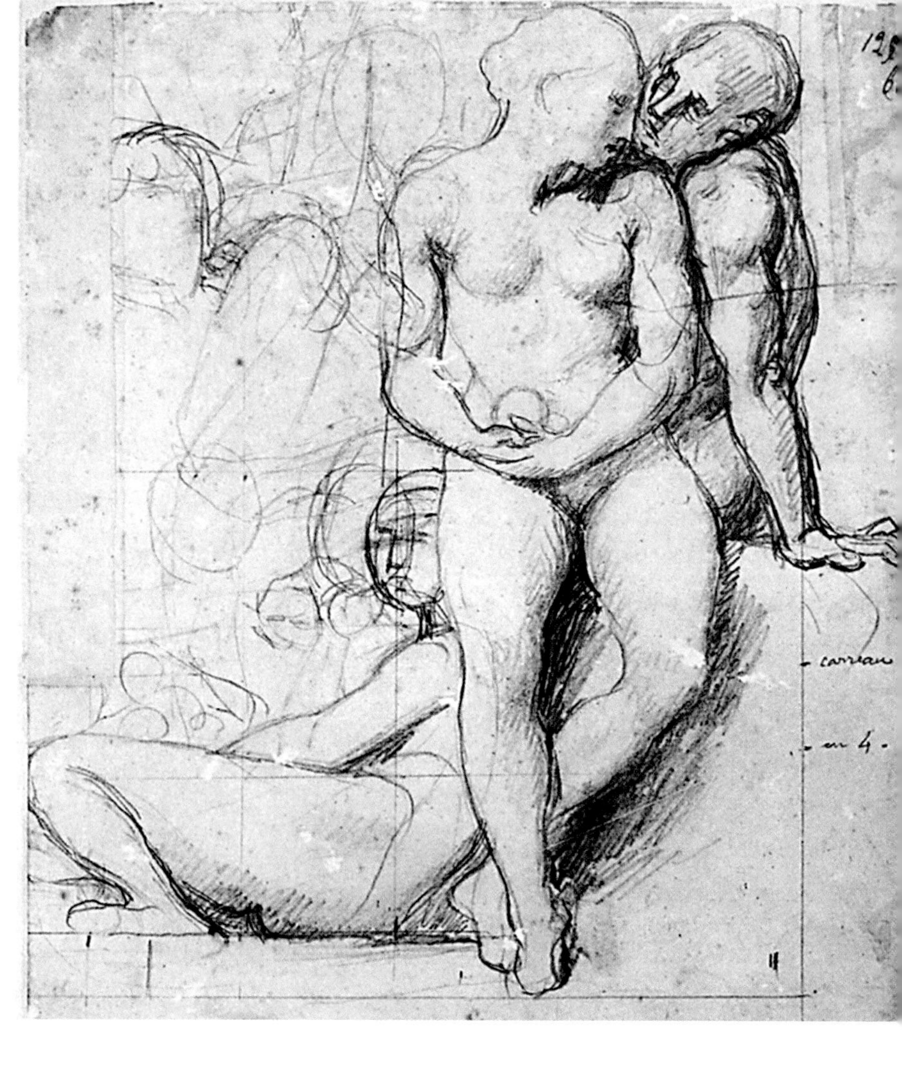
carreau
en 4

Study of a Couple for *The Golden Age*, and Figure Sketches
1842-47, pencil on paper, 22.4x19.4 cm
Montauban, Musée Ingres

Studies of Women for *The Golden Age*
1842-47, pencil on paper, 22.5x38.8 cm
Montauban, Musée Ingres

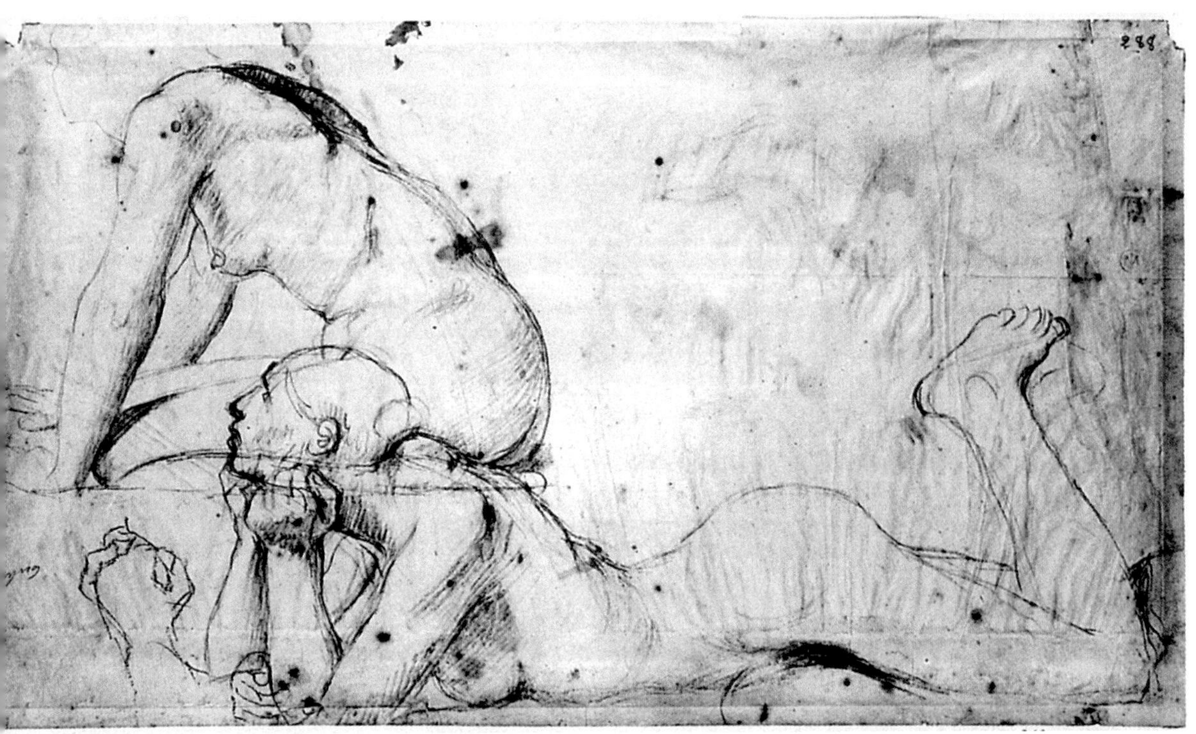

Portraits III

"Since my portraits of Bertin and Molé, everybody wants portraits. There are six that I've turned down or am avoiding, because I can't stand them." Nonetheless, there were clients among the Parisian *haute bourgeoisie* and aristocracy to whom he could not say no – even if they sometimes had to wait years. Their clinching argument, for Ingres, was their beauty: between 1845 and 1855 he painted a series of *portraits d'apparat* – the subject with objects associated with his or her daily life – that are probably the most sumptuous and awe-inspiring of his entire career.

Portrait of Vicomtesse Louise-Albertine d'Haussonville (detail)
1845, oil on canvas, 131.8x92 cm
New York, The Frick collection

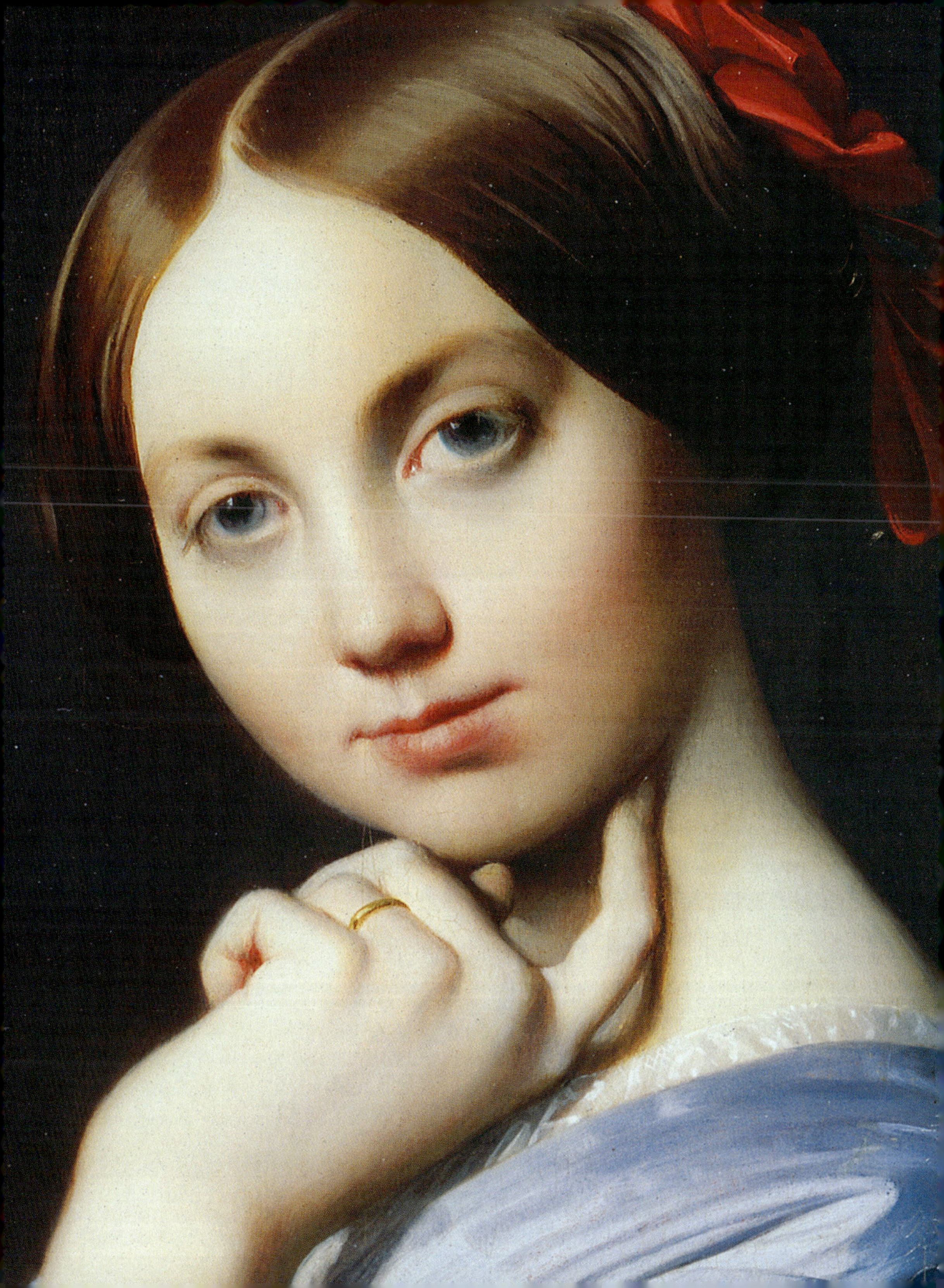

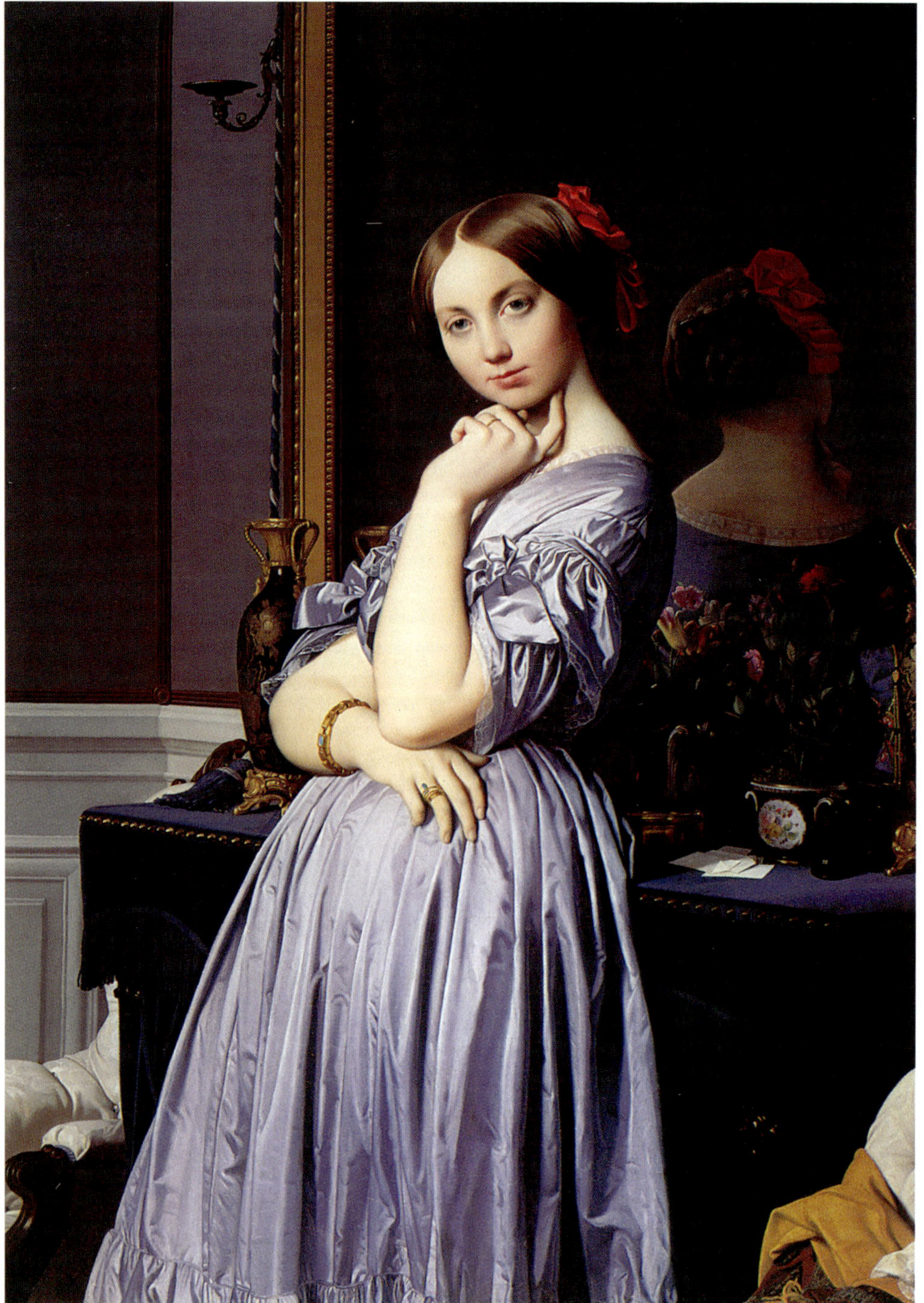

Portrait of Vicomtesse Louise-Albertine d'Haussonville
1845, oil on canvas, 131.8x92 cm
New York, The Frick collection

Portrait of Baroness Betty de Rothschild
1844–48, oil on canvas, 141.9x101 cm
Private collection

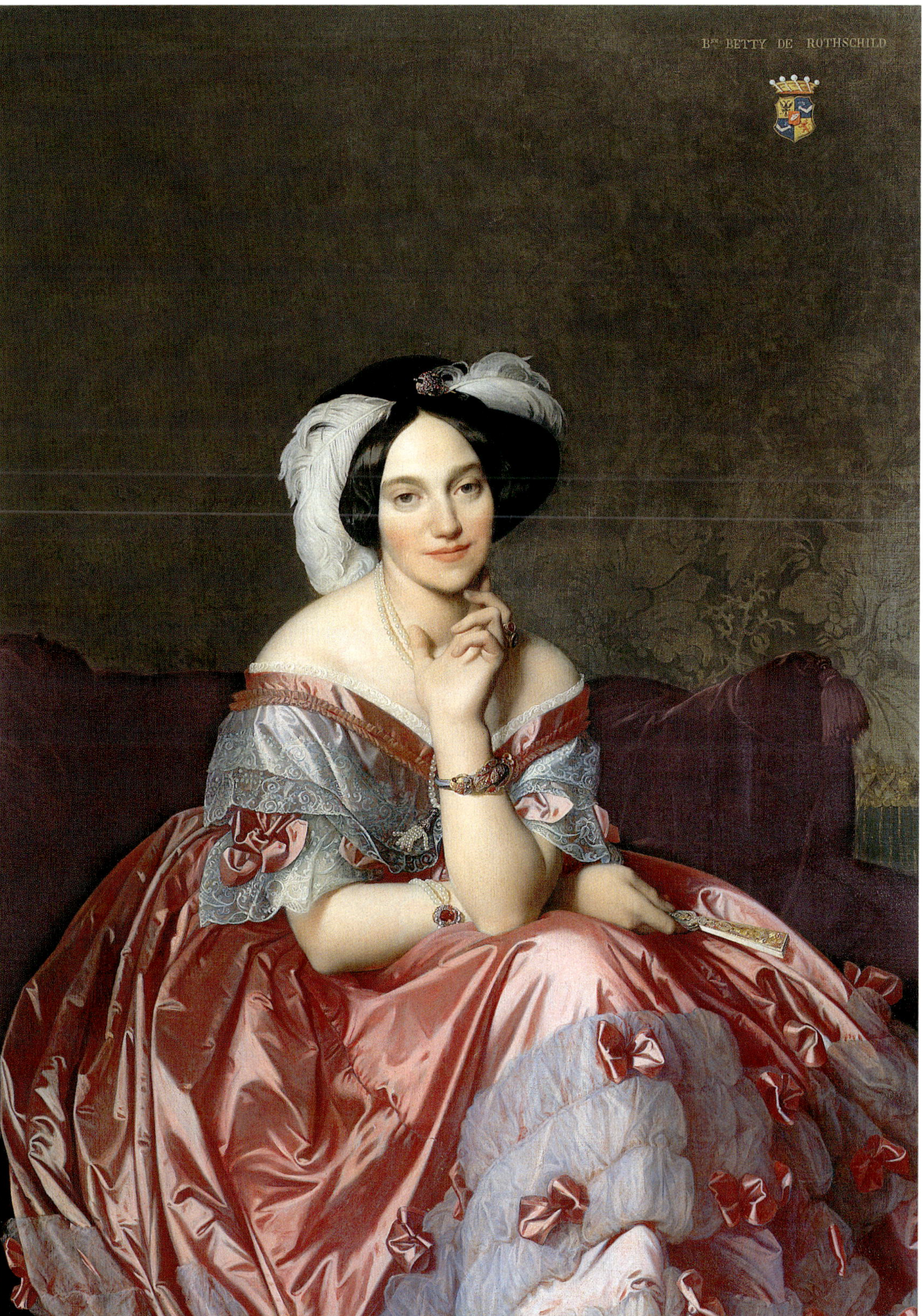
BETTY DE ROTHSCHILD

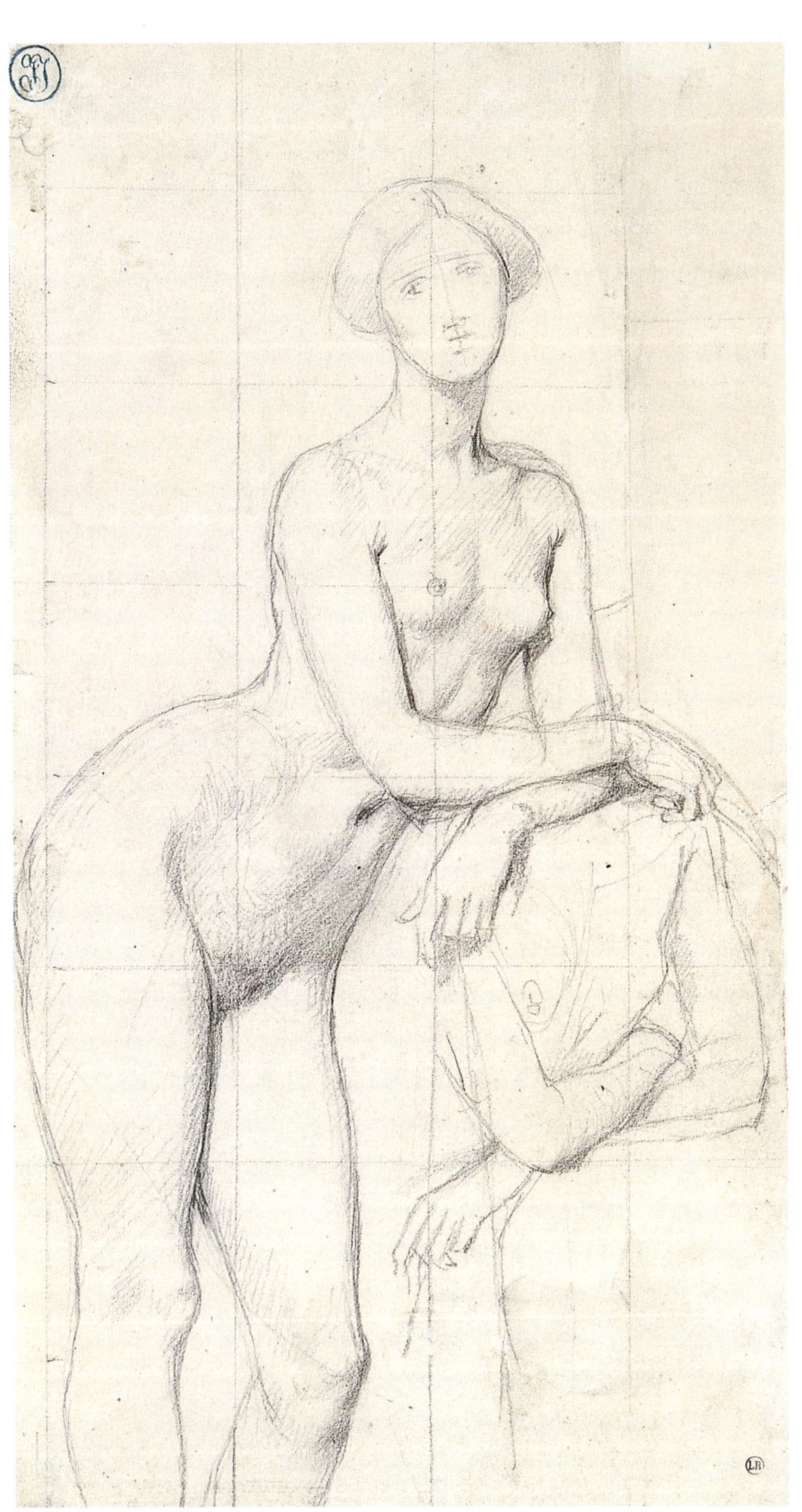

Nude Study for *The Portrait of the Princess de Broglie*
1853, crayon, 30x15.8 cm
Bayonne, Musée Bonnat

Portrait of Princess Pauline-Eléonore de Broglie
1853, oil on canvas, 106x88 cm
New York Metropolitan of Art

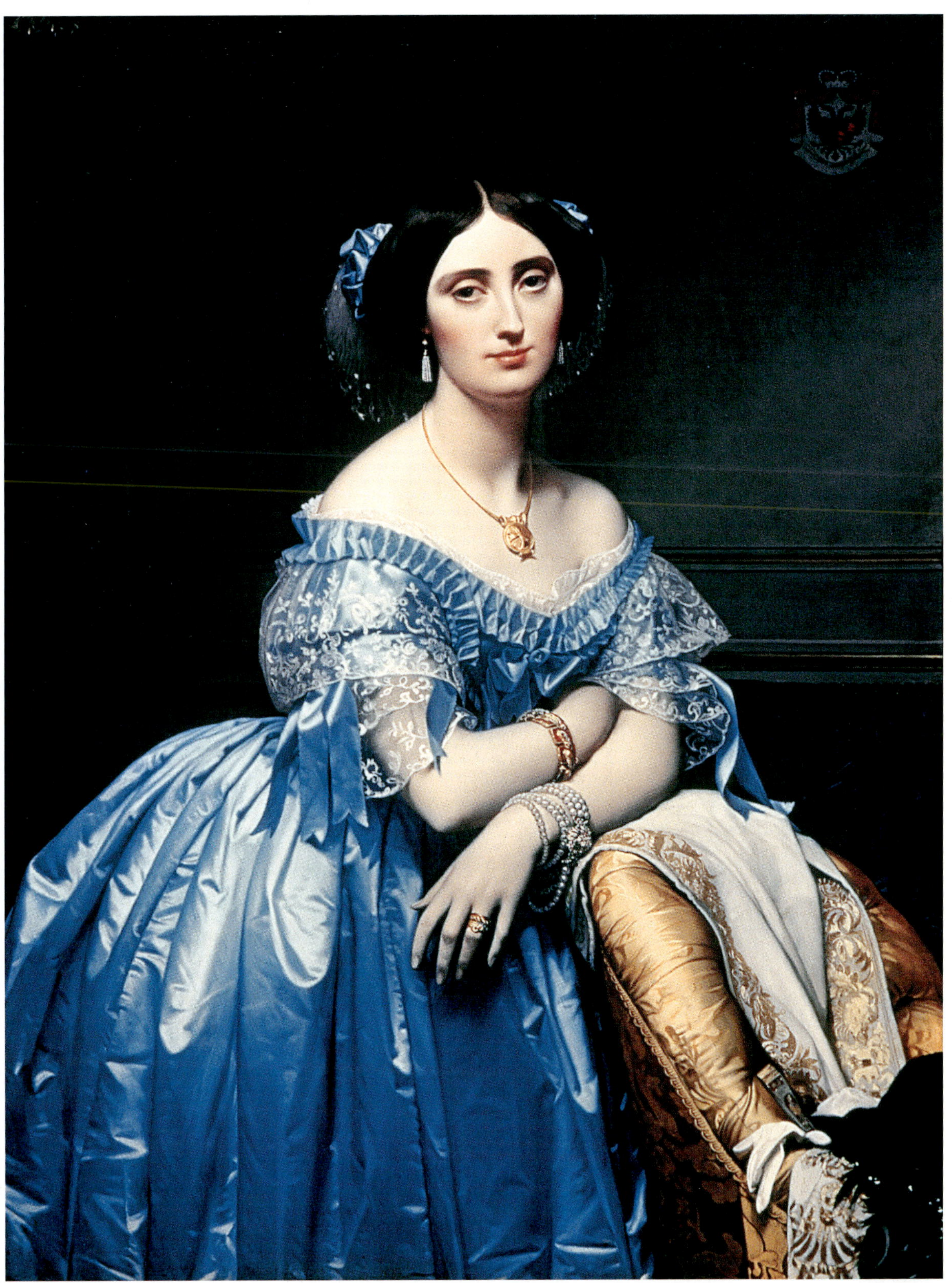

It would seem that the *Portrait of Louis-François Bertin* of 1832 oriented Ingres towards a more ambitious and monumental notion of the portrait, in keeping with the social standing of a more powerful clientele. The subjects are shown three-quarter length, a more flattering pose that heightens their elegance and allows for a display of sartorial luxury. The settings are indoor ones that expand and fill out the impression of the model's social and inner life. As in the portraits of Bertin and the Duke of Orléans, stance and gesture take on a new importance, becoming an integral part of personal expression and style.

As we have already seen, the artist very often built his figures out of ancient archetypes. This is also true of some of the portraits. Thus the pose in *Portrait of Vicomtesse Louise-Albertine d'Haussonville* – already used for Stratonice – is taken from a famous ancient statue of Modesty. Its connotations of virtue are extremely vague, but readily identifiable for the cultivated public of the time, and in addition the pose suggests untroubled reflection or daydreaming.

The *Portrait of Inès Moitessier* offers the type of majestically opulent beauty Théophile Gautier described as "Junoesque." Gautier's intuition was right, the pose being exactly that of a Roman matron representing Arcadia in a fresco from Herculaneum copied by a number of Ingres' pupils. Even the right hand, with its star-fish fingers, is taken directly from the Roman model. Ingres gave this Second Empire *bourgeoise* the pose best suited to her bloom and character: the confidence, majesty and nobility of an ancient goddess.

Yet the archetype was no mere overlay. It is fully incorporated into the image, and merges with the other components. Each of these feminine likenesses has its own social and mental character: the restraint, inwardness, delicately reflective look and nonchalant elegance of the aristocratic lady has nothing to do with the placid arrogance of this *grande bourgeoise*, whose showily lavish dress with its gaudy motifs designates her as one of the nouveaux riches.

What sets these works apart from the society portraits of the time – those of Winterhalter, for instance – is the range and richness of their artistic resources. The spectacular realism of costume and accessories transcends any descriptive intention: it is a way of introducing inherent pictorial luxury, and far from detracting from the forms, the richness of the effects highlights their unfailing density. These forms are, moreover, more ideal than realistic. As ever in Ingres' oeuvre, the persuasive charm of these female figures lies in their physical plentitude, and in the eminently sensual relationships between fabric, finery and bare flesh. Obviously this plenitude derives less from the sitters than from the artist himself: it is essential to his dream of beauty.

Some of these female portraits include a mirror placed behind the sitter, in every case very dark and adding nothing to the depth of field. Are these reflections there to reveal some additional aspect of the sitter, to complement her beauty with the charming nape of a neck, or with a profile? Perhaps, but what strikes us artistically is a summariness in total contrast with the meticulous illusionism of the rest of the picture. Moreover, there is no logic to the placing of the reflection: that of Inès Moitessier, for example, is much too far away. Like the other anomalies already noted, these point to something not covered by the system of representation, to a sort of "out of frame" aspect of the picture. One is tempted to see in these reflections the hidden face of the female sitter, her dark, mysterious side – the image, as it were, of her intimate being. This other side of the social being is the woman as lover. We recall the mirror of water reflecting the erotic undulations of Salmacis: the mirror of these portraits could well have the same function, that of gathering in the secrets of a feminine being intuited by the artist as fundamentally sensual.

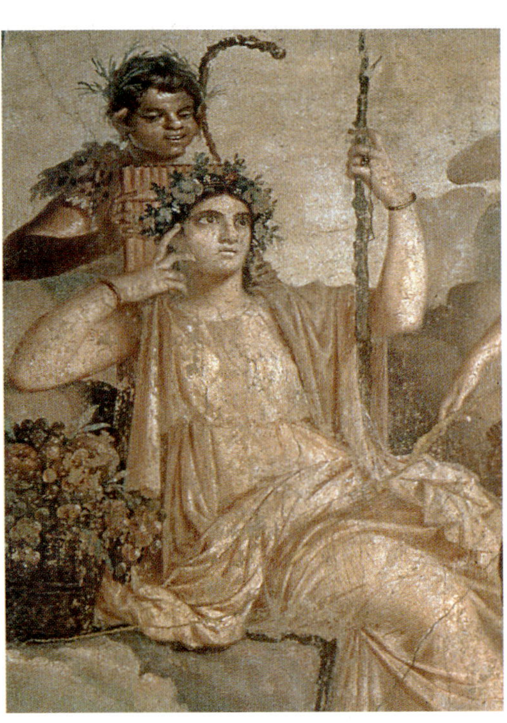

Hercules and Telephus
70 AD, mural, Basilica, Herculaneum
Naples, Archeological Museum

Portrait of Inès Moitessier
1856, oil on canvas, 120x92 cm
London, The Trustees of the National Gallery

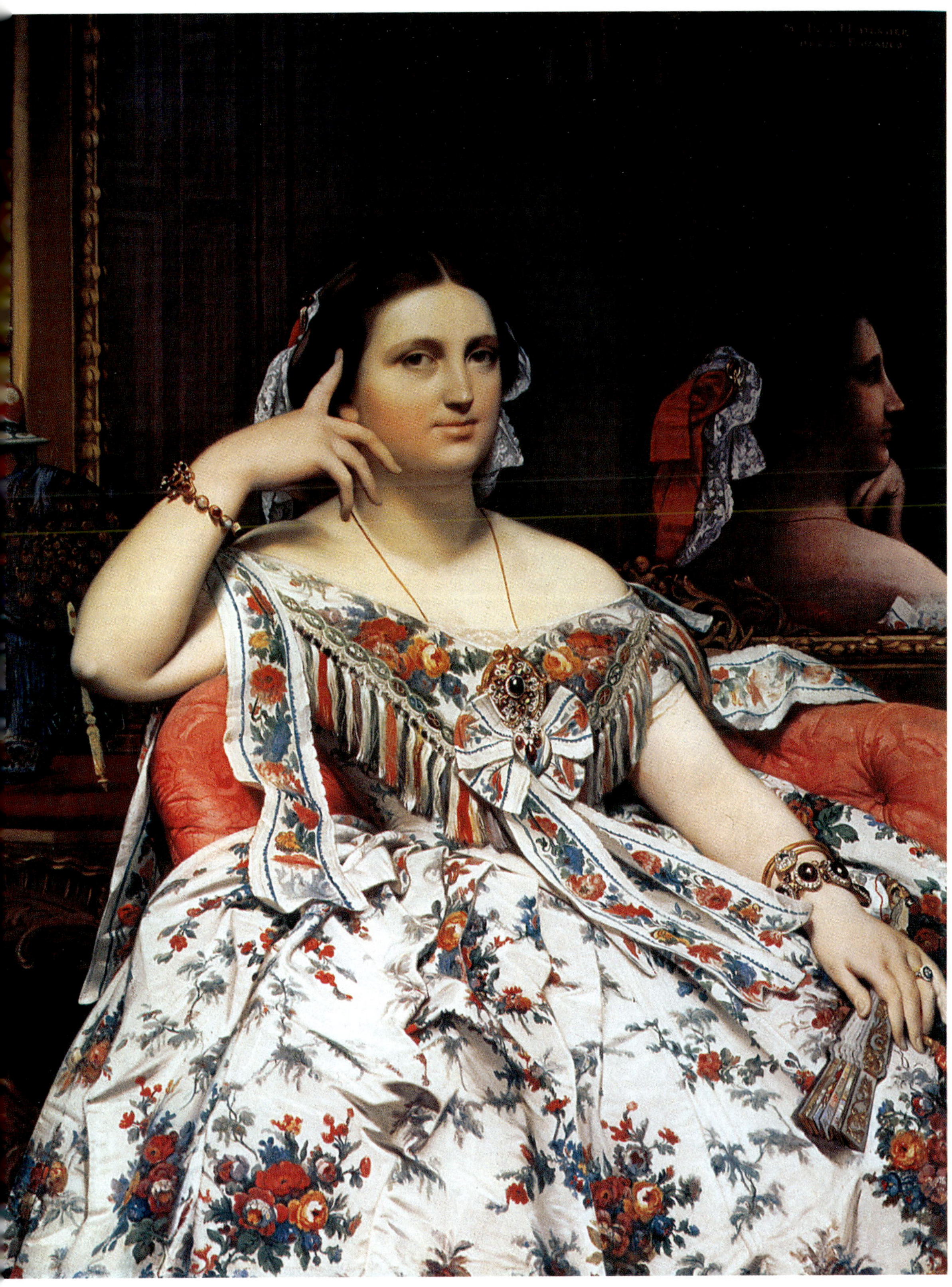

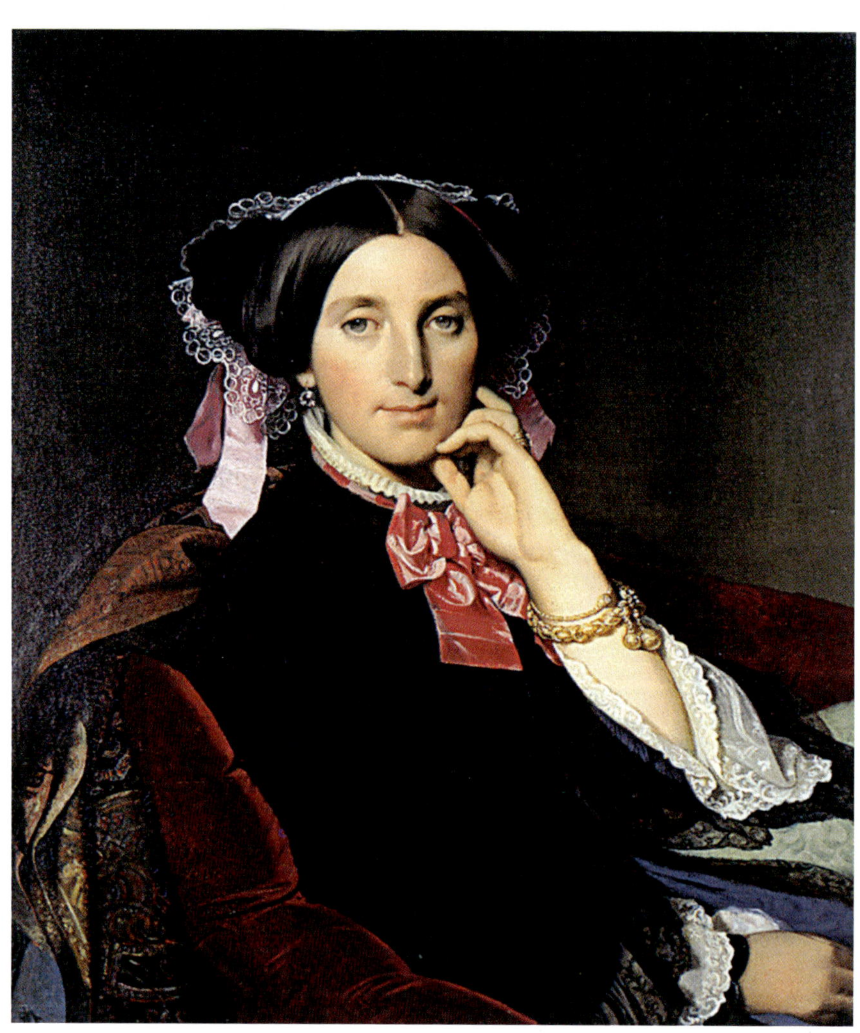

Portrait of Caroline Gonse

1852, oil on canvas, 73x62 cm

Montauban, Musée Ingres

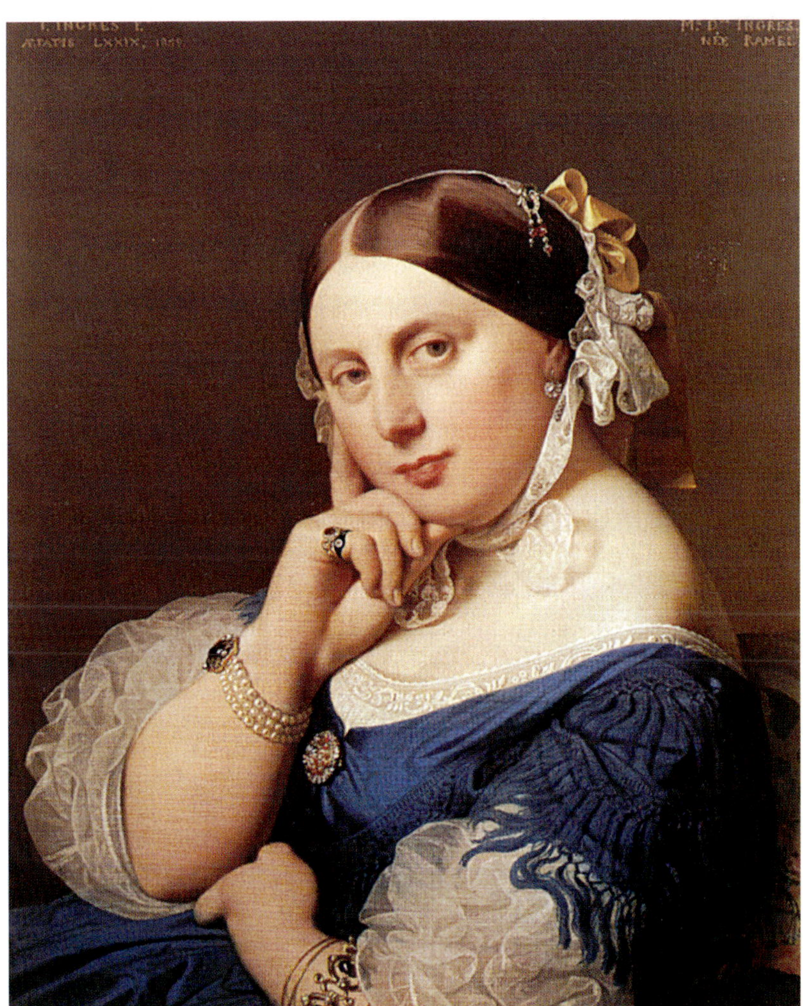

Portrait of Delphine Ingres, née Ramel

1859, oil on canvas, 63x50 cm

Winterthur, Oskar Reinhart collection

La Venus and the *Grisette*

When the Revolution of 1848 broke out, followed by the abdication of Louis-Philippe and the proclamation of the Republic, Ingres cursed the insurgents as "cannibals bearing the name of Frenchmen." This incurable bourgeois had a visceral hatred of revolution and social disorder: in politics as in art he needed the order that ensures the permanence of things. The cult of "eternal beauty" went hand in hand with respect for an immutable authority.

Nonetheless, it was in these troubled times that he calmly completed his *Birth of Venus*, originally conceived in 1807 as an academic nude. After several decades as a rough draft, it was reworked a number of times before reaching its finished form. Forty years had passed, with nothing weakening or dimming the timeless vision that had haunted the artist since the beginning.

His Venus belongs to the same world as the Thetis of 1811. In the same unrealistic climate we find the cold, blue air into which Ingres loved to plunge his Olympians. Yet we have the feeling that the gods and goddesses exist only to exalt the beauty of the human body, to abstract its forms, save them from the ups and downs of life and the world, to set them in the sphere of the eternal verities. Written in gold in the depths of the sky.

In the mid-19th century this kind of agenda could easily have seemed absurd. The erotic mythologizing of Bouguereau and Cabanel provoked gentle mockery or gnashing of teeth with its fundamental clumsiness, but Ingres is not clumsy here: part of his life and consubstantial with his being, his dream of beauty gives focus to all the resources of his art. Triviality, complacency, the accidental – none of these disturb the harmonious movement of form in space, that ideal yet living form whose pearly whorls have the infallible perfection and flawless grace of the most exquisite shells. Once again he captures the spirit of great Greek statuary. His *Venus* is a pagan, almost religious hymn to beauty seen as a sign of the divine. A hymn whose fervor convinces: this radiant body set against sea and sky, with its brightness of a cold sun in the blue night and its smooth, incorruptible substance, overwhelm the eye – and even, ultimately, haunt it.

Quite a different impression is produced by *The Source*, which uses the same figure and took almost as long to complete. Begun in Florence in 1820, it remained a rough draft until Ingres, with the help of a number of assistants, finished it in 1855-56. *The Source* is a fine example of the contradictions Ingres could become entangled in, combining as it does superb artistic qualities with intellectual banality. The hackneyed allegorical convention, the feebleness of the backdrop (attributable to the landscape painter Alexandre Desgoffe), and the intolerable dullness of a face nonetheless superbly painted all drastically undermine the value of the work. Yet we have only to block out the "pretty little *grisette*'s face" for the picture to unleash the most physically intense impression of life pouring out in all its vigor and freshness.

When he finished *The Source*, Ingres was seventy-six. He had lost his wife in 1849 and remarried three years later, to a woman almost thirty years his junior. At the Universal Exhibition in 1855 he had been able to show an authentic retrospective, being the most generously represented artist along with Delacroix, Decamp and Vernet. Was the public sufficiently alert to see the difference between Ingres and representatives of the official esthetic like Gérôme, Gleyre, Baudry, Cabanel and Bouguereau? And between Ingres and the Ingrists Amaury-Duval, Flandrin, Desgoffe, Balze and Lehmann?

Whatever the case, even though his reputation was at its height, Ingres still had his critics. "A miserly talent," said the Goncourt brothers: "Monsieur Ingres draws

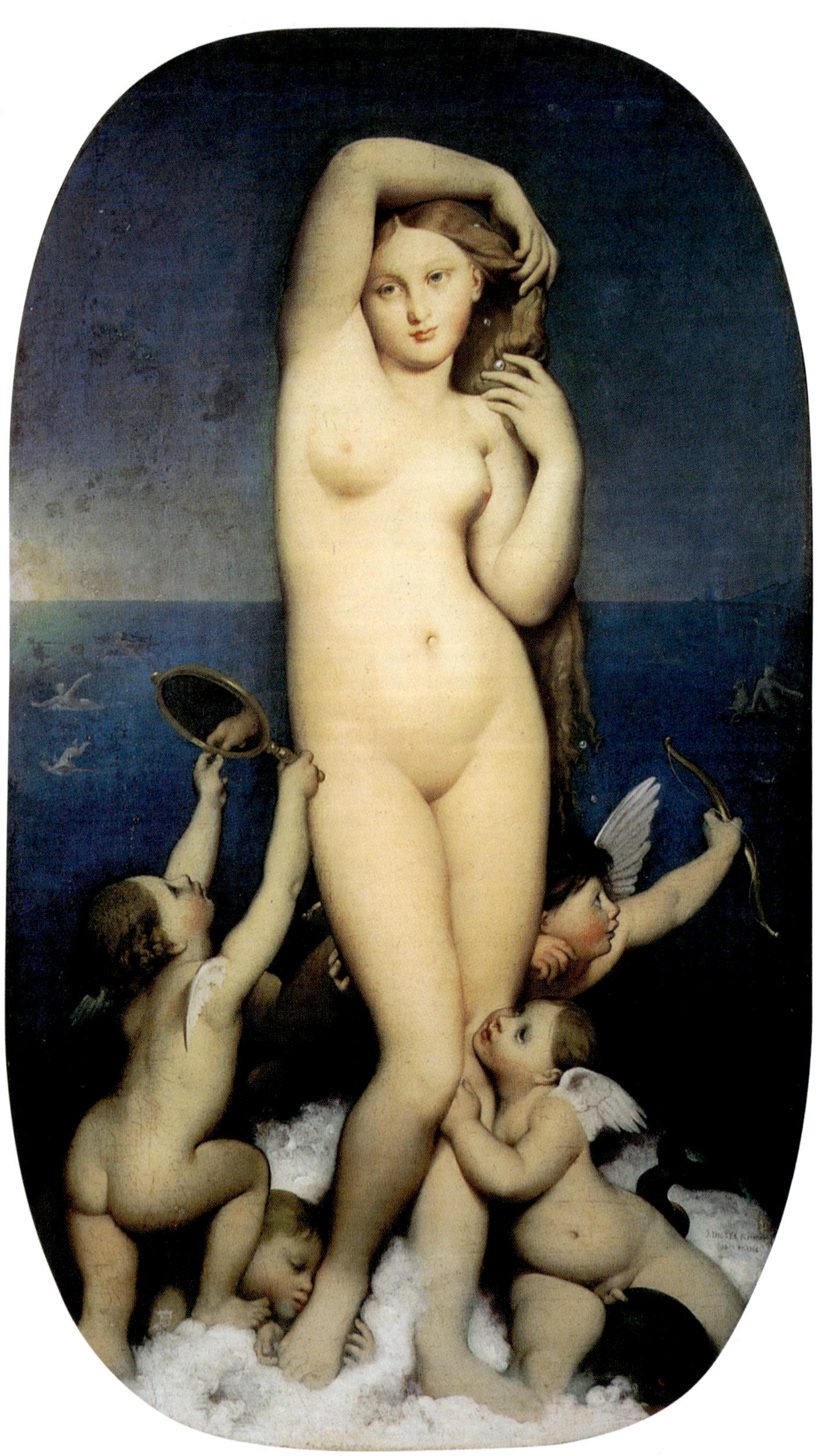

The Birth of Venus
1807–47, oil on canvas
193x92 cm
Chantilly, Musée Condé

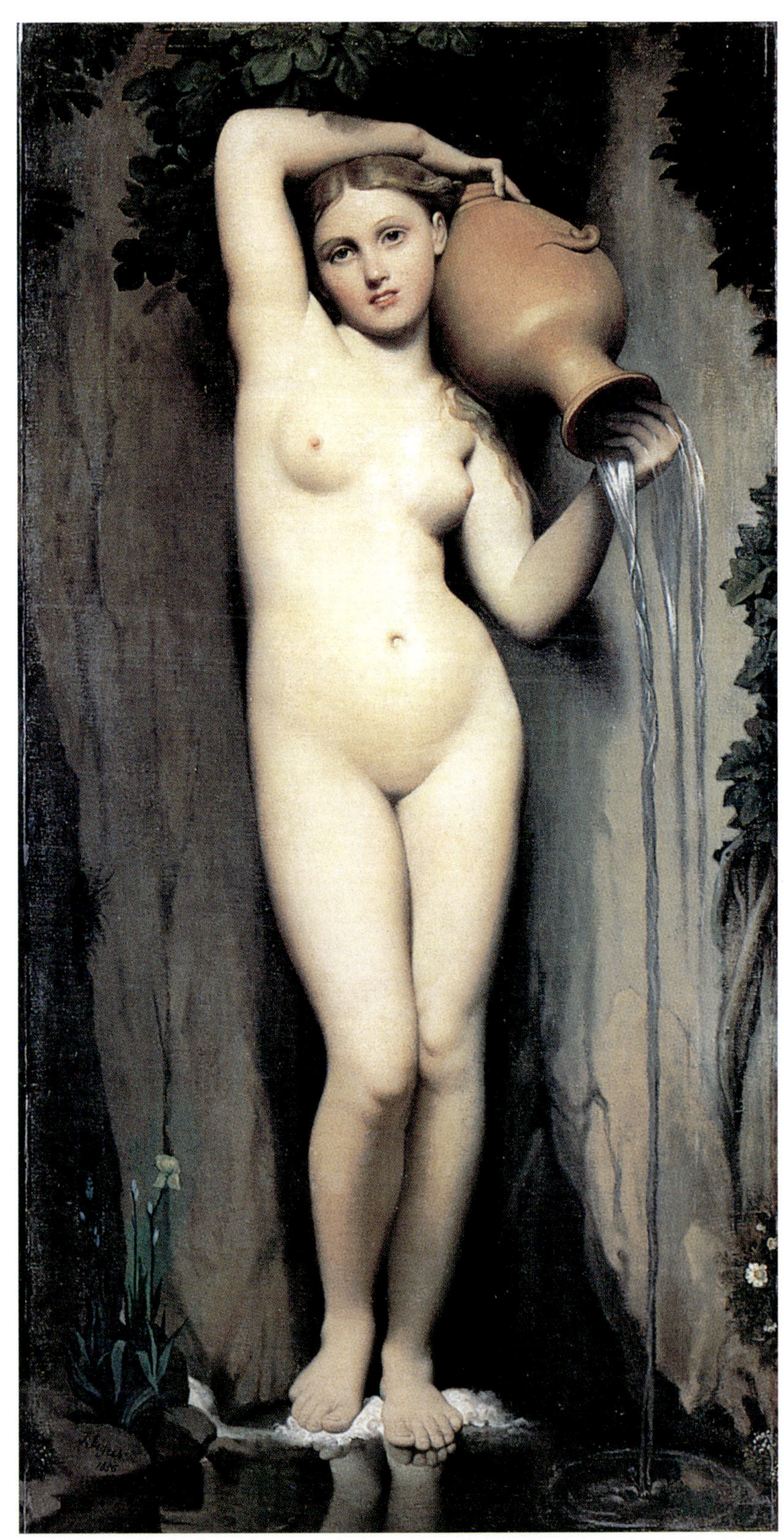

Jean Auguste Dominique Ingres,
Paul Balze and Alexandre Desgoffe
The Source
1830-56, oil on canvas, 163x80 cm
Paris, Musée d'Orsay

Study for Jesus Among the Scribes
1866, oil on canvas mounted on panel, 34x47 cm
Montpellier, Musée Fabre

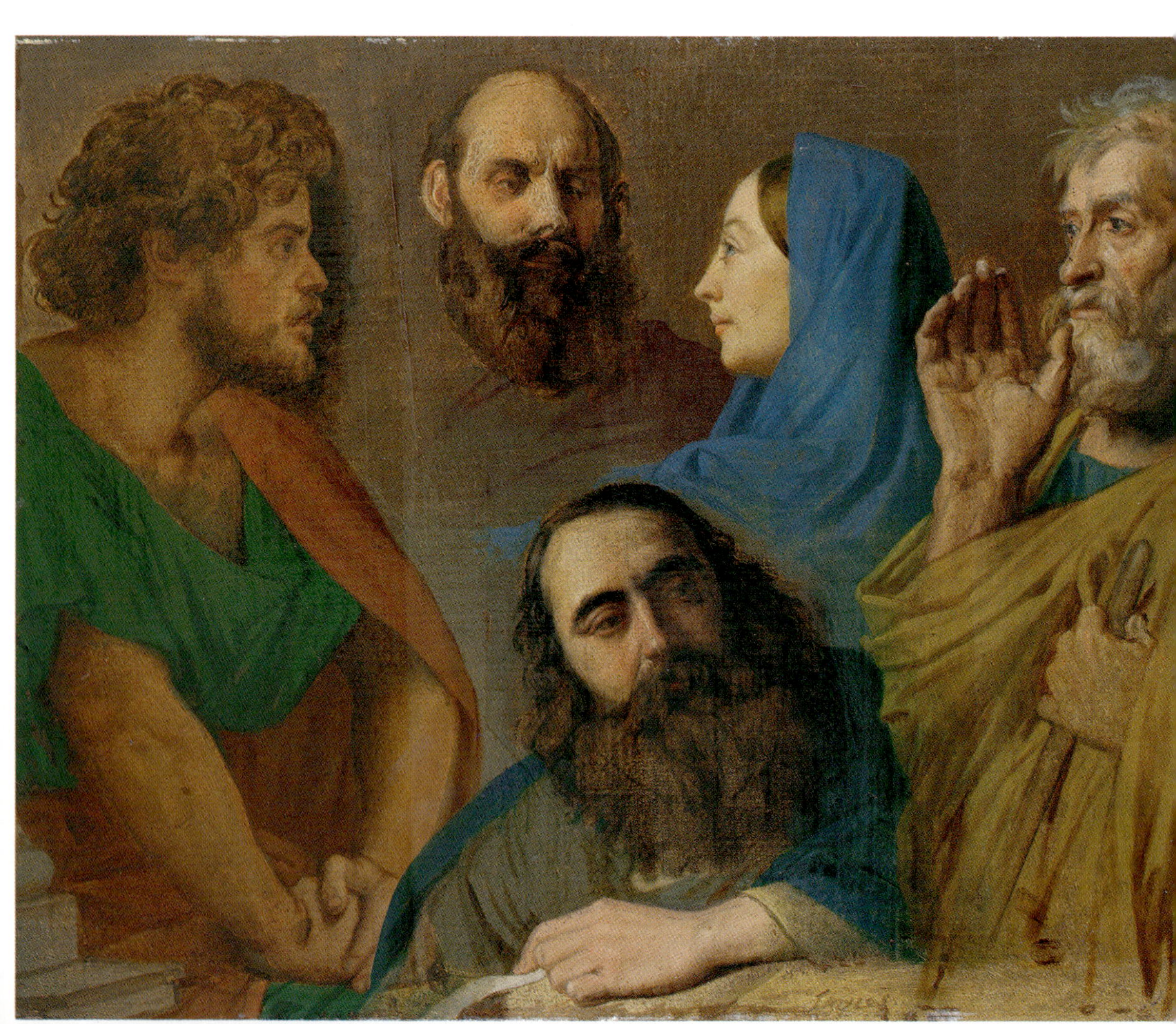

nothing out of himself. He painfully extracts his oeuvre from other masterpieces. He is seeking his soul and his glory in strenuous effort...Set face to face with history, he vainly seeks succor in a niceness of organization, decency, propriety, correctness and that dose of spiritual elevation called for by a semi-educated public. He sprinkles his figures around a focal point, placing but not grouping them. He throws in, here and there, an arm, a leg, a perfectly drawn head, and believes he has fulfilled his task when he has assembled his forms..." [42]

Baudelaire's reservations were more marked than they had ever been: "Monsieur Ingres can be considered a man of great talent and an eloquent pleader for beauty, but he is bereft of the energetic temperament that forges the destiny of a genius." [43]

In his diary for 15 May 1855, Delacroix mentions the "ridiculousness" of the Ingres exhibition, apparently presented in a fairly pompous way, and adds: "This is the complete expression of an incomplete intelligence. Effort and pretension are everywhere, but there is not a glimmer of naturalness."

The portraits aside, his pictures from the 1850s are nothing remarkable. In 1853 he had painted the ceiling of the Salon de l'Empereur at the Hôtel de Ville in Paris with an *Apotheosis of Napoleon I* – destroyed in the fire of 1871 – that a rough sketch and an old photograph give no cause to grieve for. His *Joan of Arc* and *St. Germaine of Pibrac* anticipate St. Sulpice, and his *Jesus among the Scribes*, whose execution dragged on until 1862, is perhaps the driest, least-inspired thing he ever did. As one of his pupils reported, "Ingres began by having the background painted in. He added unclothed *grisaille* drawings of the figures, then painted the parts that were to remain visible, and finished with the draperies." Is the frigidity of the work attributable to a system rationalized down into a method of working? What we can be sure of is that painting assistants specializing in certain fields – landscape, architecture – are a tangible presence in the works of the final period; and the problem may be that they were not much more than mere journeymen. Once again the result, in *Jesus Among the Scribes*, is no more than a succession of "beautiful fragments" in a well-defined space with accurately drawn, perfectly conventional architectural detail. The use of color had never been so sharply contrasted and so blatant.

The Apotheosis of Ingres

And yet the master had not said his last word. Since 1849 he had been working on another painting, whose endless stages of execution would keep him busy for almost fifteen years.

The idea had come to him during his first stay in Rome, maybe as early as 1819. In Notebook IX, under the heading "Women's bath," we find a résumé of extracts from the *Letters* of Lady Montague, wife of the British ambassador to Turkey. From these letters, published in London in 1764 and subsequently translated into French, Ingres had noted passages recounting a visit to the baths in Constantinople: "There were easily two hundred bathers...The couches were covered with cushions and rich carpets and all those present were naked. Yet there were no indecent gestures, no lascivious poses; they walked and moved with majestic grace. A number of them were very handsome, with vividly white skin and adorned only with their hair

Study of a Woman for *The Turkish Bath*
1859–63, oil on canvas, 24.9x25.9 cm
Montauban, Musée Ingres

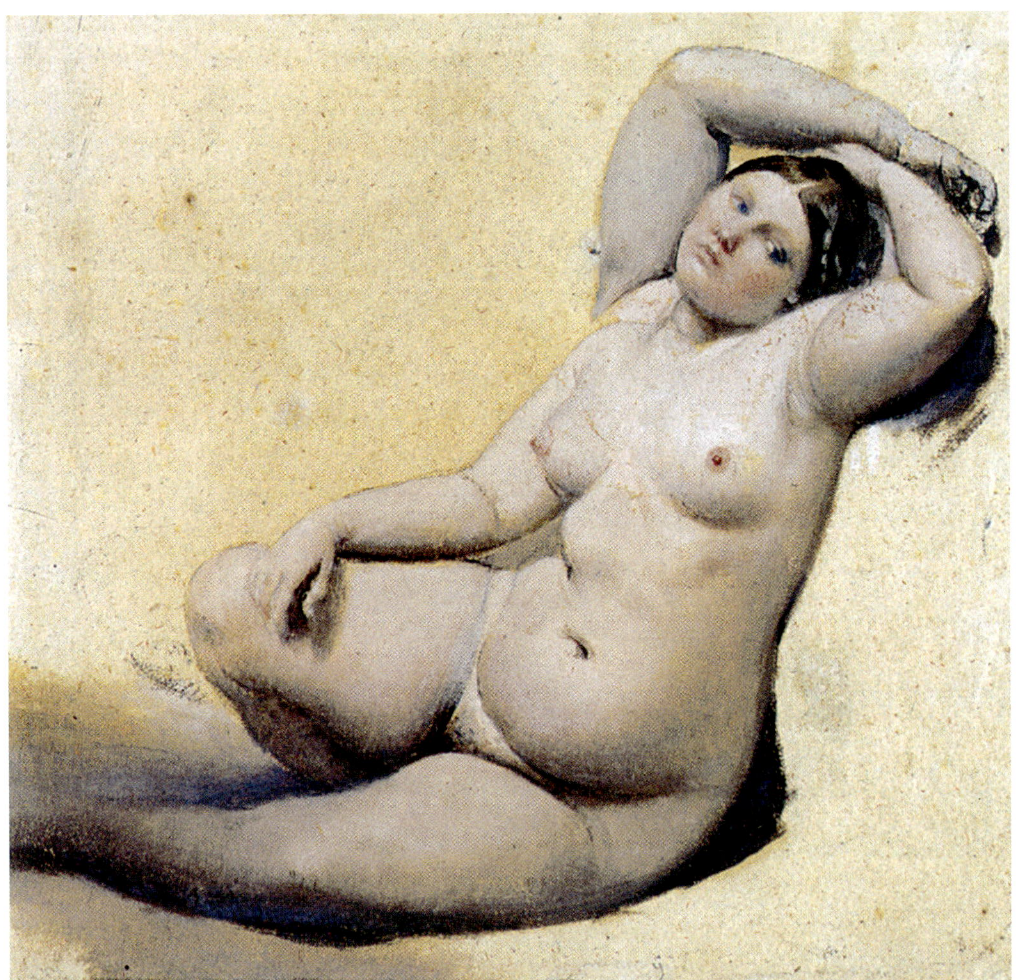

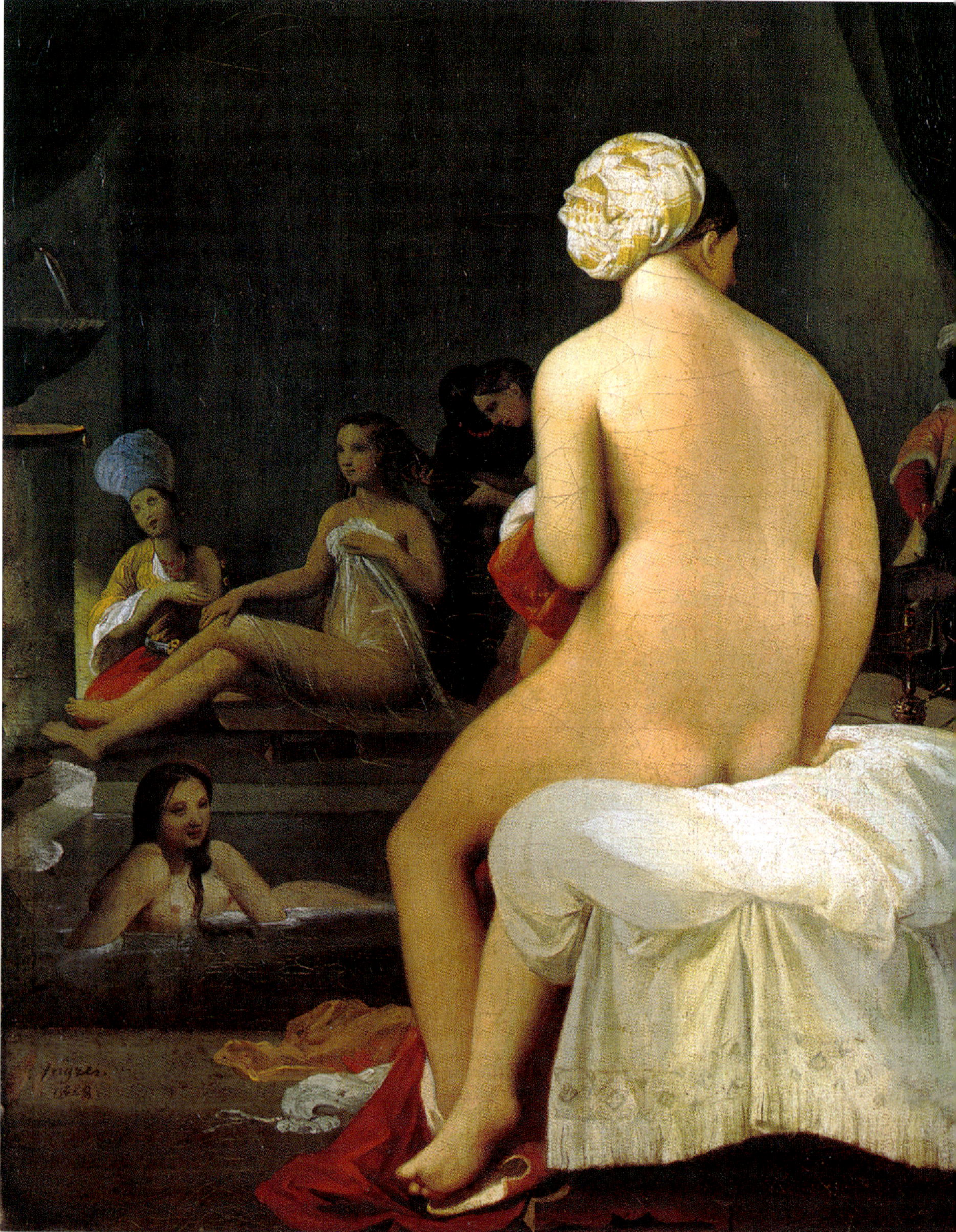

Small Bather, Interior of Harem
1828, oil on canvas, 35x27 cm
Paris, Musée du Louvre

which, dotted with beads and ribbons, fell in braids on their shoulders. Beautiful naked women in different postures, some chatting, others working or taking coffee or a sorbet. Some lying back negligently on their cushions. Pretty girls of sixteen or eighteen, busily braiding their hair in endless different ways... After the meal I was given coffee and perfume, which is a mark of great consideration: two kneeling slaves incensed, so to speak, my hair..."

The history of the *Turkish Bath* is a complicated one. Ingres had long had the idea of painting a "women's bath," but the commission from Count Demidoff did not come until 1840. The canvas was begun, then abandoned until 1849, when it was rapidly completed and acquired by Prince Napoleon. But so much nakedness alarmed Princess Clotilde and the painting was returned to its maker in exchange for another. As a photograph taken by Charles Marville in 1860 shows, it was then square, but Ingres decided to turn it into a tondo, which meant modifying the composition: of the woman whose provocative body was nestled in the bottom right corner, there remain only the hands and head, and the gap in the foreground has been filled with a still life. The full-length reclining figure facing the viewer was given arms arched over her head, which enabled the introduction of the delicious little blue "Turkish" cushion embroidered with red flowers. Further figures were added, behind the dancer and in the pool, and the background was enhanced with new niches and windows.

Truly finished only in 1864, the work was ultimately acquired by the Turkish diplomat Khalil Bey, a collector and lover of nudes who also bought a number of works by Courbet.

Ingres stayed close to the description in the letters, while adding such new elements and music and dance. Several figures were borrowed from old engravings of life in the Middle East. Most notably, however, Ingres reused quite a number of figures and motifs from his own earlier work. The *Turkish Bath* returns to and enlarges on a theme already worked on in 1827 in *Small Bather, Interior of Harem*, a work that sets the figure of the *Grande Baigneuse* of 1808 in a harem, surrounded by female companions. One young woman relaxes in the pool, another is having her hair combed: this was already an illustration of the Lady Montague text.

In the *Turkish Bath* the back of the *Grande Baigneuse* is readily recognizable, but in a sitting position which is that of the musician-slave of the 1839 painting, and with the motif of the breast under the arm to be seen in the *Bather* of 1807. The raised arms and sinuous forms of the two reclining women on the right are taken from *Sleeping Woman, Nude* and *Odalisque and Female Slave*. The face of the woman caressing her own breasts is from *The Vow of Louis XIII*,

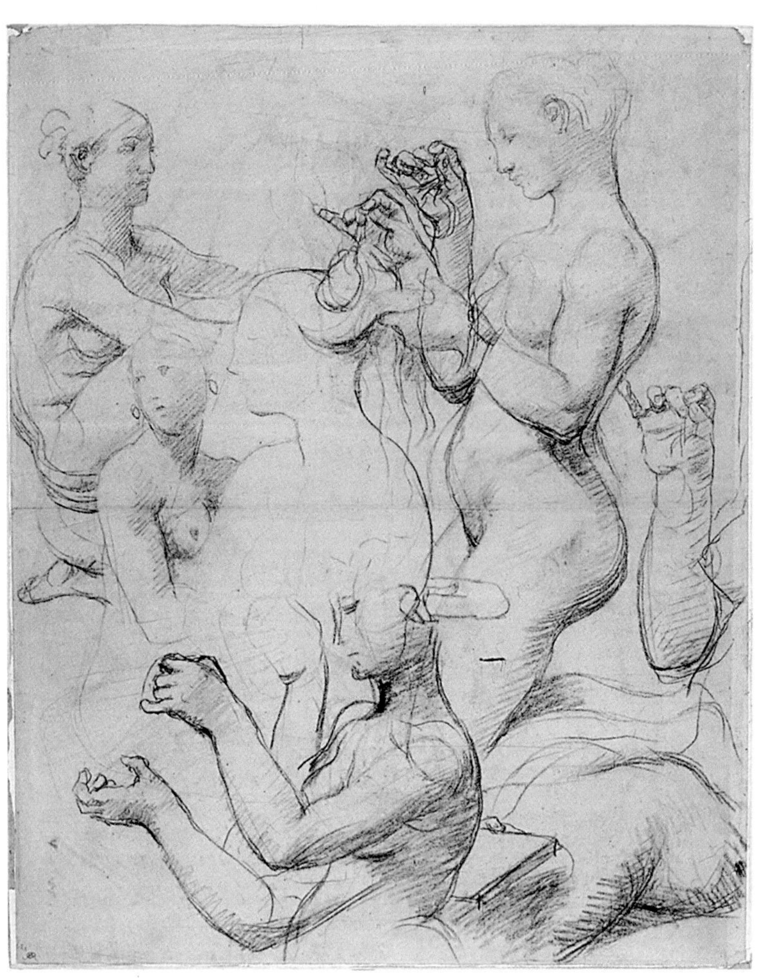

Study for *The Turkish Bath*
black chalk on paper, 64x50 cm
Paris, Musée du Louvre, Cabinet des Dessins

The Turkish Bath
photograph by Charles Marville
1859,
Paris, Musée du Louvre

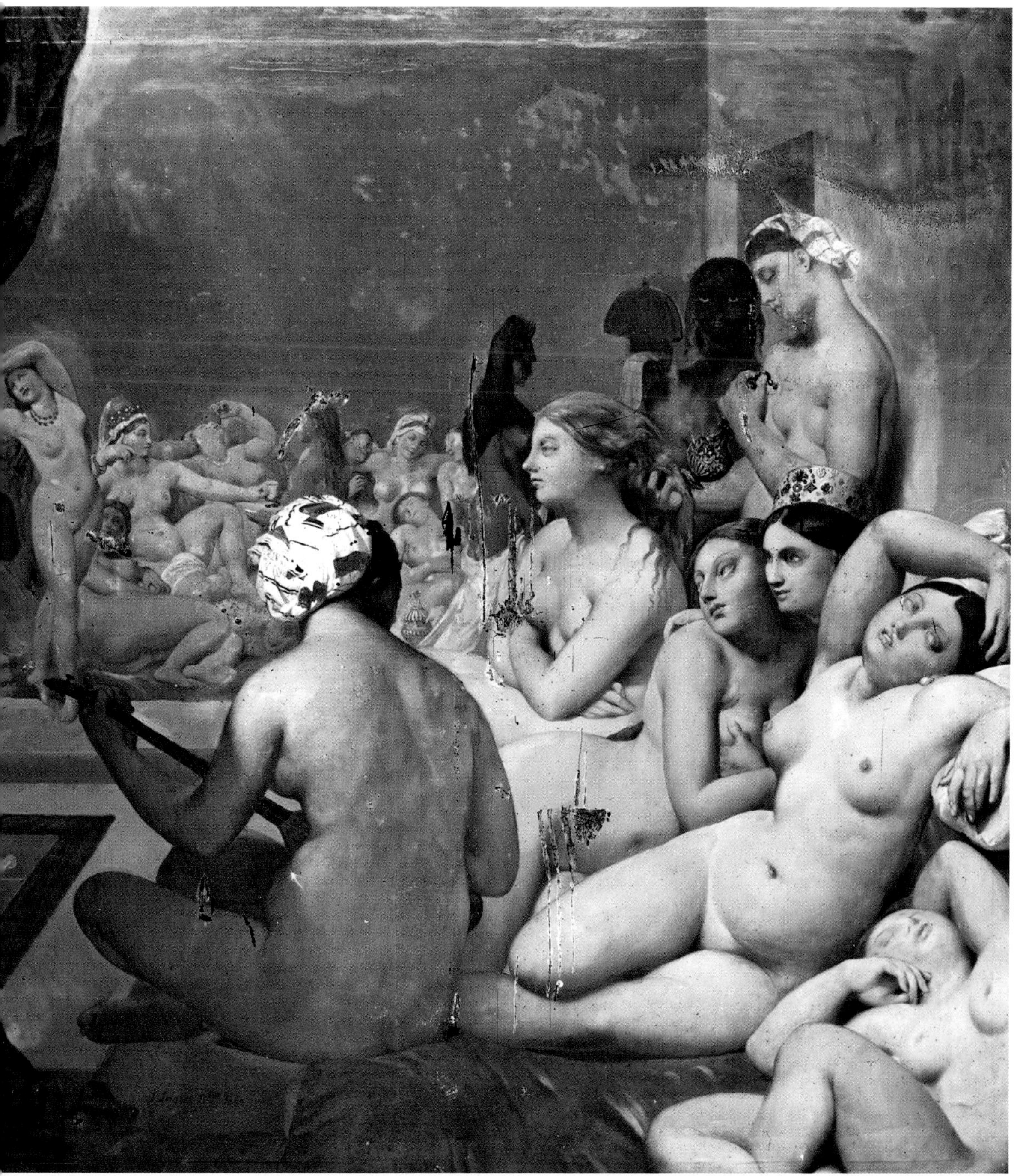

and the dancer is an adaptation of the female figure from *Ruggiero Frees Angelica*. One of the background bathers can be seen in the Golden Age, and another, in the pose of a Hindu goddess, is shown gesturing like Madame Moitessier.

Like rivers and streams converging on a vast estuary, these variations on the theme of female beauty traverse Ingres' entire career to come together in the final work. The *Turkish Bath* is the culmination and ultimate summation of his exploration of the nude.

The painter had noted the following observation in Lady Montague's Letters: "[These women] reminded me in every way of Theocritus' *Epithalamion of Helen*; and it seemed to me that the same customs had been retained since that time." Ingres could not have failed to notice this survival, in the Islamic context, of the Greek bath tradition; and the Oriental bath theme must have seemed to him a way of modernizing the dream of antiquity in its "Venusian" version. The Orient of the *Turkish Bath* is more totally fictive than any of its counterparts, not only because it is free of the veneer of ethnography resorted to by so many Orientalist painters, but also because it sets out to capture with its circular net the rekindled memory of a mythical, timeless antiquity – but the antiquity of radiant bodies, not that of the heroic virtues.

Thus the *Turkish Bath* is a multiple fusion, an artistic last will and testament, and perhaps the most moving of all Ingres' works. The old painter has brought all his treasures together in a doubly enclosed space, hermetically sealed both by its walls – the punishment for male intruders, Lady Montague adds, is death – and by its circular form. His dream of a beauty at once sensual and chaste has at last found its ideal locus and climate, that "greenhouse temperature," as Gaétan Picon put it, that brings it to full flower. And gives it significant new scope: for the work has all the complexity and monumentality of a large-scale historical composition.

The Turkish Bath
1848–64, oil on canvas mounted on panel
diameter 108 cm
Paris, Musée du Louvre

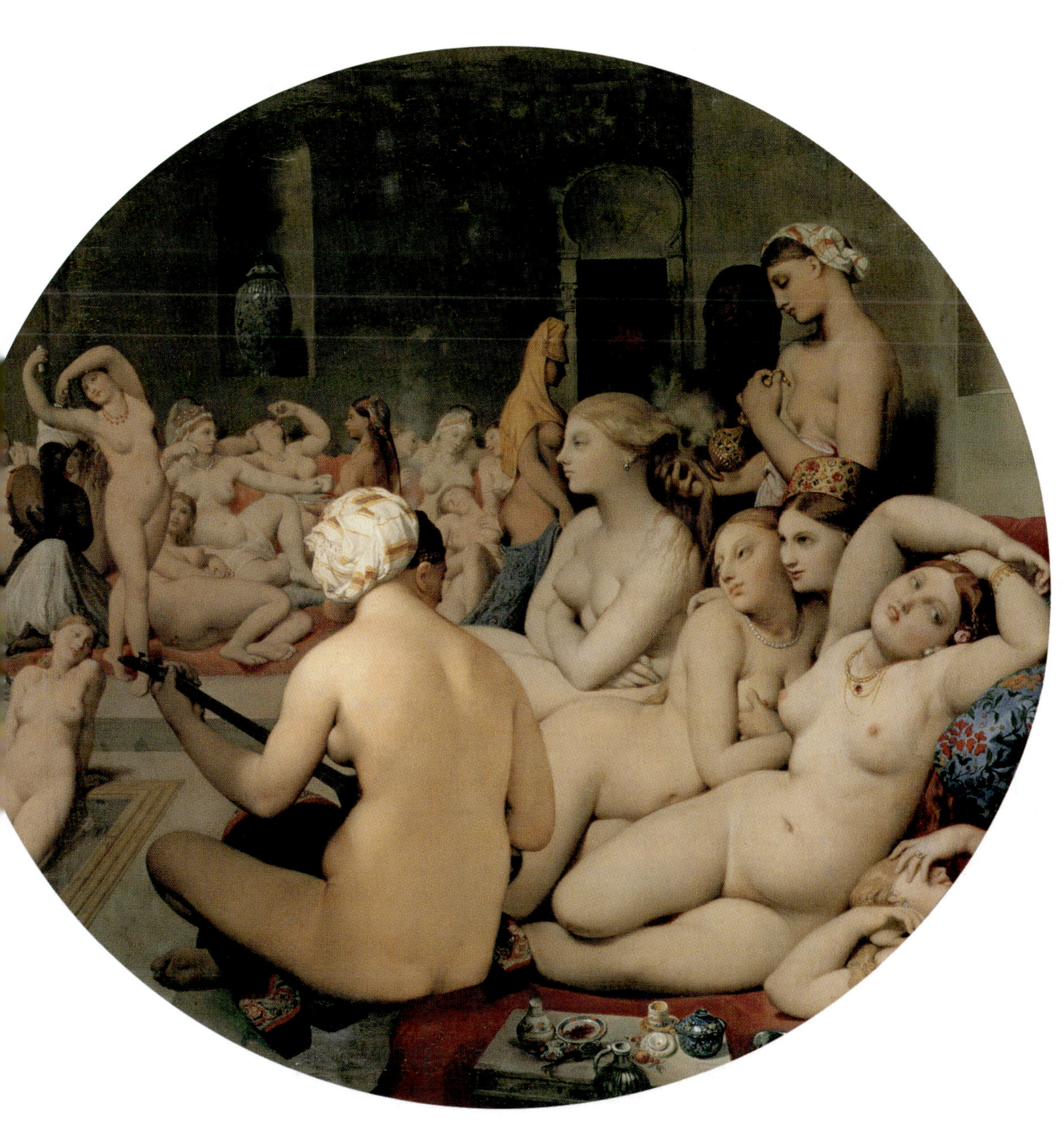

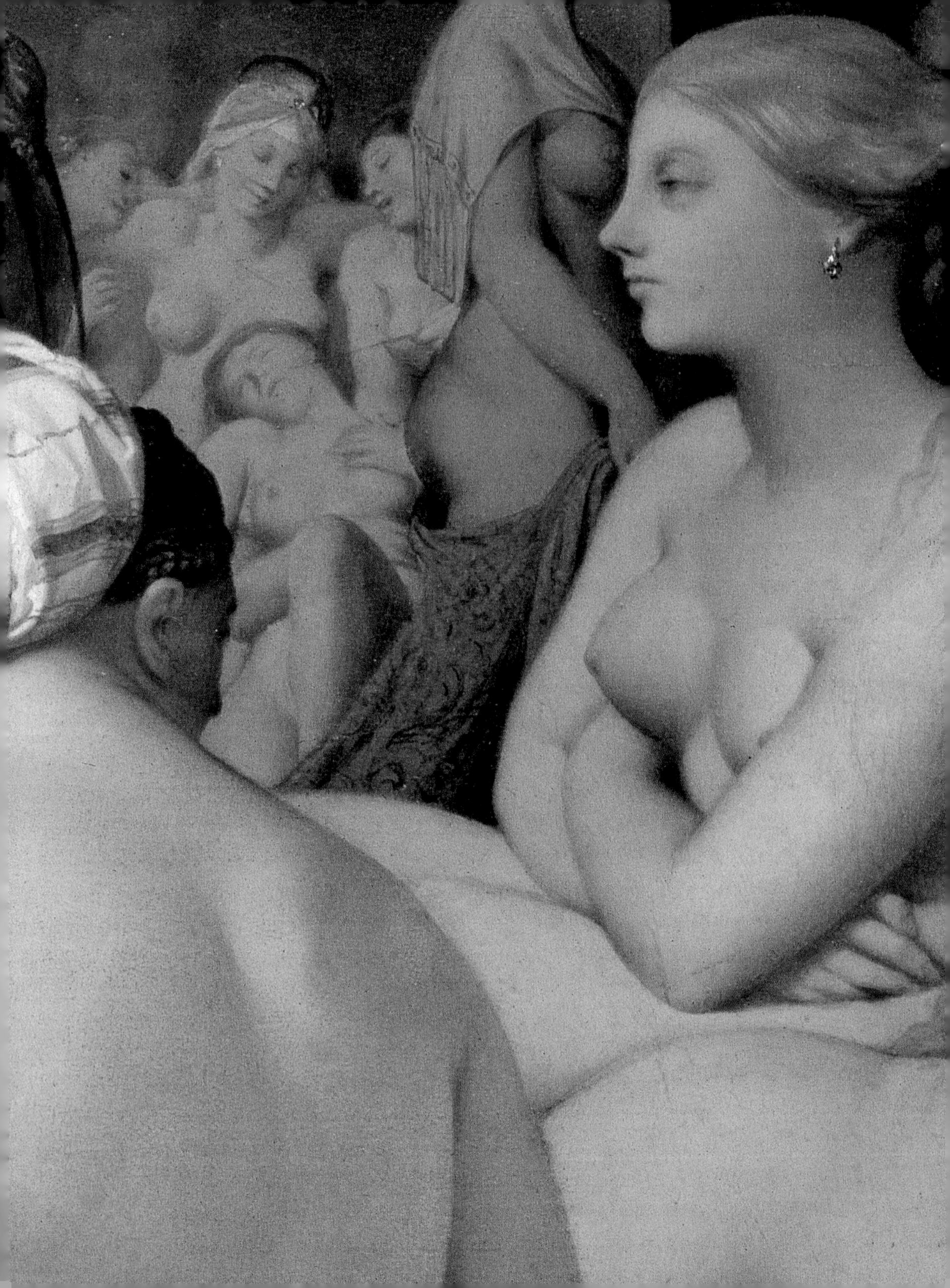

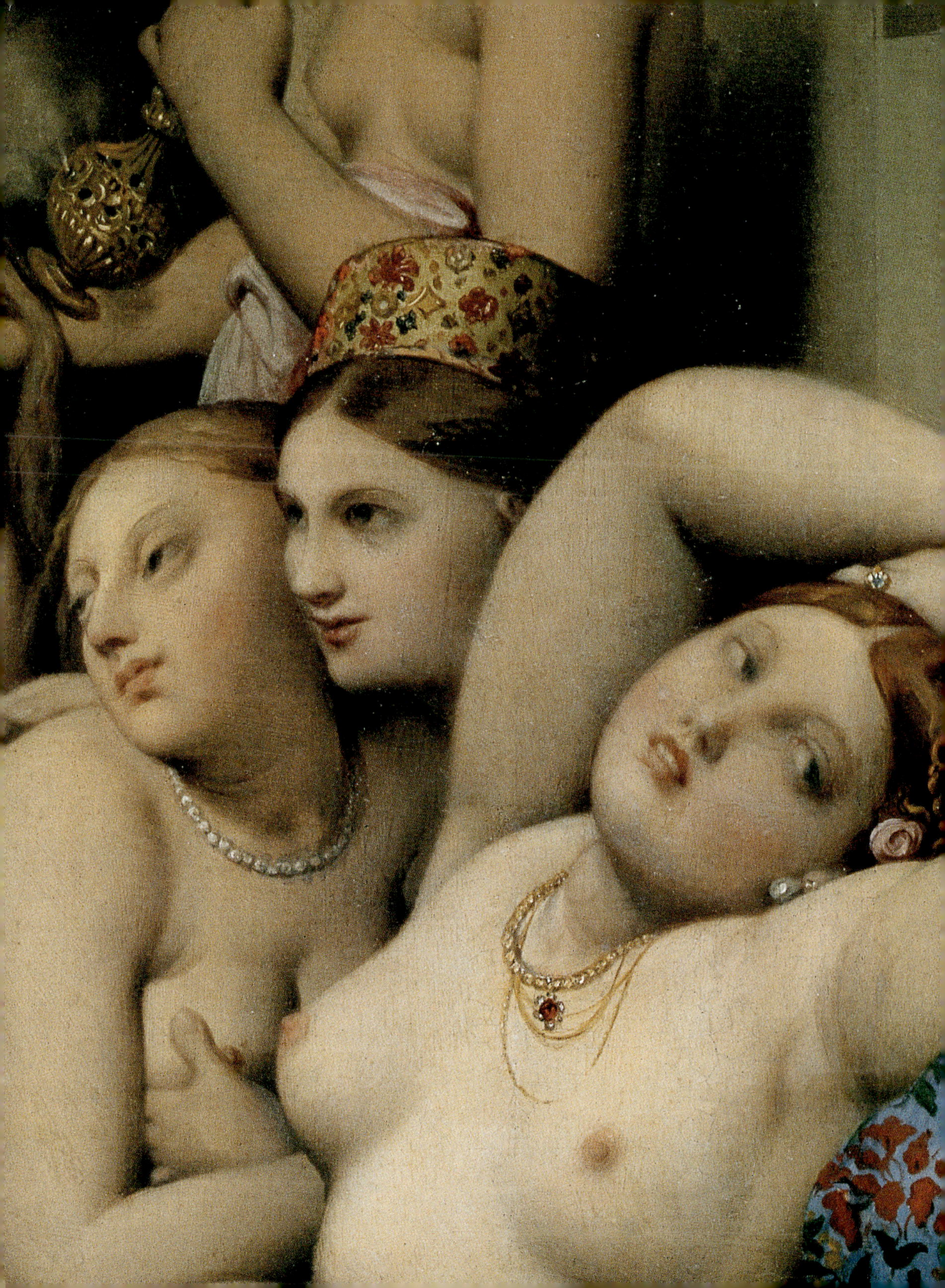

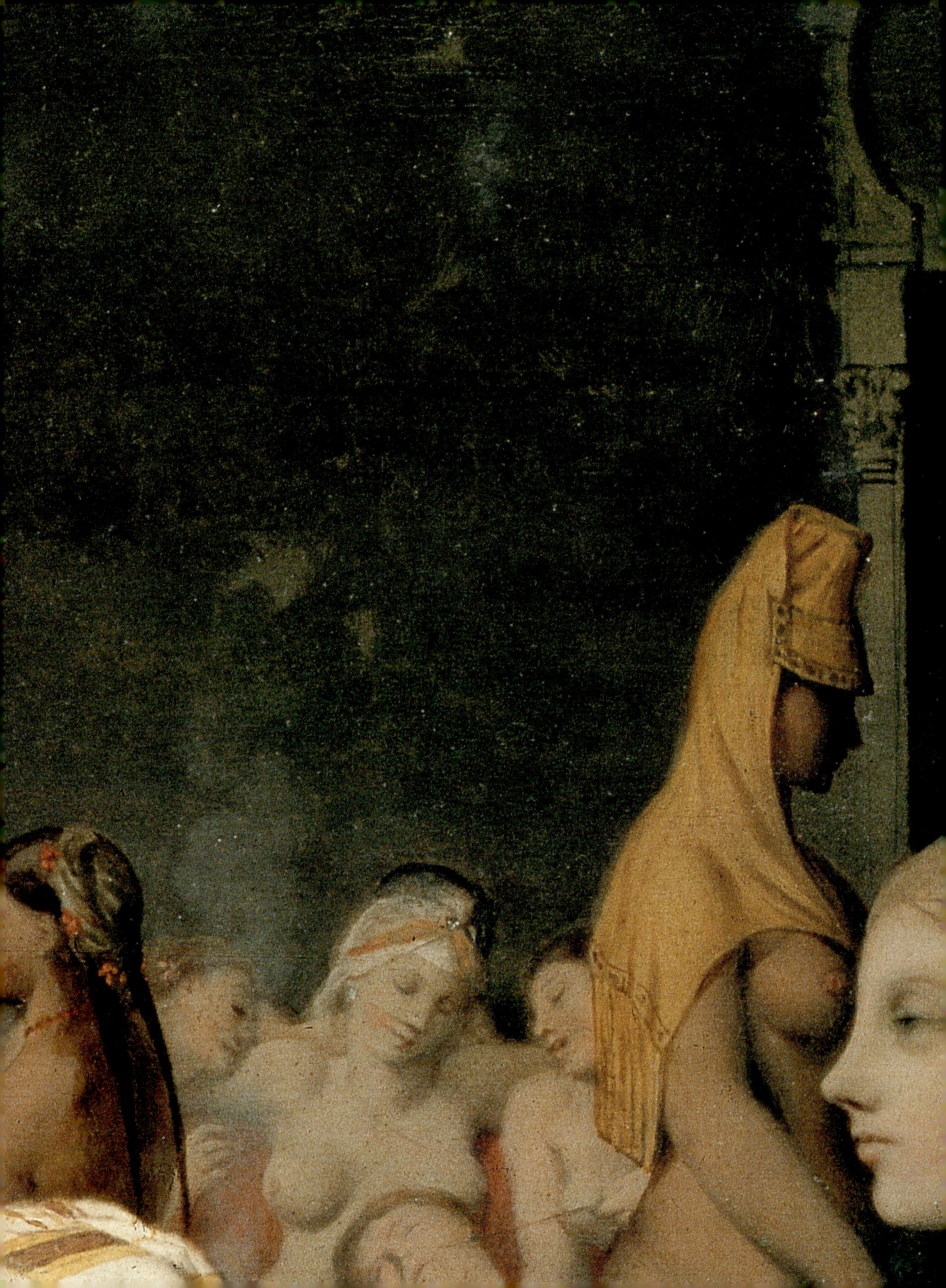

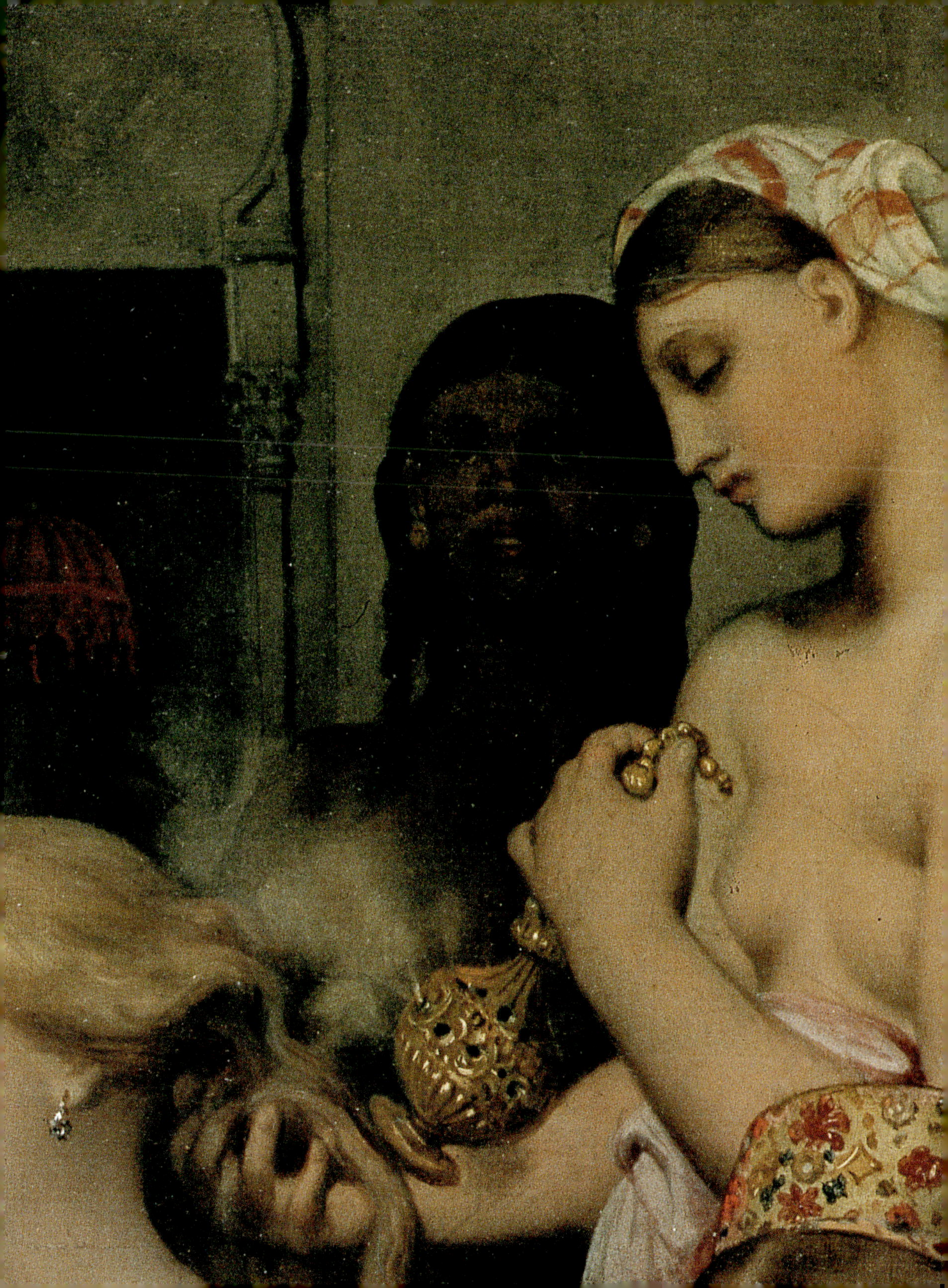

From Harem to Brothel

In the Classical and Neoclassical traditions the nude was simultaneously governed and given legitimacy by the edifying activity of history painting.

In raising the nude to the same poetic level and degree of formal inventiveness, Ingres accorded it an inherent worth and thus made it a genre in its own right, retaining for it the dignity of an "elevated" status and regenerating it with his love of living form. In other words he gained acceptance for the notion that the formal value of the nude met art's highest demands. This notion was bitterly contested and Ingres was endlessly criticized for an exaggerated love of form that led him to sacrifice expressiveness. As Théophile Silvestre put it, "David made form the servant of thought. Monsieur Ingres, believing only in form, turns painting into a voluptuous, sterile contemplation of raw matter. He professes a total indifference to the destinies of men and the secrets of creation, and with straight and curved lines pursues the plastic absolute that in his view is the beginning and end of all things. And after creating his prototypes of beauty, he does not even realize that he has forgotten to give them a soul."[44]

This pagan celebration of a totally physical beauty cost him many rebuffs, even after his death: in 1907 the *Turkish Bath* was turned down yet again – this time by the Louvre.

And yet the nude found its rightful place; so much so that it became the symbol of an academicism Ingres had managed to avoid, even as he did so much to foster it.

At the end of the 19th century Ingres' name was inevitably associated with an already moribund academic system. Nonetheless, many artists saw his oeuvre as a rejuvenated classicism, the last sound link in a still-living tradition: this could be the means of transcending Impressionism and replacing observation of shifting phenomena with ordered thinking rooted in the solidity of form and drawing.

Already, Degas had declared his unreserved admiration for Ingres. Renoir had had an Ingres period in the early 1880s. Seurat, Gauguin and Puvis de Chavannes acknowledged a debt to him. And Felix Vallotton revered him.

When the *Turkish Bath* was revealed to the public at the Ingres exhibition at the 1905 Salon, the artists of the rising generation were confronted with the originality of an oeuvre in many respects close to their own artistic concerns. Form that took precedence over content, the boldness of the distortions imposed on physique and on space, the force of a non-naturalistic approach to color, the taste for the esthetic of the "Primitives," the "constructive" rigor of the works: these added up to that "plastic absolute" denounced by Théophile Silvestre and seemed to them uniquely modern.

Matisse and Derain were among those attentive observers and the very titles of the works they painted then – Matisse's *Joie de Vivre* and *La Luxure*, Derain's *Golden Age* and *Bathers* – make no secret of their thematic proximity to Ingres. Matisse began a discreet but fruitful dialogue with the master of Montauban, whose presence can be sensed throughout his career. He seemed to adopt and extend all that was best in Ingres' drawing, notably the radiant lyricism of a line that on its own could express form totally. Even the paper cut-outs of the late years can be seen as a genial resolution of the tensions between vibrant line and ardent color that reached such a high point in some of Ingres' work.

Picasso's interest dates from his first years in Paris and surfaced on many different occasions. Like Ingres, Picasso was a great "plunderer," never hesitating to appropriate what the masters had to offer. This "cannibalism" was at the heart of his relationship to the great painting tradition, and his appropriation of the *Grande Odalisque* began with the work leading up to Cubism. It may be, moreover, that Picasso's *Demoiselles d'Avignon* (1907) was a response to the *Turkish Bath*, which the young painter had discovered two years before: we note the similarity of subject, and the recurrence of such motifs as the raised arms behind the head and the small still life in the foreground. Picasso's great painting is a kind of vital revolt against a classical tradition of which Ingres was the leading symbol and which fascinated Picasso: a tradition he had at once to smash to pieces and reinvent. This is what his *Demoiselles* do, chopping up the old Classicism with an axe and parading over the ruins in all their barbarous sexual power. Picasso's painting – a brothel scene – shattered the canons at the heart of Classical since ancient times and "savagely" desacralizes the human figure. Yet at the same time, in drenching that figure in the vitality of non-European traditions – as if in the blood of some pagan sacrifice – he gives it a new sacred dimension. No question: it was at the cost of this destruction that Picasso was regularly able to revive the great Mediterranean tradition and provide humanity with radiant myths. This was the heritage of which Ingres had been the inflexible guardian and devoted go-between.

By the 1910s Ingres had become a major point of reference in modern art: Guillaume Apollinaire, notably, saw him as closely tied to Cubism. Juxtaposition of

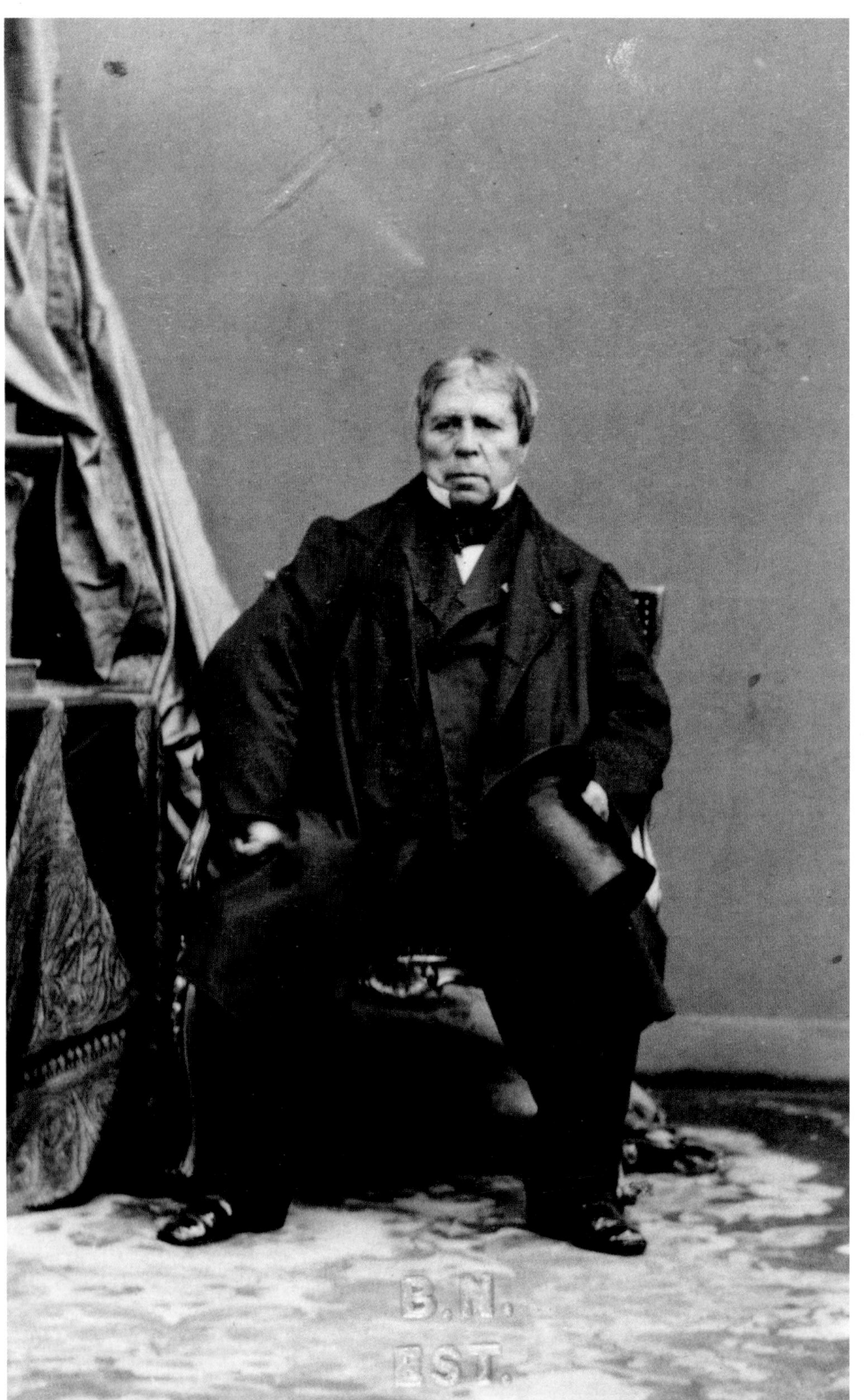
B.N.
EST.

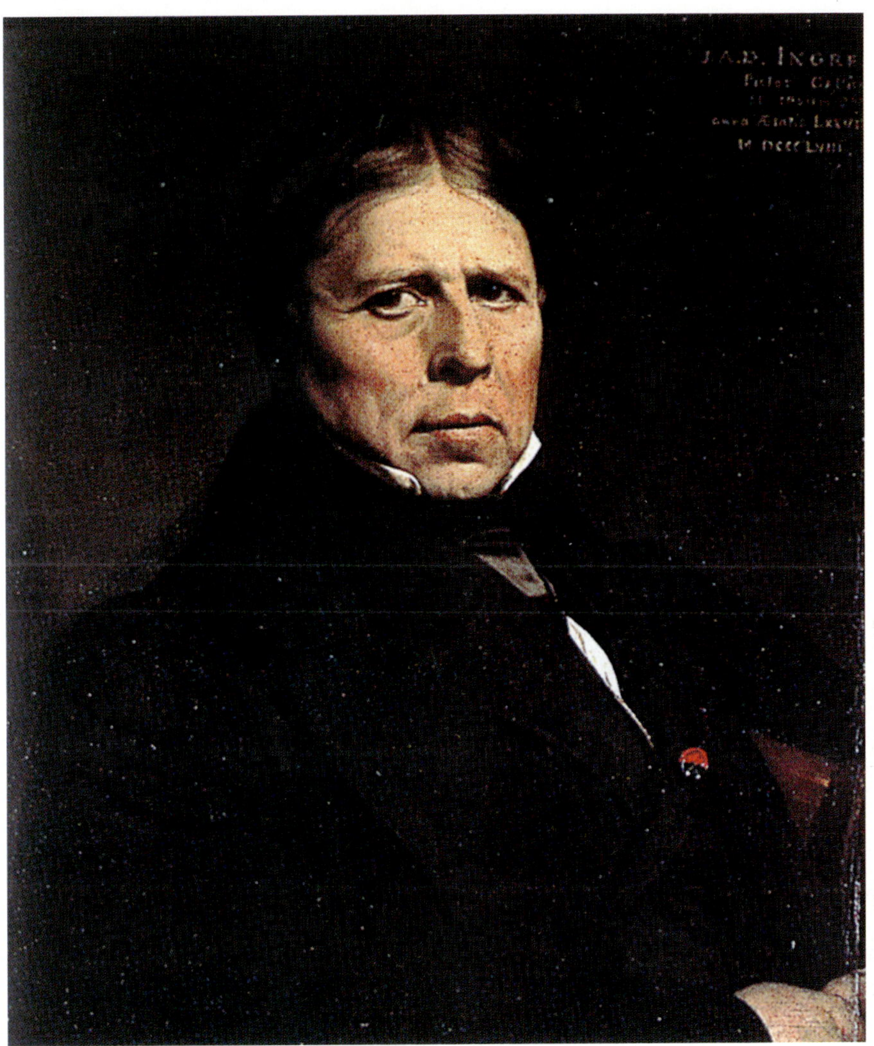

Self-portrait at the Age of Seventy-eight
1858, oil on canvas, 64x53 cm
Florence, Uffizi

Ingres
photograph by André Adolphe Disdéri
undated

planes in depthless space, and the capacity to describe multiple facets of the same object – the female body in *The Turkish Bath*, the face seen frontally and in profile in *La Grande Odalisque* – were considered pointers to the future. From Braque and Picasso to Juan Gris, André Lhote and Fernand Léger, Ingres was constantly drawn on by the Cubist painters.

However, his name was also associated with the new figurative order that followed the First World War, and especially with Picasso's spectacular return to realistic figuration. Picasso would undergo a so-called "Ingres period" whose host of drawn portraits were characterized by a virtuosity, a purity of line, and an exact realism referring specifically to his predecessor's drawings.

There is, in fact, no end to the list of Picasso's borrowings from Ingres: so much so that an entire exhibition was devoted to them in Paris in 2004. But worthy of especial note is the memorable series of engravings the Spanish artist based on *Raphael and La Fornarina* in 1968. Picasso uses the Ingres picture at the same time as he introduces an aspect of Raphael's life that Ingres had subtly veiled or coded: for according to his early biographers, Raphael's excessive sexual activity was the cause of his early death. Ever interested by such matters, Picasso set about calling a spade a spade in images showing the Italian master, armed with palette and brushes, furiously making love with his model. In no uncertain manner these engravings take the lid off the old metaphor: painting, like the sexual act, is determined by the desire of the painter and aimed at creating pleasure for the "voyeurs": the painter himself, the client who has commissioned the work, and the public. The same *eros* is at work in the act of love and the act of artistic creation. This is the message of Picasso's Raphael, simultaneously brandishing his brush and his penis. Via a picture-within-a-picture system – Ingres' Raphael as seen by Picasso – the artist applies the sexual metaphor to the artistic process with which he was so familiar: taking pleasure in the work of art, possessing and appropriating it.

There is an enormous gap between Ingres' chasteness and Picasso's erotic frenzies. And yet nobody, before Ingres, had so openly proclaimed the sensual beauty of bodies, not only as a privileged focus for painting, but as its very goal and prerequisite. The *Turkish Bath* launches us into space made flesh: stripped of all secondary considerations, the painting itself is totally and exclusively identified with the object of desire, whose image proliferates over its entire surface. In the circular enclosure of the picture the dizzying splendors on display are those of painting in all its nakedness.

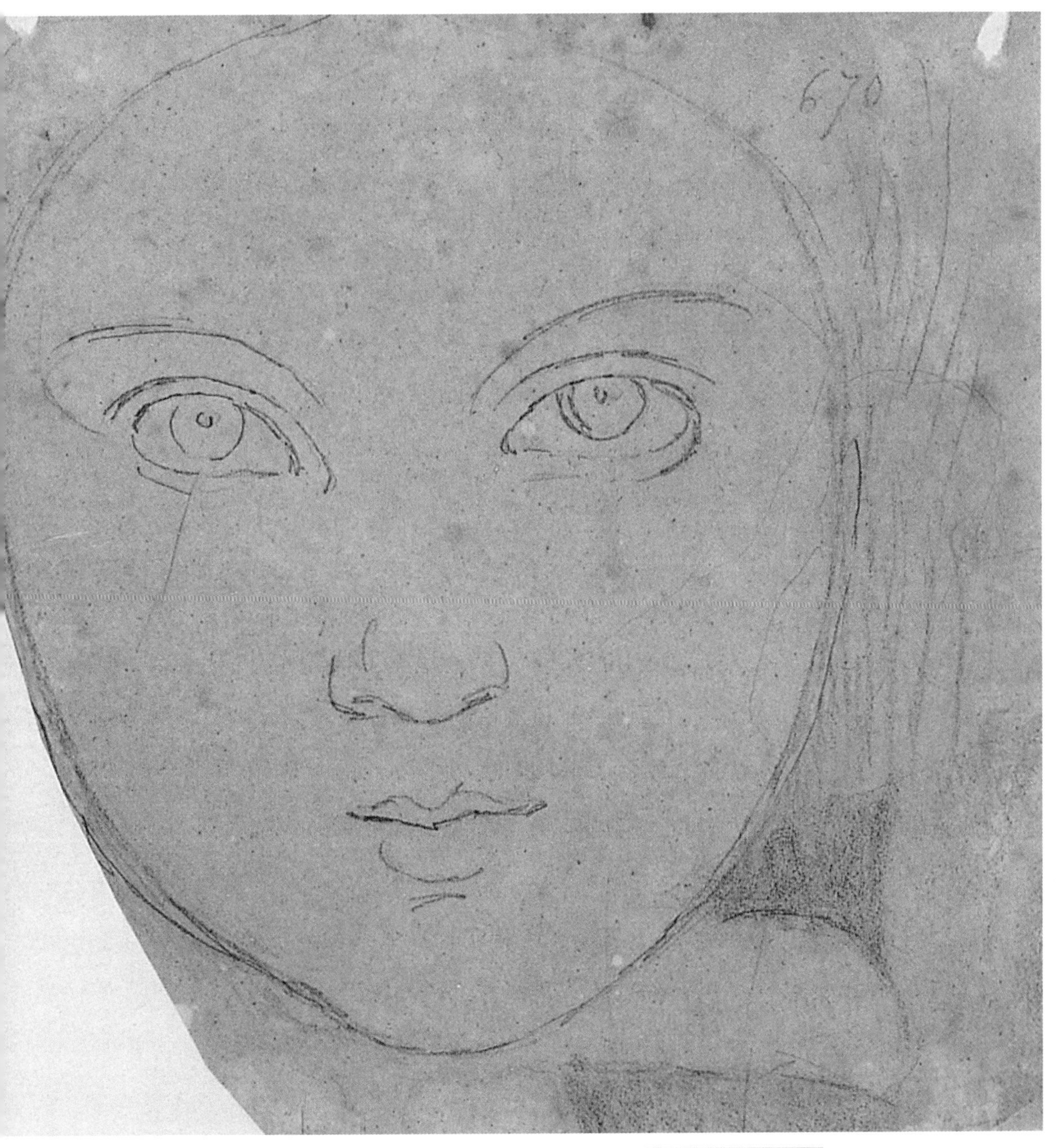

Study for the Head of Venus

1807, pencil, 165x155 cm

Montauban, Musée Ingres

Notes

1. Charles Baudelaire, *L'Exposition Universelle de 1855* ("The Universal Exhibition of 1855"). The quotations from Baudelaire in this book are from his *Esthetic Curiosities*.
2. Auguste Barbier, *Ingres, souvenirs personnels* ("Ingres, Personal Memories"), Paris, 1883.
3. Théophile Gautier, in *L'Artiste*, 1857.
4. Robert de la Sizeranne, "L'œil et la main de M. Ingres" ("The Eye and Hand of Monsieur Ingres", *Revue des Deux-Mondes*, 15 May 1911.
5. Louis Gillet, "Ingres et la Nouvelle exposition de ses œuvres" ("Ingres and the Latest Exhibition of his Work"), *Revue hebdomadaire*, 25 April 1911.
6. Baudelaire, *(op. cit.)*.
7. Théophile Silvestre, *Histoire des artistes vivants* ("Artists of Today"), Paris, 1856.
8. Baudelaire, *(op. cit.)*.
9. T. Silvestre, *(op. cit.)*.
10. Etienne-Jean Delécluze, *Louis David, son école et son temps* ("Jean-Louis David, His School and His Time").
11. Régis Michel, *David, l'art et le politique* ("David: Art and Politics"), Paris, Gallimard, 2003.
12. Pierre Chaussard, *Salon de 1806* ("The Salon of 1806"), *Le Pausanias français*, Paris, 1806
13. Letter to Jean Forestier, Rome, 22 October 1806.
14. Letter to Jean Forestier, Rome, 23 November 1806.
15. Ingres left ten notebooks, of which all but one are in the Ingres Museum in Montauban. Extracts from these notebooks were published (in French) by Henri Delaborde in 1870, and Pierre Courthion in 1947.
16. Translated by Samuel Butler.
17. Letter to Jean Forestier, December 1806
18. Louis Gillet in *Revue des Deux-Mondes*, 1932
19. Charles Landon in *Annales du musée. Salon de 1814*, Paris, 1814.
20. Théophile Gautier, *Les Beaux-Arts en Europe* ("The Arts in Europe"), Paris, 1855.
21. Paul Valéry, *Ecrits sur l'art*, ("Writings on Art") Paris, 1962.
22. T. Silvestre, *(op. cit.)*.
23. Emmanuel Amaury-Duval, *L'atelier d'Ingres* ("Ingres' Atelier"), Paris, 1878.
24. Letter to François Gilibert, Florence 20 April 1820.
25. Charles Blanc, *Ingres, sa vie et ses ouvrages* ("Ingres, His Life and Work"), Paris, 1870
26. Adolphe Thiers, *Le Salon de 1824* ("The Salon of 1824").
27. Stendhal, *Promenades dans Rome* ("Walks in Rome"), Del Litto (ed.), Paris, Gallimard, 1993.
28. E. Amaury-Duval, *(op. cit.)*.
29. C. Baudelaire, *Le Musée classique du Bazar Bonne-Nouvelle* ("The Classical Museum of the Bonne-Nouvelle Bazaar").
30. C. Baudelaire, *Le Salon de 1859* ("The Salon of 1859").
31. C. Blanc, *(op. cit.)*.
32. Quoted by Henri Mondor, *Mallarmé*, Paris, 1941
33. E. Amaury-Duval, *(op. cit.)*.
34. Charles Gounod, *Mémoires d'un artiste* ("Memoirs of an Artist") 1896.
35. Auguste Jal, *Salon de 1833* ("The Salon of 1833").
36. C. Baudelaire, *Le Salon de 1859* ("The Salon of 1859").
37. T. Gautier, *(op. cit.)*.
38. Related by Georges Sand, *Impressions et souvenirs* ("Impressions and Memories"), Paris, Des Femmes, 2005.
39. T. Silvestre, *(op. cit.)*.
40. C. Baudelaire, *Le musée classique du Bazar de Bonne-Nouvelle* ("The Classical Museum of the Bonne-Nouvelle Bazaar").
41. C. Baudelaire, *Le Salon de 1846* ("The Salon of 1846").
42. Edmond and Jules de Goncourt, *Etudes d'art* ("Studies in Art"), 1894.
43. C. Baudelaire, *L'Exposition Universelle de 1855* ("The Universal Exhibition of 1855").
44. T. Silvestre, *(op. cit.)*.

CHRONOLOGY

1775: Birth of Jean-Auguste-Dominique Ingres in Montauban.
1789-91: Studies art in Toulouse.
1797: Moves to Paris, begins studying at David's atelier
1801: Wins the Prix de Rome scholarship.
1806-1810: Resident at the Académie de France (Villa Medici) in Rome.
1810-20: Lives in Rome. Marries Madeleine Chapelle in 1814.
1820-24: Lives in Florence.
1824-34: First major success at the 1824 Salon, with *The Vow of Louis XIII*.
Receives the Cross of the Legion of Honor, is elected to the Institut de France and opens his own atelier.
Appointed teacher at the Écoles des Beaux-Arts in Paris in 1829.
1835-41: Director of the Villa Medici.
1843-47: Decoration of the great hall of the Château de Dampierre. The *Golden Age* and the *Bronze Age* remain unfinished.
1849: Death of his wife.
1851: First donation to the Montauban Museum.
1852: Marries Delphine Ramel.
1855: Presents a retrospective of his work at the Universal Exposition. Napoleon III makes him a Grand Officer of the Legion of Honor.
1862: He is made a senator, then a member of the Imperial Council of Public Education.
1866: He bequeaths his collection, several of his works, and the entire contents of his studio – over 4000 drawings – to the city of Montauban.
1867: Death of the artist.
1869: Opening of the Ingres Museum in Montauban.

Biliography

- Jean Clay, *Romanticism*, Book Sales, 1983
- Patricia Condon, *In Pursuit of Perfection: The Art of J.-A.-D. Ingres*, Indiana University Press, 1984
- Jay McKean Fischer et al., *The Essence of Line: French Drawings from Ingres to Degas*, Pennsylvania State University Press, 2005
- Uwe Fleckner, Jean-Auguste-Dominique Ingres, Könemann, 2000
- Jean-Auguste-Dominique Ingres, *Portrait Drawings: 44 Plates*, Dover Art Library, 1993
- Carol Ockman, *Ingres's Eroticized Bodies: Retracing the Serpentine Line*, Yale University Press, 1995
- Gaétan Picon, *Ingres*, Rizzoli International Publications, 1991
- Adrian Rifkin, *Ingres, Then and Now*, Routledge, 2000
- Robert Rosenblum, *Ingres*, Harry N. Abrams, 1990
- Léon Rosenthal, *Romantic Art and Artists*, Abaris, 1989
- Andrew Shelton, *Ingres and his Critics*, Cambridge University Press, 2005
- Gary Tinterow, Phillip Conisbee (Eds.), *Portraits by Ingres: Image of an Epoch*, Metropolitan Museum of Art, 1999
- Jane Turner (Ed), *From David to Ingres*, St Martin's Press, 2000
- Georges Vigne, *Ingres*, Tr. John Goodman, Abbeville Press, 1995
- Georges Wildenstein, *Ingres*, Phaidon, London, 1956

Akg-images: p. 145.
Aix-en-Provence, musée Granet:
p. 54, 69, 70 (detail).
Artephot: p. 33, 200-201, 227.
Bridgeman-Giraudon:
couverture (detail), p.9, 19, 26, 28, 30, 31 (detail), 39, 40-41 (detail), 45, 49, 50 (detail), 53 top et down (details), 63, 64 (detail), 64-65, 79, 80-81 (detail), 84-85 (detail), 90-91, 92 (detail), 94-95, 96-97 (detail), 99, 101, 102, 111, 112-113, 114-115 (detail) 128, 129 (detail), 131, 133, 135, 136-137 (detail), 138, 139, 146, 147, 148-149 (detail), 156, 158, 163, 175, 181 , 191, 194-195, 196-197 (detail), 198-199 (detail), 203, 207 down (detail), 221, 224, 225, 230, 239, 249.
Bruxelles, Musée royaux des beaux-arts: p. 73 down.
Cambridge, Fogg Art Museum: p. 109, 117.
Collection particulière: p. 172, 219.
Dominique Genet, Boulogne: p. 213.
Erich Lessing/Akg-images: p. 141, 142-143 (detail), 210.
Frédéric Jaulmes: p. 232.
Leemage: p. 73 top.
Liège, musée d'Armes: p. 37.
London, Victoria & Albert Museum: p. 88-89.
London, National Gallery: p. 127.
Lyon, musée des Beaux-Arts: p. 22, 118, 173.
Montauban, musée Ingres: p. 34-35, 134, 150, 161 down (detail), 176 top, 178-179, 214, 215, 226, 235.
Musée des Augustins, Toulouse : p. 82.
New York, Frick Collection:
p. 217 (detail), 218.
New York, The Metropolitan Museum of Art: p. 75, 124, 159.
Napoléonmuseum Arenenberg:
p. 100.
Orléans, musée des Beaux-Arts: p. 15.
Paris, Bibliothèque nationale de France : p. 21 top et down, 32, 60 down, 248.
Paris, École nationale supérieure des beaux-arts: p. 13 down (detail), 27.
Photo Roumagnac: p. 107, 153, 155, 176 down, 251.
Photo courtesy of The National Gallery, London: p. 209.
Photothèque du musée des Arts décoratifs: p. 57, 60 top.
RMN: p. 13 top (detail), 42, 43 (detail), 46, 61, 76, 103, 104-105 (detail), 125, 132, 151, 161 top (detail), 164, 168-169, 182, 186,
207 top (detail), 231, 236,238, 241, 242-243 (detail), 244-245 (detail).
RMN/R.G.Ojéda: p. 220.
Studio Basset: p. 170-171.
Washington, National Gallery of Art:
p. 121, 122 (detail).

Printed by Grafiche Zanini,
Bologna, Italy,
October 2005.